The Brazilian People

Published in Cooperation with the Center for
Latin American Studies of the University of Florida

Florida A&M University, Tallahassee
Florida Atlantic University, Boca Raton
Florida Gulf Coast University, Ft. Myers
Florida International University, Miami
Florida State University, Tallahassee
University of Central Florida, Orlando
University of Florida, Gainesville
University of North Florida, Jacksonville
University of South Florida, Tampa
University of West Florida, Pensacola

The Brazilian People
The Formation and Meaning of Brazil

by Darcy Ribeiro

Translated from the Portuguese by Gregory Rabassa

University Press of Florida

GAINESVILLE · TALLAHASSEE · TAMPA · BOCA RATON

PENSACOLA · ORLANDO · MIAMI · JACKSONVILLE · FT. MYERS

English translation Copyright 2000 by the Board of Regents
of the State of Florida
Original Portuguese publication in 1995 as *O Povo Brasileiro*
Printed in the United States of America on acid-free paper

05 04 03 02 01 00   6 5 4 3 2 1

Library of Congress Cataloging-in-Publication Data
Ribeiro, Darcy.
[Povo brasileiro. English]
The Brazilian people: the formation and meaning of Brazil / by Darcy
Ribeiro; translated from the Portuguese by Gregory Rabassa.
p. cm.
Includes bibliographical references.
ISBN 0-8130-1777-7
1. Brazil—Civilization. 2. Ethnology—Brazil. 3. Brazil—Race
relations. 4. Brazil—Social conditions. I. Rabassa, Gregory. II. Title.
F2510.R47713 2000
981—dc21 99-086541

The University Press of Florida is the scholarly publishing agency for
the State University System of Florida, comprising Florida A&M
University, Florida Atlantic University, Florida Gulf Coast University,
Florida International University, Florida State University, University of
Central Florida, University of Florida, University of North Florida,
University of South Florida, and University of West Florida.

University Press of Florida
15 Northwest 15th Street
Gainesville, FL 32611
http://www.upf.com

Here I give heartfelt thanks to those who have helped me finish this book: Mercio Gomes, my colleague, for his patience in reading the original text with me page by page; and Carlos Moreira, my comrade, whose first readings I never dispense with and who also read it, all of it, and cast his profound erudition over my text.

I must confess, however, that my greatest, deepest, and most fervent thanks must go to Gisele Jacon, my editor. This book is our joint work. If I was the one who thought it out, she put it together materially, giving it the physical consistency of something that can be touched and read. I am most grateful.

Darcy Ribeiro

Contents

Foreword

The Brazilian People is the culmination of the life's work of Darcy Ribeiro, one of Brazil's leading twentieth-century intellectuals. Ribeiro served his country as statesman, politician, educator, and novelist while becoming Brazil's most well-known specialist and advocate of Indian affairs. First published in 1995, two years before his death from cancer, this book proposes a "theory of Brazilian culture" that summarizes the author's thirty years of research, fieldwork, and contemplation on the contributions of the Indians, Afro-Brazilians, and many mixed-race variations to the distinct character of Brazilian nationality and culture. It is the last major work in a distinguished bibliography of more than thirty volumes, many of which have been translated into other languages.

The Brazilian People not only summarizes the career of a distinguished Brazilian who upheld the myth generated by earlier Romantic writers trying to explain Brazil in terms of its encounter with three races. It also closes the chapter on a scholarly tradition, dating to the sixteenth century, of works that sought to document and portray the complex and volatile reality of Brazil national identity as a product of its ethnic roots.

The first text in this series was the epic poem *Prosopopéia* by Bento Teixeira (1561–1600), who sang of the feats of Dom Jorge de Albuquerque, third landholder of Pernambuco. This text later inspired writers to explore the meaning of Brazil and to write about it. The nineteenth-century Romantic novelist José de Alencar idealized the Brazilian Indian and the sexual union of the Indian and Portuguese peoples. Paulo Prado, the early twentieth-century sociologist, coined the theory of the "sad race," and poet Mário de Andrade launched the Brazilian Modernist movement with the figure of Macunaíma, the "hero with no character," who epitomized a new world anti-hero, happy to confront Eurocentric world views and preoccupations.

Darcy Ribeiro acknowledges the particular influence on his work of three texts: *Das Capital*, Gilberto Freyre's *Casa-Grande e Senzala*, and Euclides da Cunha's *Os Sertões*. He claims never to have been Marxist but to have "consumed Marx": "Marx says in *Das Capital*, that a history of technology, of the development of technology solutions, will have the same importance for history as the theory of the evolution of species that Darwin had for science. What I began to do was to work at a theory to understand the Iberian Peninsula and its relationship to Brazil. I wanted to understand why North America, with less resources, colonized by people poorer than the Irish and the English, got it right and became rich, while a rich province like Brazil devolved" (interview with *Jornal do Brasil*, April 22, 1995). The other two books, seminal texts on the influence of minority cultures on the development of Brazilian society, explored the themes of productive tension between dominant and servile races and that of two Brazils, the urban and the rural, in the formation of contemporary Brazilian society.

The Brazilian People generated considerably controversy among critics when it first appeared in Brazil. Some dismissed the book as an extravagant movie-like script portraying Brazil as the "most fascinating place in the universe, [in which] the Indian is a superior being and the mameluke a hero like the soliders of imperial Rome" (Geraldo Maryink, *Veja*, May 3, 1995, p. 112). Ribeiro was labeled as simplistic because his villains are the irresponsible upper classes and the heroes are the downtrodden minorities who upgrade the national gene pool and character through mating forced on them by their European masters. His opponents point out that he himself was a member of the Brazilian power elite. A populist, always blaming the elite for everything, he was, according to critics, vain and authoritarian and from the ruling classes. While Ribeiro derides racism and sexism, he practices both if only in his way of expressing himself. He warns his readers, "Do not be fooled. I am not just an anthropologist, but a man of faith and party. I do politics and science moved by ethics and a profound patriotism. Don't look for objective analysis" *(Jornal do Brasil*, April 22, 1995).

Darcy Ribeiro rose from fairly modest roots to become a leader in three central spheres of Brazilian life during the critical years of the 1960s through the 1990s. Born in 1922 in Montes Claros, in the state of Minas Gerais, Ribeiro did fieldwork among Indians in Amazonas and central Brazil after finishing his studies in anthropology at the School of Political Sociology of São Paulo. He spent ten years working with the Societey for the Protection of the Indian, doing research on the culture, art, and religions of various Brazilian Indian peoples. With the support of UNESCO, he organized the Indian Museum in Rio de Janeiro (1953). During João

Goulart's presidency (1954–64), he was charged with the planning and establishment of the University of Brasília, where he served as its first rector in 1961–62. He also served Goulart as minister of education and culture and as special advisor to the president. When the military seized power in 1964, Ribeiro went into exile in Montevideo, Uruguay, where he taught anthropology at the Universidad de la República Oriental de Uruguay. During this period, the Brazilian military dictatorship censored and burned his most important book on the Brazilian Indians, *The Americas and Civilization*, in which he examines the social factors that form the different ethnic units and causes of uneven development in the Americas. In the early 1970s Ribeiro moved to Caracas, where he participated in the reorganization of the Central University of Venezuela.

He returned to Brazil in 1974 and resumed his political career, becoming lieutenant governor of the state of Rio de Janiero under Leonel Brizola from 1983 to 1987. During this period he became known for establishing a system of public schools called Integrated Centers of Public Education, an experiment in early childhood care and schooling that was held up as a model, then as a failure of public education policy. Later, as senator of the republic from 1991 to 1996, he wrote the Education Reform Act, which has laid the foundations for the modernization of the Brazilian educational process.

Ribeiro, the novelist and member of the illustrious Brazilian Academy of Letters, has also made a significant contribution to Brazilian literature. His work *Maíra* (1976) focuses on the subject of Indians in the world of whites and is narrated from the point of view of the Indians. The descriptions of Mairum society are based on Ribeiro's work with the Caduvoeo, Urubu, and other tribes. The most moving sections describe the effects of the contacts between Indians and whites, each seeking to follow the word of their own God or Maíra. *The Mule* (1982), his last novel, depicts the life journey of a mixed-breed orphaned Brazilian (Indian, black, and white) of low birth, a man who is symbolically sterile and who grows up amidst cattle ranchers in the backlands of Brazil's remote Center-West. It is an "upside-down" social novel in which the underdog survives through sheer tenacity and a book that bluntly exposes the evils of racism in Brazilian society as practiced by all classes in the interests of their power and wealth.

Ribeiro's contributions as researcher and educator have given him credibility as an anthropologist and theorist of culture. His thesis on "ethnic transfiguration" was the central concept of his work (Mercio Gomes, *The Indians and Brazil* [Gainesville: University Press of Florida, 2000], 21). In

it he states that Indian peoples will never be assimilated but at best acculturated into Brazilian society. Indeed, his role as planner, organizer, and
foremost reformer of various Latin American universities offered him a
means of testing his theories. His association with anthropologist Charles
Wagley brought his work to the attention of North American scholars.
During the years that Ribeiro spent among the tribes of Central Brazil and
the Amazon area, Ribeiro was closely associated with two other prominent anthropologists, Wagley and Eduardo Galvão. Indeed, it was
Ribeiro's ties to Wagley that led to his decision to offer the publication in
English of this book to the University Press of Florida. Charles Wagley,
author of seminal studies on Brazilian culture and society, was professor
of anthropology and Latin American Studies at the University of Florida
during the 1970s and 1980s. In his last days, Darcy was treated at Shands
Hospital at the university, and he gratefully acknowledged that the treat-
ments he was given there improved the quality of his life, allowing him to
finish his writing projects.

Darcy Ribeiro's legacy is that he is one of the few Brazilian intellectuals
to have thought of Brazil as a whole. He dwelled intensely on the paradox
of Brazil, a country of immense potential hindered by racial and class
prejudice. He states in *The Brazilian People*, "The most terrible aspect of
our heritages is that we will always carry with us the mark of the torturer
impressed on our soul, ready to explode into race and class brutality." But
he believed firmly in a Brazil that is "the most beautiful and luminous
province on earth" (conclusion). Contradictory patrician that he was,
Darcy Ribeiro bequeathed good works with a conscience lightened by a
delightful sense of humor and a distinctly poetic style, in his many scholarly and literary writings.

Elizabeth Lowe

Preface

Writing this book has been the greatest challenge I have ever proposed for myself. I have been writing and rewriting it for more than thirty years. The worst of it is that I feel frustrated when, occupied with other undertakings, I am not working on it. I have never put so much of myself into anything, never driven myself as I have to finish this always postponed task. Today I pick it up again for the third time; that is, if I count only that first time when I wrote and finished it and the second time when I rewrote it all completely, leaving out innumerable inconsequential revisions.

Of late the anguish has been sharpened because I have seen myself close to dying without having finished it. I fled the hospital to Maricá here in order to live and also to write it. If you are holding it in your hands to read today it is because I have finally won out and brought it into being. I hope so.

I have just read, half cursorily, the final version. The one I wrote in Peru, which was translated into Spanish but which I vetoed, was a good book, I now think. It could well have been published just the way it was. Or perhaps the way it was still represented a challenge. But I didn't want to release it. I was asking more of myself and promised myself that I would revise it, redo it, until it attained the form it should have. What form is that?

I don't think any book is ever finished. The author can always continue indefinitely the way I continued with this one without picking it up again. What happens is that a person gets tired of the book, that's all, and at that moment he considers it finished. I'm not sure, but I suspect that's how it's been with me.

Why have I picked it up again only now, after so many years in which I busied myself with the most varied tasks, avoiding it? I don't know! It certainly wasn't in order to rest. It was to undertake other tasks, among them that of becoming a literary man and publishing four novels, picking up once more a line of interest that I had attempted at the age of twenty.

During that long journey I also did a lot of politicking, successfully and unsuccessfully, here and in exile, and I became involved in arduous and diverse undertakings; I also almost died.

During all those years the book at hand was stuck away in a drawer, turning yellow, waiting for today. Here I am now on the beach at Maricá, where I've brought the folders containing all the reams of paper that make up its various versions.

The first attempt to write it, when it wasn't even beginning to take shape, was in the middle of the fifties, when I was directing a broad program of socio-anthropological studies in the research section of the Ministry of Education, the Brazilian Center for Educational Research (CBPE). I conceived of it then as a synthesis of those studies, with all the ambition of its being a picture of the whole body of Brazil, in its rural and urban makeup, and in its archaic and modern forms, at that moment which, to my mind, was the eve of a transforming social revolution.

And then I abandoned it—thirty odd years ago or more—to become involved in the planning and establishment of the University of Brasília. That task led me to others, such as Minister of Education and Chief of Staff of the Presidency for João Goulart, with the mission of linking up the elements of the National Movement for Basic Reform.

All of that resulted, as is well known, in my first exile in Uruguay. There the first version of this book, some four hundred dense pages, took shape after ten years of intense work. It was no longer the synthesis I had first proposed. It was in effect a version resulting from my experiences in the tragic events in Brazil in which I had played a role. The nerve throbbing beneath the text was the search for historical and scientific answers to the questions that those of us deposed by the military coup were asking ourselves. Why, once again, was the dominating class defeating us?

In truth, in order to write it I scarcely consulted the published works that came out of those investigations. Instead I read any and all texts on Brazil and Latin America that fell into my hands—ever so many, thanks to the magnificent Municipal Library of Montevideo.

Once the book was finished, my first critical reading of it startled me: it wasn't saying anything, or it was saying little that hadn't already been said. The worst of it was that it was not answering the questions I was posing, summed up in the sentence that from then on I kept repeating: why hadn't Brazil turned out right yet?

My feeling was that we lacked a general theory, the terms of which would render us explicable, based on our historical experience. The theorizing originating in other contexts was all too Eurocentric and for that reason impotent in rendering us intelligible. Since our past had not belonged to someone else, our past was not necessarily their present nor our future a future in common.

In search of answers to those questions in the years that followed, I plunged into study and came upon surprises. What was to have been a theoretical introduction in my plans for revision of the text was becoming entire books. The need for a theory of Brazil that would locate us in human history led me to the audacity of proposing a whole theory of history. The alternatives offering themselves were imposing. They would serve perhaps as a theoretical version of the European performance, but they didn't explain the history of oriental peoples or the Arab world, much less of Latin Americans. The best of them, represented in the new version put together by Engels in his *Origins* and by Marx in his *Formations,* in opposition to each other, left the theme open.

The Civilizing Process is my voice in this debate. It was heard, I like to believe, because it has been translated into the languages of our western circuit, has been published and republished many times, and has been the subject of international debates in the United States and Germany. The audacity of writing such an ambitious book provoked a certain disdain from those who suffer a sense of inferiority and will not give a Brazilian intellectual the right to enter debates dealing with such complex matters. It has suffered restrictions too, from Communists because it wasn't a Marxist text and from academics on the right because it was. That did it no harm; it has ended up being published and read more than any other recent book on the same theme.

But the *Process* wasn't enough. The explanation it offers for ten thousand years of history is too broad. Its answers, necessarily generic, give only vague outlines of our historical development. It was what could be done as an alternative to the classic texts generally dealing with that theme — a conceptual scheme closer to reality and more explanatory than those available, with the proposition that new technological revolutions, new civilizing processes, and new sociocultural formations are the driving forces of history. Seen in that light, our reality is portrayed in its most general features, resulting in an explanatory discourse useful for theoretical and comparative ends but insufficient to address the causality of our history.

I went off, then, in search of more down-to-earth explanations with more years of work. The theme I was now proposing was to reconstitute the process of formation of the American peoples in an effort to explain the causes of their unequal development. Thus I leaped from the scale of ten thousand years of general history to that of the five hundred years of history of the Americas, with a new book, *The Americas and Civilization,* in which I propose a typology of the American peoples in the form of a broad, discursive explanation.

This book has been making the rounds since then, translated, republished, and discussed, more by historians and philosophers than by anthropologists. These last colleagues of mine have an irresistible barbarian bent and a fondness for all deviant and bizarre behavior. They dedicate their meager talents to all wild themes that fall into their hands, making of civilization a series of anthropologies and refusing idiotically to use their efforts for an understanding of ourselves.

What has occurred yet again, however, is that with the task finished, I see the limits of what I have obtained in relation to what I was seeking. My book is a help, certainly, in making us intelligible, but it is clearly insufficient. Hence I delve once more, searching on a new, synchronic scale for the theories that we need if we are to understand ourselves. Three were urgently required to replace the schemes—less Eurocentric than crude—that had been relied upon.

First, we need a theory of the empirical base of social classes as they appear in our Brazilian and Latin American world. For the European world and the Anglo-Saxon overseas one made up of transplanted peoples, the accepted Marxist scheme, without too many repairs, pales visibly in the face of our Ibero-Latin reality. Here, with no progressive bourgeoisies fighting feudal aristocracies, no proletariats annointed with irresistible revolutionary propensities, but with class struggles, there must exist disguised antagonistic blocs that are difficult to identify or characterize.

Second, we lack a typology of the forms for the exercise of power and political militancy, whether conservative, reformist, or insurgent. All the copious political thought available has been made up of irrelevant analyses or philosophizing speculations that leave us more perplexed than enlightened. Discussion about liberals, conservatives, and radicals, or democracy and liberalism, and even about social and political revolution may convey in other contexts some sense of concrete definitions, but in ours it means nothing, such is the ambiguity with which these expressions are applied to the most differing agents and the most disparate orientations.

Third, lacking too is a theory of culture capable of meeting the requirements of our reality, where erudite knowledge is so often spurious and popular lack of knowledge, by contrast, reaches critical proportions, mobilizing minds into strong movements for social restructuring. How can we establish the forms and the role of our erudite culture, a transplanted product governed by European fashions, in the face of popular creativity mingling the most scattered traditions, so that we can understand that new version we have of the world and of ourselves? In order to meet that necessity I wrote *The Dilemma of Latin America*. There I propose a new schema of social classes and political obligations, locating them under the pressure of the North American hegemony with which we live, not being ourselves but being what it suits them for us to be.

In a purely didactic exercise I summed up the theoretical corpus developed in those three books in order to put together *The Brazilian People: The Formation and Meaning of Brazil*. The only new thing it brings out is the theory of culture I have mentioned. I didn't put it in the *Dilemma* so as not to have to deal with such a broad theme within a Latin American dimension.

Indians and Civilization and the other four books mentioned make up my *Studies of the Anthropology of Civilization*, even though they are the result of earlier research. What is certain, however, is that its theoretical corpus is the same, based on the concept of ethnic transfiguration. It might be called the process through which peoples rise up, become transformed, or die.

Occupied with those "preliminary" writings that have resulted in five volumes of almost ten thousand pages, I neglected the book I now take up again. In effect, they are all the fruit of the search for theoretical bases that, rendering Brazil explicable, would permit me to write the book at hand.

This was what I attempted several times in Peru, as I have said—a complete revision based on my theoretical studies. Not satisfied with the form I had reached years before, I put it aside, thinking that within a few months I would pick it up again.

That's not the way it was. The tempest of my life broke over me. A cancer was eating away a whole lung that had to be removed. In the meantime I returned to Brazil, rekindling white-hot political flames that had been dormant in me during the years of exile. All that and more brought on an irresistible passion, revealing that I was mortal and enslaving me ever since, drawing me away from the task I had set for myself.

Now a new political phase is reviving the necessity to publish this book, which, in addition to being an explanatory anthropological text, is my contribution in the new struggle for a decent Brazil.

But don't be deceived: in addition to being an anthropologist, I am a man of faith and of party. My involvement in politics and science is motivated by ethical impulses and by a deep patriotism. Don't look for any neutral analyses here. This is a book that aims to be participatory, that aspires to influence people, and that aspires to help Brazil find itself.

Introduction

Brazil and the gestation of the Brazilians as a people are what we shall here attempt to reconstitute and comprehend. We have arisen out of a melding, a collision, and a melting pot of the Portuguese invader with plains- and forest-dwelling Indians and with African blacks, both groups coerced into slavery.

Out of this blend, which took place under the rule of the Portuguese, people of disparate racial origins, distinct cultural traditions, and various social formations confronted one another and merged to give birth to a new people (Ribeiro 1970) in a new model of societal structuring. New because they have arisen as a national ethnicity, culturally differentiated from their formative matrices, with a heavy racial mix, powered by a syncretizing culture and distinguished by the resulting redefinition of cultural traits. New also because they see themselves and are seen as a new people, a new human species unlike all others in existence; a new people furthermore because they make up a new model of societal structuring, inaugurating a singular form of socioeconomic organization based on a revived type of slavery and on continued bondage to the world market. New, even, because of the unlikely joy and the astonishing will for happiness in a people who have seen so much sacrifice, which encourages and stimulates all Brazilians.

Old, however, because they function as an external proletariat—that is to say, as an overseas implant of European expansion—which exists not for itself but in order to generate exportable profits through its function as a colonial provider of goods for the world market, with resulting wear and tear on populations recruited within the country or imported.

Brazilian society and culture have been shaped as variants of the Portuguese version of traditional western European civilization, differentiated by tones inherited from American Indians and African blacks. Brazil thus emerges as a renewed mutant, expressing its own characteristics but genetically tied to its Portuguese origins, which involved unsuspected potential for existence and growth that would only be fully realized here.

This coming together of so many and such varied matrices might have resulted in a multiethnic society torn by clashes among differentiated and unmixable components. Quite the opposite has taken place: in spite of the survival of marks of their multiple ancestry in physical appearance and spirit, Brazilians have not split up into antagonistic racial, cultural, or regional minorities tied to their different ethnic loyalties and demanding autonomy from the nation.

The only exceptions are a few microethnic tribal groups who have survived as islands surrounded by the Brazilian population or who, living beyond the frontiers of civilization, preserve their ethnic identity. They are so tiny, however, that no matter what their fate, they can no longer affect the macroethnicity in which they are contained.

What Brazilians possess that differentiates them from the Portuguese comes from qualities that have their origins in indigenous and African matrices, according to the particular proportions in which they have been brought together in Brazil; from the environmental conditions encountered here; and in addition from the aims that have engaged them and brought them together.

That basic ethnic unity does not signify uniformity, however, precisely because three diversifying forces act upon it: ecology, causing the emergence of distinct human environments where the natural conditions surrounding people have brought on regional adaptations; the economy, creating differentiated forms of production that have led to functional specialization and corresponding lifestyles; and lastly immigration, which has introduced into this magma new human contingents, mainly Europeans, Arabs, and Japanese. But with the nation already formed and capable of absorbing and Brazilianizing foreigners, only a few Brazilians have been "foreignized" as differences are generated in areas or social strata where immigrants have been heavily concentrated.

Along these lines, diverse rural ways of being have taken shape historically for Brazilians, which permit them to be distinguished today as *sertanejos* (people of the *sertão*) in the Northeast, *caboclos* in Amazônia, *crioulos* along the coast, *caipiras* in the Southeast and center of the country, *qaúchos* on the southern plains, as well as Italo-Brazilians, Gringo-Brazilians, or Nippo-Brazilians, all of them marked much more by what they have in common as Brazilians than by differences brought on by regional or functional adaptations or by the miscegenation and acculturation that have given various portions of the population physiognomies of their own.

Urbanization, in spite of having created so many citified ways of being, has contributed even more to the uniformity of Brazilians on a cultural level—without, however, erasing their differences. Industrialization, as a way of life that creates its own human type, has formed industrial islands where it has taken hold. New methods of mass communication are actively at work spreading and making uniform new cultural forms and styles.

No matter how differentiated they may be in their racial and cultural matrices and in their ecological-regional functions, or in respect of being descendants of old settlers or recent immigrants, Brazilians have come to know themselves, to feel themselves, and to act as a single people, belonging to one and the same ethnicity. They are, it must be said, a national entity distinct from all others, speaking the same language, differing only in regional accents less noticeable than the dialects within Portugal. They take part in a body of common traditions that is more meaningful for all than is any one of the subcultural variants that distinguish the inhabitants of a region, the members of a class, or the descendants of one of the formative matrices.

More than a simple ethnicity, however, Brazil is a national ethnicity, a nation-people settled in a territory of its own and framed into a single state where they will live out their destiny. Unlike Spain in Europe or Guatemala in America, for example, which are multiethnic societies governed by unitary states and for that very reason torn by interethnic conflicts, Brazilians are integrated into a single national ethnicity, constituting in that way a single people incorporated into a unified nation, in a uni-ethnic state. The only exceptions are the several tribal microethnicities, so small that their existence does not affect national destiny.

But this cultural uniformity and this national unity—the great result of the process of formation of the Brazilian people—must not blind us to the disparities, contradictions, and antagonisms that subsist beneath them as dynamic factors of major importance. Indeed national unity, made visible by the successive economic integration of diverse colonial implants, was consolidated after independence as an express objective reached through the bloody struggles and political wisdom of many generations. This is undoubtedly the only indisputable merit of the old Brazilian governing classes. Comparing the unitary bloc that resulted in Portuguese America with the mosaic of diverse national tableaus that came about in Spanish America, one can appreciate the extraordinary importance of this accomplishment.

Unity resulted from a continuous and violent process of political unification; it was obtained by means of a deliberate effort at suppression of all contradictory ethnic identity and the repression and oppression of all workable separatist tendencies, even social movements that basically strove to create a more open and harmonious society. Under these conditions, the struggle for unification entrenched and reinforced social and class repressions, punishing as separatist in nature even movements that were simply republican or antioligarchic.

Lying hidden beneath Brazilian cultural uniformity is a profound social distance generated by the type of stratifications produced in the very process of national formation. The class antagonism that corresponds to all social stratification is exacerbated here and sets up in opposition to the great mass of population a very restricted privileged stratum, making social distances more unbridgeable than are racial differences.

This nation-people did not arise in Brazil from the evolution of previous forms of sociability, where human groups were structured in opposing classes that join to attend to survival needs and progress. It came from the concentration of a slave labor force alien to it, recruited to serve mercantile aims. It arose through processes so repressive and violent in governance that they constituted a continuous genocide and an implacable ethnocide.

Under these conditions the social distance between the ruling classes and the subordinate ones is exacerbated, as is that between the latter and the oppressed, causing accumulation of oppositions as traumatic dissociative tensions beneath the surface of ethnocultural uniformity and national unity. As a consequence, the governing elites, first Portuguese, then Luso-Brazilian, and finally Brazilian, have always lived and still live in panicked terror of the uprising of suppressed classes. The repressive brutality used against any insurgency and the authoritarian predisposition of the central power, which admits no alteration in the established order, clearly express this terror.

Social stratification thus separates rich and well-off Brazilians from the poor, and all of them from the wretched, and places the groups in even greater opposition than is usually the case with such antagonisms. In this respect class relations become so unbridgeable that they obliterate all proper human communication between the masses of the people and the privileged minority, which sees them but ignores them, treats and mistreats them, exploits and deplores them, as if that were natural behavior. In this way the achievement represented by the process of racial and cultural fusion is denied on what is apparently the most fluid level of social relations. Countering the unity of a cultural common denominator taken to heart by a nation of 160 million inhabitants is the tearing apart of this same people by class stratification with clear racial overtones and of the most cruelly unequal kind conceivable.

The frightful part is that Brazilians, proud of their so vaunted and so false "racial democracy," rarely perceive the deep abysses separating the social strata here. The gravest part is that this abyss does not lead to struggles aiming to bridge it, because things crystallize into a modus vivendi that separates rich from poor, as if there were castes and ghettos. The privileged simply isolate themselves behind a barrier of indifference to the lot of the poor, whose repugnant misery they try to ignore or hide through a kind of social myopia that perpetuates the separation. The mass of people, long-suffering and perplexed, see the social order as a sacred system affording privileges to a minority favored by God, a minority to whom they consent and concede everything—even the gift of existence, sometimes generous, often cold and perverse, and invariably unpredictable.

That contradiction took dynamic shape in the age-old struggles of Indians and blacks against slavery and later in the rare instances when the masses of a region organized in a struggle for an aim of their own and an alternative to the social structure, as happened with the Cabanos and in Canudos, in the Contestado, and among the Muckers.

Under such conditions of social distancing and bitterness brought on by the exacerbation of class prejudice and by the emerging awareness of injustice, anarchical convulsions could well be brought about tomorrow that will set the whole society on fire. That ever-present risk is what explains the obsessive preoccupation of the ruling classes with maintenance of order—a conclusive symptom of their knowing quite well that this might happen should the containment valves be opened. Out of that come their "preventive revolutions," leading to dictatorships, which are seen as a lesser evil than any correction of the established order.

It must be pointed out that this worry first appeared in the fear of slave revolts. Given the dark color of the poorest groups, racial fear persists when it is social antagonisms that threaten to break out with frightening violence. Its effects could take the form of a terrible social upheaval: an emotional explosion would end up in defeat, crushed by repressive forces that would restore the old unequal order on top of the rubble.

The great challenge confronting Brazil is how to achieve the necessary lucidity to chain these energies and orient them politically, with a clear awareness of both the risk of regression and the opportunities for liberation. The Brazilian people have historically paid an extremely high price in struggles of the bloodiest kind recorded in history without succeeding thereby in emerging from the situation of dependence and oppression in which they live and struggle. In these fights, Indians have been decimated and blacks have been slaughtered by the millions, always defeated and dumped into slavery. In vast regions whole populations, in the hundreds of thousands, have been bloodied in counterrevolutions without attaining, except episodically, the command of their destiny to reorient the course of history.

Contrary to what official historiography alleges, there has never been a lack here—rather, an excess—of the appeal to violence by the ruling class as a fundamental arm in the construction of history. What has always been lacking has been space for social movements capable of bringing about its reversal. What has always been lacking and is still so obviously lacking is a clear comprehension of the history that has been lived as necessary to the circumstances in which it occurred, or a clear alternative project for the social order, lucidly formulated, which could be supported and adopted by the great majorities as their own. It is not unthinkable that this social restructuring be conducted without social upheaval, through a democratic policy of reform. But it is most improbable in this country where a few thousand large landowners monopolize the greater part of the territory, compelling millions of workers to go to cities and live the life of *favela* slums on the strength of upholding a few old laws. Every time a nationalist or populist politician heads in the direction of a revision of institutional forms, the ruling classes resort to repression and force.

This book is an effort to contribute to the consideration of this call for lucidity. This is what I have aimed to do in what follows. I address matters first through analysis of the process of ethnic gestation that gave birth to original nuclei, which multiplied and came to form the Brazilian people; then through the study of the lines of diversification that have shaped our regional ways of being; and finally by means of a critique of the institutional system, notably agrarian property and working methods, in the sphere of which the Brazilian people have arisen and grown, constrained and deformed.

I

The New World

I

Ethnic Roots

The Island Brazil

For thousands of years the Atlantic coast was traversed and occupied by innumerable indigenous peoples. Fighting over the best ecological niches, they were incessantly settling, moving on, and resettling. During the later centuries, however, Indians of the Tupi language group, fine warriors, established themselves as the dominators of the immense area along the Atlantic littoral as well as up the Amazon and up main rivers such as the Paraguay, the Guaporé, and the Tapajós all the way to their sources.

In this way they gave configuration to the island Brazil spoken of by old Jaime Cortesão (1958) and prefiguration on the ground of South America to what would come to be our country. It was not a nation, obviously, because the Indian groups were not too well acquainted with one another, nor were they conquerors as such. They were, simply put, a myriad of tribal peoples speaking tongues from a common trunk, dialects of the same language, each of which as it grew would divide into two peoples beginning to show differences and soon becoming estranged and hostile to each other.

If history had given these Tupi peoples a few centuries more of freedom and autonomy, some of them might have imposed themselves on others, creating chieftainships that would become broader and broader, forcing the peoples living there to serve them, making them culturally uniform and thereby unleashing a process that would be the opposite of expansion through differentiation.

None of this happened. What happened and what changed their destiny in a thorough and radical way was the introduction of a new protagonist into their world: the European. Even though tiny, the little band of newcomers from across the sea was super-aggressive and capable of acting destructively in many different ways, mainly through deadly infection that decimated the preexisting population to the point of extinction.

The conflict took place on all levels—predominantly on the biotic level, in the form of bacteriological warfare carried out by the plagues that the white man bore in his body and that were deadly for the untouched populations. On the ecological level was the dispute over the territory and its forests and wealth for other uses. On the economic and social level was the enslavement of the Indian with the mercantilization of the productive relationship linking the new worlds to the old European one as providers of exotic goods, captives, and gold.

On the ethnocultural level this transformation took place through the gestation of a new ethnicity, which brought together in language and custom Indians released from their pagan way of life, blacks brought from Africa, and Europeans settling here. It was the Brazilian who was arising out of the building blocks of these matrices as the latter were being demolished.

The reconstruction of this process in order to understand it in all its complexity is my purpose in this book. It seems impossible, I recognize that; impossible because we have only the testimony of one of the protagonists, the invader. He is the one who speaks to us of his deeds. It is he, too, who relates what happened to the Indians and the blacks, rarely giving them an opportunity to register events in their own words. What this copious documentation recounts for us is the version of the conqueror. Reading it critically, I shall make an effort to attain the necessary understanding of this unfortunate adventure.

It is an important task on two levels: on the historical level, through the reconstitution of the singular and unique string of events through which we have come to be what we are, Brazilians. And on the anthropological level, because the general process of gestation of the people who make us up, highly documented here, is the same one that has made many other peoples arise in other times and circumstances, as in the Romanization of the Portuguese and the French, for example, of which process we have only scant and doubtful word.

The Tupi Matrix

The indigenous groups found along the coast by the Portuguese were mainly tribes of Tupi origin who, having settled there centuries before, were still dislodging earlier occupants of other cultural matrices. They may have totaled a million Indians, divided into dozens of tribal groupings, each one made up of a conglomerate of several villages of from 300 to 2,000 inhabitants (Fernandes 1949). This was no small number of people; Portugal in that period probably had the same population or a little more.

On the scale of cultural evolution the Tupi peoples were taking the first steps in the agricultural revolution, emerging thus from their paleolithic state, as had occurred for the first time 10,000 years before among the peoples of the Old World. It must be pointed out that they were doing it on their own, as were other peoples in the tropical forest, who had domesticated various plants, which brought them out of their wild state into settlements for the maintenance of their cleared fields. Among the crops was manioc, cultivation of which was an extraordinary feat because it was a matter of a poisonous plant that not only had to be cultivated but must also be given proper treatment for extraction of its prussic acid in order to render it edible. It is a most valuable plant because it does not have to be harvested and stored but can remain alive in the ground for months.

In addition to manioc they cultivated corn, sweet potatoes, yams, beans, peanuts, tobacco, pumpkins, annatto, cotton, *caroa,* gourds and calabashes, peppers, pineapples, papayas, yerba maté, and *guaraná,* among many other plants, including dozens of fruits trees like the cashew and the *pequi.* For that purpose they cleared large areas in the forest, felling trees with their stone axes and burning.

Agriculture assured them sufficient food for the whole year and a great variety of raw materials, condiments, poisons, and stimulants. In that way they overcame the condition of food shortages to which pre-agricultural peoples are subject, dependent on the generosity of tropical nature, which provides fruits, coconuts, and tubers in abundance for part of the year and at other times condemns the population to want. They remain, therefore, dependent on chance to obtain other food by hunting and fishing, also subject to seasonal differences marked by months of enormous abundance and months of scarcity (Ribeiro 1970a; Meggers 1971).

Hence the importance of privileged spots where abundant fish and game guaranteed the survival of the group with greater regularity and permitted them to maintain larger settlements. In certain especially rich locales along the seacoast as well as in the more fertile valleys, those exceptional settlements reached populations as high as a thousand inhabitants. They were, however, pre-urban conglomerates (undifferentiated agricultural villages), because all of the inhabitants were compelled to work in the production of food. Only freed from it, exceptionally, were a few religious leaders (*pajés* and *caraíbas)* and some warrior chiefs (*tuxáuas*).

In spite of the linguistic and cultural unity that allows these groups to be classified as a single macroethnicity in opposition overall to the other peoples designated by the Portuguese as Tapuias (or enemies), the Indians of the Tupi branch were never able to unite in any political organization that would have permitted them to act in consort. Their very evolutionary state of peoples on the tribal level led each ethnic unit, as it grew, to divide up into autonomous entities, which, moving apart from one another, would become reciprocally more differentiated and hostile.

Even in the face of the new all-powerful enemy from beyond the sea, when open conflict arose the Tupi managed to put together only ephemeral regional confederations that would soon disappear. The most important of these, known as the Confederation of the Tamoios, had an opportunity through an alliance with the French established on Guanabara Bay. Between 1563 and 1567 it brought together the Tupinambá of Rio de Janeiro and the Carijó of the São Paulo plateau—aided by the Goitacá and the Aimoré of the Serra do Mar coastal range, who were of the Jã linguistic group—to wage war on the Portuguese and on other indigenous groups supporting them. In that implausible war of Reformation versus Counter-Reformation, of Calvinist against Jesuit, in which both the French and the Portuguese fought with native armies of thousands of warriors—4,557, according to Léry; 12,000 on both sides in the final battle of Rio de Janeiro in 1567, according to the figures of Carlos A. Dias (1981)—the future of the colonization was at stake. And the natives did not even know why they were fighting. They were simply incited by the Europeans, who exploited their reciprocal aggressiveness. The Tamoios won several battles, destroyed the captaincy of Espírito Santo, and seriously threatened that of São Paulo, but in the end they were defeated by native troops enticed by the Jesuits.

In those wars—like the ones before (that of the Paraguaçu in the Recôncavo of Bahia in 1559, for example) and the ones that followed until consolidation of the Portuguese conquest (like the campaigns of extermination against the Potiguara in Rio Grande do Norte in 1599 and in the following century the War of the Barbarians and the wars in Amazônia) —the Indians never established a stable peace with the invader, forcing him into a continuous effort over decades to dominate each region.

That resistance can be explained by the very simplicity of their egalitarian social structure, which, not relying on a higher order that could set up a valid peace or on lower groups conditioned to subordination, made it impossible for them to organize as a state, while at the same time their domination became impossible to realize. After each skirmish against other Indians or against the European invader, if victorious, they took prisoners for cannibalistic rites and went on their way; if defeated, they tried to escape with the aim of regrouping their forces for new attacks. When they were decimated and therefore incapable of attack or defense, the survivors fled beyond the frontiers of civilization. This is what is happening today, 500 years later, with the Yanomami of the northern frontier region of Brazil.

Each Tupi nucleus lived in permanent conflict with other tribes settled in their areas of expansion and even with their neighbors from the same cultural roots (Fernandes 1952). In the first case the conflicts were caused by disputes over the places best suited for planting, hunting, or fishing. In the second they were motivated by a culturally conditioned animosity, a kind of intertribal interaction that took place through warlike expeditions for the purpose of capturing prisoners for ritual cannibalism.

The cultural and collaborative character of these ceremonies made it almost imperative to capture for sacrifice warriors from within the same Tupi group. Only these—by sharing the same set of values—could fulfill to perfection the role prescribed for them: that of a proud warrior who spoke haughtily with his killer and those who were going to eat him. This dynamic is confirmed by the text of Hans Staden, who was borne to cannibalistic ceremonies three times, and three times the Indians refused to eat him because he wept and befouled himself begging for mercy. They did not eat cowards. Cannibalism was also an expression of the relative backwardness of the Tupi peoples. They ate their prisoners of war because, with the rudimentary state of their productive system, a captive would render little more than he consumed, there being no incentive yet to integrate him into the community as a slave.

Many other indigenous groups played a role in the formation of the Brazilian people—some, like the Paresi, as preferred slaves because of their familiarity with the technology of the old Paulista pioneers; others as irreconcilable enemies, useless as slaves because their adaptive system contrasted too much with that of the Tupi peoples. That was the case, for example, of the Bororo, the Xavante, the Kayapó, the Kaingang, and the Tapuia in general.

The greatest contrast was seen between those of mixed blood called Mamelukes (*mamelucos*) and a rival really capable of threatening them, the Gauikuru, also called horseback Indians. Adopting the horse, which for other Indians was nothing but new game multiplying on the prairies, the Gauikuru restructured themselves into pastoral chieftaincies that vigorously confronted the invader, inflicting upon him defeats and losses that came to threaten European expansion.

One of the chroniclers of the civilizing expansion across their territories tells us clearly that "they were close to exterminating all Spaniards in Paraguay" (Félix de Azara, cited in Holanda 1986, 70). Francisco Rodrigues do Prado (1839, 1:15), a member of the Frontier Commission for Spanish and Portuguese America, put the number of Paulistas killed by the Gauikuru along the routes of communication with Cuiabá at 4,000.

Those Guaikuru Indians seem to have been made for that evolutionary path. First, because of their very physical makeup, at which all Europeans who observed them in the fullness of their performance marveled. They are described as gigantic warriors, quite well proportioned, about whom, we are told, "I doubt that there is any people in Europe who, among so many, could be compared to these barbarians" (Félix de Azara, cited in Holanda 1986, 78). Sánchez Labrador (1910, 1:146), the Spanish Jesuit who catechized them over long years, spoke, however, of Indians huddling under skins to escape the pitiless cold snaps that sometimes fell over those regions, and he tells us that "there is no image more fitting than that of a painted Hercules."

Even more explicative of their drive is the fact that before the arrival of the Europeans, the Guaikuru had already imposed their suzerainty over agricultural peoples, forcing them to supply food and slaves. Reports dating from the early years of the sixteenth century speak of these Indians as intelligent people who dominated the Guaná, imposing on them a relationship that the writer compared to that of the Tatars over their vassals. The Mbayá-Guaikuru became even more dangerous when they allied themselves with the Payaguá-Guaikuru, pirate Indians, who fought with their oars transformed into double-tipped lances and who decimated several Paulista expeditions loaded down with gold from Vila Bela in upper Mato Grosso.

Sérgio Buarque de Holanda (1986, 82) collected data from primary sources that estimated from 300 to 600 and even 1,800 to 3,000 pounds of gold stolen from the Paulistas for barter with people in Asunción, who must have accumulated great fortunes in that way.

The *herrenvolk* propensity of the Guaikuru, armed with the strength of cavalry, brought about their rise from an undifferentiated tribal state to pastoral chieftainships able to take captives for slaves, who would be incorporated into their chieftainships, and to have sovereignty over numerous agricultural tribes.

For the Iberians fighting over the rule of those vast hinterlands rich in gold, nothing could be better than to form an alliance with the Guaikuru, to hurl them against adversaries. Both Portuguese and Spaniards managed to do this at one time or another. But over the long run the Spaniards were doubly excited by that alliance because in their case, greed was added to competition. The fact is that the Guaikuru learned quickly about barter, capturing black slaves and also European men and women and many Mamelukes, as many as they could, to sell in Asunción.

On describing these alliances, Sérgio Buarque de Holanda bristles: "It is the contribution of two diverse humanities, so heterogeneous, so ignorant, yes, of each other, that a deadly state of intolerance is interposed between them" (1986, 59).

The Guaikuru were alternately allied with Spaniards and with Portuguese without holding any loyalty to either because they had never accepted any domination. Goaded and indoctrinated by the Jesuits, whose missions were sheltered among their tents, they hurled themselves against the Portuguese, attacking Cuiabá and Vila Bela (Labrador 1910). When the Jesuits were expelled, the Indians turned even more strongly against the Spaniards, attacking the environs of Asunción.

The Mbayá ended up settling in the southern part of Mato Grosso, which, thanks in large measure to that alliance, has remained Brazilian, and the Payaguá in the Asunción region. The Paraguayan War gave both of them their last moment of glory, attacking and sacking Paraguayan and Brazilian settlements. They ended up finally despoiled of their herds of cattle and horses, which were weakened by plagues and stolen. Nevertheless they maintained their haughtiness until the end and still keep it in the form of the proud identification they have of themselves, setting themselves firmly apart from all other Indians, to which I can bear witness from the years I lived among them in their villages around 1947.

The Portuguese

In contrast to the peoples they found here, all of them structured in autonomous, anarchic tribes and not stratified into classes, the horde of invaders was the local vanguard of a vast and ancient urban and classist civilization. Its center of decision was Lisbon, where the court retained many functions, notably that of the powerful Overseas Council, which anticipated, planned, arranged, and supplied everything.

Another powerful coordinator was the Catholic Church, along with its repressive arm, the Holy Office. Listening to denunciations and calumnies in its search for heresies and bestialities, it judged, condemned, imprisoned, and even burned alive those who were most audacious. Not even here in the vastness of these immense jurisdictions did the civilizing structure that was being imposed on the nascent Brazil end. It was an interactive conglomerate of equal entities in active, sometimes bloodthirsty competition with one another.

A most important absence stood out at first in the complex: that of Spain, an object of special attention, with the shadowy and permanent threat of absorption and liquidation of the Portuguese hegemony. Coming later as entities actively aligned against Portugal in the dispute over its new worlds were England and Holland. Over all of them hovered Rome, the Vatican, the Holy See, as the center of the legitimization and canonization of every worldly undertaking and the center of the faith established in its name by a vast clergy in countless churches and monasteries. There followed a powerful apparatus of armed mercantile states, hostile among themselves and barely held in check by papal authority, respected by some, attacked by others.

That complex of Portuguese power was being activated in the previous decades by the transforming energies of the mercantile revolution, based especially on the new technology in seafaring, with new sails for the high seas, a fixed rudder, the compass, the astrolabe, and above all a bank of war cannons. Along with it came Gutenberg's printing press, expanding the availability of books, and cast iron for producing the tools and appurtenances of war.

Its sciences were an effort to link the experiences being accumulated with knowledge, and especially to put that knowledge into practice for the discovery of any land that might be found, with the result that the whole earth was structured into one single world ruled by Europe. All of this had the aim of bearing away all the wealth that could be plundered and, after that, everything that came out of the productive capacity of the conscripted peoples.

It was humanity itself that was entering a new moment in its existence, when thousands of peoples would be extinguished, along with their languages and their own singular cultures, giving birth to macroethnicities larger and more inclusive than had ever been seen.

The driving force of this expansion was the civilizing process that had given birth to two national states—Portugal and Spain—which had just been established as they overcame the feudal fractionalization that followed the decline of Rome. This was not how they, the movers of that expansion, saw themselves, naturally. They gave themselves the luxury of proposing motives more noble than mercantile, defining themselves as those who were spreading Catholic Christianity to peoples who existed and would be found to exist overseas. They planned to remake the globe in a mission of salvation, fulfilling the supreme task of the white man, who had been destined for it by God: to bring together all men in one single Christianity, lamentably divided into two faces, the Catholic and the Protestant.

Even before the "discovery" of Brazil, the Vatican had established the basic norms for colonizing action by setting the rules, with eyes still on Africa, for the new crusades that were to be launched, not against the heretical worshipers of another God but against pagans and innocent peoples. That is what can be read in the bull *Romanus Pontifex,* of January 8, 1454, by Pope Nicholas V:

> It is not without great joy that it has come to our knowledge that our beloved son Prince Henry, burning with the ardor of his faith and zeal for the salvation of souls, is striving to make known and venerated the whole globe over the glorious name of God, bringing to His faith not only Saracens, its enemies, but also all other infidels. Guineans and blacks taken by force, others acquired legitimately have been brought to the kingdom, which we hope will lead to the conversion of all the people or at least many more. Now therefore, having pondered the matter with all due consideration, we concede to the aforementioned King Afonso complete and free license, among other things, to invade, conquer, and subjugate any and all Saracens and pagans, enemies of Christ, their lands and their possessions, to reduce all to servitude and to keep everything for his own use and that of his descendants. We declare that everything shall rightfully belong in perpetuity to said King Afonso and his descendants and to the prince. If anyone, individual or group, shall infringe on these determinations, let him be excommunicated. (In Baião 1939, 36–37)

Later on, always with foresight, the Vatican, in the bull *Inter Coetera* of May 4, 1493 — in almost the same words as in the previous bull — decreed that the New World, also, could be legitimately possessed by Spain and Portugal and that its peoples also could be enslaved by whoever might subjugate them:

> Through our own liberality and certain knowledge and with full Apostolic power, all islands and mainlands found and to be found, discovered and to be discovered, to the west and to the south, with

a line drawn from the Arctic Pole . . . whether they be mainlands or islands found or to be found in the direction of India or in the direction of any part, which line shall lie at a distance of a hundred leagues toward west and south from one of the islands commonly called Azores and Cape Verde. . . . To you and to your heirs and successors (Kings of Castile and León) by the authority of Almighty God conferred on us through Saint Peter along with the vicarate of Jesus Christ, which we exercise on earth forever, by this present text we give, concede, and hand over to you with all their realms, cities, fortresses, towns, villages, laws, jurisdictions, and all things pertaining thereto. And to you and to the aforementioned heirs and successors, we make you, constitute you, and deputize you as masters of the same with full, free, and omnifarious power, authority, and jurisdiction. . . . Subjecting to you, through the favor of Divine Clemency the mainlands and islands mentioned above and the dwellers and inhabitants thereof, and to bring them to the Catholic Faith. (In Macedo Soares 1939, 258)

It must be recognized that this is, even today, the law that obtains in Brazil. It is the base upon which there was disposition, through exception, for the awarding of a small territory to an indigenous people or else, through exception, the episodic and temporary declaration that the people of such and such a tribe were not open to enslavement. It is the basis, furthermore, of the right of the large landholder to the land that was once awarded him along with the rule over all the people there, who merely formed a work force, with no destiny of their own, and whose function was to serve the landlord, whose origins derived from these bulls.

2

The Confrontation of Worlds

Opposing Views

The Indians looked upon the arrival of the Europeans as a fearsome event, understandable only through their mystical view of the world. These must be people coming from their god, the creator—Maíra—people who had arrived miraculously over the waves of the broad sea. There was no way to interpret their designs: they could as easily be fierce as peaceful, despoilers as benefactors.

They must be generous people, the Indians thought, because in their world it was more beautiful to give than to receive. There no one ever despoiled anyone and no person was ever denied praise for his bravery and creativity. The new arrivals coming out of the sea were visibly ugly, smelly, and sickly. It could not be denied. It was true that after a bath and a meal their looks and manners improved. The hopes of those first Indians were probably greater than their fears, so much so that many of them went confidently about the first vessels, believing that they would be taken to the Lands without Evil, the dwelling place of Maíra (*Newen Zeytung*, 1515). So many of them went that, after brazilwood, Indians came to be the principal merchandise for export to the mother country.

That idyllic vision would not last long. Over the following years it was erased and quite the opposite came to prevail: the Indians began to see the hecatomb that had befallen them. Could their god Maíra be dead? What explanation could there be for his chosen people to have suffered such afflictions? So fearsome and terrible were these that many Indians found it better to die than to go on living.

Later on, with the destruction of the bases of indigenous social life, the negation of all their values, despoilment, slavery, a large number of Indians lay down in their hammocks and let themselves die, as only they have the power of doing. They died of sadness, certain that any possible future would be a most horrible negation of the past, a life unworthy of being lived by real people.

Onto these Indians, frightened by what was happening to them, the preaching of the missionaries fell like a lash. Through it the Indians discovered that what had happened to them was their fault and was due to their iniquity, their sins, that the good God in heaven had fallen upon them like a savage dog, threatening to hurl them into hell forever. Good and evil, virtue and sin, valor and cowardice were all so mixed up, changing beauty into ugliness, evil into good. Nothing of what had been of greatest value to them was worth anything from then on: gratuitous bravery, a desire for beauty, creativity, and solidarity. Christianity appeared to their eyes as a world of sin, painful and mortal illnesses, cowardice, a usurpation of the Indian world, everything infected with corruption, everything rotting.

The peoples who could still flee into the forests did so, horrified at the fate offered them by living with the whites, whether in the Christianity of the missions or the sinfulness of the colonies. Many of them carried in their contaminated bodies the illnesses that would decimate both their own groups and the unaffected peoples they were approaching.

But the irresistible attraction of tools, adornments, adventure made them come back. Every generation wanted to see with its own eyes the strange people settled on the shore who received ships laden with such precious goods. Some approached and stayed on, preferring the adventure of living with the new masters as archers in their wars against wild Indians to the routine of tribal life, which had lost its exuberance and glow.

That was the first effect of the fateful encounter that took place here. All up and down the Brazilian coast in 1500 they faced each other, startled to see each other just as they were, savagery and civilization. Their conceptions of the world, life, death, and love, not only different but opposite, collided cruelly. The sailors, bearded, hairy, smelly after months of sailing the sea, scabby with the marks of scurvy, looked with wonder at what seemed to be innocence and beauty in the flesh. The Indians, in feathered nudity, splendidly vigorous and handsome, holding their noses against the pestilence, were even more startled as they looked at those creatures coming out of the sea.

For those arriving, the world they were entering was the arena for what they would gain in gold and glory, even if the latter was mainly spiritual, or seemed to be so, as was the case with the missionaries. In order to attain it, everything had been given them, for their overseas activities—base and brutal as they might come to be—had been previously blessed by the bulls and words of pope and king. They were, or so they saw themselves, new crusaders destined to attack and sack the tombs and temples of the heretics of the Indies. But what they saw here with surprise was something that looked like an Edenic humanity, precursor to the one that had been cast out of Paradise. A new era had opened up with this encounter, in which no innocence could even soften the fury with which the invaders hurled themselves against the heathens, ready to subjugate them for the honor of God and for Christian prosperity. Only today, rethinking this encounter on an intellectual level, can one arrive at its true meaning.

For the Indians who were naked on the beach there the world was a splendor to be lived, so rich with birds, fish, roots, fruits, flowers, seeds, a world that could provide the joys of hunting, fishing, planting, and gathering for all the people it might come to have here. In their wise and simple conception, life was a gift from good gods who had endowed them with splendid bodies, good for walking, running, swimming, dancing, fighting. Fine eyes to see all the colors, their lights and shadows. Ears capable of the joy of hearing strident or melodic voices, somber or sharp songs, and every kind of sound there is. Noses competent to sniff and smell stenches and perfumes. Magnificent mouths to enjoy sweet or bitter meals, salty or bland ones, drawing from each the pleasure it gave. And, above all, opposite and complementary sexes made for the joys of love.

The newcomers were practical people, experienced, forbearing, aware of their faults, beginning with the sin of Adam, predisposed to virtue with a clear notion of sin and eternal perdition. The Indians knew nothing of this. They were, in their own way, innocent, confident, without any vicarious conception but with a clear feeling of honor, glory, and generosity, and fitted as no people ever was for living together in solidarity.

In the eyes of the newcomers those handsome Indians—who gave eyes pleasure by just being seen, men and women, their bodies in bloom—had one capital defect: they were loafers, living a useless and worthless life. What did they produce? Nothing. What did they save? Nothing. They lived their futile full lives as if all that were asked of them in this world was living.

In the eyes of the Indians the ones coming out of the ocean seemed too distressed. Why did they work so hard? Why did they accumulate so much, getting more enjoyment out of getting and keeping than giving and exchanging? Their avidity would have been disguised had it not been so visible in their drive to pile up logs of red wood, as if in order to survive, they had been condemned to cut wood and load it on board without any respite. Could they have been afraid perhaps that the forest would cease to be and with it birds and prey? That rivers and sea would dry up, killing all the fish?

> Our Tupinambás are very puzzled why the French and other foreigners set about looking for their red wood. Once an old man asked me: Why do you other people, Maírs and Perôs [French and Portuguese], come from so far away to get wood to warm yourselves with? Don't you have any firewood in your lands? I answered that we had plenty but not of that quality and that we didn't burn it, as he imagined, but that we extracted dye from it to color things, just as they did with their cotton cords and feathers.
>
> The old man immediately retorted: Is it possible that you need so much of it? — Yes, I replied, because in our country there are merchants who own more cloths, knives, shears, mirrors, and other items than you can imagine, and one of them alone will buy all the brazilwood that many ships have come loaded down with. — Ah! the savage responded, you are telling me many wondrous things, adding, after reaching a good understanding of what I had told him: But that man so rich that you speak to me about, does he not die? — Yes, I said he dies like all others.
>
> But savages are great discoursers and it is their custom to follow any matter to the end. Therefore he asked me once more: And when they die, who gets what they have left behind? — Their children, if they have any, I answered. If there are none of these their brothers and sisters or their closest relatives. — Really, the old man went on, who, as you no doubt can see was no fool, I now see that you other Maírs are great madmen, because you cross the sea and suffer great hardships, as you say when you arrive here, and you work so hard to pile up riches for your children or for those who survive you! Can it be that the land that nourished you is not sufficient to feed them too? We have fathers, mothers, and children that we love, but we are certain that after our death the land that has nourished us will also nourish them. That is why we can rest and have no great worries. (Léry 1960, 151–61)

That divergent view of the Indian peoples who filled the beaches marveling at the swollen sails, and who were looked upon with fascination by the newly arrived bearded sailors, also reflected the fatal biotic confrontation of health and morbidity. The Indians were not familiar with illnesses other than rashes or dizziness from a momentary loss of consciousness.

The white men carried everything from dental caries to smallpox, whooping cough, tuberculosis, and measles. Unleashed there from the very first moment was implacable biological warfare. On the one side were peoples winnowed over centuries and millennia through diseases that they survived and for which they developed resistance. On the other side were untouched, defenseless peoples who began to die in droves. That is how civilization takes over, first as an epidemic of fatal illnesses, then through decimation by means of exterminating wars and slavery. These, however, were only the initial steps of a growing calvary of untold sorrows of genocidal and ethnocidal extermination.

For the Indians life was the peaceful fulfillment of existence in a bountiful world and a harmonious society. They had their fights, of course, their wars, but all as fights in which they could demonstrate their valor. A warrior would fight bravely in order to take prisoners, for the glory of attaining a new name and a new tattoo mark by capturing enemies. A fight could also serve to have him offered up as a captive in a feast in which hundreds of people would eat him, converted into *paçoca,* a manioc stew, in a solemn rite of communion to absorb his bravery, which would go on living in their bodies.

A woman would weave a hammock or fashion a basket as perfectly as she could for the pleasure of expressing herself in her work, which would be the mature fruit of her enormous will for beauty. Youths with bodies adorned with feathers scarlet from annatto or blue-green from *genipap* would wrestle in sporting struggles, body to body, into which they put the energy of warlike combat in order to enliven their vigor and their joy.

For the newcomers it was quite the contrary—life was a chore, a difficult obligation in which everyone was condemned to work and everything was subordinated to profit. Wrapped in cloth, shod with boots, and wearing hats, they placed their luxury and their vanity in those items, in spite of these being filthy and ragged more often than elegant and beautiful. Armed with iron spears and thundering blunderbusses, they felt themselves to be the flower of creation. Their obsessive desire was to multiply themselves in the wombs of Indian women and to put the women's arms and legs in their service to plant and harvest their crops and to hunt and fish for what they ate. The men served mainly to fell and gather dyewood or to produce other merchandise for the newcomers' profit and well-being.

These captive Indians, condemned to the vilest sadness, were also the providers of their joys, especially the women, with good sex organs for fornication, good arms for work, and fertile wombs to be impregnated.

The strongest drive of those heroes from overseas was to stand over those living people as their harsh masters. Their vocation was that of command with a cutlass over animals and forests and people in the immense spread of lands that they were appropriating for themselves in the name of God and the Law.

The contrast could not be greater or more unbridgeable in reciprocal misunderstanding. Nothing that the Indians had or did was looked upon with any appreciation except the people themselves, as diverse objects of pleasure and as makers of what they did not understand and producers of what they did not consume. The invader, on the contrary, came with his hands full and his ships well supplied with axes, knives, jackknives, shears, mirrors, and crystal beads in opal-like colors. How many maddened Indians shot arrows against other Indians and even against their own people for the love of those treasures! Unable to produce the items, the Indians had to find and undergo all manner of ways to pay their price, and the goods became indispensable for them. Such goods were, essentially, the merchandise that integrated the Indian world with the market, with the prodigious potential of subverting everything. That was how the newly discovered Lost Paradise was undone and made uniform.

Divergent Motives

In face of the European invasion, the Indians defended their way of being and living to the utmost, especially after losing the illusions of the first peaceful contacts and perceiving that their submission to the invader meant their dehumanization into beasts of burden. Into that conflict of life and death the Indians on one side and the colonizers on the other put all their energies, weapons, and wiles. Every tribe, however, fighting individually, unaided by the rest—except on the few occasions when they formed confederations, aided by the Europeans living among them—came to be conquered by an enemy not great in numbers but better organized, more advanced technologically, and consequently better armed.

The European victories were mainly due to the higher evolutionary state of the incipient neo-Brazilian communities, which permitted them to come together in a single entity served by a literate culture and activated by a missionary religion that had a powerful influence over the Indian communities. Paradoxically, however, it was the very backwardness of the Indians that made them more resistant to subjugation, bringing on a long, drawn-out war of extermination. That can be seen by comparing the rapidity of conquest and pacification where the Europeans faced high civilizations—as in Mexico and Peru—with the slowness of the conquest of Brazil, which continues to this day with remote tribes making armed resistance to the invasion of their territories beyond the frontiers of civilization.

Colonial chronicles make copious mention of this war without quarter between Europeans armed with cannons and muskets against Indians who relied only on clubs, blowguns, and bows. Even so, the chroniclers take pleasure and pride in exalting Lusitanian heroism. This is the case of the poems of Father Anchieta in praise of Mem de Sá, the subjugator of aboriginal populations in order to enslave them and place them in the hands of the missionaries. Anchieta, putting aside the good sense that should have corresponded to his future sainthood, praised the brave governor in these terms:

Who will be able to tell of the heroic deeds of the Chief
At the head of his soldiers in the immense wilderness?
One hundred sixty villages burned,
A thousand houses destroyed by the devouring flames,
Fields laid waste with their riches,
Everything under the blade of the sword.

These are some of the 2,000 lines of praise written in Latin by José de Anchieta (1958, 129) in the poem *De Gestis Mendi de Saa* (circa 1560).

The praise is all the more understandable when one recalls that Mem de Sá, with his wars of subjugation and extermination, was rigorously executing the plan of colonization proposed by Father Nóbrega in 1558. This cruel plan is the most expressive document of the Indian policies of the Portuguese Jesuits. In its frightful eloquence, one of the arguments used is the allegation of the necessity of putting an end to cannibalism, which will only be stopped, it says, by doing away with "the hellish mouth that has eaten so many Christians." Another argument, no less expressive, is the expediency of enslaving all Indians immediately so that they not be enslaved illegally.

If Your Highness wishes to see them all converted, order them to be subjugated, and you should send Christians inland and divide among them the services of those Indians in order to help them conquer and rule, as is done in other parts of new lands. . . .

By subjugating the heathens, an end will be made to the many cases of illegal slavery and many scruples, because men will have legitimate slaves taken in a just war and will have the service of

Indian vassals and the land will be populated and Our Lord will gain many souls and Your Highness will draw much profit from this land because there will be many stock farms and many plantations, even if there be not much gold and silver. . . .

This also seems the best way for the land to be populated by Christians and it would be better than sending poor settlers, as some have come not bringing anything with which to buy a slave, beginning their new lives unable to maintain themselves and thus forced to return or dying of worms; and it seems better to send people who can dominate the land and are ready to accept any good way to make a living from it, as did some of those who came with Tomé de Souza. . . .

There should be a protector of Indians to have them punished when necessary and to defend them from harm that might come to them. He should be well paid, chosen by the priests, and approved by the governor. If the governor is diligent this should be sufficient.

The law that would be laid down is to prohibit them from eating human flesh and making war without the governor's permission, to make them have only one wife, wear clothing, as they have plenty of cotton, after they are Christians at least to take away their witch doctors, keep them at peace among themselves and with Christians, have them live quietly without moving to other places unless they go among Christians, have lands divided up sufficient for them, and have priests from the Society there to indoctrinate them. ("Notes on Things in Brazil," May 8, 1558, in Leite 1940, 75–87)

Such was the Jesuit master plan to rule and maintain colonization: a summary of fatal violence, intolerance, despotism, and profit. All the vilest qualities were joined together to form Nóbrega's civilizing plan. Applied with fire and steel by Mem de Sá, that program brought despair and destruction to nearly 300 Indian villages on the coast of Brazil in the sixteenth century.

The balance of that hecatomb is given us by Father Anchieta himself in these words:

The number of people who have passed away around this bay in the last twenty years is something that cannot be believed, because no one had ever thought that so many people could ever die.

If one goes to the plantations and farms of Bahia now he will find them full of blacks from Guinea and very few people from the land,

and if he asks about so many people, they will tell him that they died. ("Report on the First Settlements in Bahia," circa 1587, in Anchieta 1933, 377–78)

Nevertheless, even more than swords and muskets, the great weapons of the conquest mainly responsible for the depopulation of Brazil were the illnesses, unknown to the Indians, with which the invaders contaminated them. The magnitude of this lethal factor can be seen in the registry of the effects of the first epidemic that struck Bahia. Close to 40,000 Indians, foolishly gathered together by the Jesuits in villages around the bay during the middle of the sixteenth century, were attacked by smallpox, and almost all of them died. The 3,000 survivors were so weakened that it was impossible to reconstitute the mission. Often the priests themselves served as involuntary contaminators, to which their own letters bear witness. In some of these they comment on the relief from "chest sickness" that the good air of the new land brought them. In others they tell how the Indians died, covered with flies, spitting blood, with only their souls to be saved.

Even more barbarous was the opposite plan, also defended on the ideological level and much more efficient on the practical plane. The best expression of it comes from Domingos Jorge Velho in a letter to the king dated 1694, where the great captain of the São Paulo Mamelukes arrogantly declares, speaking of his fighters, that "they are not people registered on Your Majesty's rolls, they receive no pay or any help in clothing or ammunition. They are groups some of us have brought together, each one gathering his slaves and weapons." He goes on to say that they do not go into the forest to capture Indians, as "some try to make Your Majesty believe, in order to civilize savages." They go, in his words, "to acquire the wild heathen Tapuia, eaters of human flesh, in order to bring them to a knowledge of urbane humanity and human society." He further alleges that "anyone who tries to make them into angels before making them men labors in vain" ("Letter to the King from Barriga Hill," July 15, 1694, in Ennes 1938, 204–7).

After a few decades the indigenous populations that the caravels of discovery had found all along the Brazilian coast, and whom the first chroniclers had contemplated with wonder, had disappeared. In their place three new types of population had appeared. The first and main one was made up of concentrations of African slaves for plantations and ports. Another, spread out in settlements and villages along the coast or through the open cattle ranges, was formed mainly by people of mixed blood and poor whites. The third consisted of Indians incorporated into the colonial enterprise as slaves of other nuclei or concentrated in villages, some of which preserved their autonomy, while others were governed by missionaries.

In spite of the fact that the Jesuit plan for the colonization of the nascent Brazil had been formulated without any humanitarian scruples, such was the ferocity of the lay colonization that some decades later a serious conflict broke out between the priests of the society and the inhabitants of the agrarian-mercantile settlements. For the priests, the Indians, in decline then and threatened with extermination, had come to be seen as creatures of God and as the original owners of the land, with the right to survive if they gave up their heresies and became part of the Church's flock in the status of workers for the colonial enterprise, and being safeguarded in the missions. For the colonists the Indians were human livestock, whose nature, closer to that of animals than of people, made them good only for slavery.

The Portuguese Crown nominally supported the missionaries, although it never denied authorization for the "just wars" demanded by the colonists to capture and enslave both wild and hostile Indians and those who were simply unsociable. The Crown almost always looked the other way when indigenous slavery was involved, thus making it inevitable, given the character of the colonial enterprise itself, especially in poor regions. Prevented from buying black slaves because they were too expensive, the colonists in São Paulo and other regions turned to the contingency of using the forest dwellers or of making their principal business the capture and sale of Indians to those who needed their labor in subsistence tasks, which for a long time were handled by Indians.

In diverse regions—but especially in São Paulo, Maranhão, and the Amazon country—there were great conflicts between Jesuits and colonists, each defending his solution with regard to the aborigines: missionary reduction or slavery. In both the long and the short run the colonists won out, using Indians as guides, oarsmen, wood gatherers, hunters and fishermen, domestic servants, artisans, and above all using Indian women, engendering in their wombs a vast number of mixed-blood offspring who would later make up the majority of the people in the land: Brazilians.

Almost all religious orders accepted without resistance the role of taming Indians for their incorporation into the workforce or armed expeditions of the colony. The Jesuits, however, regretful of their initial role as seducers of the Indians for the colonists, and inspired by the experience of their Paraguayan confreres, attempted to put into practice in Brazil too a utopian plan for the intentional reconstruction of the social life of the detribalized Indians. Such were their missions, where the Indians were concentrated—after having been attracted by the priests or subjugated by the secular arm—in communities tightly organized as self-sufficient economies, although they might also have some mercantile production. That would take place in the second wave of evangelizing in the Amazon region.

The Jesuit project was in such clear opposition to the colonial one that it is fantastic to think that the two had been attempted simultaneously and in the same areas and under the same rule of the same kingdom. The conflicts resulting from disputes over the domination of the Indians prevented the Jesuit missions from attaining, in Brazilian territory, the dimensions in the number of Indians brought together or the level of organization and prosperity that the Society of Jesus had reached in Paraguay.

Contributing to this failure were two types of factors. The first involved the aforementioned open opposition of the Portuguese settlers to a project that disputed their right to Indian labor and that was taking place in the very areas the settlers occupied. Second, the illnesses brought in by the whites, propagating in the human concentrations of the missions, caused great carnage. After a few decades the Jesuits recognized that in addition to not having succeeded in saving the souls of the Indians—which was clear in the failure of their conversion but which was not serious because "awakening faith is the task of God," not of the missionary (Nóbrega, cited in Dourado 1958, 44)—they had not saved lives either. Quite the contrary. The depopulation of the whole coast was obvious and, looking at the facts today, one has to recognize that the Jesuits themselves were one of the main agents of the extermination.

The role they played was as diplomat-peacemakers, going into action whenever the Indians seemed able to win a battle. This was what happened in Peruíbe when Anchieta, passing himself off as a miracle-working *paí*, ran back and forth trying to dissuade the Indians from attacking the Portuguese, who if attacked at that moment might have been defeated. In fact, he is credited quite correctly—he and Nóbrega—with having saved São Paulo and Portuguese colonization itself on that occasion.

Equally disastrous was the role of the Jesuits in bringing the Indians out of their scattered villages and concentrating them in the reductions, where, in addition to working for the priests and not for themselves and dying in the wars of the Portuguese against hostile Indians, they were the ready victims of the plagues with which the Jesuits, without wishing to, were infecting them. It is obvious that in both cases the explicit plan of the Jesuits was not to destroy the Indians, but the result of their policy could not have been more lethal had it been intended thus.

The most negative activity of the Jesuits, however, was based on the very ambiguity of their double loyalty to the Indians and the Crown— though they were more predisposed to serving the Crown against warlike Indians than to defending them effectively against it. This was especially the case in the first century of colonization, when the priests' main function was to undermine the ethnic loyalties of the Indians by a strong appeal to their religious feelings, with the aim of having people break with their tribes and attach themselves to the missions. The efficacy attained in this alienating role was as extraordinary and as great as the Jesuits' responsibility in the decimation that resulted from it.

In the second century, already enriched by their sad role and represented now by figures more capable of moral indignation, like Father Antônio Vieira, the Jesuits assumed great risks in the protection and defense of the Indians. For that reason they were expelled first from São Paulo and later from the colonies of Maranhão and Grão-Pará by the colonists. In the end, the Crown itself, through the person of the Marquis of Pombal, decided to put an end to that precocious socialist experiment, expelling them from Brazil. Then the saddest thing of all took place.

The priests obediently handed over their missions to the rich colonists, Pombal's people, who were given the ownership of lands and Indians, while the priests were arrested and shipped off to Europe to ponder bitterly for years the sad role of subjugators they had played.

Salvationism

Over the decades of the finding, exploration, and invasion of Brazil, ever more detailed descriptions of the new lands appeared. In that way they went on being appropriated by the invader through his knowledge of their rivers and forests, animals and sprites. At first this involved absorbing the copious indigenous wisdom of previous millennia of growing familiarity with the surrounding nature, classifying and giving names to places and things, defining their uses and utility. Later the process moved through successive redefinitions, sometimes retaining the old names and at other times renaming things, but in both cases forming a new body of knowledge turned toward different values and aims.

It was the people found there who aroused the greatest curiosity. The Indians, seen at first as the good, handsome people who generously received the first navigators, afterward went on to be seen as cannibals, the completely detestable eaters of human flesh. With contact, just as the Indians began to distinguish different nations and characteristics in the Europeans, so too the latter came to differentiate the Indians into groups of allies and enemies, speaking different languages and having different customs.

Thus, a reciprocal ethnology was emerging through which each people portrayed the other. Corresponding to it in Europe was a compendium of interpretations of the startling novelties that arrived in letters from the navigators, later on in chronicles and testimony, and finally in this incipient ethnology. Curiosity arose and passed into the realm of the theologians, who were astonished by certain news items that had been unthinkable until then.

Those Indians, so different from the Europeans who saw them and described them but also so similar—could they also be members of the human race, made of the same clay by the hands of God in His image and likeness? They had fallen into impiety. Could they have salvation? It soon became evident that their souls needed a strong bath of lye, befouled as they were by so many abominations, like eating their enemies in savage banquets, the base way in which they were manipulated by the devil through their witch doctors, the lascivious way they made love with the naturalness of beasts, the sloth of their full and useless lives, lacking in mercantile productivity.

That curiosity bloomed soon after into a theology for barbarians, in which the treatises of Frei Francisco de Vitória, Nóbrega, and later those of Vieira and so many others offered learned discourses portraying the Indians on the theological, evangelical, apostolic, providential, cataclysmic, and eschatological levels. Thus was a discourse ever more rational and ever more insane being composed concerning the reality of what had happened to the Indians: crushed and enslaved by the colonizer, who was blind and deaf to any reasons that did not have to do with pecuniary actions and needs.

In spite of these cruel pieces of evidence, a few holy men, in their illuminated alienation, continued to believe that they were fulfilling a Christian calling as the builders of the Kingdom of God in the New World, as apostolic soldiers of universal Christianity. Therefore, they put together a hallucinatory and messianic theology that saw in the Iberian expansion, with the successive discovery of widespread and unknown lands and countless pagan peoples, a divine mission that was being fulfilled step by step. Tordesillas, in that context, must have been a prophetic vision of the Iberian destiny of evangelization to create a Church that was at last truly universal.

Those discourses answered an equally imperative necessity, that of attributing some formal dignity to the war of extermination that was being waged, to the brutality of the conquest, to the perversity of the elimination of so many people. The Iberian Empire, sanctifying itself through the New World, was taking on the hues of Rome. It promised that Indian depravity would be succeeded by Christian prudence and piety, to the point of converting the infidel servants of the devil into Christians, fearful of sin and perdition, worshipers of the true God.

The European who, misinterpreting biblical tradition, had turned the god of the Hebrews into the king of men, now had to include that pagan Indianhood in the humanity of the past, among the children of Eve expelled from Paradise, and in the humanity of the future, among those destined for eternal redemption. The polemic concerning this theme broke out everywhere with lively arguments over which parts of the ancient tradition applied to them or otherwise. Had the Flood with Noah and his animals also occurred in the New World? What evangelical pastors had the carrying of the word of God there as their duty? Why had Christ's comrades failed in their mission? Or were the Indians also guilty of original sin? Would the next Messiah come to save them too? Would the apocalyptic cataclysms of the Last Judgment apply to Indians as well as whites? Could the prophesied Son of God have been born among them as an Indian perhaps?

The only thing in the whole debate that gleamed as bright as the sun for the Crown and for the Church was the salvationist mission: it fell to Christianity to undertake, with fire and steel if necessary, to bring the new peoples into the flock of king and Church. It was an imperative mandate on the spiritual plane, an express destiny, a mission under the charge of the Crown, whose right to make vassals of the Indians, to colonize, and to bring a flow of riches out of the new land was part of the sacred duty to save the natives through evangelization.

On the secular side the legitimacy of European hegemony had been completely established. On the divine side, however, the Jesuits and Franciscans claimed that they were destined to create pious and seraphic republics of holy men with the newly discovered Indians, so that, as prescribed in the Book of Acts, all who believed could live together, holding all their goods in common.

In this way two cruelly opposing outlooks stood out, each seeking predominance in the domination of the New World. On one side were the colonists with their commercial interests; on the other, the religious with their missions. At first, in such vast territory, with each group working in their own province, they were able to grow along parallel lines, but soon the contrast turned into open conflict. The colonists were working to reproduce here a healthy mercantile world, moved by their greed and usury. The monks were making ancient Joachinist heresies echo in the New World—like that of Prince Henry with his preaching that since the age of the Father, governed by the Old Testament, had passed, as had that of the Son, addressed in the New Testament, the Era of the Holy Spirit had arrived, which would bring about the millennium of love and happiness in this world, with the Indians converted and changed into people who praise the glory of God.

History would have the opposite plan prevail, obliging the evangelizers themselves to fulfill the colonial project through genocidal war against all Indians and through ethnocidal missionary activity, to their regret.

In the tasks for the conversion of the pagan and his integration into Christianity, the main soldiers were the Jesuits, the Franciscans, and the Carmelites. The followers of Ignatius were inspiring, supporting, and urging on the secular arm so that by making war and bringing people into vassalage, they would place the humiliated natives at the priests' feet in the missions. There, apparently, they would contritely live the lives of humble Indians. In truth, they were inventing a new sad life of catechumens for the Indians, one that was bearable only in the face of the alternative, which was to fall captive to the colonists. In this way they were building, day by day, year by year, the Christian City, virtuous and operative, unthinkable in the Old World but feasible here with the docile clay that formed the Indians—innocent, simple, and pure, especially the children, still with their milk teeth, as Gilberto Freyre has said. In the end it became clear to the missionaries that they could hope for nothing from rotten and corrupt Europe. The Apocalypse would be the only possible hope of salvation for it. In the New World, on the other hand, every day they saw their hopes of concretizing the biblical prophecies being confirmed.

The task that the missionaries proposed for themselves was not to transplant European ways of living and being into the New World. It was, on the contrary, to re-create the human being here, developing the best potentialities in order to implant, finally, a mutual, egalitarian, prayerful, and pious society on the bases dreamed of by the prophets.

That socialistic and seraphic utopia would flourish in the Americas, going back to the traditions of primitive Christianity and the most generous messianic prophecies. It would be based in equal measure on the

Adamic innocence that so surprised the missionaries and on the Edenic sense of solidarity that they came to see in the Indians as they lived among them.

The Franciscan mystics, who saw themselves at the head of a caste system of Indians that was a holdover from pre-Columbian civilizations, went along recruiting them to convert pagan pyramids into sumptuous Christian churches for the greater glory of God. They dreamed of organizing indigenous life according to the rules of Sir Thomas More's *Utopia*, inspired anachronistically by the original Indian culture. They even believed that it was possible to spread that alternative to the conquest, making European expansion the universalization of Christianity. Incarnate in indigenous bodies, Christianity would enter the Joachinist Millennium, where happiness would be attained in this world. In Brazil the Jesuits were ahead of the Indians along the same path, reinventing history.

Those utopias were so cruelly opposite to colonial plans that war soon broke out between colonists and priests. The colonist, wishing to put Indian labor to work for his enrichment, was aided by the secular clergy, who were regularly disposed to bless the earthly city, giving to God what was God's and to the king whatever he demanded.

It was a disaster. Even where the missions had come to be productive and profitable for the Crown itself—as occurred with those of Sete Povos in the south and in the north in the more laggardly missions of the Amazon region—the will of the colonist, which saw in the Indians a workforce that he needed to prosper, prevailed.

The startling thing for someone who ponders that drama today is the vigor of the missionary faith of those holy men, who went as far as subversion in the struggle for their ideal. After having compromised without limits, interpreting in a transcendental tone the conquest as a necessary evil, the gateway to the path that would open onto the road of faith through sacrifice, they recovered their senses and began to see their own conniving role.

For decades they had spoken not a word of pity for the thousands of dead Indians, for the burned villages, for the men, women, and children enslaved by the millions. They had watched all this in silence—or had even, like Anchieta, sung of those acts in thousands of servile lines of poetry. For them all of that grief was necessary grief to color the cheeks of the dawn they saw breaking. Only tardily did they come to realization, seeing themselves defeated first in evangelization and then in the reclusion of Indians in the missions. Nevertheless, no historical disaster, no previous utopian project had aimed so high, because no hope until then had been so positive or could have been carried so far forward, demonstrating the feasibility of intentionally reconstructing society according to a plan.

The Jesuit utopia fell apart and the Ignatians were expelled from the Americas, turning over their catechumens unprotected and unmanned to sacrifice and slavery at the grasping hands of the colonists. The same thing happened to the marvelous dream of the Franciscans, reduced to a vision of the savageness of the colonial world, impious and brutal.

One must ask here whether it was their very success that brought the utopian projects of the Jesuits and Franciscans to failure. Seeing the unbridgeable incompatibility between themselves and the colonists, and by extension between the missionaries' plan and the royal one, they withdrew to create their own European province. They tried to give Iberian expansion the monk's alternative of the restoration of a Christianized Indianhood, which would speak its own indigenous languages and would have fealty only to itself. The Crowns, both of them, favored the colonial plan. The mystics had already fulfilled their function of dignifying the act of conquest. Now they should make way for practical men who would set up and consolidate the bases of the greatest empire ever seen. Instead of holy, pious kingdoms under missionary kings in the service of the Church and God, the kings of Spain and Portugal wanted the kingdom of this world.

3

The Civilization Process

Germinal Peoples

The civilizing process, driven by the technological revolution that made oceanic navigation possible, transfigured the Iberian nations, structuring them as *mercantile salvationist* empires. This is the explanation for the extraordinary vitalization of those nations, which suddenly took on an inexplicable expansive energy, both in a simply feudal form and also in a capitalist form. This latter arose in England and Holland only much later.

It is a fact that explanatory theories of world history offer no theoretical categories that can explain either the singular power that Arab civilization held for over a millennium of splendor or the Iberian expansion, which created the first universal civilization. That lack is what obliges us in our study of the civilization process (Ribeiro 1968; 1972) to propose, with respect to the Arab world, the category of *despotic salvationist empire,* emphasizing the atypical character of its salvationism, which never attempted to convert anyone. They simply conquered an area, shouted *Jihad,* and let the people live. At a certain moment, as has happened with all civilizations, they went into obsolescence and became feudal, giving way to a new kind of salvationism. For the Iberian world we propose the category of *mercantile salvationist empire,* generated by the same technical revolution, the mercantile one, that gave access to the overseas world. Technology had been generated in the Arab world and in the Orient, but was gathered in and strung together first by the Portuguese.

The Iberians, as a first step, had freed themselves of the age-old Arab occupation and had expelled their Jewish contingent, assuming complete command of their territory through a centralized power that left no space for any feudal autonomy or commercial monopoly.

In a second step they expanded over the seas, plunging into wars of conquest, sack, and evangelization against the peoples of Africa, Asia, and principally the Americas. In that way they established the bases for the first world economic system, interrupting the autonomous development of the great American civilizations. Simultaneously they exterminated thousands of peoples who had previously been living in prosperity and happiness, spread out over all the land, along with their languages and their original cultures.

At the same time they molded themselves into new socioeconomic formations and new historical-cultural configurations, which covered areas and subjugated populations infinitely larger than those of Europe (Ribeiro 1970). It was during the course of this self-transformation that the indigenous populations of America, including Brazil, saw themselves conscripted, to their sorrow, for the tasks of the nascent civilization. They were useful because of their indigenous knowledge, which permitted Europeans to adapt to other latitudes, and they largely provided the workforce that brought the colony into the world market then taking shape.

Like Rome in the past, the Iberians, the English, and the Russians were germinal nations in the modern world. Each of them gave origin to a ponderable variant of humanity—the Latin American, the neo-Britannic, and the Slavic—creating peoples as homogeneous among themselves as they were different from the rest. Strangely, Germany, France, and Italy, so advanced and accomplished as branches of western civilization, were not germinal. Closed up inwardly, feudalized, busy with dissensions among their internal variants, they never became organized at the time as national states, nor did they exercise seminal power.

The Slavs expanded simultaneously over their steppes and tundras and reached Alaska, but held back by the sclerosis of their archaic, rigidly stratified society, they reined in their drive without conquering new worlds.

The English expanded as hard-working Puritan farmers or as industrialized and business-oriented city dwellers who carefully weighed every act. Intent on a different type of colonization, their task was that of transplanting their landscape to the world outside, re-creating little Englands, paying little heed or indifferent to what existed where they had arrived. Refusing to see or understand the age-old reasoning and justifications of the Vatican, they simply proposed conquering their slice of the American pie. At best it was to flush excess humanity out of their own kingdom, giving them new nations to build. They also managed, first by the hands of pirates, corsairs, and smugglers, to take all the gold they could from what the islanders were carrying to the Old World. Subsequently, through the mechanism of mercantile exchange, they took possession of an even greater chunk of those riches.

Later on they settled in northern areas of the continent, populating it with colonies. Neighbors of the Caribbean islands and their rich sugar plantations worked by slaves, the colonies were poor and backward. They flourished only slowly, gaining subsistence from the trade in food and artifacts with the slaveholders of the islands and producing the merchandise of the poor.

The Iberians, on the other hand, plunged into the overseas adventure to open new worlds, driven by the most fanatical fervor and the most ungovernable violence in search of riches by sacking or from what could be produced by slavery, certain that they were new crusaders fulfilling a salvationist mission of bringing the whole world under Roman Catholic rule. They always landed without illusions, ready for new worlds, aiming to rule them, rebuild them, convert them, and mix racially with them. Consequently they multiplied prodigiously, fertilizing native wombs and creating new human types.

As has been seen, the primary cause of the overseas expansion and therefore of the discoveries was the precocious national unification of Portugal and Spain, moved by a technological revolution that gave them access to the whole world with their armed vessels, giving birth to a new civilization. Freed of the Saracen occupation, relieved of Jewish exploitation, rid of the local powers of feudal nobility, a national state arose in each region. These were the first in the modern world.

Out of this, therefore, came entities capable of great enterprises, like the discoveries and the golden enrichment overseas, along with their institution as an empire with hegemony over America, Asia, and Africa. Their power grew so much that at one time Spain tried to exercise its sovereignty over Europe as well. Portugal saw itself compelled to make an alliance with England in order to maintain its independence.

During those worldwide conflicts, Iberia grew so weakened that it ended up succumbing as head of the world empire so often dreamed of. It succumbed, however, back there, in conflicts with its peers. Here in the New World its seeds continued the prodigious fertilization of an American racial mixture; its languages and cultures continued to spread. In that way it went on finally to make up one of the broadest, richest, and most homogeneous provinces on earth, Latin America. England, which was the third nation to become structured, founded on its wealth and the Judaic wisdom it had taken in, ended up taking possession of the other half of the Americas, over which it expanded as a second macroethnicity, immensely homogeneous and neo-Britannic.

The dimensions of these dominions were those of the world they had just occupied. The original ethnic heterogeneity of that world, on the contrary, was without parallel in human history. It was broken and reconstituted only through the continuous effort over the centuries that wiped out any ethnic inconstancy or any right of self-determination of the people held in vassalage.

So it was that Iberia and Great Britain, so filled with the stiff resistance of the peoples of their home territories, whom they would never succeed in assimilating, here absorbed and razed almost everything. When they came upon high civilizations, the people were killed, infected with diseases, cut off from their leaders, converted into mere animal energy for slave labor. Those undone people managed to hold only in their breasts the feeling of themselves as a people, the language of their ancestors, and the echoes of ancient greatness.

In Brazil Portugal's colonial work with Indians and blacks was also something radical. Its real product was not the gold so eagerly sought and found or the merchandise produced and exported, or even what so much wealth permitted to be built in the Old World. Its real product was a nation-people forged principally here through racial admixture, a people who multiplied prodigiously as a dark humanity in bloom and awaiting its full destiny—a clear, uncomplicated destiny of simply being one among peoples and existing for themselves.

Nothing was more continuous or as permanent over these five centuries than the ruling class, exogenous and unfaithful to its people. In the drive to use up people and forests, animals and things, for profit, they have destroyed the most amazing forests on earth. They have reduced innumerable hills in search of minerals. They have eroded and leveled lands without count. They have used up people by the millions.

Everything has been incessantly transformed over the centuries. Only the ruling class has remained the same, exercising its interminable hegemony. Old domains are succeeded by new ones, super-homogeneous and in solidarity among themselves in a heavily armored ironclad union and predisposed in every way to keep the people moaning and producing not what they want and need but what they are told to produce, in the form imposed on them, with indifference to their destiny.

The members of the ruling class have not even managed the minor deed of generating a generalized prosperity for the working classes here, as has been attained under similar regimes in other places. Even less successful have been their efforts to become integrated into industrial civilization. Their aim today is to force us over to the margins of the civilization that is emerging.

The Baroque and the Gothic

Two styles of colonization were inaugurated in the north and in the south of the New World. Up north was the haughty gothic of cold Nordic peoples brought over in entire families to re-create by a new form of agriculture the landscape from which they had come as surplus labor. For them the Indian was a detail who soiled the landscape that had to be Europeanized; they had to be rid of Indians. Let them go and live where they wanted, free to be different but far away, over the other sea if possible, into the Pacific.

Here in the south was the baroque of the miscegenated Iberian peoples, who had mixed with the Indians without recognizing any rights for them except that of multiplying in order to provide more workers. To the apartheid of the northerners they placed in opposition the assimilation of the melting pot. On the one side we have the proud and arrogant tolerance of those who know themselves to be different and wish to remain that way. On the other we have the oppressive tolerance of those who wish to live together by ruling over the bodies and souls of the captive Indians and blacks, whom they can conceive of only in what these people should be tomorrow—their equivalents—because any difference is intolerable to them.

Acting with the ethic of the adventurer who improvises at every moment as he faces the challenge he must confront, the Iberians did not produce what they wanted but rather what resulted from their often unrestrained actions. It is clear that the colonization of Brazil was a persistent and stubborn effort to implant a Europeanness here that was adapted to these tropics and was incarnated in these racial mixtures, but it always ran up against the obstinate resistance of nature and the whims of history, which have made us what we are today in spite of those designs, so contrary to whiteness and urbanity, so inwardly de-Europeanized as de-Indianized and de-Africanized.

Those gothic gentlemen and ladies who expected no great wealth from their new homelands acquired terrain so as to live a virtuous rural existence. As it was not necessary to subject the new homeland to the European world they had left behind, or necessary to subject it to slave labor, since it was incapable of producing any worthwhile product, it gave them land and liberty.

None of that occurred in the baroque world. Here Europe was faced with a multitude of exotic peoples, some savage, others civilized, who could be mobilized as an indispensable labor force to bring forth the wealth that was in plain view here or that could easily be produced.

Here no land was wasted on the people who worked it. The ruling class appropriated all of it, less for their own use, as there was much too much of it, than with the aim of obliging the subjugated pagans to work on other people's land. Nor was any freedom permitted, because it was a matter of heretics to be catechized, freeing them from eternal perdition.

There was nothing more natural than thinking in those terms for Iberians who had just expelled Saracen and Jewish heretics who had dominated them over the centuries. Still, with the fervor of the glorious crusades against the Moors, they raged now against the American pagans. The state itself assumed priestly functions expressly conferred by the pope to fulfill the destiny of the City of God against the European Reformation and against American impiety. To attain that, the pope reached the point of transferring to the Iberian Crowns the most important of his privileges, which was papal patronage, and he gave them the right to name, transfer, and revoke bishoprics and other ecclesiastical offices. As a counterweight to what God was giving it in wealth and vassals in the antipodes, Rome blessed the possession of the new worlds with the condition that the Iberians continue there the fight against the Moors, with war and the conversion of the new and recently discovered infidels, perhaps even transforming them through preachers into a final Christianity.

As a consequence, here, in our Catholic and baroque universe, more than there in their reformist and gothic world, the ruling classes tended to define themselves as the agents of western and Christian civilization, considering themselves more perfect, prudent, and pious, so much advanced over savagery that their destiny was to impose themselves as the natural rule of the good over the bad, of the wise over the ignorant. That rule was attained through the action of war, through intelligence in business, through conscription for work, and through refuge in missions. In their view the rulers were simply forcing those inactive Indians to live a destiny more in conformity with the will of God and the nature of man. The colonist became rich and the workers were saved for their eternal life.

This was the dialectic of the natural mastery of the Christian over the likewise natural servitude of the barbarian. With the passage of the ages, the latter would end up coming out of his pagan infancy, innate indolence, lewdness, and sin. No ideology before or after was so convincing for the one who exercised hegemony or as unavoidable for the one who bore it, slave or vassal. Dispossessed of their lands, enslaved in their bodies, converted into livestock for uses that their master assigned them, they were also despoiled of their souls. That was attained through the conversion that invaded and brought their very consciences into vassalage, making them see themselves as poor, pagan, and sinful humanity, which, unable to save itself in this vale of tears, could only hope through virtue for the vicarious compensation of an eternity praising the glory of God in Paradise.

Such is the strength of this ideology that it still arrogantly rules today. It convinces the governing class in their minds that they are leading and civilizing their underlings, making them overcome their innate laziness in order to live more productive and profitable lives. It also makes the oppressed think they are learning to see the social order as something sacred and their role in it prescribed, that of God's creatures being tested on the road to eternal life.

Those formative lines on the northern side correspond to the formation of a free people, masters of their own destiny, which takes in all white citizens. In our south, what is engendered is an elite of landowners and civilian and military rulers riding herd on the mass of an oppressed subhumanity with no recognized rights. The evolution of both these formations opens the way along similar lines, on the one side for the maturation of a democratic society founded on the rights of its citizens, which has recently come to include blacks as well; and on the opposite side a latifundist establishment hostile to its people, condemned to arbitrary acts, ignorance, and poverty.

On the historical-cultural level, the northerners have realized some of the potentialities of western civilization as an insipid and legitimate extension of it. We, on the contrary, are the promise of a new civilization marked by singularities, principally of African origin. Therefore we appear to European eyes as a strange people, which, added to our Indian tropicality, makes us appear exotic to those same eyes.

We are not—and no one takes us to be—an extension of the whiteness that has been thought to be the most normal form of being human. Not we. We have other standards and other ways that derive from more different peoples.

This, remember, does not make us any poorer but rather richer in humanities; that is to say, more human. This strange and bizarre singularity of ours has been threatened a thousand times, but fortunately it has managed to become consolidated, even as Europe poured in multitudes of immigrants whom we took in, or even recently with the large number of Asian people who have settled here. All of them or almost all have been assimilated and Brazilianized.

Historic Updating

In contrast to the tribal ethnicities that survived side by side for some time, the nascent colonial society, bizarre and precarious, was and acted as an overseas offshoot of European civilization in its Portuguese version. It must be noted that it was already a bisected society, with one rural condition and another urban one, stratified in classes, served by an erudite and literate culture and integrated into the economy of international scope that navigation had made possible.

That higher evolutionary position did not represent, obviously, any ascension of original indigenous societies from their tribal condition to the status of an urban and stratified civilization. It was a simple projection of the civilizing advances reached by Europeans as they came out of the Middle Ages onto the remnants of the aboriginal formation that had been there before and onto the blacks brought in from Africa as a slave labor force.

We now face the results of a civilizing process which, as it interrupted the previous evolutionary line of Brazilian indigenous populations after subjugating them, has recruited those who remained as the slave labor of a new society that was already being born and integrated into a higher period. In this case the step was taken through the incorporation or *historic updating*—which presupposes the loss of ethnic autonomy on the part of the engaged nuclei, their domination, and their transfiguration— which established the bases on which Brazilian society would be built henceforth.

Such bases can be clearly defined by the establishment of the first sugar plantations, which, connecting their former extractive nuclei to the world market, made possible their existence in the socioeconomic condition of an "external proletariat," structured as a mercantile-slaveholding colony of the Portuguese homeland.

On the *adaptive level*—that is, relative to the technology with which the material conditions for existence are produced and reproduced—the Brazilian colonial nuclei were established on the following bases:

- Incorporation of European technology as applied to production, transportation, construction, and war, with use of metal instruments and their multiple applications;
- transoceanic navigation, which integrated the new worlds into a world economy as producers of merchandise for export and as importers of black slaves and consumer goods;
- establishment of sugar plantations, based on the application of complex agricultural, chemical, and mechanical procedures for the production of sugar, and later gold and diamond mining, which involved the mastery of new technologies;
- introduction of cattle, which would furnish meat and hides in addition to being beasts of burden and traction, as well as the raising of hogs, chickens, and other domestic animals, which, in association with tropical indigenous cultivation, would provide subsistence for the colonial nuclei;
- adoption and diffusion of new species of cultivated plants, for both food and industry, which would later come to assume a decisive importance in the economic life of diverse variants of national society;
- use of simple Portuguese technology for the production of tiles and fabrics, shoes and hats, soap, cane liquor, cart wheels, bridges, boats, etc.

On the *associative level*—that is, in what concerns the ways of organization of social and economic life—the nuclei were structured as the implantation of a civilization thanks to:

- substitution for the elementary solidarity founded on kinship, characteristic of the egalitarian tribal world, by other forms of social structuration that divided society into rural and urban components and stratified it into antagonistically opposing classes, even though they could be independent through the complementary nature of their respective roles;
- introduction of indigenous slavery, later replaced by the traffic in African slaves, which permitted the most dynamic sectors of the economy to have no need for the original population in the recruitment of a work force;
- integration of all local nuclei into a single sociopolitical structure that would provide a dominating class for the patronage of enterprises and a ruling noble elite, whose main functions were to make colonial enterprise viable and economically profitable and to defend it against slave revolts, Indian attacks, and foreign invasions;

· availability of financial capital to underwrite the establishment of enterprises, to provide them with slaves and other productive and competent resources, and to secure the income they produced.

On the *ideological plane*—that is, as relating to forms of communication, knowledge, beliefs, artistic creation, and ethnic self-image—the culture of the neo-Brazilian communities was shaped by the following elements:

- · the Portuguese language, which spread out slowly, century after century, until it became the only vehicle of communication among Brazilian communities and with the mother country;
- · a tiny stratum of learned people, who through their domination of erudite learning and the European technology of the time could direct complex activities and operate as a center for the diffusion of knowledge, beliefs, and values;
- · an official Church associated with a salvationist state, which, after arranging the submission of indigenous nuclei through catechizing, imposed a Catholicism of messianic stamp and exercised a rigorous control over the intellectual life of the colony in order to impede any diffusion of other ideologies and even of scientific knowledge;
- · artists, who exercised their activities in obedience to European styles and types, principally the baroque, within the canons of which the new society began to express itself when and where there was any sign of opulence.

Those technological innovations, combined with the aforementioned more advanced forms of social order and ideological instruments of control and expression, provided the bases on which Brazilian society and culture were built as a European colonial implantation. The society and culture were not so much determined by the resulting singularities of the incorporation of multiple traces of indigenous or African origin as by Portuguese colonial rule, which brought the various entities into conformity as the Lusitanian branch of European civilization.

All of it is explained by the absence of a dominating native class. Those who played that role, whether as agents of economic exploitation or in the position of organizers of political hegemony, were really agents of colonial domination. The dominated classes themselves did not constitute a people dedicated to the production of their own conditions of existence—or even capable of reproducing it passively. They are a disparate conglomerate composed of Indians brought from distant places who could barely understand one another, along with people torn from their African roots, all brought together against their will, to find themselves changed into mere slave labor to be consumed in work—people whose very renewal was brought about more through the importation of new contingents of slaves than through their own reproduction.

With a base in this atypical community and in their sociopolitical lot, the new entities were soon able to confront two crucial challenges: one was to wipe out those indigenous groups who, not having been captured and made to work as slaves, had fled the coast and from the interior would attack the neo-Brazilian nuclei settled on the coast. Another was to maintain Portuguese colonial rule over the neo-Brazilian nuclei, which as they grew maintained their internal social stratification and their dependence on the motherland.

II

Ethnic Gestation

4

A Human Nursery

Cunhadismo

The social institution that made possible the formation of the Brazilian people was *cunhadismo*, or "in-lawism," an old indigenous usage for incorporating outsiders into the community. It consisted of giving a man an Indian girl as a wife. As he took her on, he automatically established a thousand links of kinship with all members of the group.

Its reach was based on the Indians' system of classifying kinship as relating all members of a people to one another. In that way, by accepting the girl, the outsider went on to have *temericó*, or kinship, with her, and all her relatives of her parents' generation became his parents or parents-in-law. Likewise with his own generation, where all became his brothers and sisters or brothers- and sisters-in-law. All of the following generation were his children or children-in-law. These terms of blood relationship or affinity went on to classify the whole group as related or incestuous. With the first, he had to maintain relationships of avoidance, as is proper with mothers-in-law, for example. Open and enjoyable sexual relationships obtained in the case of the so-called brothers- and sisters-in-law; likewise with the generation of sons- and daughters-in-law. This practice has been amply recorded by chroniclers and its importance for Brazil has also been evaluated by Efraim Cardoso (1959), of Paraguay, and by Jaime Cortesão (1964).

Spanish documentation, richer in this matter, reveals that in Asunción there were Europeans with more than eighty temericós. The importance of this was enormous: it meant that such a foreigner could rely on a multitude of relatives who could serve him, whether for his personal comfort or for the production of merchandise.

Since every European along the coast could make numerous such marriages, the institution functioned as a vast and efficient form of recruiting laborers for the heavy work of cutting dyewood, transporting it, and loading it on board ship as well as for hunting and taming parrots and *saki* monkeys. Later it also served for the taking of prisoners of war, who could be ransomed in exchange for merchandise instead of suffering the traditional fate of being ritually eaten in a feast.

The Indians would not have it any other way. Enthralled by the riches Europeans were able to bring on their ships, the Indians made use of the newcomers to provide themselves with highly prized possessions that soon became indispensable, things like metal tools, mirrors, and adornments. When they were well provided with those items, other merchandise was given them. And finally it became necessary to go from cunhadismo to warfare for the capture of slaves when the need for native workers became too great.

The role of cunhadismo in the new civilizing establishment was bringing about the rise of a widespread class of people of mixed blood, who effectively occupied Brazil. It is quite possible that the colonization itself was only brought about through the development of this practice. It had the defect, however, of being accessible to any European who disembarked near native villages. That was precisely what happened, and it brought a growing number of ships and the incorporation of the Indians into the mercantile system of production. For Portugal it represented a threat, as she was now losing her conquest to French, Dutch, English, and German shipowners whose ships knew where to find their cargoes.

Without the practice of cunhadismo, the creation of Brazil would have been impracticable. The European populators who ended up here were a handful of castaways and deportees left by the ships of discovery or were sailors who had run away to seek a new life among the Indians. By themselves they would have been but a passing intrusion along an Atlantic coast populated by completely indigenous groups.

But on the basis of cunhadismo, breeding grounds for people of mixed blood were established in the centers where castaways and deportees had settled. First they settled among the Indians in villages, where they took on local customs, living like the Indians, piercing their lips and ears and even taking part in anthropophagous ceremonies, eating people. They quickly learned the language and became familiar with indigenous culture. Many of them enjoyed it so much that they decided to remain in that good life of the Indians, who were friendly and useful. Others formed groups apart from the villages, made up of the new arrivals, their multiple Indian women, and their numerous children, always in contact with the countless relatives of the women. Survival was assured by the Indians in a way almost identical to how they assured their own. The Europeans effected a highly noxious activity, however: the mercantile economy, capable of acting as a civilizing agency through the intermediary of barter, with the exchange of European articles for the products of the land.

The first and principal nucleus of this kind was the one in São Paulo, set up quite early on the coast, perhaps even before the arrival of Cabral. It was centered about João Ramalho and his companion Antônio Rodrigues. It seemed to be so specialized in the ransoming of captive Indians to be sold to ships that the anchorage of the vessels they dealt with came to be known as Port of Slaves.

The village of Ramalho, founder of the future state of São Paulo, had several visitors who described him. The German adventurer Ulrich Schmidel, who in 1553 visited Santo André, one of João Ramalho's villages, said he felt safer in a village of Indians than in that lair of bandits. He went on to note that Ramalho was capable of raising a force of 5,000 Indian warriors, while all the Portuguese government could manage was less than 2,000.

About João Ramalho himself Governor Tomé de Souza, filled of admiration, says in a letter to the king in 1553: "He has so many children and grandchildren, great-grandchildren, and descendants that I dare not tell Your Majesty. He has not a single gray hair on his head or face and he walks nine leagues before dining" ("Letter from Tomé de Souza to the King with Several Items of News about the Lands of Brazil," June 1, 1553, in Cortesão 1956, 271).

Nóbrega, in that same year, was horrified by Ramalho, whose life he considered a monument to scandal:

> He is a major hindrance for us with our pagans because he is so well known and closely related to the Indians. He has many wives. He and his sons go with their sisters and have children by them, both the father and the sons. They go to war with the Indians and their festivals are those of the Indians, and they live that way, going about naked like the Indians themselves. Since we have tried everything with him and nothing has succeeded, we have left him alone. ("Letter to Father Luís Gonçalves da Câmera," June 15, 1553, in Nóbrega 1955, 173–74)

The Jesuits used all manner of wiles, first to attract Ramalho and his people to them, then to make him leave, so vexing was his position of undisputed rule over the Indians, and they had hopes that he might assume an attitude of submission to the priests. They could not do without him in face of the threat represented by the Tamoio, in confederation against the Tupinambá nucleus of São Paulo and ultimately instigated by the French, who were established on Guanabara Bay. Only with the support of Ramalho and his allies could the Jesuits confront the enemy that was causing them even more horror, namely the presence of the Reformation embodied by the Calvinists, where the Jesuits, as the Counter-Reformation, were attempting to create a realm of pious men.

Another pioneering nucleus of great importance was that of Diogo Álvarez, Caramuru, the heraldic father of Bahians. He settled in Bahia in 1510, also surrounded by an extensive Indian family. He succeeded in maintaining a certain balance between the Indians, whose life he shared in cunhadismo, and the Portuguese who were arriving. In that way he became in essence the base of the Portuguese settlement in Bahia. He even helped the Jesuits and left them something in his will.

A third nucleus was that of Pernambuco, where several Portuguese associated with the Tabajara Indians produced a number of *mameluco* mixed-bloods, including the famous Jerônimo de Albuquerque, the great captain of the war for the conquest of Maranhão, which had been occupied by the French.

In Maranhão itself there were reports of a warrior who had survived a failed expedition thanks to his skills as a craftsman, Peró by name; he had probably bred with a number of the mamelucos who played an active role in the colonization of that area.

The French also had their breeding farms based upon cunhadismo, so many that according to Capistrano de Abreu, it was not known for a long time whether Brazil would be Portuguese or French, such was the strength of the French presence and the power of their influence with the Indians. Their main base was the one established in Guanabara, with the Tamoio of Rio de Janeiro, which had more than a thousand mamelucos who lived along the rivers emptying into the bay and on Governador Island, where they would establish Antarctic France.

Other mamelucos were bred by the French with the Potiguara in Paraíba and with the Caeté in Pernambuco. They attained a certain prosperity from the merchandise they induced the Indians to produce and to haul to many ships. Their merchandise was mainly dyewood, but they also dealt in local pepper, cotton, and in curiosities like saki monkeys and parrots.

The Spanish similarly took part in the cunhadismo phase of European settlement on the Brazilian coast. The chronicles speak of a Pero Galego, a Castilian interpreter among the Potiguara, who had his lips pierced like theirs. His influence must have been great, as evinced by the role he played in the expulsion of the Portuguese from Paraíba and later on in the fighting in Maranhão, always on the side of the French.

The General Government

In order to preserve its interests, which were threatened by widespread cunhadismo, the Portuguese Crown in 1532 put into effect the system of land grants. Almost all those chosen came to take possession with the aim of populating the grants and making them productive, lifting the colonial economy to a new level.

The royal plan was to confront its enemies by populating Brazil though the forced importation of deportees. The letter of grant and the charter conceded to Duarte Coelho (1534) states that the king, attending to many vassals and with the appropriate aim of populating Brazil, is pleased to declare asylum and refuge for all criminals who care to live there, even those condemned, including those under the penalty of death, excepting only those whose crimes have been heresy, treason, sodomy, and counterfeiting (in Malheiro Dias 1924, 3:309–12).

The grants, distributed to the upper nobility—people close to the throne and with their own fortunes to colonize the lands—were veritable provinces. They were immense allotments of dozens of craggy leagues along the sea and reaching inland to the line established by the Treaty of Tordesillas.

Some of them were successful, such as those of Pernambuco and São Vicente. Others failed disastrously, sometimes in a most tragic way, like that of Pereira Coutinho in Ilhéus—he ended up being devoured by the Indians. Lopes de Souza was completely uninterested and did not even take possession of the concession he had received. Almost all of the grants had new European populators and were organized on a completely new basis, whereby the Indian was no longer a relative but a source of labor who could be recruited as a slave.

The system of land grants was most vigorously organized by Martim Afonso, who brought in the first cattle and the first sugarcane plants. There is no record of his having brought blacks from Africa to be left here, but as the Portuguese were already living surrounded by slaves in Lisbon, it is quite improbable that he and his captains would have come unaccompanied by their servants.

Pero Lopes reports on Martim Afonso's works in these words:

> This land looked so good to all of us that Captain Martim Afonso was determined to populate it and he gave all the men land where they could set up farms: and he founded a village on the island of São Vicente and another nine leagues into the backlands on the bank of a river called the Piratininga: and he divided the people between those two villages and made them officials: and he did everything in a just way, from which the people drew great consolation as they saw themselves populating villages and having laws and sacrifices and celebrating marriages and living in communication with the arts: and each one master of his own things: and taking care of his own problems: and having all other comforts of a secure and sociable life. (In Marchant 1943, 68)

The grantee was a high nobleman invested with feudal powers by the king to govern his estate for thirty leagues in every direction; with the political power to found villages, grant pieces of land, and license artisans and merchants; with the economic power to develop his lands directly or through intermediaries; and even with the right to impose capital punishment. Martim Afonso, the most important of the grantees, came with 400 people. He also brought nine noblemen, seven knights along with two youths from the royal court. It was the greatest injection of nobility that Brazil has ever received. From their seed came the pretentious native nobility, almost all of it a failure.

Work along the coast grew more and more intense. Ever more numerous were the ships that made port, sent out by shipowners from different European countries, mainly Holland and Germany. The cargoes they took on were not small. They could total 3,000 logs of brazilwood, 3,000 jaguar skins, much wax, and as many as 600 chattering parrots. The equivalent in tools and trinkets must have been a respectable amount. Putting all of this together must have occupied a great many Indians and a great deal of time as they cut trees at distances measured in leagues and transported them to the coast—work in great contrast to their habitual manner of living and producing.

Cargoes of this size were stored at trading posts by the Portuguese. The French, unable to maintain posts, used the ships themselves for this, anchoring them for the time necessary for the Indians to collect or harvest everything they wanted to trade. The work was naturally performed under the direct supervision of the interpreters or *truchements,* also called *caramelus* by the French, a name later given to the mamelucos with whom they bred.

Many were the difficulties arising out of that growing prosperity. Failure was due largely to the hostility of the Indians, mainly in the case of those who had settled in areas of Indians allied with the French, like Itamaracá, or in Ilhéus, where as noted the grantee himself ended up being devoured.

Fortune followed varying routes in each province when the Crown, not content with what had been accomplished, placed the surviving grants under its control. For that purpose it appointed a governor general in the person of Tomé de Souza, who now set up villages—each with a pillory, an armed military contingent, and fortifications—and also brought numerous populators to Brazil.

The first governor arrived in Brazil in 1549 with three men-of-war, two caravels, and a brigantine. They carried military and civilian functionaries, soldiers, and artisans—more than a thousand people all told, mainly deportees. With him came new colonists as well as the first Jesuits. Nóbrega, older and more experienced than most, was at their head, along with three more priests and two brothers. Anchieta, a stout youth of nineteen, arrived with the next batch.

The government was set up in Bahia, establishing the town with the people it had brought and with the aid of Caramuru's Indians and mamelucos. The quantity and quality of the professional people is noteworthy: they included surgeons, barbers, and bleeders along with a large number of stonemasons, sawyers, tanners, locksmiths, tinkers, woodcutters, charcoal makers, goldsmiths, street pavers, canoe makers, fishermen, and shipbuilders.

No single women came except, as far as is known, for a slave, probably Moorish, who was the object of a lively dispute. Consequently, the new arrivals mated with Indian women, taking on, as was the custom in the land, as many as they could, going on to produce more mamelucos. The Jesuits, concerned over such shamelessness, sought the ear of the government at home. They called for women of all classes, even harlots, because "there are all classes of men here . . . and in this way sin will be avoided and the population in the service of God will be increased" ("Letter," 1550, in Nóbrega 1955, 79–80). They especially wanted so-called orphans-of-the-king, who would marry good and rich men here. They did not get many.

In 1551 three sisters arrived; in 1553 nine more came; in 1559 another seven. These few Portuguese women did not play much of a role in the making of the Brazilian family.

A discreet success was reached in the importation of juvenile delinquents from Lisbon to live with the young Indians in the Jesuit colleges. In 1550 a band arrived in Bahia that was described as made up of "lost boys, thieves, and evil-doers who are called rascals here." Ten or twelve went to São Vicente in the same year. The Jesuits hoped to civilize the urchins and Indians together and have them learn Latin grammar in joint classes. It was a difficult task, as could soon be seen when the street boys, under siege by the Indian women, could not resist the temptation and ran off with them. The priests immediately changed tactics, abandoning the teaching of Latin in order to dedicate their energies to the training of lay brothers and priests who could handle the language of the land, Tupi-Guaraní, well enough to help attract Indians to their missions for religious doctrination.

Nóbrega points out that it was not necessary to send any women or boys to Pernambuco as there were many daughters of white men and native Indian women, "all of whom now will marry with the aid of the Lord" ("Letter," 1551, in Nóbrega 1955, 102). They were the *mamelucas,* entering the history of Brazil along with their mothers before them. No longer Indian, they were trying to find a place in some category of respectable people. The only one open to them was that of contrite faithful to the Catholic saints, enthusiastic followers of the ritual. That was the only conversion that the priests managed. These women were, in fact, the ones who implanted popular *santeiro* Catholicism in Brazil, as is documented in the following text from Nóbrega:

> We work hard to care for the free Indian women who for a long time have been living in sin with Christians so that they will not go into the backlands since they are now Christians, and we have had a house built for them at the expense of those who keep them in order to settle them there and they will marry some working men in time. They all show great fervor and the wish to make up for their sins and the more intelligent among them are already going to confession and they know quite well what to say. By winning these over a great deal is won, because there are more than forty in this settlement alone, many others outside who are in other settlements, and they bring in others from the backlands, both Christians and those still pagans. Some of the oldest of these preach to the others. We have made one of them a supervisor as she is so diligent in the call to doctrine that

Our Lord should be praised for it. ("Letter to the Priests and Brothers of Coimbra, Pernambuco," September 13, 1551, in Nóbrega 1955, 92–93)

The hardest bone for the new governor and especially the Jesuits to gnaw on was the confrontation with Antarctic France, established at that time on Guanabara Bay based on the numerous nuclei of French mamelucos who lived there. Besides Villegaignon, a dozen Calvinists had come and a larger body of people whom he describes as rustics, lacking in honor and civic virtues, composed of Norman and Breton sailors and interpreters. Those who came with Villegaignon himself numbered 600, mainly soldiers and artisans. With Léry came 300 more, including five young brides, who after many disputes were married here.

The religious fervor of Villegaignon, half-monk, half-soldier, played an important role in the failure of Antarctic France. Conflicts immediately broke out among Huguenots, Calvinists, and Catholics and tore the nascent community apart. The situation was aggravated by the revolt of the Indians, who refused to accept the new role assigned them in the colonization of Brazil.

The cordial and egalitarian sociability of cunhadismo was being replaced by the discipline of a pious community in an unbearable climate of tension. The pastors, wishing to calm the more erotic rather than religious fervors of their faithful, hanged a few of them, punishing also the Indian women with whom they had transgressed.

It was in that critical situation that the French had to confront the attack by the Indian forces of the Jesuits, who had poured all their ardor into it. Created as soldiers of the Counter-Reformation, the Jesuits had run into the Reformation in the new land, trying to create its own utopia with the native Indian population.

A real economic revolution was taking place with the leap from multiple indigenous cultivation, which mingled dozens of different plants, to monotonous plantations of sugarcane. It was a step from plenty to hunger for those who worked the land, because in order to produce merchandise, they were no longer cultivating what they ate and wore.

For a long time it was easy to seduce the Indians into those immense efforts, such was the attraction of tools and gewgaws. Over the years difficulties arose because the Indians wanted better compensation for their services, because dyewood was getting scarcer and farther away, or because the cultivated fields they were opening for the whites in exchange for barter were getting larger and larger with the increase in the number of

Europeans, or because the Indians had enough of the articles the whites were giving them. At that time slavery began to be imposed as a means of conscripting workers.

Records show that, indeed, the number of Indian slaves working for the land grantees was beginning to grow. In São Vicente there were close to 3,000 Indian slaves working on six sugar plantations. There was also an increase in battles with neighboring Indians for the capture of slaves, and from then on an ever greater number of the expeditions called *bandeiras* went out to search for slaves farther and farther away.

At the time of Mem de Sá's arrival as governor, the situation was critical in Bahia, which had been assaulted by epidemics and famine (1563–64). The Indians, in revolt against the colonists, refused to plant and were driven into territory farther inland. The situation in Guanabara, where the French occupation was being consolidated with the strong support of the Indians, was even more serious.

Mem de Sá, advised by the Jesuits, simultaneously called for the cruelest of wars against the Indians and for a peace of the victor, which was his surrender to the missionaries. Close to 34,000 Indians were gathered together in eleven parishes under the direction of the Jesuits, giving birth to the missions, or reductions, and hamlets organized as villages with a pillory.

There all Indian life was organized into groups according to sex or age, each having a prescribed task to fulfill from dawn to dusk by schedules marked by the ringing of bells: a time for working in the field, hunting, fishing, spinning, weaving, etc. A time to read, a time to pray, a time to fornicate, because the population was visibly decreasing. Attending to the demand for workers by the colonists, the governor declared that a state of war existed against the Caeté. Disagreement broke out because the colonists, instead of attacking those Indians in their distant villages, went hunting for those already pacified who were living in the Jesuit missions. These were quickly depopulated.

Missions with approximately 12,000 souls in a short time saw themselves reduced to a thousand. It was during that desperate situation that the smallpox epidemic of 1562 and 1563 broke out, not touching the Portuguese but killing more than 30,000 Indians and blacks in three months. A new epidemic arose that killed more than a quarter of the surviving Indian population. The villages, filled with unburied dead and with starving and desperate people, were abandoned by many Indians who surrendered to the whites as slaves in exchange for a handful of flour.

All through the backlands, too, despair reigned, either because the epidemics were reaching there or because the colonists were attacking villages. People spared were induced by all manner of trickery to go to Bahia, where they were enslaved. Data from Anchieta in his "Report on the First Settlements" show that the Indian population in the Bahia area, estimated at 80,000 was reduced to less than 10,000. The smallpox epidemics, along with deadly fevers, completed the destruction.

Antonio Blásquez describes it thus:

> At that time the usual dancing and jollity was not seen among them, all was weeping and sadness, some of them finding themselves without parents, others without children, and many widows without husbands, so that anyone who saw them in that abandonment and remembered times past and how many they had been and how few now and how before they had had something to eat and now were dying of hunger and how previously they had lived in freedom and were now seen in addition to their misery attacked at every turn and forcibly made slaves by the Christians, pondering and ruminating on that sudden change, could not help but to pity them and shed many a tear of compassion. ("Letter," 1564, in Blásquez 1931, 405)

It was during the time of Mem de Sá that the three plagues of the white man—epidemics, war, and slavery—grew in ferocity and fell with deadly fury upon the Tupinambá. In the end their survivors were compelled to pay further penalties by rebuilding fortresses and sugar mills.

A new enemy then rose up: the Aimoré and other Tapuia, who until that time had been held back by the Tupinambá, began to attack the colonists, depopulating previously prosperous areas like Ilhéus. With the defeat of the Indians came consolidation from then on in Bahia and its subsidiaries in Espírito Santo, in São Vicente and Piratininga and their extensions to the south. Pernambuco, too, after liquidating the resistance of the Caeté and their allies and the French in Paraíba and Ceará, imposed its rule beyond in Maranhão. Only there and among Indians who had moved in flight from the whites would the Jesuits find more Indians to catechize. They, too, all along the Atlantic coast, had been defeated as an alternative way in the colonization of Brazil.

In 1570 Portuguese domination was solidly established in places with around 4,000 households (eight to twelve people in each), which corresponded to a population of 30,000 or 40,000 inhabitants. And the majority of those were mamelucos, because all of the Portuguese in Brazil did not number more than a fourth of this population. Four settlements stood out in that grouping with growing prosperity: Bahia, Pernambuco,

Espírito Santo, and São Paulo. Three others began to decline and would disappear completely: Itamaracá, which had once seen prosperity, was abandoned by the Portuguese because of the attacks of Indians allied with the French. The same happened in Ilhéus and Porto Seguro, which had reached populations of 200 households each but which also succumbed to attacks by the Aimoré.

Attacked by the same Indians, Espírito Santo managed to survive because, founded on an island, it did not have to destroy its Indian neighbors and, indirectly, relied on them.

The Captaincy of São Paulo, composed of three towns on the seacoast, São Vicente, Santos, and Iperoig, and one up in the hills, the then Piratininga, was a second-rate colony. Its sugar plantations had not prospered and there was no other agriculture. Even the production of brazilwood was always less than that of other provinces. The Jesuit missions, too, were slow in developing there, bringing together only a small cluster of Indians. What was strong in São Paulo was the association of mamelucos with free and slave Indians. All living the same kind of life together, they ended up growing in size by capturing Indians for their own use or for sale.

Portuguese Rio de Janeiro, founded after the expulsion of the French in 1565, was living in peace with the Tupinambá, their allies, because they relied on a number of slaves from among the vanquished Tamoio. The Jesuits had two missions outside the city with about 3,000 Indians.

Bahia was the largest Portuguese nucleus. It was successful in maintaining around the city under the control of the Jesuits diverse indigenous communities that aided in the defense of the city and provided labor and provisions. There were thirty or so plantations, worked by 3,000 or 4,000 black slaves and 8,000 Indians. The black African component in that proportion would grow steadily.

The same had happened in Pernambuco, which had more than a thousand inhabitants concentrated on the islands of Olinda and Igaraçu and in neighboring communities. It already had two productive plantations worked principally by African labor. Its original population had been practically exterminated by war, famine, pestilence, and also by drought. It was so small that the Jesuits could not establish any missions there. The two ports on Pernambuco Bay were beginning to be entryways for the workforce that would thenceforth come to build what was to be built, produce what was to be produced in Brazil: the African slaves.

The Jesuits, with stern Ignatian discipline, were able to attain a certain prosperity of a different type from that of the colonists because, fundamentally working to provide for their own Indians, they were able to assure breadth and a degree of luxury in their buildings. Each mission also had men and weapons that could be rushed to the governor's call whenever requested, and often it was against other Indians as well as mutinous black slaves. From this they received food and maintenance. The municipalities, through a complex system of labor bartering by both towns and plantations—in negotiations that were becoming more and more difficult—were reaching the point where the colonists no longer had this as a source of labor. The majority of Indians had disappeared, a larger portion than those incorporated into the Portuguese establishments, because the forest was close by and there they could reorganize their lives in the backlands.

At the same time in the sugar-producing Northeast, a new type of Brazilian was arising. Composed originally of mamelucos or "Brazilindians" bred by the mixture of European and Indian, the area soon saw the early and ever stronger presence of African slaves. These included some few women who went on to breed mulatto men and women, who by default were already born as proto-Brazilians since they were not assimilable by Indians, Europeans, or Africans and their admixtures.

Because of that black and mulatto presence and especially as its differentness was later recognized, this matrix soon became quite prominent. Thus was born the Creole culture, centered on the great house and the slave quarters, with an enveloping patriarchal family and vast multitude of servants. These Creole people, quite similar to the Brazilindians of São Paulo, could also be differentiated by their specialization as subordinate service people, providers of goods, and fishermen.

A fraction of that matrix who took on the function of cattle herding also emerged, adjusting to pastoral tasks. They became even more distinctive because they came into successive contact with various Tapuia peoples of a culture specially adapted to the aridity of the *caatinga* brushlands, people with whom they crossed and gave birth to a new phenotype, the Northeastern *cabeça-chata,* or flathead.

On the linguistic level, Tupi-Guaraní for centuries remained the lingua franca of São Paulo Brazilindians, but in the Northeast it was soon supplanted by Portuguese. That was because the main population of slaves and people of mixed blood were compelled to adopt the speech of the foreman in order to communicate with other slaves, and this helped consolidate the Portuguese language in Brazil. Later the heavy slave traffic into the mining region in the center of the country would play the same role of introducing the Portuguese language. The first wave of settlement, composed of São Paulo people, gave almost all bodies of water, hills, and landmarks names in Tupi, a language never spoken by the Indians native to the region. The Brazilindian of the dry Northeast—who spread out most widely of all through Brazil, herding cattle—did not adopt any language of the regions he inhabited and was another spreader of the Portuguese tongue, because he had most certainly been "Lusitanized" when he left the coast.

That was how over decades and centuries there arose Brazilian ways that were as differentiated from each other by their singularities as they were homogenized by the much larger amount they had in common. Such are, for example, the Bahian from lush Bahia, the Pernambucan with his black *massapé* soil, the São Franciscan from Bahia do Bode, the northeastern backlander or sertanejo.

Other variants would arise along the same lines, among them the Amazonian *caboclo,* adapted to life in the forests and on the waterways, the one who maintained the greatest amount of his original indigenous heritage. There original communities have been kept alive and holding sway over their world by multiple and prescribed forms of interaction with their surroundings, which give their culture not only an indigenous flavor but also an extraordinary richness. Looking the world over, I can compare the caboclos only to French peasants because of the extraordinary richness of their lives as small farmers. Goat cheese, wines, pâtés, and so many other things are the European equivalents of *tacacá no tucupi,* a dish made of tapioca, manioc juice, pepper, garlic, and shrimp; *maniçoba,* manioc shoots with meat or fish; and *muçuão,* turtle soup. Lamentably, this culinary wealth of ours is disappearing with the decline of caboclo culture, while the French flourish ever more.

Another typical variant of being Brazilian is that of the gaúcho, specializing in herding, but with two distinct components: people eager for war and for the frontier, and cattle hunters, rather than breeders, who exploited the herds that had multiplied on the open plains of the south, their main value as merchandise being for leather.

Indigenous Slavery

Indigenous slavery predominated all through the first century. Only in the seventeenth century would black slavery surpass it, as Brandão points out: "In some captaincies there are more of them than natives of the land, and all the men who live on it have put almost their entire wealth into such merchandise" (Brandão 1968, 115).

Even so, in pioneering areas the native population still served as a source of cheap slaves, useful for auxiliary functions. No colonist ever doubted the usefulness of indigenous labor, even though he might prefer black slaves for mercantile export products. The Indian, on the contrary, was considered an ideal worker for transport of loads or people over land and water, for cultivation of commodities, for preparation of food, and for hunting and fishing. His role was also preponderant in wars against other Indians and fugitive black slaves.

Colonial documentation emphasizes the aptitudes of Indians for craftsmanship as carpenters, joiners, locksmiths, and potters. In the Jesuit missions they had an opportunity to become typographers, plastic artists, musicians, and writers.

The basic function of captive Indians was, however, that of laborer in subsistence production. For that the legally free were hunted down in the forests and taken on as slaves, appropriated by their masters through all manner of stratagems, licenses, and subterfuges.

Beginning with the royal charter of 1570, in which King Sebastian authorized the taking of Indians in just wars, one law of enfranchisement followed another authorizing captivity through paralegal procedures such as official auctions for the sale of Indians, taxes collected for an Indian sold as a slave, and royal decrees for the capture and sale of allotments of Indians to pay for public works and even to build churches, as occurred with the cathedral of São Luís do Maranhão.

In fact, despite the copious legislation guaranteeing the freedom of the Indians, it can be stated that the only indispensable requirement for an Indian to be enslaved was that he still be a free Indian. Even those already incorporated into colonial life—as happened to those gathered at the missions—were attacked and hunted innumerable times. That was what happened, for example, when Mem de Sá authorized a war of vengeance to enslave the Caeté Indians for having eaten Bishop Fernandes Sardinha. The colonists, basing their action on that order of vengeance, fell on the Jesuit missions, and out of 12,000 catechumens, only a thousand were left when the rider was revoked.

Thousands of Indians were incorporated into colonial society in that way—incorporated not to be integrated into it with the status of members but to be worn down until death serving as beasts of burden for the one who had taken them over. That is how it was over the centuries every time that a new front for expansion opened up in a new area with the sudden appearance there of remote tribes. They became a source of captive workers and captured women for agricultural work, the breeding of children, and domestic slavery.

Costing one-fifth the price of an imported black, captive Indians became poor people's slaves in a society where Europeans had ceased to
perform any kind of manual work. Every wearisome chore outside of the
privileged plantation work for the export economy, which was reserved
for blacks, fell upon Indians.

Their seizure was always held to be a praiseworthy practice, even as a
technique for conversion. Nóbrega himself, in his plans for colonization,
advised against the coming of colonists so poor that they could not immediately buy captive Indians to place in their service, suggesting that only
those grantees who had the wherewithal to acquire these captives should
be sent here. It is clear that he, like the other Jesuits, wanted to put an end
to the greed of the colonists, which had degenerated into practices that
were using up the Indian population and were harmful to colonization.

While his position as a competitor arose as soon as he had a different
destination to give the Indians, what is certain is that he had a clear vision
of the great need for large concentrations of Indians in missionary towns
and in the service of landowners as the principal consolidating mechanism
for the colonial enterprise.

The support the Crown gave the Jesuits in their efforts to regulate the
captivity of Indians was not always based on the religious and moral reasons that it alleged. It was based, in fact, on administrative interests. Ac-
tually, the missionary villages were concentrations of people who were
recruitable and available at any time, at no cost whatever, for wars against
hostile Indians, foreign invaders, and rebellious blacks. They were also an
important source of provisions for a hungry population because they were
primarily occupied in the production of food. Plantations only took care
of products for export. The concentration of Indians at the missions also
often coincided with the interests of slavers, who in a single attack could
reap a large harvest of captives.

The contradiction between the political aims of the Crown and the
Jesuits on one side and the immediate concerns of the traffickers in Indians
on the other was never resolved by a royal decision either for freedom or
for captivity. The legislation regulating the matter is the most contradictory and hypocritical that has ever been seen. Dozens of times law decreed
just war against Indians considered guilty of great offenses or simply hostile, limiting such war immediately afterward, only to authorize it again in
an endless cycle of iniquity and falsehood.

The administrative acts that governed Indian slavery likewise went
back and forth between enticement and chicanery, at once prohibiting
captivity and instituting it. Indians could be legally enslaved if taken in a

just war or if obtained by means of a just ransom or if captured in an authorized attack or if freed from the captivity of a tribe that threatened to eat them—or if they were part of an allotment that went to make up a portion of the 20 percent tax paid to the local government.

The missionaries finally arrived and, unable to counteract the general feeling [in favor of indigenous slavery], they made a pact with it. In one of those capitulations of conscience for which Jesuits are noted, they found a means of reasoning that "the broader the entry of legitimate captives, all the more slaves who would enter the Church and set out upon the road to salvation" (Vieira, "Reply to the Chapters," 25). Thus, agreeing to the practice of slavery, they accompanied the troops and, as arbiters, decided on justice for the captives. In that concession lay the ruination of their work and, what was worse, of their reputation. No one will ever free them from the blemish of having directly assisted in the destruction of the unfortunate race they set out to save. (Azevedo 1930, 169)

But that is not all. Also instituted was the voluntary slavery of Indians over the age of twenty-one, who in cases of extreme necessity were authorized to sell themselves to anyone charitable enough to buy them, after making it perfectly clear to them what it was like to be a slave (Leite 1965, 119, 124). Likewise legal was the purchase of Indian children from their parents to be reared and trained for work, which is the height of effrontery, since there are no people more extremely close to their children than in societies based on kinship. Legal, too, and even meritorious was the purchase of children brought in by Indian trackers or traders to be instructed in the Christian faith, a practice that is still going on today in the backwaters of the Amazon. It was equally legal to hold as a captive an Indian who mated with a slave woman and even to register the child born of that match as a slave.

It is quite difficult to estimate the number of Indians enslaved and torn from their tribes. They must certainly number in the millions even by a cautious estimate. That is what is indicated by the few figures we have, like those of Simonsen, who estimated at 300,000 the Indians captured and enslaved by the *bandeirante* pioneers from São Paulo, a third of them destined for slave traffic and sent off to other provinces. Or the figures of Justo Mancilla and Simón Masseta (1951, 1:337), who estimated that from the Jesuit missions in Paraguay, the São Paulo pioneers had taken away 200,000 captives. The capture and bringing to the coast that was annually carried out among the Indians along the distant rivers of the

Amazon region over the centuries for the missions and principally for slavery could not have involved any lesser number.

Central Brazil, the forest zone of Minas Gerais, Espírito Santo, and Bahia, as well as the pine forest regions in the south of Brazil provided a vast supply of captive workers at the same time as they were being deforested. In all of these regions the slavery of Indian peoples who resisted the expansion was decreed by the king of Portugal as legal because they were taken in just wars. Since the captured Indians were a fraction of the defeated tribe—for many of them died in the struggle for their freedom while others fled along the roads or died from ill-treatment, from revolt, and from rage in captivity—the process of capture as a form of recruiting a native labor force for the colonization constituted a genocide of gigantic proportions.

The breadth of the diverse forms of legitimization of this slavery is expressed quite well in the case of the São Paulo pioneers, who brought home so many enslaved Indians that they had to develop a whole nomenclature in order to enter them as items in their inventories. Thus they spoke of service items, *gente roja*, obligatory services, people from Brazil, servants (Machado 1943, 31–36, 165–76)—all of it so that the items mentioned would pass down from father to son as private property, with no mention made of slavery.

The Jesuit reductions themselves can only be considered a form of slavery. The missions were permanent settlements of Indians taken in war or attracted by the missionaries to live there under the direction of the priests. An Indian there had neither the status of slave nor that of servant. He was a catechumen, meaning a heretic who was being Christianized and thereby restoring his human dignity, with eternal salvation being his reward. On the juridical level he would be a free man, placed under tutelage in conditions similar to those of an orphan given over to the care of a guardian.

For the priests they would be rational but misguided souls placed in free bodies but lacking in protection and vigilance. Being there, however, they would have to work for their sustenance and to help the community of which they had become a part to prosper. They could be recruited at any time for war against any force that threatened colonial interests, because these had come to be their own. They could also be sent to towns for compulsory work in the public interest in the building of churches and forts and other urban facilities, in the opening of highways, and as oarsmen and cooks and helpers on great expeditions or in whatever seemed necessary, always for the benefit of the collectivity of which they had become a part. They could, finally, be rented out to colonists at wages of two yards of cotton cloth, building up in that way a private purse, which, if they got to receive it, they would learn to spend wisely with the priests, perhaps in some work of charity.

Worse even than the Jesuits were other missionaries, as none of them ever entered into conflict with anyone to show indignation over the extermination or captivity of the Indians. And worse still were members of the regular clergy, accused over and over again of vile avarice, some even reaching the point of being disciplined and punished by the colonial government for the abuse with which they exploited the Indians who fell into their hands.

When the Jesuits were expelled the situation deteriorated yet further, because the missions in the north were handed over to the families of grantees, who went on to exploit them as private plantations. In other regions some missions were turned over to religious orders occupied with that function because they were even more likely to serve the government and the colonists with their slaves than the Society of Jesus had been. Some were placed under the direction of civil administrators, who, able to collect a percentage from the Indians they hired out or to put the Indians to work on their own holdings, made a good business out of it—so good that some of them succeeded in the supreme privilege of becoming the hereditary owners of the former missions. The number of Indians exploited in this fashion must have been great, since documents from the close of the seventeenth century speak of 400 villages with civil administrators in São Paulo and 4,000 in other captaincies (Gorender 1978).

The expulsion by Pombal, ostensibly aimed at freeing the Indians in the Jesuit missions by integrating them into the colonial community as equals and even with certain privileges, was an enormous hoax. The regulation handed down at the time abolished compulsory work as well as alternate six-month turns at work outside the mission and being rented out to different colonies.

In reality that practice only grew from then on, plunging the nominally free Indians into a generalized state of slavery more serious than the previous one. The situation of those Indians who were rented out was worse than that of the slaves held by their master with proper title since the latter, as human capital bought with good money, had to be cared for, at least to preserve their purchase value, while the leased Indian, costing only the price of his rent, would bring in more profit if he ate less and if he fulfilled quickly the tasks for which he had been rented. That human waste of captive workers constituted another terrible form of genocide imposed on more than a million Indians.

5

Human Gristmills

The Brazilindians

The expansion inland of Portuguese rule in the formation of Brazil was the work of Brazilindians or mamelucos. The offspring of white fathers, the majority of them Portuguese, and Indian women, they spread Portuguese rule well beyond the limits of the Treaty of Tordesillas, going much farther than might have been expected.

The Portuguese in São Paulo were the main progenitors of these Brazilindians or mamelucos. The motive that moved those old Paulistas was essentially the poverty of the São Paulo trading post, nothing but a little town established on the upland plain, a four-day journey from the sea, made with difficulty along turbulent jungle streams and over craggy ridges. In the words of Sérgio Buarque de Holanda, they were driven by the "exigencies of a sad domestic daily life: they fought stubbornly against poverty and in order to make up for it, they did not hesitate to cover distances that became greater and greater, challenging the treacheries of an unknown and perhaps hostile world" (Holanda 1986, 26).

What they were looking for in the depths of the forests, at unmeasurable distances, was the only item of merchandise within their reach: Indians for their own use or to be sold, countless Indians to supply their needs and to be replaced as they were used up, Indians who would clear plots for them, hunt, fish, cook, produce everything they ate, used, or sold, Indian beasts of burden who would carry all their loads over the longest and harshest trails.

When the enslavable Indians living close by had been used up, the São Paulo Brazilindians went out searching for the nooks and crannies where others might be. For that they were organized into huge bands of mamelucos and their slaves, bands that went out for months and even years, walking barefoot on bandeira expeditions or paddling canoes on river explorations called *monções*. During the farthest and most pioneering expeditions that lasted years, they would travel for a few months and then set up camp and plant garden plots, where they could harvest food to supply them so that they could continue into the backlands through forests and across natural clearings. An advance guard would scout the way, looking for Indian villages or missions with Indians who could be taken, ever on watch for attacks by hostile Indians. This profession of people-hunting became a way of life for the Paulistas, and they grew skilled and prominent in its execution, singling out for high honors those they viewed as the bravest and most active.

The most successful among them gained not only such prosperity as that poor economy could afford but also public recognition for their deeds and the greatest satisfaction with themselves. It was a strange, unusual way of life, without a doubt; compared with any other kind of rural life, such as farming or herding, it stood out singularly.

The Brazilindians were dubbed *mamelucos* by the Spanish Jesuits, who were horrified by the brutality and lack of humanity on the part of those scourges of the aboriginal Indians, their own maternal people. No other designation could have been more appropriate. The term originally referred to a caste of slaves whom the Arabs had taken from their parents to be reared and trained in their nurseries, to develop whatever talents they might have. They would become janissaries if they showed promise as skillful cavalry soldiers or, if cowards, they would better serve as policemen and spies. Castrated, they would become eunuchs in harems if they had no other merits. But they would be able to reach the high status of Mameluke if they revealed a talent for the exercise of command and Islamic sovereignty over the people from whom they had been taken. It is obvious that applied to the Paulistas, the epithet showed the bitter resentment of a Jesuit—probably Father Ruiz Montoya, author of the *Spiritual Conquest,* which tells of the terrible suffering of the Jesuit missions in Paraguay attacked by bandeirantes from São Paulo.

Our mamelucos or Brazilindians were, despite themselves, civilizing heroes, servants of the king, imposers of the domination that oppressed them. Their greatest value as agents of civilization comes from their very rusticity as half-Indians, tireless on long marches and especially in the chore of paddling from sunup to sundown for months on end. They were accustomed to the savage brutality of the tropical jungle, heirs to the age-old knowledge accumulated by Indians about soil, plants, and animals of what for Europeans was the New World but for them was their ancestral home.

Another value to note was their flexibility as newly created people, able to be molded by any new environment, "with the consistency of leather, not iron or bronze, giving way, folding, molding themselves to the harshness of a rude world," as Sérgio Buarque de Holanda says (1986, 29).

The Brazilindians or São Paulo mamelucos were victims of two drastic rejections. First was that of their fathers, with whom they wanted to identify but who looked down on them as impure sons of the land, taking good advantage of their work while they were children and youths and later integrating them into the bandeira expeditions of which many made a career. The second rejection was that of their maternal people. The Indians' concept was that a woman is simply the sack into which the male deposits his seed. The one who is born is the child of the father and not of the mother, as the Indians see it. Unable to identify himself with either of his ancestral lines, which both rejected him, the mameluco fell into a no-man's-land out of which he shaped his identity as a Brazilian.

So it was that by means of cunhadismo carried to extremes, a new human breed was created, which was not recognized or seen as such by Indians, by Europeans, or by blacks. That breed of people reached an almost unattainable efficiency as agents of civilization. They spoke their own language, had their own vision of the world, and were masters of a technology for adaptation to the tropical forest, all of it colored by their compulsory living among Indians of Tupi roots.

Their adventurous life must have been more attractive to young Indians than the apathy of the villages. There is considerable documentation of the spontaneous allurement of Indians who preferred living the destiny of the Brazilindians, making themselves the mamelucos' slaves.

Unlike the Spaniard who, whenever he could, commanded on horseback, the mameluco opened his vast world walking barefoot in single file over trails and narrow paths, with loads carried on his own back and on those of captive Indian men and women. These were the bearers of all things, of the sick and even the dead, but also of ladies and many people from the mother country who had themselves carried by Indians in hammocks and chairs.

Friederici (1967), comparing them to their counterparts in Canada, the coureurs de bois who proliferated during the early centuries, supposes that no other historical path would be open to them except extermination when more structured European societies based on regular families colonized those areas. Curious at least is the contrast between the historical performance of those northern woodsmen in leather clothing, wearing moccasins, and speaking only native languages, in comparison to the driving energy of the mamelucos or Brazilindians who went on to make Brazil.

Those woodsmen of the north played an important role. They were the ones who opened up Canada and occupied it until the sale of the territory to the English. I think that their descendants are the Québecois, who live bitterly as the hostile neighbors of the Anglo-Canadians who occupied the territory in a colonization made with regular families.

Other Mamelukes were the ones who opened up what is today Argentinean, Uruguayan, and Paraguayan territory. Many of these people can be seen in Buenos Aires, where they are called *cabecitas negras* (black heads) and are looked down upon by the millions of gringos who came after them. All in Argentina are ignorant of the fact that the country was really conquered, organized, and led into independence by close to 800,000 Mamelukes.

In Brazil their success was immensely greater because they went on to make up the very core of the nation and, numbering some 14 million, along with Brazilianized blacks, they were able to withstand the gringo invasion, maintaining their own face and identity.

The Brazilindian, as a new type of person, even came to define his own ideology, opposed to that of the priest and the neo-Lusitanian. The best expression of it can be found in the aforementioned letter in which Domingos Jorge Velho, the leader of the Paulistas, complains to the king of the ineptitude and hypocrisy of those opposed to the activities of the mamelucos.

It was not an easy task for the mamelucos to become a major agent of Brazilian history. They were faced on one hand by the hatred of the Jesuits and the ill will of the Portuguese and on the other by all the immense difficulties of their hard life as expeditionaries. This included the hostility of wild Indians aware of the tragic fate they would face if captured—like the Aimoré of Bahia, the Botacudo of Minas Gerais and Espírito Santo, the Kaingang and Xokleng of the south, the Xavante of Mato Grosso, and above all the Bororo and Kayapó, who covered extensive areas of overgrown wasteland beyond the Araguaia and Tocantins rivers.

The Tapuia were, in the main, people of an adaptive system adjusted to the conditions of the wasteland, very much in contrast to the way of life of the farmers of the tropical forests. Their very way of waging war was unique: they preferred to inflict blows with a club or run their enemy through with a spear. As captives they were almost useless, not having any familiarity with the agricultural customs of the Tupi-Guaraní adopted by the mamelucos, and especially in that they required a permanent watch so they would not flee and if possible kill their captor.

Accustomed to covering immense distances in their moves, the Tapuia, principally the Kayapó, would always attack unexpectedly at the most distant points, taking prisoners whenever they could, especially young girls and women, whom they would incorporate into the tribe. That characteristic turned them into the terror of the bandeirantes and, later, over the centuries, of the backland settlements within their reach.

Facing these Indians schooled in confrontations with the agents of civilization, even the initially indisputable advantages of firearms were nullified. Wise and wily, the Indians would cover long distances to attack people unawares with a rain of their silent, sometimes poisoned arrows. While a bandeirante was fixing his carbine into its forked brace and working its complicated loading mechanism, the Indian would have got off three or four arrows at him.

It was absolutely necessary, however, to pass through the territory of those hostile Indians in order to reach the tribes of manioc and corn planters, more docile as slaves and more useful for small chores ever since the earliest times. That was because the basic adaptive culture of those Indians had been and continued over the centuries to be that of the Tupi peoples, whose tongue was spoken by the Brazilindians and whose customs and practices were almost the same.

The life of a captive Indian could not be any harder than as a bearer or oarsman, which were their principal chores. Belonging to the one who took him prisoner, he was livestock, worked with the greatest indifference, as if it were his destiny, because there was an apparently inexhaustible supply of Indians to replace those used up. Some colonial texts dealing with indigenous groups who facilitated the settlement of Europeans and collaborated with them call for some thought, principally about those Indians who, under frequent attack by other Indian tribes, might find the hard life and suffering under the Christians less terrible than remaining on their land at war against their enemies. One can also imagine that a young Indian recruited by a bandeirante as a warrior might stand out by capturing other Indians and being rewarded for it or by being praised as an extraordinary hunter, guide, and woodsman, with sharp eyes and great knowledge for traversing jungle and wasteland.

Some tribal groups, although brought into the colonial economy, managed to maintain a certain autonomy with the status of allies of whites in their wars against other Indians. The important thing in this case is the fact that instead of maturing for civilization—passing progressively from a tribal to a national status, from village to town, as so many historians have supposed—these autonomous nuclei remained irreducibly indigenous or were simply extinguished by the death of those constituting them. Wherever there have been concrete data, one can observe that the coexistence of an indigenous village with a colonizing nucleus was followed by the growth of the latter and the extinction of the former, its population diminishing year after year until it disappeared. In the rare cases in which a few natives have managed to survive, all of them have maintained their ethnic identity.

Ethnological investigations that I have undertaken have revealed the high degree of resistance of these tribal ethnic groups who still hold the loyalty of their members and continue to define themselves as Indians, even when submitted to acculturating and assimilative pressures over decades (Ribeiro 1970a). All those who moved against that ethnic resistance have got nowhere, either then or now. Equally useless were the threats of massacre and the integrative pressures exercised by the missionaries with total intolerance, as were the so-called persuasive methods of official organs of assistance.

Indians and Brazilians oppose each other as ethnic alternatives in an irreducible conflict that will never bring about a fusion. Wherever a tribal group has the opportunity to preserve the continuity of its own tradition by parents and children living together, ethnic identification is preserved no matter how great the assimilative pressure may be. Through that acculturative living together, however, the Indians become less and less Indian on the cultural level, ending up by being almost identical to the Brazilians of their region in the language they speak, their methods of work, their diversions, and even in the traditions they cultivate. Nevertheless, they keep on identifying themselves by their tribal ethnicity, and that is how they are identified by the representatives of the national society with whom they maintain contact. The step taken in this process is not, then, as is supposed, a transition from the status of Indian to that of Brazilian but from the status of specific Indians, invested with their attributes and living according to their customs, to the status of generic Indians, more and more acculturated but still Indians in their ethnic identification.

The Afro-Brazilians

The blacks of Brazil were brought in principally from the coast of western Africa. Arthur Ramos (1940, 1942, 1946), continuing the studies of Nina Rodrigues (1939, 1945), divides them by cultural types into three large groupings. The first of the Sudanese cultures is represented principally by the Yoruba groups, called *nagô;* by the Dahomey, designated generally as *gegê;* and by the Fanti-Ashanti, known as *mines;* along with representatives of smaller groups from Gambia, Sierra Leone, Ghana, and the Ivory Coast. The second group brought Islamic African cultures to Brazil, principally the Peul, the Mandinga, and the Hausa, from northern Nigeria, identified in Bahia as *malé* blacks and in Rio de Janeiro as *alufá* blacks. The third African cultural group was made up of Bantu tribes of the Congolese-Angolan group, coming from the area made up today of Angola and the "Counter-Coast," the present-day territory of Mozambique.

The cultural contribution of the black was of little relevance in the formation of that original proto-cell of Brazilian culture. Brought in to increase sugar production, he would constitute the basic labor contingent. In spite of his role as cultural agent having been more passive than active, the black had a cultural importance, both for his presence as a laboring mass producing almost everything made here and for his stealthy but tenacious and continuous introduction, making its strong mark on the Brazilian racial and cultural amalgam.

Just as happened with the whites who came later and were integrated into Brazilian ethnicity, the blacks, finding that Luso-Tupi proto-cell already in place, had to learn how to live within it, planting and cooking the foods of the land, calling things and spirits by Tupi names that had been incorporated into Portuguese, smoking long tobacco cigarettes and drinking *cauim,* made of fermented manioc and other fruits.

The blacks of Brazil, brought principally from the western coast of Africa, were captured haphazardly from among hundreds of tribal peoples, who spoke dialects and languages unintelligible to one another. Africa at that time was, as it still is today, an immense Babel of languages. Although more homogeneous on the cultural level, Africans at the same time varied broadly in this sphere. All of this prevented racial uniformity from corresponding to a linguistic-cultural unity, which could have brought unification when they were all brought into slavery. Religion itself—which today, after considerable effort over several generations, has become an expression of black consciousness—at that time disunited instead of uniting them. It even served as a factor of discord, according to what the Count dos Arcos has admitted.

The linguistic and cultural diversity of the black contingents brought into Brazil added to the reciprocal hostilities that they brought from Africa, and the policy of avoiding any concentration of slaves from the same ethnic group on the same plantation and even on the same slave ship impeded the formation of nuclei of solidarity where people might have retained their African cultural heritage.

Finding themselves dispersed over the new land alongside other slaves, their equals in color and servile condition but different in language and tribal identity, and frequently hostile because of the aforementioned conflicts of origin, blacks were compelled to incorporate themselves passively into the cultural universe of the new society. In spite of such adverse circumstances, they were a step ahead of other populators in learning the Portuguese tongue with which the overseers shouted at them and which they would subsequently use to communicate among themselves. They would end up making Brazil Portuguese as well as influencing in multiple ways the cultural areas where they were most concentrated, which were the sugar-producing Northeast and the mining zone in the center of the country. Today those populations preserve obvious African features in the color of their skin, the thickness of their lips, and the flatness of their noses as well as in cadences and rhythms and in special feelings in color and taste.

In both cases, on plantations and in mines, the black slaves saw themselves incorporated into atypical communities because they were not meant to care for the needs of their own population but rather for the mercenary designs of the master. As they wore themselves out producing what they did not consume, they were radically decultured through the eradication of their African culture. Simultaneously, they went along being acculturated into Brazilian ways of being and doing, such as these were represented in the simplified cultural universe of plantation and mine. In that way they had access to a body of adaptive, associative, and ideological elements from that Tupi ethnic proto-cell, which had been allowed to survive in enterprises for the exercise of extra-productive functions.

Only through great and continuous effort would the black slave go about reshaping his capacities as a cultural being, as Africans of diverse origins lived among the people of the land who had previously been incorporated into Brazilian proto-ethnicity, which would introduce him to a broader and more satisfactory range of new perceptions. In that way the black passed from the condition of *boçal* (ignorant, uncouth) — still held in his autochthonous culture and capable only of establishing elementary communication with the others who made up his new social surroundings — to that of *ladino* (astute, clever), more integrated now in the new society and the new culture. That primitive black, who still spoke no Portuguese or only a very garbled version, was, however, perfectly capable of performing the heavier and more basic chores in the division of labor on plantations or in mines.

Concentrated in great masses in areas of the most intense mercantile activity, where the Indian was becoming ever scarcer, the black would exercise a decisive role in the formation of local society. He would be the incomparable agent of Europeanization who would spread the language of the colonizer and would instruct newly arrived slaves in the techniques of work and the norms and values of the subculture into which they were being incorporated. He succeeded, thus, in exercising an influence, both by giving his touch to Portuguese speech and by impregnating its whole context with the little he had been able to preserve of his African cultural heritage. Since this last could not be expressed in the forms of the adaptation—the means of providing subsistence in Africa differing considerably on the ecological and technological levels—or in the ways of association either, these being rigidly prescribed by the structure of the colony as a stratified society into which he was being incorporated in his status of slave, that heritage would survive mainly on the ideological plane because that was the most recondite and personal. That is, it survived in religious beliefs and magical practices to which the black clung in a strong effort to console himself for his fate and in order to counter the threats of the adverse world into which he had been plunged. Along with these spiritual values, blacks retained in their innermost part both rhythmical and musical reminiscences and culinary tastes and preferences.

That scant African heritage—half cultural and half racial—in association with indigenous beliefs, would bring unique changes to Brazil's cultural ideology. It was in this sphere, for example, that a popular Catholicism appeared that was much more discrepant than any of the Christian heresies so persecuted in Portugal

Confined to the ghettos of slavery, Brazilian blacks participated and made Brazil participate in the civilization of the time, not in the forms that so-called western civilization assumed in its central nuclei but with the deformations of a spurious culture serving a subordinate society. No matter how much effort was devoted to achieving an ideal model of Europeanness, it was never attained, not even approached, because by the nature of things it was not applicable to overseas trading posts destined for the production of exotic items for export, of value only abroad. Their normal existence was the anomaly of a captive community that did not even exist for itself, governed by an internal law for the development of its potentialities, since it lived only for others and was governed by external wills and motivations, which wanted to degrade it morally and waste it physically in order to use its men as beasts of burden and its women as brood mares. The differences between the two models, not being a matter of degradation or illness, could never be restructured or cured. It was Brazil, in fact, that was constituting itself in correspondence to its ecological base or colonial system of monoculture and slavery, out of which an entirely new society was born.

The enterprise of slavery, based on the appropriation of human beings through the cruelest violence and permanent coercion, exercised with the most atrocious punishments, acted as a dehumanizing and deculturating millstone of incomparable efficiency. Subjected to that compression, any people will be dispossessed of itself, ceasing to be itself—first to become nobody, as it sees itself reduced to the status of beasts of burden, then to become someone else, transformed along lines allowed by the master, which are those most compatible with the preservation of his interests.

The astonishing thing is that anyone placed in this deculturating position managed to remain human. The Indians managed it by means of an unprecedented effort at self-reconstruction during the flow of the process of their undoing. They had no other way out; the only escape from the condition of slave was through the door of death or that of flight. These were narrow doorways, through which many Indians and blacks did escape, whether by the willful flight of suicide, which was quite frequent, or by running away—even more frequent and quite daring, as it almost always turned out to be fatal. Every black bore an illusion of flight in his breast and was sufficiently bold to attempt flight when there was an opportunity; he was therefore closely watched during his seven to ten years of active working life. His destiny was to die of exhaustion, which was his natural death. Once worn out, he might even be manumitted as worthless so that the master would not have to feed a useless black.

A premature death in an attempt at flight was better, perhaps, than the life of a slave brought from so far away to fall into the hell of that most painful existence. Feeling that he was violated, knowing that he was exploited, he resisted as much as possible. "They will stop doing good work if they are not appropriately beaten," noted a German observer, "and if we disregard the first iniquity they have been subjected to, that is, their introduction to forced submission, we must still ponder the punishment their masters impose on them" (Davatz 1941, 62–63). There we have the rationale of slavery, so foreign to the human condition that once it has been instituted, it can only be maintained through perpetual vigilance and the atrocious violence of preventive punishment.

Captured at the age of fifteen in his land, as though he were prey caught in a snare, he was dragged by the trader—an African dealer in slaves—to the coast, where he would be exchanged for tobacco, liquor, and trinkets. From there he would be convoyed, tied neck to neck with other blacks and pulled along by a rope, to the port and the slave ship. Placed on board he was left in the midst of a hundred others, occupying as best he could the small space of his size, eating poorly, defecating right there, in the midst of the foulest stench. If he survived the crossing, he landed in another market on this side where he was examined like a skinny horse. Assessed by his teeth, by the thickness of his ankles and fists, he was auctioned. Convoyed again, in chains this time, he was brought inland to the owner of mines or a sugar plantation to live the life that civilization had prescribed for him, working eighteen hours a day every day of the year. On Sundays he would cultivate a small plot, hungrily devouring the sparse and filthy animal rations with which he would restore his capacity for working until he was exhausted the next day.

Without anyone's love, without family, without sex, except for masturbation, without any possible identification with anyone—his overseer might be a black, his companions in misfortune enemies—ragged and dirty, ugly and smelly, mangy and sick, without any pleasure or pride in his body, he lived his routine, which was to suffer every day the daily punishment of scattered lashes so that he would be alert and work hard. Every week there was preventive instructive punishment so that he would not think of running away, and if he attracted attention, exemplary punishment would fall upon him in the form of the mutilation of fingers, the notching of breasts, burning with hot coals, having all his teeth judiciously broken, or being whipped on the pillory, with 300 lashes at one time to kill him or fifty daily lashes if he was to live. If he ran away and was caught, he could be branded with a hot iron, have a tendon cut, live shackled to an iron ball, or be burned alive over days of agony at the mouth of a furnace or thrown in all at once to burn inside like a piece of oily kindling.

No people passing through this as the routine of their life over the centuries would come out of it without being indelibly marked. All of us Brazilians are the flesh of this flesh of those tortured blacks and Indians. All of us Brazilians are, likewise, the mad hand that tortured them. The tenderest softness and the most atrocious cruelty come together here to make us the sensitive and long-suffering people that we are and the insensitive and brutal people that we also are. Descendants of slaves and slave owners, we will always be slaves to the distilled malignancy installed in us, both because of the feeling of the pain intentionally produced in order to give more pain and because of the exercise of brutality over men, women, and children that has been the nourishment of our fury.

The most terrible aspect of our heritages is that we will always carry with us the mark of the torturer impressed on our soul, ready to explode into racist and classist brutality. It is what still burns today with so much of Brazilian authority predisposed to torture, abuse, and crush the poor people who fall into their hands. By provoking growing indignation, however, it will give us the strength tomorrow to rein in the madmen and create a society of solidarity here.

The Neo-Brazilians

Thanks to the self-identification they were cultivating and also to their access to multiple sociocultural and technological innovations, the nascent neo-Brazilian communities were able to take two evolutionary steps. First, these communities included a larger number of members than the Indian villages, freeing large sectors of people from subsistence tasks and for the exercise of specialized functions. Second, they incorporated all members into a single ethnic identity structured as a socioeconomic group integrated in the world economy.

In spite of having a high degree of self-sufficiency, they depended on certain imported articles, especially metal instruments, salt, gunpowder, and other things they could not produce. They no longer lived, however, as Indians, closed up within themselves and turned fundamentally toward providing their subsistence. On the contrary, they maintained external commercial links in order to provide themselves with the aforementioned goods in exchange for their main item of export, which initially had been dyewood, then Indians taken as slaves, and which finally became certain products grown for export. The production of this merchandise went on to be their way of life.

For a long time, however, the basic population of these neo-Brazilian nuclei gave an appearance that was more indigenous than black or European, by the way they lived, by what they ate, by their view of the world, and by the language they spoke. Such Indianness was no doubt more apparent than real, because the appeal of indigenous ways of adaptation to nature, the survival of old traditions, and the very use of the indigenous language were placed now in the service of a new entity much more capable of growth and spread. As we have pointed out, while the growth of the indigenous population led only to the participation of tribes in microethnicities that tended to become differentiated, independent, and dispersed, the new communities constituted social units capable of growing conjointly in the form of a macroethnicity.

The Tupi language was the mother tongue in daily use by those neo-Brazilians until the middle of the eighteenth century. As a matter of fact, Tupi initially spread more than Portuguese as the language of civilization (on the formation and diffusion of the lingua franca, see Cortesão 1958 and Holanda 1945). The lingua franca or *nheengatu,* which arose in the sixteenth century out of the effort of speaking Tupi with a Portuguese mouth, spread rapidly as the principal tongue not only of the neo-Brazilian nuclei but also of the missionary ones.

It first filled the function of the language of communication between Europeans and the Tupinambá all along the Brazilian coast immediately after the discovery. Later it was the mother tongue of the mamelucos of Bahia, Pernambuco, Maranhão, and São Paulo. Later still it expanded along with the population as the common language both of the reductions and of the villages that the missionaries and colonists founded in the Amazon basin, just as it was in the gaúcho nuclei established in the extreme south facing Spanish populators. It must be noted that as this lingua franca was a variant not too differentiated from the Guaraní spoken in those centuries both in Paraguayan territory, where it was converted into a mother tongue, and in the Argentina and Uruguay of today, where such would not occur, we have before us a huge Tupi-Guaraní linguistic area, certainly the broadest of all American linguistic areas.

That was how it was before the arrival of the Europeans, since tribes of the Tupi trunk occupied almost the whole Atlantic coast of present-day Brazil and reached inland into vast regions of the Amazon basin and through the drainage of the River Plate. This linguistic area, loosely speaking, corresponds to the present-day territories of Brazil, Paraguay, and Uruguay. That was what the neo-Brazilians made theirs, speaking Tupi in order to communicate with the tribes who lived there and whom they succeeded ecologically in the same space.

The replacement of the lingua franca by Portuguese as the mother tongue of Brazilians would be completed only in the course of the eighteenth century. Since a long time before, however, it had been taking place in a more rapid and radical way where the economy was more dynamic and, consequently, the concentration of black slaves and Portuguese settlers was greater, and more slowly in economically marginal areas like the Amazon region and the extreme south. Along the Rio Negro the lingua franca was spoken until the twentieth century in spite of the fact that the Tupi had never reached north of the Amazon. Introduced as a civilizing language by the Jesuits, *nheengatu* remained after their expulsion as the everyday speech of the local Brazilian population and continued as the predominant language until 1940 (Nation Census of 1940).

In the south the presence of a vast Guaraní area in the River Plate basin can be seen on the one hand by the predominantly Guaraní toponymy of zones long occupied by Uruguay and Argentina and on the other hand by the present-day use of Guaraní as the vernacular language of Paraguay.

The same process of succession took place with productive technology. The initially indigenous technology was steadily replaced over the centuries by European techniques, all the more rapidly as each zone was completely integrated into the mercantile economy and modernized. Even so, all through the centuries the technology of rural Brazil was and continues to be basically indigenous with regard to subsistence—based on the cultivation and preparation of manioc, corn, pumpkins, and sweet potatoes along with many other plants—just as indigenous techniques of hunting and fishing persisted.

From early on, this indigenous technological base was enriched by European contributions that gradually increased its productivity. Such was the case with iron tools—axes, knives, machetes, scythes, hoes, fishhooks; firearms for the hunt and for war; and mechanical devices like the press, which often replaced the indigenous *tipiti,* a braided straw basket for squeezing manioc. Similarly, there were the *monjolo,* a large water mill for grinding corn, and mills for grinding cane; the waterwheel, ox cart, potter's wheel, loom, cotton gin, and even metal pots and pans, which replaced ceramic toasters for the treatment of manioc flour; and lastly there were domestic animals—chickens, hogs, oxen, horses—used for food, hunting, transport, and hauling.

The houses of the new nuclei were much reduced in size as compared to the indigenous communal huts, because instead of sheltering extended families, taking care of hundreds of people, they now sheltered smaller families or slave groups. Building techniques were improved with the use of plaster and adobe in construction of the more modest houses and tiles, stones, and bricks for those of the masters. Simultaneously the residences of wealthier people were embellished with more elaborate furniture, with sleeping hammocks replaced by beds, woven baskets replaced by leather hampers or wooden chests, to which tables, benches, cupboards, and oratories would be added later on. All of this was accompanied by techniques for the preparation and use of salt and soap, liquor, oil lamps, tanned leather, new medicines, sandals, and hats.

The main unifying elements of the new nuclei were an administrative and political rule represented locally by secular and ecclesiastic authorities and a socioeconomic agency under the charge of producers and merchants. The unity of command in this power structure allowed the nascent communities to grow and become more and more differentiated, with a rural component and an urban one. The first was based mainly on plantations under the governance of their owners but worked by black slaves in mercantile production and with administrative functions, defense, and the production of food falling to people born on the land. The second was the urbanized sector of the population, ruled by captains and prelates and including the activities of laborers, artisans, businessmen, functionaries, and priests. Their role was to administer the colonial enterprise and make it conform as a Portuguese possession, molding it to fit the canons of Portuguese culture and to be completely faithful to the Apostolic Roman Catholic Church.

A superior group soon stood out in the body of this colonial population, one removed from productive tasks and made up of three educated sectors, participants in certain erudite matters of Portuguese culture. They were a colonial bureaucracy governed from Lisbon, exercising the functions of civil and military government; a religious bureaucracy, which played the role of an apparatus for the indoctrination and catechizing of Indians and the ideological control of the population under the direction of Rome; and a third sector managed the export economy and was represented by financial houses and ship owners intent on the interests of and under the orders of European port cities that imported tropical articles. Those three sectors, along with their personnel established in the ports, made up the ruling class of the whole structure. They formed an urban component as important as that of European societies of the time. These, too, had been formed in the main by rural populations. The urban component was, in fact, a substructure of the European metropolitan network, less independent than its other components because Lisbon was the intermediary.

The Brazilians

There are special factors in the formative process of the American peoples that defy explanation. Why have some of them, even those poorest during the colonial period, progressed at an accelerated pace, becoming integrated into the industrial revolution in a dynamic and effective way, while others fell behind and are still struggling to modernize? Evidently the *transplanted people* whose ethnic identity came from Europe perfectly defined have found facilities in their own configuration for their incorporation into a new civilization that rises out of their roots. The case is different for peoples who were making a configuration of themselves that was totally different from their roots and who faced the task of spreading it to the peoples they had brought together and who were so different from one another. It was thus their task to define their ethnic identity, which could not be only that of overseas Europeans.

Another argument posed by history concerns the reasons for the linguistic uniformity of the American peoples. In the north, as in the south, the languages spoken by millions of people are the same—English, Spanish, Portuguese—and they do not offer any dialects. As none of this has occurred in any other place on earth, one must ponder why it happened here.

The name *Brazil,* usually identified with the dyewood, is really much more ancient. Old letters and legends of the ocean-sea carry mention of an island called Brazil, probably referred to by Iberian fisherman in search of cod (cf. Gandia 1929). The name was almost immediately applied to the new land, however, even though the Portuguese government tried to give it holy names that did not stick. The oldest maps of the coast already referred to it as "Brazilian," and the children of the land were also immediately called Brazilians. But use of the name as a generic term that a people applied to themselves arose only much later.

The name took root when it became necessary to give a differentiating denotation to the first neo-Brazilian nuclei, most often formed by Brazilindians and Afro-Brazilians, where the new historical-cultural configuration began to take shape, enveloping its components in a world that was not only different from but the opposite of that of the Indian, the Portuguese, and the black.

Full awareness of that opposition would be reached only much later, but a perception of the antagonisms and the differences was noted from the earliest decades. It was revealed in the prejudice of the native toward the mother country and, in counterpoint, in the disdain the mother country had toward the people of the land. It showed up in the perplexity of the missionaries, who found in Brazil not families formed according to the European model but a regular breeding ground for people of mixed blood, sired by a white father with his multiple Indian women. We have noted the concern of royal functionaries as to whether, two centuries after the discovery of Brazil, that mixed-blood mass who communicated in Tupi-Guaraní would ever come to speak Portuguese.

It is quite probable that the Brazilian began to arise and recognize himself more out of the perception of foreignness that he brought out in the Portuguese than because of his identification as a member of a new socio-cultural community; also, perhaps, because he was desirous of marking his difference and superiority vis-à-vis the natives.

In that search for his own identity he might even have been upset by the idea that he was not European, as he, too, considered everything native or black as inferior. Even the son of white parents who was born in Brazil, the so-called *mazombo,* occupying a position in his own society inferior with respect to those who came from the mother country, would be quite upset with his status as a son of the land, rejecting any treatment as a native and discriminating against the Brazilindian mameluco as an Indian.

The first Brazilian to be aware of himself was perhaps the mameluco, that Brazilindian mixed in both flesh and spirit who—unable to identify with those who were his American ancestors, whom he despised, or with the Europeans, who despised him, and being an object of ridicule by European and native-born Portuguese—saw himself condemned to the pretense of being what had never been or existed before: the Brazilian.

From these opposing poles and from a persistent effort to put together his own image and awareness as one belonging to a new ethnocultural entity, what was gradually emerging and taking shape was "Brazilian-ness."

It is quite possible that all of this became settled only after the local society was enriched by strong contributions from the descendants of African contingents, thoroughly de-Africanized now by the acculturative millstone of slavery. Those mulattos were either Brazilians or nothing, since identification with the Indian, the African, or the Brazilindian was impossible. In addition, as they helped spread Portuguese as the basic language, the mulattos, along with the mamelucos, soon made up a majority of the population that would go on, even against its will, to be seen and accepted as the Brazilian people. Although ecological-regional specialization—sugar, cattle, gold, rubber, etc.—would lead to strong local differentiations, that basic community, originally Luso-Tupi, would be maintained, always providing a line of continuity that strongly reveals its ethnic specificity while at the same time showing opposition to the roots from which it arose and which it got rid of as it took shape.

That cultural proto-cell formed during the first decades, while the African element was still absent or rare, operated from then on as the common denominator of the popular way of life for future Brazilians of all regions. Their basic heritage was made up of the Tupi peoples' age-old techniques of adaptation to the tropical forest as that lifeway was integrated into the cultural inheritance of the mamelucos.

As a matter of fact, the new nuclei were able to spring up and grow under such improbable conditions and in a milieu so different from the European one precisely because people had learned from the Indians how to identify, name, classify, and use all of tropical nature, distinguishing useful plants from poisonous ones and those good for food from those that had other uses. They had also learned from Indians about techniques efficiently adjusted to local conditions and to the different seasons of the year as concerned the cultivation and preparation of various things they planted, their hunting in the forests, and their fishing in lakes, rivers, and the sea. From the Indians, too, they learned to make ceramic utensils and to weave mats and baskets for home and outside use and sleeping hammocks and slings for carrying children. It was from the Indians, likewise, that they learned how to build the simplest of houses, adjusted to the climate, like the huts made from materials of the land where the common people lived, and to make canoes from bark or a dugout from a single tree. It was upon that base that the European technological heritage was later added, modernizing the nascent Brazilian society and allowing for its better integration with the peoples of the time.

Thus, working productively in an environment different from the European and the African ones, under climatic conditions that were also different, they met the requirements necessary for survival in the tropics. The technocultural heritage on which the ecological adaptation of Brazilians was based was essentially the same as that of all agricultural tribes in the tropical forest. It had, however, many peculiarities that made it recognizable as of Tupi origin. Notable in this regard were the language spoken by the neo-Brazilians, nheengatu, which was an offshoot of the Tupi trunk; the specific ecological formula for survival in the tropics, based on their agriculture, which was also Tupi; and the very genetic makeup of the mameluco nuclei, formed by European fathers and mainly Indian women from the coast, who were predominantly Tupi. All of that together gives the original Brazilians a flagrantly Tupi physiognomy.

In fact, neo-Tupi was what the Brazilian mameluco nuclei were, as opposed to other indigenous groups—treated generically as Tapuia— ethnocentrically looking down on them as inferior people because they did not speak the same language, eat manioc meal, or behave as was proper in true men. Only in the present century has Brazilian ethnology been able to distinguish the multiplicity of peoples mingled under that generic designation and to appreciate their true cultural characteristics. Curt Nimuendaju's investigations have demonstrated the specialized and relatively advanced character of the Jê cultures.

In that sense Brazil is the final and painful realization of those Tupi peoples who reached the Atlantic coast one or two centuries before the Portuguese and who, deformed and transfigured, have come to be what we are: Latino latecomers from across the sea darkened in a fusion of whites and blacks, deculturated of the traditions of their ancestral roots but carrying surviving remnants of these to help contrast us so much with Lusitanians.

As can be seen, an extraordinarily fortunate formula had already been shaped for people's adaptation to the tropics as a civilization linked to the Portuguese world but profoundly differentiated from it. Onto that mass of neo-Brazilians formed by the transfiguration of their roots would fall the task of making Brazil.

The assumption of their own identity by the Brazilians, as it is for any other people, was a long and dramatic process of diversification. No Indian reared in a village ever became a Brazilian, I think, so irreducible was his ethnic identification. But an Indian woman's son sired by a foreigner, white or black, would wonder what he was, since he was no longer an Indian, nor white nor black. Could he be the proto-Brazilian, constructed as a negative, created out of his absence of ethnicity? Seeking a recognizable group identity in order to stop being a nobody, he was forced to give birth to his own identification.

The black slave, acculturated in an African community, remained himself in his original identity until his death. Set down in Brazil, he was always in search of some brother from his distant community with whom he could fraternize. Not a companion, a slave, male or female, like himself, but someone coming from his African people, different from all those he saw here, since they were black slaves.

Surviving all ordeals in the transition from *boçal* to *ladino*, learning the new language, the new tasks, and the new habits, that black man was profoundly remade. He did not get to be a somebody, however, because he never reduced his own being to the simple common quality of black in race and slave in condition. His son, born here in the new land, racially pure or mixed, knowing himself not to be African like the boçal blacks he saw arriving, or white, or Indian, or their mixtures, felt challenged to rise up out of nobodyness, building his own identity. Thus he too would be a proto-Brazilian by default.

The Brazilindian and the Afro-Brazilian existed in a no-man's-land, ethnically speaking, and it was due to that essential lack, in order to free themselves of the nobodyness of non-Indians, non-Europeans, and non-Africans, that they found themselves obliged to create their own ethnic identity: Brazilian.

The Portuguese, no matter how much he identified with the new land, liked to look upon himself as part of the mother country. He was a native of the realm and that was his one undeniable superiority. His son, also, would certainly prefer being Portuguese. What it took for the mazombo to cease still being Portuguese was for the mamelucos and Indians and people who were part black to become an entity with a collective identity.

We have two lines of resort here. First is that of being formed within an ethnicity, always irreducible by its very nature, which embittered the fate of the exile, the landless person, forced to survive in what he knew to be a community of strangers and he a foreigner to it, all alone. The other is being at the same time torn away as a child of the land who did not fit, however, into the ethnic entities constituted here, rejected by them as an outsider, living in search of his identity. What opened up for the new Brazilian was an ambiguous space. Knowing himself to be different, he had within his consciousness the desire to remake himself, to approach those like him and form a viable collectivity with them. It would take a great deal of effort to define this new entity as human and, if possible, better than all others. Only by that tortuous route would all the new categories of people cease to be an isolated people, nobodies in the eyes of others.

It was essentially a case of constructing reciprocal representation as a new ethnic entity with sufficient cultural and social awareness to make it viable for its members and recognizable by outsiders by the dialectical singularity of its speech or by other singularities. It was also necessary for it to be sufficiently cohesive on the emotional level to withstand the inevitable animosity of all those excluded from it and to integrate its members into a unitary entity in spite of the internal diversity of those members, frequently greater than their differences with respect to other ethnicities.

When was it that one could speak of a new operative ethnicity in Brazil? When was it that Brazilians arose, conscious of themselves and, if not proud of their own being, at least resigned to it? That would take place when millions of people came to see themselves not as Indians of a certain tribe or as either tribal or generic Africans, because they had left all that behind, and much less as European or American Portuguese, but rather, starting with the rejections they suffered, felt themselves free and challenged to build a new ethnicity and national identity, that of Brazilians.

The fact is, however, that a collective representation of that identification must exist outside individuals so that they will identify with it and thus plausibly assume that the rest will accept them in a common shared status. The first element of this is the recognition of their own peculiarities, which are as different and opposite from the characteristics of those who do not possess them as they are similar to the features of those who bear the same peculiarities. When one says "our blacks," the reference is to the color of the skin; when people speak of mixed blood they are pointing to secondary characteristics. The relevant part, however, is that both are Brazilians, a general quality that transcends their peculiarities.

The birth of an inclusive Brazilian ethnicity that can include and take in the varied peoples joined together here calls for getting rid of ethnic identifications such as Indian, African, and European, and for a lack of differentiation among the various forms of mixture such as mulatto (black and white), caboclo (white and Indian), or *curiboca* (black and Indian).

Only by this path will all of them come to be one single people recognizing themselves as equal in something so substantial that it removes their differences and places them in opposition to all other peoples. Within the new grouping each member, each person will remain unmistakable but will go on to be included in the definite collective identity.

Being and Conscience

Lamentably, the process of the making of ethnicity left no recognizable marks except in the registry of a group as exotic and ambiguous as the writers of the period. The people of letters—few and rare—were viewed in one of two ways because they were fanatically identified either with the ethnicity of the Portuguese colonizer or with its Luso-Jesuitical variant.

Valuable in this sense are the aforementioned commentaries of Nóbrega and Anchieta on João Ramalho. More expressive still are the texts of Gregório de Matos (1633–96), one of the first Brazilian intellectuals, who in Bahia, with great delight, set about mocking all the people of that city, which was still new and exotic in flavor. On the nobility of Bahia he tells us:

In every corner a great counselor,
Trying to govern us in our shacks and vineyards,
Unable to govern their own kitchens,
They want to govern the whole world. (Matos Guerra 1990)

On people of mixed blood:

Noblemen to our very bones we think,
that's what makes the finest coat-of-arms . . .
of those who used to eat their grandfathers. (Matos Guerra 1990)

Picturing a Bahia already filled with blacks and mulattos, Matos leaves a
fine record of how they were looked upon by whites:

I don't know why being born
in this plague-ridden Brazil
a white man is honored
without any other race.
A crass and vulgar land
that has respect for no one
except for someone with a touch
of the Mulatto. (Matos Guerra 1990)

The whole multiracial world of Bahia comes out in these lines:

The black man insults you, the white man curses,
But nothing wounds you:
And for your lack of flavor and your little grace,
You're a tale at home but a joke in the street.
Oh! May the bullet that carried off your arm
Come back and carry off your face! (Matos Guerra 1946, 79)

We are also indebted to him for an express reference to mamelucos in his
portrayal of the governor of Bahia:

He gave birth to a cuckoo in his time,
A monster, inhuman, I must say,
Who was a toucan in his beak,
A *mameluco* in his blood . . .
Without being asked,
A trace of nobility came to him,
Pedestrian knighthood,
All with a punctured beak . . .
Before getting on his feet,
And before being what he is,
He didn't speak Portuguese,
But spoke in Cobé . . . .
We wager he's a white man,
Rational as a rock;

A *mameluco* to the fourth degree
And malignant to the core. (Matos Guerra 1946, 80–83)

Speaking of the petty noblemen of Bahia, Gregório de Matos rolls with laughter, but he also suffered, as the following lines quoted brought about his deportation to Angola.

Nicely woven palm-leaf breeches;
Annatto shirt; chief of the Arara,
Instead of a knife, bow and arrow;
A flamingo feather for a cap;
Lip pierced, no fear of his father's
death, run through with a palm-leaf;
His mother pounding the stone,
Holding back the blood that doesn't flow.
Savage without reason, brute without faith;
With no law but what he wants; and when wrong
From a monkey he becomes a loyal man.
I don't know how he ended up or in what war:
I only know that from this Adam of Maçapé
Some noblemen of this land descend. (Matos Guerra 1946, 148)

The best testimony of those times comes from Frei Vicente do Salvador, a native of Bahia. He was the first intellectual endowed with the new wisdom of the nascent people, capable of seeing our world and the world of others with our eyes, in solidarity with our people, with no doubts about our identity, and even with a touch of pride appropriate for this critical awareness. Almost all subsequent writings up to the present lack those qualities of love for the land and make of us a mindless people, because they lack our own native intellectual qualities, which could illuminate the view of our people among others as we face our destiny.

A graduate of Coimbra, a Franciscan monk, Frei Vicente helped build the monastery of Santo Antônio in Rio de Janeiro and rose to be vicar-general of Salvador in a quite successful career. In 1627 he finished his *History of Brazil,* saying: "I am 63 years old and now it is time to deal only with my own life and not that of others." He lived ten more years with hopes of seeing his work published. This happened only in 1888 in a first partial edition of excellent quality by Capistrano de Abreu. Portugal never mentioned him. It silenced all voices that spoke of Brazil, especially those speaking with praise.

The monk must have been a man with a good sense of the comic, for he wrote with great good humor. He tells us that his father was rescued from a shipwreck when he was coming to Brazil in flight from his stepmother. Of Governor Mem de Sá, who killed and mistreated the Indians, he reveals that "he died pleased" with his victories. Of Duarte Coelho, the founder of Pernambuco, the only effective grantee, the monk speaks of his returning to the homeland and that "there he died, annoyed that the king had received him with gibes and little favor." He adds to the colonial chronicle the news what the powerful Tomé de Souza, who waited impatiently for years for permission to return to the kingdom, must have said when it was granted: "The truth is that I was most desirous and my mouth watered when I thought of going to Portugal. But I don't know why it is that my mouth has dried up so much now that when I try to spit I can't" (Salvador 1982, 18).

But Frei Vicente was also just. For example, of Albuquerque, in addition to praising his unparalleled bravery, he notes that "his hands were always clean" — a rare thing, praiseworthy among us even today. He extols our rivers, our forests of cedars, *vinháticos,* and other trees, many providing vines to fasten fences and houses together, oakum for chinking, rafters for roofing, and huge trunks dug out by Indians into boats fifteen feet long that were powered by twenty oarsmen.

His judgment of the colonists is without praise. According to the monk the Portuguese "do not know how to settle or take advantage of the lands they have conquered." And they are most ungrateful "because services are rarely paid for in Brazil."

In certain passages our monk goes on to complain, for example grumbling about the king's neglect of us, that he preferred being lord of Guinea to being that of Brazil.

Of the settlers he tells us further that "no matter how rooted in the land or rich they might be, they all want to take back to Portugal all the wealth and possessions they can talk about, just as the first thing they teach parrots is 'parrot of the king to Portugal I bring,' because they want everything to go there; all of them use the land not as owners but as a usufruct, only to get as much out of it as they can and then leave it in ruin" (Salvador 1982, 57–58).

His history is largely a testimonial chronicle. Besides living half a century with eyes for everything that was happening about him, he listened to many old men who could speak of their own experiences and what had happened in previous periods.

Although succinct, our monk continues with a presentation about miraculous resins, medicinal balms, aromatic oils. He is charmed by the fruits of mighty trees like the *massaranduba* and even more by the genipap, the watery juice of which stains Indians black for weeks. He is greatly pleased with the cashew and the pineapple. Beans here are incomparably superior to those of the mother country. He describes a sensitive plant, so sensitive that it curls up at the slightest touch. In the chapter on food he mainly extols the merits of manioc and the sweet cassava.

Speaking of animals, he shows us peccaries, capybaras, tapirs, anteaters, foxes, a variety of monkeys, jaguars capable of downing and devouring bulls, and he mentions snakes. He even narrates the evil habits of one of them. It is the case of a woman in Pernambuco "who after having given birth, had a snake come to her on several nights to suckle at her breasts, doing it so gently that she thought it was her baby, and after she discovered the deception she told her husband, who lay in wait the following night and killed it" (Salvador 1982, 72).

He went on from there about chiggers, lice, and bedbugs. Sometimes he exaggerates, for example when he speaks of mermen who had been seen coming out of the water after Indians in order to eat their eyes and noses. He speaks at length about fish, mussels, and crustaceans, and especially about the blue *guaiamu* crabs, which emerge from their burrows with the first rains and enter houses.

His description of the Indians is summary, but he notes that "they have no king over them or whom they obey, only a captain, more for war than for peace" (Salvador 1982, 78). He also comments on the teary emotion with which the Tupi Indians received visitors they liked, including Portuguese who spoke their language. They greeted these visitors with great weeping and lamentation:

> The poor fortune that their grandfathers and earlier ancestors had had in not coming upon such worthy people as the Portuguese, who are owners of all the good things they bring to the land and which were lacking before and now are in abundance, like axes, scythes, fishhooks, knives, shears, mirrors, combs, and clothing, because previously they cleared the forest with stone wedges and took many days to fell a tree, fished with thorns, took care of their hair and nails with sharp stones, and when they wanted to adorn themselves they would use a pool of water as a mirror, and in that way life was a great chore, but now they do their planting and everything else with great ease, for which they owe them great esteem. (Salvador 1982, 79)

An important item is the one about a prisoner of war destined to be eaten but worth an ax or a scythe in ransom by the Portuguese. Since those possessions quickly became indispensable, one can imagine that an enormous number of Indians were saved in that way from the barbecue to be lost in slavery.

The mischievous monk even allows himself to speak ill of Anchieta, relating a bothersome episode concerning the execution of a French Calvinist. He tells us: "Seeing that the executioner was not very skilled at his trade and that he was delaying in killing the prisoner and therefore was making him anguished and putting him in danger of denying the truth that he had already confessed, he scolded the executioner and instructed him to do his duty quickly." And he adds judiciously: "Cases like this are more to be amazed at than imitated" (Salvador 1982, 167).

The monk anticipated by centuries a feeling of Brazilianness that would reach maturity only expressly with Tiradentes' comrades, who used "Brazilians" as the political designation for the people they wished to rouse to rebellion.

Also, the native movement of the previous century called Indianism was an assumption of the worth of non-Portuguese natives, who were found to be quite superior to the Portuguese. There is much talk about identity in psychological and philosophical terms that adds little to the concrete and visible fact of the emergence of the Brazilians, constructed by themselves, now fully aware that they were a new and unique people and, if not hostile to, at least wary of all others.

6

Bellies and Ballocks

De-Indianization

Since we cannot count on any trustworthy series of statistics for the past, as we do not even have them for the present, we shall make broad use here of what I call hypothetical demography—that is, a historical series set up and based on the few concrete and complete data that seem plausible.

It is quite probable that the total indigenous population of Brazil at the time of the invasion amounted to 5 million or somewhat more. In any case, it was likely much greater than current estimates suppose, as studies in historical demography show (Borah 1962, 1964; Dobyns and Thompson 1966). Based on analyses of the documentation at hand done in the light of new criteria, these studies have increased old estimates of the original indigenous population of the Americas.

On both the Portuguese and the Spanish sides there has been an obvious tendency on the part of scholars to minimize the original indigenous population. Either scholars believed that there was exaggeration in the primary sources of the chroniclers who effectively saw the Indians with their own eyes, which is absurd, or there was the tendency prevalent for a long time—and perceptible even today—to exalt the role of the conquerors and colonization, concealing the weight of their genocidal impact on American populations, which is even more absurd.

There are still no studies assembled in light of this new perspective for the reestimation of the original indigenous population of Brazilian, Paraguayan, and River Plate territories, but it must surely have been greater than the indirect calculations, apparently well founded, such as those of Julian Steward (1949, 666), which put it at a little over a million; Lugon

(1968), who raised that number to 3 million; and Hemming (1978, 487–501), who reduced it to 2,400,000.

The number we shall use for reference for the whole area (5 million) will consequently have to be viewed with reserve until we can rely on direct studies of the matter with a basis in the documentation at hand and in accord with the new methodology of historical demography. It is doubtless a question of a large number, even in comparison with the population of Portugal in 1500, which was a little over 1 million inhabitants.

Our estimate of the original indigenous population of Brazil, however, cannot be an exaggeration because it matches the primary sources, and in establishing it we have kept in mind the figures of tribal population that followed the first century of contact. In fact, the numerous concrete cases of depopulation resulting from the first contacts of which we have direct knowledge (Ribeiro 1970a, 261) confirm the figures of the demographic studies cited, which is on the order of twenty-five to one. That calculation is based fundamentally on the collapse of the Mexican population immediately after the conquest, when it fell from 25,300,000 to 1 million between 1519 and 1605 (Cook and Borah 1957). This means that the 100,000 Brazilian Indians of the first half of the twentieth century must represent a population originally numbering 2,500,000 at least. Since, however, we are considering on the one hand an area that includes the territories of Paraguay and Uruguay, highly populated, and on the other, a period of four centuries in the course of which many indigenous groups became extinct, it must be imagined that the original indigenous population had in fact been much greater, probably double, which brings us to the figure we are using.

Following that line of reasoning, we suppose that those 5 million Indians of 1500 would have been reduced to 4 million a century later by decimation through epidemics among the peoples along the Atlantic coast, who suffered the first impact of civilization, and by the contamination of tribes in the interior by the plagues brought by the Europeans and by war. In the second century, from 1600 to 1700, the depopulation continued, brought on by further epidemics and by a wasting away through slave labor along with extermination through war, reducing the indigenous population from 4 million to 2 million.

This is how it was with the erosion of isolated tribes living in areas of recent colonization, and especially in the southern region, where the São Paulo mamelucos liquidated enormous concentrations of Guaraní Indians at the Jesuit missions. It is probable that in that century more than

300,000 were enslaved, brought to São Paulo, and sold for shipment to Bahia and Pernambuco (Simonsen 1937). That capture of slaves was also conducted through the intermediary services of any number of captive Indians enticed by the bandeira expeditions. The proportion of Indians to "whites" in the bandeiras was 700 to 200 according to Cristóvão de Barros, and 900 to 150 according to Antônio Dias Adorno in 1574, and 1,000 to 200 in the bandeira of Raposo Tavares to the Jesuit reductions in Itatins (1648). Nassau himself sent a failed expedition of 700 Indians and 100 mulattos along with 300 Dutch soldiers against Palmares in 1645. Palmares was destroyed a half century later by the men of Jorge Velho, who came down from Piauí to fight first the Janduí Indians (1688) and then Palmares (1694) with a troop of 1,300 Indians and 150 "whites." Indians also made up the major part of the force with which the Portuguese fought the French in Guanabara and later in Maranhão as well as the force used against the Dutch in Paraíba.

In the third century, from 1700 to 1800, another million must have been *used*—to employ the bizarre term of colonial chroniclers—principally in Maranhão, Pará, and Amazonas, reducing the remaining population of isolated Indians from 2 million to 1 million. This last million has been diminishing ever since with the occupation and gradual exploitation of vast forest areas in Minas Gerais, São Paulo, Paraná, and Santa Catarina along with the opening up of broad fronts of expansion in central Brazil and the Amazon region.

In every century and in every region, indigenous tribes untouched by contact and free of contagion were successively experiencing the impact of the main drives and plagues of civilization, and the demographic losses from which they have never recuperated. The decimating effect of unknown illnesses, abetted by compulsory enlistment in the workforce and deculturation, brought the greater part of indigenous groups to complete extinction. In many cases, however, remnant populations have survived, which as a rule correspond to that proportion of one to twenty-five of the original population. Beginning with that minimum figure, the population has slowly begun to increase.

According to what has been seen, the original population of Brazil was drastically reduced through a genocide of frightful proportions that took place through wars of extermination, exhaustion in slave labor, and the virulence of new illnesses. This was followed by an equally decimating ethnocide, which acted through demoralization by catechizing, by the pressure of plantation owners who were taking over their lands, through the failure of their own attempts to find a place and a role in the world of the invaders. Genocide and ethnocide were accompanied by the wars of extermination authorized by the Crown against Indians considered hostile, like those of the valley of the River Doce and the Itajaí. A great number of them were dislodged and destroyed. In spite of everything, amazingly, some indigenous tribes have survived as islands in the growing mass of the Brazilian rural population. These are the Indians who have been integrated into national society as a remainder of the original population.

We have already pointed out that this integration does not correspond to an assimilation that converts them into undifferentiated members of Brazilian ethnicity. It means, quite simply, the establishment of a most precarious modus vivendi, through which they move from the status of specific Indians with their own peculiar race and culture to that of generic Indians. Even though mingling increasingly in blood and culture, they still remain "Indians," in an alternative status from "Brazilians," because they are looked upon and suffer as Indians, and this is how they are seen and treated by the people with whom they come in contact.

There is copious documentation, starting with the first century, of generic Indians concentrated in villages, some autonomous, others administered by religious missions or by official protection services. They have survived over decades or for centuries, still unassimilated, the remnants of the hecatomb of the impact of civilization, always irreducibly Indians as opposed to Brazilians. No basis in fact can be found, so far as can be seen, for the idea that these Indians, through the processes of acculturation, have matured enough for civilization.

The classic tale so beloved of historians and according to which the Indians were maturing for civilization in such a way that every village was changing into a town is completely lacking in authenticity. The study we undertook for UNESCO, hoping to show Brazil as a country of assimilation par excellence, has shown precisely the opposite. The Indian has been irreducible in his ethnic identification, as has occurred with the Gypsy and the Jew. Greater persecution only drives them more decidedly into themselves. Assimilation has not been attained by official protection services, generally turned over to missionaries, or by the latter either. There are peoples like the Bororo, for example, who after more than a century of missionary life remain Bororo, little changed by missionary activity, or the Guaraní, with more than four centuries of contact and domination.

Some "success" has been attained by very retrograde missions like the Salesians of the Negro river, who, intent on westernizing and catechizing the Indians of that area, have brought together the children of different tribes in the same schools, thus fulfilling the essential condition for de-

Indianizing the Indians, which is to break the old transmission relationship from parents to children. What they got were not little Italians but marginalized girls and boys who did not know how to be either Indians or civilized people and lived in terrible sadness there.

The incorporation of natives into the Brazilian population took place only on the biological level and through the process mentioned so many times of the breeding of mamelucos, sons of the dominators by women torn from their tribes, sons who identified with their fathers and were added to the paternal group. Along that path, over the centuries, the Indian woman went along shaping the Brazilian people in her role as the main ethnic breeder. In a society lacking women, Indians and blacks taken for slaves rarely had female companionship. Saint-Hilaire, speaking of the region of Rio Grande do Sul, observes that the enslaved Indians "were of no use for populating the land since they were far from their territory and found no women they could marry" (Saint-Hilaire 1939).

In the first decade of the twentieth century the situation of the native in Brazil was highly conflicted. Missionaries appropriated the lands of the Indians they were catechizing and divided them into parcels, causing great rebellion on the part of the Indians. Vast areas were given over to colonization by foreigners, principally Germans, and were in turmoil caused by Indian fighters paid by the colonists to rid their lands of the inconvenient "invaders." The director of the Paulista Museum, an eminent scientist, asked the government to choose between savagery and civilization. If it was their aim to civilize the country, they would have to undertake a war of extermination with government troops in order to solve the problem.

It was in that situation that the principal Brazilian humanitarian, Cândido Rondon, arose. He had much experience in dealings with the Indians because he had strung thousands of miles of telegraph lines in Indian territory without coming into conflict with them. Rondon demanded of the nation respect for its original population. His appeal was answered not only by the government but by dozens of officers of the armed forces and professionals of all types, who decided to dedicate their lives to the salvation of the indigenous peoples. Based on the principles of Auguste Comte but going far beyond them, Rondon and his companions established a body of directives that for decades oriented official Indian policy. They maintained that the objectives should not be to exterminate or transform the Indian but to make him a better Indian, giving him access to tools and a suitable orientation. What should be done in essence was to assure that indispensable minimum to every Indian people, namely the right to be Indian through the guarantee of a territory where they could live in peace, safe from attack, and could reconstitute their lives and customs. The necessity of opening new frontiers of colonization had to be preceded by careful work among the Indians.

The main innovation put forth by Rondon, however, was the establishment of the pioneering principle, recognized internationally only today, of the right to be different. In place of the bland proclamation of the equality of all citizens, the Rondonians said that since they were not equals, equality served only to turn the Indians over to their persecutors. What was called for was setting the norms of a compensatory right by which the Indians would have the same rights as Brazilians—voting and performing military service, for example—but those rights should not be imposed on them as if they were duties.

Curt Nimuendaju, one of the most important ethnologists with a knowledge of the Indians of Brazil, sketches a profile of the civilized Indian in his "Trip to the Negro River" report to the Service for the Protection of Indians, dated September 1927:

> More than in any other part of Brazil known to me, in Içana and Uaupés I found the relations between Indians and civilized people— whites as they are called there—destroyed: a chasm has opened between the two elements, barely perceptible at first, disguised by the veil of a *modus vivendi* set up by both sides, but showing itself immediately in all its impassable depth as soon as one tries to gain the confidence of the Indians and penetrate the intimacy of their psyche. Of course, the majority of the civilized people, not understanding or needing any of this, never get to see this chasm, considering themselves perfectly satisfied with the *modus vivendi* and probably often presenting it as the result of their civilizing processes. (Nimuendaju 1950, 173)

In the bygone times of 1954, when I was working for the International Labor Organization to establish the rights of indigenous peoples, the Rondonian thoughts I presented there so impressed two intellectuals from India that they called for an interpreter and had lunch with me, wanting to hear about that great Brazilian of whom they were unaware. I pointed out to them that there had been no connection between Rondon and Gandhi. They were simply two parallels of humanitarianism. It is curious to remember that they wanted to know if I had taken an oath. I had trouble understanding their question when they said that they had taken an oath for the cause of the minorities and oppressed peoples of India. That is, they had promised that in the ten years following their university degrees, they would dedicate their minds and hands to that cause alone.

Prodigious Growth

The great achievements in Brazilian history were the conquest of a continental territory and the building of a population that went beyond 150 million. Neither of these acts was gratuitous. Portugal—which had lived for a thousand years obsessed with a frontier, fearful of being swallowed by Spain—here, from the very first moment, tried to mark out and extend the bases of its territorial possessions. It established forts a thousand leagues from any other settlement. Over the years it maintained, through war, fixed points along its boundaries, such as the Colony of Sacramento.

The building of a population, if not done with any deliberate plan, was the effect of a spontaneous demographic policy that resulted both in the depopulation of millions of workers and in the increment of other millions.

On the genetic level, the Brazilian population was built simultaneously through the most atrocious decimation as well as by the most prodigious increment. Through the widespread utilization of the immense availability of the wombs of enslaved indigenous women, the growth of the mixed-blood population was nothing less than miraculous.

In 1584 Father José de Anchieta estimated the population of Brazil at 57,000 souls, 25,000 being "native whites"—meaning principally people of mixed blood fathered by Portuguese men with Indian women—18,000 Indians, and 14,000 blacks. The number would have been much greater if the estimate had taken in the area occupied by Brazil today, and especially if it had included those Indians who, although living autonomously, were already in permanent interaction with the nascent society, estimated to have been at least 200,000. Anchieta, however, was referring only to the population involved in the colonial enterprise, which at that time probably took in no more than twenty-five square miles.

That population was essentially established in the Northeast, occupied in the embryonic sugar economy and in the exploitation of dyewood. There were probably fourteen settlements then, the principal ones being Olinda, with 700 inhabitants; Bahia, and Rio de Janeiro, with 500; and the remainder with an average of 400, which represented an important urban component that coordinated the colonial enterprise.

Based on Anchieta's estimate and on the data furnished by other chroniclers of the time, the assumption can be made that in 1600 the neo-Brazilian population was 200,000 inhabitants (Capistrano de Abreu 1929, 123) — that is, the population directly involved in the colonial enterprise plus the indigenous groups that were in direct and peaceful interaction with the colonizers and who represented 120,000 people. As for the non-indigenous contingents, they must have reached a figure of around 50,000 for those defined as white, almost all of them of mixed blood, and 30,000 black slaves. The urban contingent probably reached 6,000 to 8,000 inhabitants, from the growth of settlements reported by Anchieta as well as the creation of new nuclei that would occupy an area of 25,000 square miles. Celso Furtado (1959) estimates that 120 sugar plantations were operating then and that herds of cattle had probably reached 680 head. The annual production of sugar probably reached 2 million *arrobas* (around 50 million tons), the value of which would have been 2.5 million pounds sterling at that time. As he points out, such extraordinarily high revenue made the Portuguese colonial enterprise the most prosperous of the period and, for that very reason, the one most coveted by the Dutch and the French, who from that time on would fight over its possession.

The demographic balance of that first century of occupation gives us one principal result: the decimation of one million Indians, killed mainly by the epidemics that raged on the coast and reached the interior immediately thereafter, and also dying from captivity in missions and from war. Simultaneously the number of mixed-blood offspring of some Indians grew like wildfire.

In 1700 the neo-Brazilian population probably reached some 500,000 inhabitants, of which 200,000 were natives integrated into the colonial system, doubling its area of occupation. Blacks probably numbered 150,000, concentrated mainly on sugar plantations but also in the zones recently opened to mining. A portion of them took refuge in *quilombos,* settlements of runaways, beyond the frontiers of civilization; but Palmares, the main nucleus, which had brought together 30,000 blacks, had already been wiped out. The "white" population, which probably consisted of 150,000 inhabitants, formed in the main by people of mixed blood with European fathers and native mothers, spoke mostly nheengatu as their mother tongue. In rough contrast to that parcel of Brazilindians was a considerable number of mulattos formed by diverse crossings — the *banda-forra* (white and black), the *salta-atrás* (mameluco and black), the *terceirão* (a recrossing of white with mulatto) — who, being largely acculturated and speaking Portuguese, would help the colonizer thenceforward in culturally inculcating the mamelucos.

The economy was concentrated fundamentally in sugar production, which led all exports; in cattle, which probably reached 1.5 million head and had taken on a certain importance as a source for the export of leather; and in tobacco, which had also become an important article of export, principally to pay for the importation of African slaves. The production of gold from recently discovered veins was growing with extraordinary vigor and in succeeding decades was destined to form the most dynamic sector of the economy. As such it would draw to the gold-mining zones in the center of the country large populating contingents of whites coming from the mother country and from areas of previous occupation and especially of blacks transferred from plantations or imported directly from Africa.

Gold mining (1701–80) and later diamonds (1740–1828) would bring about a substantial change in the scattered rural aspect of the early colonial nuclei. The first consequence was the rapid attraction of a new population—more than 300,000 in the first sixty years—to an area of the interior previously unexplored, incorporating the territories of Minas Gerais, Goias, and Mato Grosso into the economy of the colony.

To judge the importance of mining, we have only to consider that it probably produced close to a thousand tons of gold and 3 million carats of diamonds, the total value of which was the equivalent of 200 million pounds sterling—more than the export value of precious metals from all the rest of the Americas.

The gold-bearing region was the object of the greatest dispute that has taken place in Brazil. On one side were the São Paulo people who had made the discovery and demanded the privilege of its exploitation, and on the other were the Bahians who had arrived in the region first with their herds of cattle and had taken the care to register their territorial properties—a certain Guedes, a notary from Bahia, registered for himself a huge holding that stretched from Bahia to the middle of Minas Gerais. The war between the disputing parties brought on an enormous increase in violence, with betrayal, murder, and theft. A father ordered his son hanged; a son set his father adrift in a flimsy skiff on the Rio das Velhas, praying for him to reach the sea and Portugal.

But its impact was even greater. Rio de Janeiro was born and grew into the port for the mines. Rio Grande do Sul and even Argentina, suppliers of mules, were tied to Minas Gerais, just as were the owners and a large portion of the slaves of the Northeast. All of this made Minas the knot that tied Brazil together, turning it into a single unit.

The lands were so rich in gold, and such was the avidity to find it, that slaves were able to buy their freedom when they exceeded their regular production. So it was that a few strange black nabobs arose. Startling, too, was the hunger of people who would buy a hen for its weight in gold.

Decades of a skillful policy of accusation and subornation finally brought peace to the area, calming the mobs of miners, but not before everything was almost lost to Portugal in a plot hatched between the miners and the government of the United States, organized by the most unlikely subversives—poets, magistrates, military men, priests, etc. The plot ended up being crushed with the hanging and quartering of the main hero, in order to set an example for the people, and the other plotters left to rot in exile in Africa.

In Ouro Preto and its environs, when gold was no longer so plentiful, the highest expression of Brazilian civilization was seen to flourish, with extraordinary figures of artists like Aleijadinho, poets like Gonzaga and Cláudia Manoel da Costa. Allow me, unable to resist the temptation, to provide for your reading the chapter "Quicklime" from my novel *Migo* on the spirit of Minas.

Seeing Minas here, so miserable, who but someone out of his mind would say that we are the people of the future? We're a tepid people with outstanding heroes. There they've been, over the centuries, gathering in our love of liberty. Filipe shouts, Joaquim José answers:

"*Libertas sera tamen.*"

"Freedom, here and now. Now!"

How did they do away with Filipe? Quartering him? The strongest horses in all Brazil were there, champing at the bit, foaming at the mouth, kicking at the pavement of the square. There were four of them. One horse was tied to his left arm. Another horse to his right leg. The third horse to his right arm. The last horse to his left leg. Each horse was mounted by a trooper in armor.

Whipped, spurred, the four horses took off, each in its own direction. But they remained there, halted, drawing sparks out of the paving stones with their shoes, tied as they were to Filipe's firm flesh. Lashed, spurred till they bled, finally, with Filipe torn apart, the horse with his right arm went off, freed, carrying along with the arm a piece of his chest. Quickly, instantaneously, the three other horses took off, tearing Filipe to pieces, each with a part of him.

What did they do when the sweating horses, far off now, stopped, when the revolting order had been carried out? There they went, dragging their four pieces through the streets to the dung heap of an old gravel pit. There, into the dark hole, there, into the midst of the quicklime, they threw what remained of the flesh and bones of the hero and they threw more lime on top of it. Filipe, death boiling from his scant flesh. They had killed him in such a way that he would be remembered forever.

A half century passed with the people in wait for the time of another appointed one. Destiny acted, this time crowning the head of Joaquim José, condemned by the Mad Queen to die a natural death on the scaffold, to be quartered and displayed as a lesson for the people. Torn apart, pieces of him remained rotting there until time consumed them, as Dona Maria had wished. The four quarters stuck there stinking on the Queen's Highway, his head with its thick hair and beard raised on a tall pole in Ouro Preto, watched over by patiently by hungry vultures with steely wings, sharp beaks. They, and only they, were his gravediggers. Finished like that, so completely finished, without even the charity of quicklime, Tiradentes never came to an end, nor will he ever. He goes on throbbing inside us. Over the centuries he will continue to call out in the flesh of the grandchildren of our grandchildren, gathering in with each one his dignity, his love of liberty:

The beards, the beards, the beards,
Here they will remain,
Awaiting another face, another shame.

These are our appointed heroes, symbols of a hidden grandeur that once was—that still is, I like to believe, rarer than the others yet to be mined.

Greater than those two, however, is the multitude I am going to summon. Watch:

"Come, I call you, come one and all. Come here and tell of lacerated nerves, worn-out muscles. Come one and all, with your sad faces, your withered illusions, come clothed or naked, just as you were buried, if you were. Come once more to die your ignominious deaths here.

"You come first, unknown man of Minas who stole the skull of Tiradentes, prayed for his soul, and buried it. But come one and all!"

Do you see them? They were millions of souls clothed in mortal, aching bodies that were wasted here in Minas. Take another look at them, take a good look. Just look. In the beginning they were mostly native Indians and a few imported light Mulattos. Then mainly blacks from far away, from Africa. But slowly, slowly, just look: no, they were swarms of mixed-bloods, born here, right here.

These millions of so many people are the mules of this Gehena of sluiceways. See how they are all looking at us, eyes lowered, fearful, asking in soft voices:

"Who are we? What do we exist for? Why? For nothing?"

We are the people with outstanding heroes, but we're also the people of these frightened multitudes, deceived and wasted. The people punished in the flesh and in the soul. We are the people who saw and still see. The people who watch and wait.

Starlike Minas, firmament, mother of iron, mother of gold and mercury. Mineral mother, sulfuric glow. Astral Minas, Portuguese emblem of living rock buried overseas.

Ancient Minas, cruel satrapy of gall and agony, It is I who beg you to put an end to this agony, for a flash of lightning now, ask for death. Die! Die and be reborn. Let rocks roll from out of the petrified sea, roll, crumble the granite wall that imprisons people and time, enslaving, bleeding, starving, murdering.

Minas of the tall tree. Minas of blood, tears, and wrath. Minas, mother of men. Minas of sperm, of corn, of flowers, of spades, of dynamite. Carnal Minas of bloom and seed. Minas, mother of pain, mother of shame. Minas, my twilight mother.

We shall have a dawn. The world is tinted with the hues of the predawn's glow. (Ribeiro 1988, 376–78)

Our greatest glory as a people is that these people existed and expressed themselves in such a lofty way. They are our glory. Their works, in the form of architecture and sculpture, erudite music of the highest quality, poems and books, are our pride.

That explosion of prosperity would have multiple consequences. Among others was that of bringing to the interior the colonial effort, which until then—before the inroads of the bandeirantes—had been limited to the land along the coast, people "content to crawl up and down the coast like crabs," Frei Vicente do Salvador said. And, above all, it started bringing the scattered Brazilian nuclei together in the unification of national territory.

Until then Brazil had been an archipelago of colonial settlements, isolated like islands apart from one another by thousands of miles. Now a network of commercial exchange was growing that would have enormous import in the future because it would provide an economic base for national unity.

Another effect of the surge of gold was the retaining in the interior of the country of a mass of resources that permitted the rapid building of an urban network in the mining zone, creating prodigiously wealthy and beautiful cities. There and in the old ports a gold civilization flourished, expressed in sumptuous churches and mansions, the construction and decoration of which employed vast numbers of workmen specialized in arts and crafts. Wealthy Brazilians became wealthier and showier, emerging from the crudeness of São Paulo and the mediocrity of the Pernambuco and the Bahia of the first two centuries.

With the petering out of the veins of gold came the diaspora. That ever-so-civilized population of blacks, mulattos, and others of mixed blood spread out through the uncultured grant lands of Minas, implanting the ways of living, eating, dressing, of being silent, of being sad, and even of committing suicide that are unique in Brazil. It is the Minas way.

Even more significant was the second Portuguese invasion. From one day to the next almost 20,000 Portuguese, fleeing the troops of Napoleon, disembarked in Bahia and Rio.

The wise king knew quite well that his effective kingdom was there. So it was that when he saw Portugal invaded by Napoleon he ended up here, dragging along his mad mother. He brought with him the cream of Portuguese bureaucracy. It was an immense naval undertaking, with thousands of Portuguese embarking for Brazil and fighting for space on the decks of the English ships called in for the operation. Its influence was tremendous.

Brazil, which had never had universities, suddenly received a most competent ruling class, who naturally paid themselves by appropriating the best there was in the country. But they taught us how to govern.

While Spanish America broke up and in every port a not too viable nation was put together, here, in spite of the immense regional differences, unity was maintained. All uprisings, even those defamed as republican, were confronted by the king's generals with cannons on the one hand and epaulets and decrees of amnesty on the other. It is true that many of those battles were so fierce that the king was obliged to order the shooting of a great many priests, who were the intellectual rebels of those times. But when the strife was over there was complete reconciliation.

By 1800 the population of the territory of Brazil had regained its original figure of 5 million—but now with an inverted composition. Half of it was now made up of Brazilian "whites," predominantly *pardos*—meaning people of mixed blood and mulattos—who spoke mostly Portuguese as their mother tongue and were completely integrated into neo-Brazilian culture by this time. Black slaves numbered a million and a half, a third of them *crioulos,* meaning blacks born in Brazil, broadly acculturated. The remainder of the original indigenous population who had been subjugated and integrated into the neo-Brazilian population as slave labor, either directly subjugated or incorporated into the system through missions and directories of Indians, numbered half a million. Beyond the frontiers of civilization, in flight or resisting conscription into the labor force and vassaldom, another million intractable and hostile Indians probably lived, concentrated mainly in the Amazon region but also scattered throughout the country wherever zones of impenetrable forest provided them with refuge.

The year 1800 represented a turning point in Brazilian history. The export economy was going through a period of decline, which certainly meant a respite for the population. In fact, with the pace of sugar production reduced and the period of exploitation of gold and diamonds over, these endeavors having occupied the main contingents of workers, black and white, people spread out in search of independent means of survival. Sugar production, which was experiencing a crisis because of the expansion of new productive centers in the Antilles, made up half the value of exports, but was considerably reduced. Cattle raising had spread prodigiously throughout the interior backlands and southern pasturelands. The most dynamic sector at the time was the cultivation of rice and, after that, cotton, in Maranhão, the principal cotton purchasers being English mills in competition with producers in the United States.

The fundamental result of three centuries of colonization and successive projects of economic viability in Brazil was the makeup of its population at the time—at 5 million inhabitants one of the most numerous in the Americas—with the simultaneous ethnic deculturation and transfiguration of its diverse constituent matrices. Until 1850 only Mexico

(7,700,000) had a larger population than Brazil (7,200,000). The real product of the process of colonization at that time was the formation of the Brazilian people and their incorporation into an ethnically and economically integrated nationality. This last result seems to have been reached a few decades before, when almost all Brazilian nuclei were already being integrated into an internal economic network and this went on to be more important than the external market. The reverses experienced by the various regional export economies and the consequent fall of the large landholders and the commercial power of their monoculture appears to have opened up for Brazilians at that moment an opportunity to structure themselves as a people who existed for themselves. That might have occurred had not a new export product appeared—coffee—which would lead to the restructuring of the whole workforce into a new means of integration into the world market and to the reincorporation of Brazilians into the status of an external proletariat.

It could well be, however, that even without the rise of coffee, this reversal, or turning inward, of Brazilians might not have taken place. Brazil, a product of the expansion of the world economy, would need deep transformations in order to exist outside it. The indispensable decisions for that—abolition of slavery, agrarian reform, autonomous industrialization—were beyond the capacity of the ruling class as long as there was economic profit for them in the importation of goods manufactured in European centers and in the exportation of tropical products. Added to this was the fact that since there were no existing models for the intentional reconstruction of society, a purely autonomist reversion would have resulted at most in a feudal autarchy. As in all cases of feudalization, that would represent a break in the mercantile system, which would make slavery impractical because there would be no way to obtain new slaves and because it would render them useless in their main function, which was the production of merchandise. But it would condemn the emerging society to a historical step backward, which would probably render it incapable of defending its possession of the land that it occupied and of avoiding the threat of falling under the rule of another dominating colonial system of one of the new emerging industrial powers.

For better or for worse, Brazil was a marginal component, dependent on an agrarian-mercantile civilization on its way to industrialization. In any of these types of civilization the failure of one line of production for export only brings about the discovery of another line, which, replacing it, would revitalize the colonial economy and consequently fortify external dependency and an internal oligarchical order.

The Black Stock

The "white" colonizer and his descendants kept on growing in number, century after century, not through the input of new European contingents but mainly through the multiplication of mixed-bloods and mulattos. The black population in turn grew, keeping pace with the whites, but unlike the latter, blacks only increased through the yearly introduction of large contingents of slaves destined both to replace those worn out through work and to increase the supply available to take care of new productive projects.

On the following pages we shall reconstruct this biological process of the consumption of blacks and the discreet multiplication of mulattos that took place simultaneously with their deculturation and incorporation into Brazilian society and culture.

The first contingents of blacks had been introduced into Brazil in the final years of the first half of the sixteenth century, perhaps in 1538. They were not very numerous, as can be deduced from the difficulties historians have had in documenting these first arrivals. Immediately thereafter, however, with the development of the sugar economy, blacks began to arrive in great numbers. The hunt for slaves in Africa and their transport and sale here went on to constitute a major business for the Europeans, in which immense capital was invested and which in the future would absorb at least half the value of sugar and later of gold.

The Crown allowed each plantation owner to import up to 120 "items," but there was never any limit to his right to buy blacks brought in for the slave markets. With a basis in that legality, the holders of royal concessions in the slave traffic had one of the most solid businesses in the colony, one which would last for three centuries, allowing them to move millions of Africans to Brazil and in that way to absorb the greater part of the profit made from the enterprises in sugar, gold, cotton, tobacco, cacao, and coffee, which went into the cost of slave labor. It has been calculated that the cost to the Brazilian economy of the acquisition of African slaves during the 300 years of the traffic was 160 million pounds in gold.

The huge business in slaves was rarely the object of reservations. On the contrary, it was considered meritorious to undertake human hunts, killing those who resisted, as a means of freeing the black from his backwardness and even as a pious act in bringing him to the god of the whites.

The earliest estimates of the number of black people introduced into Brazil during the three centuries of slave traffic vary a great deal. They range from exaggeratedly high numbers like the 13.5 million estimated by

Calógeras (1927) or 15 million by Rocha Pombo (1905) to much smaller figures, like 4.6 million suggested by Taunay (1941) and 3.3 million by Simonsen (1937).

Unfortunately there are no carefully gathered demographic figures that permit the substitution of a well-founded estimate for such inaccurate numbers. In a study made on the basis of official registrations filed in Bahia, P. Curtin (1969) notes that 959,000 slaves were brought in from 1701 to 1760; 931,800 from 1761 to 1810; and finally 1,145,400 from 1811 to 1860. This means a total of 3,036,800, which, added to the probable 810,000 previous arrivals, would give us a total of 3,846,800. The utilization of customs data as a basis for computation leads one to suppose that this is much lower than the true figures. In fact, no account is made in the proper amount for the smuggling and concealment of slave contingents in order to avoid the payment of taxes, leading one to suppose that the true figure might well be double what has been put forth.

A closer estimate of that number, thanks to M. Buescu (1968), seems nearer to the true number of slaves introduced into Brazil. Starting with the total number of slaves generally allowed for in primary sources for each century, Buescu applies the rate of replacement that he supposes to have been necessary in order to maintain the volume of population—keeping in mind that its natural growth was negative—and he adds additional rates for the periods in which the slave mass increased. As a result of his calculations, considering a yearly decreasing rate of replacement that goes from 5 percent in the sixteenth century to 2 percent in the nineteenth, he allows for a total increase of 75,000 blacks for the sixteenth century, 452,000 for the seventeenth, 3,621,000 for the eighteenth, and 2,204,000 for the nineteenth century, which adds up to a total of 6,352,000 slaves imported from 1540 to 1860. These figures, from a hypothetical demography, do not jibe with the number generally accepted from primary sources.

The composition of the slave population by sex and age is even more difficult to calculate. All that can be relied on for this is vague estimates and a few scattered reports on the numbers of blacks recorded locally, especially in Minas Gerais. For the total and for longer periods, we have to extrapolate, contenting ourselves with vague figures.

The generally accepted proportion of men to women in the importation is four to one. Some authors, analyzing the births among African slaves, accept estimates like 162 percent or 138 percent male in areas like Pernambuco for the middle of the last century. Data collected in Vassouras, in the state of Rio de Janeiro, for the same period allow for a balanced population between men and women.

How could so many women not registered in port statistics have arrived here? It was a question of purloined black girls who brought high prices, sometimes twice that of robust mulattos, if they were pretty. They were luxuries for landowners and foremen. They produced any number of mulatto women, who had better lives in the big house. Some of them became private maids and were even incorporated into the family as wet nurses, as Gilberto Freyre so admiringly describes.

The black mistress, after serving the master—at times provoking jealousy on the part of his wife, who might order her teeth extracted—would fall back into the life of hard labor on the plantation or in the mines.

Ever so tempting was the wish to establish breeding farms for blacks in order to free the owners from the need of importation. The young blacks bred there, very wily, would discover ways of escaping by making themselves pass as emancipated, which made the business quite burdensome. Added to this was the fact that a young black who did not begin hard work in the cane fields at an early age, about twelve, could never adapt to the harshness of that work.

A relative of mine has a letter sent by a foreman who made a good estimate of the relative advantages of using captive or imported blacks, opting quite frankly for the latter as the most economical.

More is spent on these useless slaves for their clothing, generally two *côvados* of baize and six yards of cotton cloth that cost at least 2,500 réis apiece and totally 290,400 réis, making their annual clothing and keep come to 3,181,200 réis, in addition to the curing of their illnesses, which always costs more than when they are in good health.

This expense is faced annually by the plantation with the breeding of children and with the invalids and the decrepit through charitable obligation toward one and all, hoping that boys of fifteen and over will be workers and make up for the lack of Africans.

There is no controversy over the fact that half of those born die before the age of ten, and, calculating that the expenses of a native-born slave until working age amount to 24$600 annually, by the age of fifteen that amount will be 369$000 réis, while an African of that same age can be purchased for 150$000 réis. Therefore, you have the native costing more, exceeding the African by 219$000 réis.

Another observation proved by experience is that the African slave stands up under the hard work on plantations better than the native-born black because the latter has a less robust constitution and from the age of fifty on he can no longer be counted on in the way of service, while the African can go on up to sixty-five or thereabouts, which generally does not happen with native-born blacks, Mulattos, and halfbreeds. ("Matta Plantation, January 1818. Report on Slaves Incapable of Field Work on the Plantation," letter from the administrator in Bahia to the owners at the Casa da Ponte in Lisbon, in Ribeiro Pires 1979, 298)

III

The Sociocultural Process

7

Adventure and Routine

The Wars of Brazil

It is sometimes said that our essential characteristic is cordiality, which ought to make of us a gracious and peaceful people par excellence. Can that be so? The nasty truth is that all manner of conflicts have left their scars on Brazilian history, ethnic, social, economic, religious, racial, and so on, each tinged with the colors of the one that would follow.

What is of import here is a factor predominant in characterizing every concrete conflict. Thus, the Cabanos War, containing as it did interracial tensions (whites against Indian mixed-bloods) and those of class (masters against servants), was essentially an interethnic conflict, for in it one ethnicity was fighting for hegemony, trying to stamp its ethnic image onto society. The same happened in Palmares in 1695, where what is often considered to have been a class struggle (slaves against masters) seems to have had racial confrontation as its principal component. Also, those in the quilombos (settlement of runaways) were attempting to create a new way of social life in opposition to the one they were fleeing. They did not succeed in bringing to maturation a viable alternative to the powers that ruled society, but in their struggle they did pose a threat to those powers.

A third example is Canudos (1897), which also shows those three forms of tension. The class aspect prevails because the backlanders, brought to revolt by the Conselheiro, were in fact fighting the plantation order, which by compelling people to live in a world divided up completely among plantations made them serve one landowner or another, without their ever having a piece of land of their own. As a consequence of this they had no possibility whatever of caring for their own needs. Rumbling in all this, however, were racial and other conflicts, including those involving religion.

The formative process of the Brazilian people brought about by the mutual collisions of Indian, black, and white contingents was filled with conflict. It could even be said that to all intents and purposes, we have been living in a state of latent war, which has frequently turned cruel and bloody.

Interethnic conflicts have always existed, pitting Indian tribes against each other, but this took place with no major consequences as none of them had any possibility of imposing hegemony on the rest. The situation changed completely when a new type of contender entered the conflict, one of irreconcilable character, the European conqueror and the new human groups he set about gathering in, subjugating, and transforming into an expansionist macroethnicity.

From 1500 to the present those confrontations have been seen to break out into armed struggles against every tribe that stood in the way of the national society during its inexorable expansion across the territory as it has gone about expropriating its own piece of the world: the physical basis of its existence. The Yanomami and the conflicting emotions they evoke between those who defend them and those who wish to dislodge them are only the latest episode in this centuries-old war.

Interethnic conflict becomes a process in the course of an age-old movement of ecological succession between the original population of the territory and the invader who harasses the aboriginals with the aim of implanting a new type of economy and society. It is, consequently, a question of a war of extermination. In it no peace is possible except under a provisional armistice, because the Indians cannot surrender to what is expected of them—namely, to cease being themselves and to enter individually into a new society where they will live a different form of existence not their own. Their opponents, the Brazilians, will not surrender either, with the feeling that there is no room in this land for any other ethnic identity but theirs, which, having been taken on by so many Europeans, Africans, and Asians, should also be accepted by the Indians.

That conflict does not take on the appearance, of course, of a debate in which both sides present their arguments. The Brazilian who captured Indians to use as slaves did so with the opinion that it would be useless to let them go on living with no purpose. The Indian, rejecting the slavery that would turn him into a thing, preferred death to submission—not out of any heroism but by an ethnic imperative, since ethnicity is exclusive by nature.

The forces that confront each other in these struggles could not be more cruelly unequal. On the one side are tribal societies structured on a basis of kinship and other forms of sociability, armed with a deep ethnic identification in the brotherhood of a way of life that is essentially one of solidarity. On the other side is a state structure based on the conquest and domination of a territory, the inhabitants of which, whatever their origins, make up a society divided into classes that are, it might be said, antagonistically opposed but imperatively joined together for the fulfillment of economic goals that are socially unresponsive. The first of these is the occupation of the land. Wherever an ethnically foreign contingent tries to maintain its own traditional way of life within this territory or to create for itself an autonomous way of existence, bloody conflict will break out.

There are also virulent conflicts among the invaders, however, the most noteworthy with regard to its motivations (although noteworthy, too, were components that derived from class, race, and ethnicity) being the long war without quarter between the colonists and the Jesuits. At a very early point, misunderstandings arose between the communal project of the Ignatians for the native population and the Portuguese colonial process, which reserved for them the role of laborers in colonial undertakings. In this way it came to pass that the priests abandoned their envisioned function of pacifiers of the Indians and set themselves up instead as protectors of the natives.

For two and a half centuries here, there was one conflict after another on the administrative level, leading in the end to the expulsion of the Jesuits by the colonists, first from São Paulo and then from Maranhão and Grão-Pará, followed by their return to Brazil by order of the Crown. There were also serious confrontations between catechumens and colonists, which the priests attempted to avoid, given their pledge to bring about a spiritual conquest with never an appeal to force.

From the very first days of colonization, the Jesuit plan was laid out as an ethnic alternative that would bring about a different kind of society, unlike the one that arose in areas of Spanish and Portuguese colonization.

It was structured on the basis of the tradition of solidarity among indigenous groups and was coupled to the missionary experiments of communal organization with a proto-socialistic character. In this way, too, it was in cruel contrast to the model that the colonists were setting up. That divergence reached complete maturity in the case of the Paraguayan missions, which attained a high degree of prosperity and autonomy. The same opposition, however, was evident in Brazil, principally in the regions where the missions had been established with the greatest success, especially in the lower Amazon. Most threatening in both cases was the fact that the language used by the Jesuit missionaries in their reductions in order to reorganize the Indians and to civilize them was neither Spanish nor Portuguese but *nheengatu.*

The most important motivation, however, was the greed awakened in the colonists by the extraordinary enrichment of some of the missions. Exploiting the lands of the natives and using them as a labor force, the Jesuits had begun to operate as prosperous provinces that were provided with practically everything, thanks to the large number of artisans they could count on, and they even produced surpluses, exploiting drugs of the forest which, along with the products of their fields and other mercantile items, made them one of the principal economic forces in the incipient colonial market.

Equally important as sources of wealth were the rich donations they received from colonists who gave everything in search of the salvation of their souls. Several contributions were famous, like the one for which the Society of Jesus promised to say five daily masses and one weekly high mass until the end of the world for the salvation of the soul of Garcia D'Ávila.

The size of the Jesuits' holdings at the time of their confiscation (1760) was enormous. It extended from the north of the country to the south in the form of missions and territorial concessions from the Crown, where they had set up their fifty catechizing missions, the material base of which consisted of sugar plantations (seventeen), dozens of cattle ranches with herds estimated at 150,000 head, along with farms, sawmills, and many other holdings.

The missionary society was probably also the largest urban property owner, judging by the number of houses in towns that held their schools, seminaries, hospitals, noviciates, and retreats under the care of 649 priests and lay brothers. In Bahia alone they owned 186 buildings, in Rio 70, and in São Paulo they still had around 6 left, with many more in Maranhão, Recife, Belém, and elsewhere, from which they received a grand rental income.

The greed that such wealth provoked was proportionate to it and increasing every day on the part of those who demanded its expropriation with hopes of taking over all that wealth for themselves. The necessity of such expropriation was defended by the bureaucracy, which was upset by the religious bodies' fiscal privilege of not paying taxes or tithes. The dream of the bureaucrats and the colonists was finally realized, and some of them enriched themselves as "caretakers" of the priests' wealth and of the Indians themselves, who had been declared free but who in fact were held in captivity that was as rigid as the slavery of the blacks.

The departure of the Jesuits from the Indian villages, when they were deprived of rule over these a short time before the final expulsion, was marked by an acceleration of mercantile activity described by Lúcio de Azevedo:

Adornments, images, and vestments, everything the priests had was loaded onto boats, often indecorously concealed among commercial items, the remnants of the profits of which they did not wish to deprive the community. Where there were cattle and canoes, these they sold in exchange for goods. And as the boats slipped away from so many places down river, sloshing with the weight of their cargoes, they looked more as if they were returning from predatory expeditions than the return to the monastery of catechizers interested only in preaching the Gospel. . . . And not just [cargoes] from the land and the products of its cultivation, but also from the Indians who worked it, slaves, in the words of the Jesuits converted from their former altruism and now rebuking freedom. The priests appealed to the king and queen with teary pleas, complaining, among other things, of the violent acts of Mendonça, stating that taking away their slaves was the same as depriving them of their last means of subsistence. (Azevedo 1930, 325–26)

The Cabanos War, which so often took on an aspect of genocide with the object of slaughtering mixed-blood populations, is the clearest example of interethnic confrontation. What took place was a life-and-death struggle by the former population of the Amazon region, which could be characterized as neo-Brazilian because it was no longer indigenous but rather aspired to live apart, autonomously, in opposition to the basically Luso-Brazilian ruling class, planning out an existence that corresponded to the occupation of other areas of the country. The civilizing contingent, with the help of forces from outside, confronted the Cabanos, destroying them nucleus by nucleus. The Cabanos won many battles, even managing to assume the central power in the region, occupying Belém, Manaus, and other cities, but they experienced the dramatic counterprivilege of not being able to lose a single battle. That was what finally happened and they were decimated.

Another important aspect of the conflict is one of predominantly racial confrontations. Here we see the three matrices of society up against one another, each armed with racial prejudices against the other two. These antagonisms reach their vilest aspect as they confront blacks brought from Africa to be slaves, who find themselves condemned to fight for their freedom and even after abolition must continue fighting against the humiliating discriminations of which they are victims as well as against multiple forms of deferment. The battles are inevitably bloody because only by force can the status of slave be imposed and maintained. Ever since the arrival of the first blacks and until today they have been in a struggle to escape the inferiority that was originally imposed on them and that is maintained by all means of oppression, making extremely difficult their integration into the status of ordinary workers equal to others or of citizens with equal rights.

Palmares is the exemplary case of interracial confrontation. There blacks fleeing from sugar plantations or towns organized themselves into a form of an economy of solidarity and an egalitarian society. They did not return to entirely unworkable African ways. They turned to new forms, archaically egalitarian and precociously socialistic. Since their destruction was required for the survival of a slaveholding society, conflicts were inevitable, whether to recover fugitive slaves or to guard against new flights, but also to prevent what could come to be a worse threat than foreign invasions—a general uprising of blacks.

A third type of conflict involving Brazilian populations is of an essentially classist character. Here facing each other we have on one side the privileged landowners, predominantly white, holding the means of production, and on the other the great mass of workers, mainly black or of mixed blood.

While classist components can always be found in the other two types of conflict, because in all of them the concern for recruiting labor for mercantile production is present, under certain circumstances the conflicts take on the specific character of a confrontation of classes. This happens when they are not contingents differentiated into racial or ethnic opposition but multiracial and multiethnic human groups or social strata ready to create new forms of socioeconomic order irreconcilable with the plans of the ruling class.

Canudos is a good example of that type of confrontation and the great outbreak of that form of struggle. There backlanders bound to an archaic universe of beliefs, but crudely subversive because they dared to confront the existing social order and followed values different from and even antagonistic to those of their opponents, were lined up against a society based on the ownership of land and the power of the owners over whoever lived on their domains. From the beginning the Counselor's faithful were looked upon as a growing group of farm laborers who were leaving the plantations and organizing by themselves and for themselves without any bosses or middlemen, and therefore they appeared to be and were viewed as something extremely dangerous.

When the situation came to a head, that human contingent was capable of facing up to and defeating first the local authorities and plantation owners, attracting gunmen, and then state troops, and finally various armed expeditions sent by the federal government. They kept on winning right up to their total defeat because no peace was possible between people fighting to remake the world in the name of the most sacred values and armed forces who were fulfilling their role of maintaining that world just as it was, aided in that drive by all the forces of global society.

Euclides da Cunha gives us the sharpest picture of that unlikely confrontation. He reports that at the end of the fighting, among the few survivors, there was not to be seen

> a single male face or an arm capable of holding a weapon or the heaving chest of a conquered champion: women, countless women, spectral old women, aged girls, old and young indistinguishable in the same ugliness, cadaverous and filthy, with children straddling them. . . . Canudos did not surrender. A unique example in all history, it resisted until it was completely drained. Conquered foot by foot in the literal meaning of the term, it fell on the fifth day at dusk when its last defenders fell, all of whom died. There were only four of them: an old man, two grown men, and a child, against whom 5,000 soldiers roared with rage. (Cunha 1945, 606, 611)

Examples of prolonged conflicts are repeated throughout that text. What they have in common and what is most relevant is the insistence of the oppressed in opening and reopening a fight to flee the fate prescribed for them and, on the other hand, the unanimity of the ruling class, which forms up and controls a servile parliament, the function of which is to maintain the institutional basis of latifundia, all of it guaranteed by the swift repressive action of a national body of armed forces, which yesterday lent itself to the role of slave hunters and today lends itself to the function of the strong arm of a sterile minority standing in opposition to all Brazilians.

Brazil as Enterprise

On the economic level Brazil is the product of the implantation and interaction of four types of commercial activity, each with a distinct function, varying forms of the recruitment of a working force, and with different degrees of profitability. The main one, because of its high operative efficiency, was the slave trade, dedicated either to the production of sugar or the mining of gold, both enterprises based on a workforce imported from Africa. The second, also highly successful, was the communal enterprise of the Jesuits, based on Indian slave labor. Even though it succumbed in competition and in conflicts with the colonial system, it too attained noteworthy importance and prosperity. The third, of much lesser profitability, unimportant as a source of enrichment but with substantially greater social importance, was the multiplicity of microenterprises for the production of the means of subsistence and livestock raising, based on different forms of attracting a workforce, from spurious types of partnership to the enslavement of natives, openly or surreptitiously.

The slave trade, dependent on latifundia and monoculture, had always been highly specialized and essentially mercantile. The Jesuit enterprise, although taking over extensive areas and producing items for local and overseas commerce, was not so much a true business as an alternative form of colonization of the tropics through the detribalization and integration of the original population into a different type of society, which was to be pure, pious, and seraphic. Subsistence microcommerce really functioned in a complementary way to the large-scale export and mining enterprises, which, thanks to the existence of the subsistence sector, found themselves without any obligation to produce food for the population or for their own use in the regions of greatest economic prosperity—they concentrated their entire workforce on their essential objective. Those microenterprises are, in fact, what established Brazil as a people, bringing forth at an early stage the cells that through multiplication produced what we are. It was the key because the missions would have brought about a theocratic society and the plantations could not even have survived without the viability they received from the support and sustenance of a local population.

In reality, although competing, these three forms of commercial organization joined to guarantee, each in the fulfillment of its own specific function, the survival and success of Portugal's undertaking in the tropics. Enterprises based on slavery integrated nascent Brazil into the world economy and assured the long-standing prosperity of the rich, making Brazil a fine business for them. The Jesuit missions undermined the resistance of the Indians, contributing decisively to their liquidation, starting with the ones brought into the reductions, who in the end were handed over, defenseless, to their exploiters. Subsistence businesses made possible the survival of all and mingled European mixed-bloods with Indians and blacks, giving shape to what would be the main body of the Brazilian people. They formed, above all, a breeding ground of people.

The main body of rural Brazil, its constituent threads—flesh, blood, bones, skin—has, in fact, been built upon those subsistence microenterprises, shaped in their various ecological-regional variants. It is onto this body—acting like a mechanism that sucks out its substance but also discards on it human matter useless for its mercantile ends—that agro-exporting and mining enterprises have fastened themselves like carcinomas.

Above these three commercial spheres of production there hovers a fourth, made up by the coastal nucleus of bankers, ship owners, and export-import entrepreneurs. This parasitic sector was, in fact, the predominant and most lucrative component of the colonial economy. It occupied itself with the thousand intermediary chores between Brazil and Europe and Africa in maritime traffic, exchange, buying and selling, in the fulfillment of it essential function: the exchange of more than half the sugar and gold produced here for slaves hunted down in Africa in order to restock the ever-declining supply of labor needed for production.

For centuries that mad exchange had been the most powerful driving force of western civilization, the one that most affected the fate of humankind by the frightful number of peoples and beings it mobilized, consumed, and transformed. It was always carried out in an efficient way, in a most impersonal and cold form, by honorable dignitaries with the feeling that they were involved time and again in a business ennobled by the great mission of the white man as a civilizing and Christianizing hero.

We are dealing here with commercial leaders. They would be inexplicable, however, without their counterparts, the aristocratic bureaucracy. All colonial life, in fact, was presided over and ruled by a civil bureaucracy of government functionaries and tax collectors and by the military, with their corps for defense and repression. Operating alongside in solidarity was the ecclesiastic bureaucracy of the servants of God, blessing and honoring those who were occupied with earthly matters, taking over especially the major part of resources that remained on the land so as to exalt with them the glory of God through the buildings and churches of their orders. That lofty group, whose elite came almost entirely from the mother country, formed along with the commercial and mercantile leaders the ruling class of the colony, essentially united as it faced the other bodies of society and in spite of the open opposition of their interests.

That dominant commercial-bureaucratic-ecclesiastical class, even though working as agent for its own prosperity, acted also in a subsidiary way as the guiding force in the formation of the Brazilian people. We are what we are because of the shape it imprinted on us, since we were formed according to what corresponded to its culture and interests. This included the reduction of what would be the Brazilian people as a civic and political entity into an offering of servile labor.

Nothing less than prodigious was the capacity of that ruling class for recruiting, unmaking, and reshaping peoples by the millions. This was done over the course of a centuries-old enterprise, the most prosperous of its time, where the objective was never to create an autonomous people, but the main result was to cause the emergence of a new people with an ethnic identity and a cultural configuration through the detribalizing of Indians, the de-Africanizing of blacks, and the de-Europeanizing of whites.

As it tore them from their roots so as to cross them racially and change them culturally, what it did was to give birth to us Brazilians, such as we essentially were and are. A ruling class, consular and commercial in character, socially irresponsible, was facing a mass of people treated like so many slaves, who produced what they did not consume and had only marginal cultural activity, on the outside of the literate civilization in which they were immersed.

Between that narrow peak and that broad base, a contingent of those who had escaped the general poverty and ignorance looked for institutional breaches where they could place themselves so as to make a Brazil according to their propensities. In the beginning they were mostly priests and subversive military men, simply because they alone were literate and had a minimal education in a subworld of colonial oppression.

An Early Assessment of the Colony

Father Cardim, who was rector of the Colégio da Bahia, liked to describe the world he saw. In my opinion he was one of the first and one of the most outstanding Brazilian intellectuals. In his *Treatises of the Land and People of Brazil,* identifying with our things and our people, he describes with enchantment forests, farms, fisheries, always with a most vivid interest (Cardim 1980).

There could not have been a better critical balance than his as regards the work of the Jesuits on one side and that of the colonists on the opposing one. He manages to maintain an extraordinary objectivity when speaking of both. The contrast could not be sharper: the extinction of the Indians and the coming of wild prosperity. As he visited various missions between the years 1583 and 1590 in the company of Father Cristóvão de Gouveia, the good Cardim tells us of the few Indians who were left in each one, all living in the most abject poverty, pretending an unlikely conversion, but full of unction and even adulation before the priests.

In his history he includes a general account of the native peoples living along the seacoast and into the backlands where the Portuguese had penetrated and among whom he distinguishes between Tupis and Tapuias. The first, divided into ten principal nations, lived from Pernambuco to São Vicente. They spoke "a single language and it is the one the Portuguese understand. It is fluent and elegant, soft and opulent. Its difficulty lies in its many constructions." He goes on to say that almost all of the Portuguese in Brazil "get to learn it in a short time, and their children, men and women, know it even better" (Cardim 1980, 101).

What interests us most in Cardim's account is the report of the slaughter of the population that was taking place and before which he himself was horrified: "There had been so many of the group that it seemed impossible for them to be wiped out, but the Portuguese pressed them to such a degree that almost all of them are dead and they have such fear that they have abandoned the coast and fled into the backlands up to distances of three to four hundred leagues" (Cardim 1980, 101).

As he goes on telling of one people or another, he reveals a progressive extermination. Of the Viatã of Paraíba, who had been quite numerous, he says that "there are no longer any of them left because, being friends and kinsmen [to the] Potiguaras, the Portuguese turned them [the two peoples] into enemies [of each other], supplying them with food so they could make war [against each other] and take them as slaves, and, finally, when there was great famine, the Portuguese, instead of coming to their aid, made captives of them and sent them off on fully laden ships to be sold in other captaincies." He adds that "in that way the nation was exterminated and the Portuguese were left without [friendly] neighbors to defend them against the Potiguaras" (Cardim 1980, 102). Concerning the Tupinaquins, who occupied all the coast from Ilhéus and Porto Seguro to Espírito Santo, he informs us that "they derived from those in Pernambuco and had spread out along a strip of the backlands, multiplying greatly, but now there are few of them" (Cardim 1980, 102). Concerning another nation yet, relatives of the Tupinaquins, Cardim says that "there were uncountable numbers of them. They are dying out because the Portuguese go hunting for them to make them slaves and those who escape flee far off to avoid servitude" (Cardim 1980, 102). Another nation, the Tememinó, "are very few now." And, further, about the Tamuya of Rio de Janeiro, he adds that "the Portuguese wiped these out when they settled Rio and there are very few of them" (Cardim 1980, 103).

Neither he nor the "visitor" from the Society of Jesus in whose name he wrote was very moved by all that. They probably consoled themselves that this must have been the will of God: a process of ecological succession by which the original population of the coast of Brazil, which had numbered a million Indians, had been succeeded by a few hundred who were meeting their end there.

After taking stock of the extermination of the Indians who had had first contact with the invaders, Cardim complacently surveys the future victims—the Carijó, who lived "80 leagues beyond São Vicente, enemies of the Tupinaquins. Of these there is an infinite number and they extend from the seacoast and backlands all the way to Paraguay, inhabited by the Castilians" (Cardim 1980, 103). In due time these Carijó or Guaraní began to be the principal victims of the slave-hunting Paulistas and the main objects of the detribalizing conversions of the Jesuits. Even more expressive is the picture Cardim draws for us of the concrete results of three decades of Jesuit preaching in the Brazilian jungle. Accompanying the principal visitor of the society, he goes along telling what he sees, village after village, through the settlements left over by the reductions. It is the fruit of a painful harvest. They visited

> the village of Espírito Santo, five leagues from Bahia, with some thirty Indians who came with their bows and arrows to accompany the father and in relays of twos they carried him in a hammock. . . . We reached the village in the afternoon; a good quarter of a league before that the celebration that the Indians had prepared took place along a pathway through very tall and cooling trees, out of which they emerged singing, playing instruments in their fashion. Others lay in wait and came out with great shouts and howls, which terrified us and caused us to tremble. The Cunumi children, lifting up a great many bundles of arrows, gave their war cries and, painted different colors and naked, came with uplifted hands to receive the father's blessing, saying in Portuguese, "Praised be Jesus Christ." Others came out doing a shield dance, Portuguese style, the *trocado*, and they danced to the sound of a guitar, timbrel, tambourine, and flute, and, along with that, they put on a brief dramatic dialogue, singing some pastoral songs. It all brought out a great feeling of devotion in the middle of a forest like that in a strange land, all the

more so as festivities like that were not to be expected on the part of such barbarous people. (Cardim 1980, 145)

As can be seen, a few customs of the savages had survived, changed into buffoonery. One of them was fear of the hated Anhanga, who was rising up out of the jungle now to frighten the Indians but incarnated in a Portuguese priest. Another was the Ereiupe ceremony, the tearful greeting with which the Tupi received esteemed visitors. In it aged Morubixabas greet the visitor with "'Have you come?' and, kissing his hand, they receive his blessing." During this "naked women (something quite new for us), lifting up their hands to Heaven, also gave their Ereiupe, saying in Portuguese 'Praised be Jesus Christ'." (Cardim 1980, 146).

Also surviving was the most solemn custom of the Tupinambas of giving counsel, which was a duty, perhaps the principal one of a Morubixaba. Cardim says:

> That night the principal Indians, their great tongues, preached about the father's life in their own way, which is as follows: they began preaching at dawn, lying in their hammocks for the space of a half hour, then they arose and went through all the village, step by step, very slowly, and their preaching was also quite measured, cautious and slow; they spoke the words gravely many times. In these preachments they tell of all the difficulties, storms, deadly perils that the father must have suffered, coming from so far away to visit and console them and at the same time they incited their people to praise God for the grace received, and they should bring the father presents in thanks. (Cardim 1980, 146)

A beautiful surprise awaited them on their visit to the village of São Mateus in Porto Seguro. The visitor and his acolytes were going along calmly on the pleasant beach when "coming down from a high hill was an Indian woman dressed in their manner with a porcelain pot from India filled with sugar cheesecakes along with a mug of cool water, saying that their lord Father Joseph was sending this to the Provincial" (Cardim 1980, 148). That Joseph was none other than Anchieta himself, who was bringing up the rear, with his cassock hiked up, barefoot and quite weary after so many years of life and so many years of preaching in Brazil.

In that village and in all the others visited, traveling all the time in hammocks carried by Indians, who took turns so that no one would be left out of the glory of being bearer, they were greeted with the same joy by the few surviving Indians. Our ingenuous Cardim never tires of being startled,

whether when confessing Indian men and women through interpreters
and seeing that "they are ever so innocent and live in much less sin than the
Portuguese" or at the candor of the children. "Some sixty children went
along with us, stark naked, as was their custom. Along the way they made
a great celebration of the father; sometimes they ran about him, at others
they surrounded him, at other times they imitated birds in a very natural
way, at the river they played many even more graceful games, and in the
water they have a great deal of charm in anything they do" (Cardim 1980,
155).

Far away from there, Cardim would be even more enchanted "by a
dance of Indian children, the oldest must have been eight, all completely
naked and painted with different pleasant colors, rattles on their feet and
arms, with legs, waists, and heads showing a variety of diadems of feathers, necklaces, and bracelets they had put together" (Cardim 1980, 169).

On the daily routine of the old missions Cardim tells us that

> in the villages, large and small, they hear mass early every day before
> going to their jobs, and before or after mass they are taught prayers
> in Portuguese and in their language, and in the afternoon they are
> instructed in the dialogue of faith, confession, and communion.
> Some of the more clever of them, both men and women, recite the
> rosary of Our Lady; they go to confession quite often; they do them-
> selves great honor when they receive communion, and even go to
> extremes, as far as abstaining from their wines, to which they are
> much given, and it is the most heroic thing they can do; when they
> are urged to commit some sin of vengeance or immorality, etc., they
> reply that they have received communion and cannot do such things.
> Those who take communion stand out among them as examples of
> good life, modesty, and observance of doctrine; they hold the priests
> in extraordinary love, belief, and respect and they do nothing with-
> out their advice, and in that way they ask permission for everything,
> no matter how small, as if they were novices. (Cardim 1980, 156)

Their main recreation now, Cardim says, consists of religious festivities.

> The first is that of the bonfires on St. John's Day, for their villages
> glow with fire and as they leap over the fires there are no clothes to
> hamper them, although sometimes they singe their hides. The second
> festival is Palm Sunday, and it is something to see as they bring forth
> words, flowers, and daisies, the festive way they carry them to the

mass and how they try to have the holy water fall onto the branches. The third, which they celebrate more than any other, is Ash Wednesday, because usually no one is missing and the ashes have come from the ends of the earth and they rejoice in having a large cross drawn on their foreheads. (Cardim 1980, 156)

In most villages

there are schools for reading and writing where the priests teach the Indian children; and some of the brightest are taught to figure, sing, and play instruments; they do it all well and there are many who play the flute, the guitar, the harpsichord, and they take part in masses with songs for the organ, things of which their parents are most proud. These children speak Portuguese, chant doctrine along the streets at night, and pray for the souls in Purgatory.

In these same villages there are confraternities of the Blessed Sacrament, Our Lady, and of the dead. The stewards are the principal and most virtuous men; they have their table in the church, with its cloth, and they wear their capes of baize or other fabrics in red, white, and blue; they serve by visiting the sick, helping to bury the dead, and at mass. (Cardim 1980, 155–56)

Quite impressive is the contrast between this panorama of poverty and humiliation and the sumptuous glory of the plantations, which were enjoying full prosperity. He was probably witnessing the most magnificent moment of that history, antedating the Dutch invasions, internal strife, and international competition.

The fact is, Brazil had discovered a rich lode that seemed inexhaustible and that, during those years, gave it the most prosperous and showy position on the planet. Let us continue with his description. In Bahia he finds

a land teeming with provisions, beef, pork, chickens, mutton, and the meat of other animals; it has 36 plantations, where the best sugar on the coast is produced; it has many types of aromatic woods in different colors and fetching a high price; the city has within its boundaries perhaps 3,000 Portuguese inhabitants, 8,000 Christian Indians, and 3,000 or 4,000 slaves from Guinea; it has its cathedral chapter of canons, a temporary vicar general, etc., with ten or twelve parishes in the outskirts, not to mention the many churches and chapels that some wealthy landowners have on their plantations. (Cardim 1980, 144)

The Society of Jesus had also become notably wealthy, as can be seen from Cardim's description of the Colégio da Bahia.

The priests have a new college here, almost completed; it is a whole city block, with a fine chapel, a library, and some thirty cubicles, most of which have windows facing the sea. The building is all of stone and oyster-shell mortar, as good as the stones of Portugal. The cubicles are large, with doorways of stone, doors of angiliwood covered with cedar; from the windows we can take in a large part of Bahia and we can see schools of fish and whales leaping in the water; the ships are so close that they seem almost within earshot. The church is capacious, quite full of rich ornaments of white and purple damask, green and carmine velvet, all with gold trim; it has a cross and a censer of silver, a fine monstrance for Holy Thursday services, and many holy panels depicting the life of Christ and all the Apostles. All three altars have canopies with curtains of crimson taffeta; it has a gilded silver cross of marvelous workmanship, with the Holy Rood, three heads of the 11,000 virgins, along with other great relics of saints, and a very beautiful and holy image of Our Lady of Saint Luke. (Cardim 1980, 144)

Grander still was the pomp of the plantations, at which Cardim marveled.

One thing that amazed me on that trip was the great facility they had in caring for their guests, because at any hour of night or day in which we arrived, very quickly the five of us of the Society (not counting the boys) were given all manner of meat to eat, chicken, turkey, duck, suckling pig, kid, and others, all of which had been raised there, and all kinds of fish and shellfish, of which there was always a good supply in the house as certain fishermen slaves were assigned to that, and the house was so replete with everything in such quantity that they seemed like counts, they spent so lavishly. (Cardim 1980, 157–58)

It was the rich Bahia of the bay area, so much the opposite of the goat-herding Bahia of the São Francisco River backlands, where the surviving Tapuia and Cariri were at total war against the invader at that time. In the first civilization that had been implanted, opulent and refined, through the work of black and Indian slaves,

great were the honors and welcomes everyone rendered the Father Visitor, all trying to outdo themselves, not only in displays of love, respect, and reverence but also in the reception and the conversation given him, and much more in the great expenditure of delicacies, the cleanliness and care of the service, the rich beds and couches of silk (which the father would not accept because he brought along a hammock that served as a bed, following the custom of the land). (Cardim 1980, 157)

Receptions followed one after the other:

That night we came to the house of a rich man who was expecting the Father Visitor: he is second in wealth in this Bahia by dint of owning seven or eight leagues of coast land where the best amber found in these parts lies and in one single year he collected 8,000 *cruzados* worth without its costing him anything. He has so much livestock that he does not know how many and he supplies the king's forces just with strays and those that have died. He received the father in his house, furnished in embossed leather with a sumptuous bed; he always served us birds, turkey, blancmange, etc. He himself, bareheaded, served at table and helped us at mass in his chapel, the most beautiful in Brazil, made all of stucco and with marvelous detail in moldings, festoonery, and cornices; it is built with a hexagonal vault and three doors, sumptuously decorated. In this and other hermitages I was reminded of Your Reverence and everything else in this province. (Cardim 1980, 154)

In Pernambuco the sumptuousness was even greater and no less were the receptions, enjoyments, and enchantment of the visitors with the town.

The father was visited frequently by the bishop, the chief magistrate, and other worthies of the area, and they sent him ample quantities of veal, pork, turkey, chicken, and other items such as preserves, etc.; and there was someone who at the very first moment sent more than fifty cruzados worth of meat, wheat flour from Portugal, a quart of wine, etc.; and, not content with that, they would sometimes take him to their plantations, which are larger and richer than those of Bahia; and there they received him with great honors and receptions, with such expense that I would not know how to add it up, because, leaving aside the great banquets with extraordinary delicacies, they honored him with beds of crimson damask, trimmed in leather, and with sumptuous mattresses from India (but the father used his hammock, as was his custom). (Cardim 1980, 161)

Cardim himself sang high mass at the main church in Olinda,

> at the request of the stewards, who are the most important people in the land and some of them owners of plantations worth 40,000 cruzados and more in value. Six of them, all dressed in velvet and damask of different colors, accompanied me to the pulpit, and this is not rare in civilized behavior in Pernambuco. . . .
>
> The people of the area are honorable: there are very rich men, worth 40, 50, and 80 thousand cruzados: some are deeply in debt because of the great losses in the slave trade with Guinea, where many slaves die on them, and from the great excesses and expenses they have in their maintenance. They dress themselves and their wives and children in all manner of velvets, damasks, and other silks, and there is great excess in this. The women are great ladies but not very religious; they do not attend mass, sermons, confession, etc. The men are so vigorous that they buy thoroughbred horses worth 200 and 300 cruzados, and some own three or four expensive mounts. They are quite given to festivities. When a distinguished young lady married a man from Viana, both of them notables in the area, the relatives and friends dressed in crimson velvet, others in green, and others in damask and various silks of different colors, and the bridles and saddles of the horses were of the same silks they were wearing. That day there would be bullfights, jousting, and they would pay a visit to the college to see the Father Visitor; and for those festivities one can judge their excesses, which were quite normal and usual. They are especially fond of banquets, where usually ten or twelve plantation owners come together to eat, and taking turns in this way they spend everything they have and ordinarily each year drink 50,000 cruzados worth of wines from Portugal; in some years they drank 80,000 cruzados, as was recorded. Finally, in Pernambuco one finds more vanity than in Lisbon. (Cardim 1980, 162, 164)

At last they reached Rio de Janeiro, where Cardim's fascination with the land of Brazil reached its peak:

> The city is situated on a hill, with a good view of the sea, and inside the harbor mouth it has a bay that looks as if it had been painted by the supreme painter and architect in the world of Our Lord God, and it is so beautiful, the most pleasant there is in all Brazil, that it cannot be matched by the view of the Mondego or the Tagus; it is so broad

that it must be twenty leagues roundabout, half filled with many cool islands that have large groves, all in sight of one another, which gives it beauty. The harbor mouth is a half league from the town and in its middle there is an outcropping sixty fathoms long and quite wide that cuts it in half, but along both sides it has deep enough water for ships of the India route; on this outcropping the King has had a fort built and it is probably impregnable, for no ship will be able to hide from it; the town has 150 inhabitants with their vicar and a large number of native slaves. (Cardim 1980, 170)

Even in Rio, success was enormous, with one peculiarity here. The de-Indianized population, especially the women, seeking a new identity for themselves, fervently identified with the figure of King Sebastian.

Sebastian was the young king lost on a mad crusade that brought death to Portugal's nobility and out of which came the loss of national independence and the surrender of Lisbon to domination from Madrid. But Sebastian was also the Roman saint who is always represented by a nude statue and being stoned to death.

The priests here have the best spot in the city. They have a broad view of the cove that faces the windows: they have already begun the new building and it has thirteen cubicles of stone and mortar now, equal to those of Coimbra, with the advantage of its fine view. They are lined with cedar; the church is small, of dried mud and plaster. They are now beginning work on a new one of stone and mortar. It has fine ornaments, with a monstrance of gilded silver for Holy Thursday, a head of the 11,000 virgins, the arm of Saint Sebastian, along with other relics and an image of Our Lady of Saint Luke. (Cardim 1980, 171)

That prophetic king, whom Portuguese and Brazilians of rustic background are still waiting to see reincarnated, has melded with the Roman saint, bringing out effusions of religious faith. Even today in Rio de Janeiro the procession for Saint Sebastian is joined by thousands of people who do not know what they believe in. But that matters not, because what they want is to have an identity of their own, which they can fully attain this way. The aforementioned relic of Saint Sebastian—brought, as it happened, by the visitor—was a beautiful piece mounted on a silver arm. It was received with great celebration, as this is the city of his name and he is its patron and protector.

The Father Visitor, with the governor himself and the principal people of the land and some priests, went aboard a big barge festooned with banners and wreaths; an altar had been set up on it and the quarterdeck was carpeted and had a canopy over it; some twenty canoes came alongside, fully manned, some of them painted, others plumed, and their paddles were of various colors. Among them came Martim Afonso, a Commentator of Christ, a trustworthy and young-looking old Indian, a fine and valiant gentleman who had been of great help to the Portuguese in the taking of Rio. There were great festivities on the water with naval skirmishes, drums, fifes, and flutes, with much shouting and uproar on the part of the Indians; and the Portuguese of the region with their flintlocks and also the people in the fort fired off a few rounds of artillery, and with those festivities we drifted for a distance under sail and the holy relic was on the altar in a fine litter with a grand array of lighted candles, organ music, etc. Disembarking, we went in a procession to the Misericórdia church, which is near the beach, with the relic under a canopy; the handles were held by members of the chamber, important citizens, old men and conquerors of these lands. There was a stage by the door of Misericórdia with a canopy made from a sail and the holy relic was placed on a fine altar while a holy dialogue about the martyrdom of the saint was presented, with weeping and several richly dressed figures; and a young lad tied to a pole was shot with arrows: the spectacle brought out many tears of devotion and joy for the whole city as it represented the living martyrdom of the saint, and not a single woman was missing from the festivities. (Cardim 1980, 169)

Quite different is the picture he gives us of São Paulo and its four poor towns. Cardim describes São Vicente as

situated in a low, melancholy, and gloomy place, on an island two leagues long. This was the first village and settlement of the Portuguese in Brazil; it had been wealthy, now it is poor, because the seaport and former harbor mouth through which Martim Afonso de Sousa and his fleet entered has silted up; also because the land has been exhausted and there are no Indians to cultivate it; it is being depopulated; it has around eighty inhabitants and their vicar. Here the priests have a house where usually six of the Society reside; the site is ghostly, with no view, even though quite healthy. (Cardim 1980, 174)

Santos, he says, has

> eighty inhabitants with their vicar. Itanhaém, which is the third
> settlement on the coast, probably has fifty inhabitants but no vicar.
> The priests visit, give consolation, and help as best they can, minis-
> tering the sacraments out of goodness. (Cardim 1980, 174)

And Piratininga

> is the town of the invocation of the conversion of Saint Paul; it is
> twelve leagues from the sea in the backlands; it is very healthful land;
> there are great frosts and freezes there and good, calm weather; it is
> full of old people, over a hundred years old, because when four living
> people are brought together the years add up to 500. They dress in
> coarse wool and brown and blue jerkins, as were worn in olden
> times. They go to church on Sunday with robes without a cape. The
> settlement is located in a good spot along a fast-running river. There
> must be 120 inhabitants, with many native slaves; they have no cu-
> rate or any other priests except those of the Society, for whom they
> have great love and respect, and in no way do they wish to have a
> curate. (Cardim 1980, 173)

No better critical assessment than Cardim's can be found regarding the
practical results of the missions and colonization. The first settlers, having
given their blood and their energies in the making of a new society, survived only in the bodies of the Brazilindians as a genetic inheritance that
will persist over the centuries, marking out the physiognomy of Brazilians.
The colonial venture was the most successful European implant overseas,
which came to have sumptuous churches and colleges outstripping those
in any other place. Yet the colony lived and still lives in the life of an
external proletariat, its fortunes dependent on the oscillations of the world
market.

It could be said, perhaps, that the greatest failure was that of Jesuitical
Stalinism, which attempted a precocious and unlivable socialism and
failed. Success, on the contrary, belonged to its opponents; and failure,
too, because by not being a people for themselves in search of their own
conditions of prosperity, they remain a people for others.

8

Chaotic Urbanization

Cities and Towns

We have determined that Brazil, although following an evolutionary pattern of historical modernization, had already been born as an urban civilization. This means that it was divided into separate rural and urban elements, different but complementary and governed by erudite city groups. First came Lisbon, which does not count. Our first de facto city was Bahia, already in existence in our first century, when Rio de Janeiro and João Pessoa also sprang up. In the second century four more cities appeared: São Luís, Cabo Frio, Belém, and Olinda. In the third century urban life reached the interior, with São Paulo, Mariana in Minas, and Oeiras in Piauí. In the fifth century the network expanded, covering all of the territory of Brazil.

Over the course of these centuries cities grew and became embellished as marvelous centers of urban life, comparable only to those in Mexico. The Dutch enriched Recife; mining wealth was displayed in Ouro Preto and other cities during the gold boom, beautifying Bahia and, later on, Rio. Wealth from sugar brought plantation owners to Recife and Bahia, where they built their townhouses and lived the life so well described by Gilberto Freyre (1935). Independence scattered large numbers of Portuguese all over the country, most of them deeply involved in commerce as agents of English companies. The American Civil War brought about growth in São Luís, which in the census of 1872 was larger and wealthier than São Paulo. Abolition, providing some opportunity for the free movement of blacks, filled the cities of Rio and Bahia with so-called African nuclei, which developed into today's *favela* shantytowns.

The unemployment crisis that occurred in Europe at the end of the nineteenth century sent us 7 million Europeans. Four and a half million of them remained in Brazil permanently, mainly in São Paulo, where they completely revitalized local economic activity. They were the ones who brought about the first surge of industrialization, which later would expand and replace imports.

The urbanized sector, increased tenfold while the total population of the country grew two and a half times, from 30.6 million in 1920 to 70.9 million in 1960. During that same period the metropolitan network grew from six major cities of 100,000 inhabitants to thirty-one. Greater still was the increase in small and medium cities, which in 1960 formed a network of hundreds of urban nuclei distributed all across the country in the form of constellations connected to national and regional urban centers.

The cities and towns of the colonial network, corresponding to the agrarian culture, were essentially centers of colonial rule, often created by an express act of the Crown for the defense of the coast, places like Salvador, Rio de Janeiro, São Luís, Belém, Florianópolis, and others. Their main activities were commerce, through importation and contraband, and providing services for the productive sectors as well as being royal agencies for the collection of fees and taxes, the awarding of land grants, legitimizing the transfer of possessions through inheritance or sale, and rendering judgment in cases of conflict. In addition to these functions they offered the services of religion, almost always associated with education at the primary level and propaedeutic duties on the part of the priesthood. Cities also provided medical attention for desperate cases resistant to traditional domestic remedies. Life revolved around these activities and a second basic function: providing an emporium for the importation of slaves and manufactured goods and for exportation of sugar and later gold, precious stones, and other items of merchandise.

The principal buildings were churches, convents, and forts, which were also the towns' main attractions. On religious feast days, the rural aristocracy would leave the plantations to live in the city for a brief period of festive urban conviviality. Outside of these occasions the cities lived a quiet existence, enlivened only by the weekly market, masses and novenas, and by the arrival of some ship in port. Beyond that they stirred only with the tinkling bells of the mule trains coming from the interior or the groaning of oxcarts that came in from the farms, loaded down with provisions and firewood.

The urban upper class was made up of functionaries, scribes, bailiffs, military officers, and priests—who were the only educated people—and businessmen. Except for the top civil and ecclesiastical hierarchy, all these people were considered "of second degree" in relation to the rural land-owners, proud of their holdings, their isolation, and convinced of their social superiority. An intermediate group of whites and free people of mixed blood, extremely poor, struggled to survive in the shadow the rich or the well-to-do.

Every plantation owner or merchant had and maintained household servants, who served devotedly without any salary whatever, in return for the favors they occasionally received and which constituted their liveli-hood. These people filled the houses, helping out in all domestic chores and in the simple handiwork of fabrics and hammocks, sewing and em-broidery, the manufacture of soap or sausages and sweets. Some indepen-dent craftsmen worked on assignment making saddles and riding gear, leather shoes, or as blacksmiths and mechanics in workshops attached to the buildings. At the bottom of the heap were the slave servants, there to give polish to the status of the rich and well-to-do, carrying them about along with their possessions and offal, nursing their newborn, serving them, in short, from head to toe.

The growth of urban centers gave birth to a civil and ecclesiastical bureaucracy of the highest level and to independent commerce, composed almost exclusively of people from the mother country. Even these, how-ever, could attain respectable social status and become integrated into the ruling class only when they, too, became landowners and masters of plan-tations. Only in the mining regions, as we have seen, was a true urban network established independent of agricultural production, based on a considerable intermediary group with a city-bred way of life.

Smaller groups appeared in the interior in every productive area for the exercise of special functions as the population grew and became concen-trated. Such were settlements along highways, serving as resting places on long journeys between established centers in the interior or appearing where the need arose to transfer cargoes from road to navigable river or to cross rivers. Such was also the case with cattle markets all through the interior midlands, some of which became quite important, such as those at Campina Grande, Sorocaba, Feira de Santana, Campo Grande, and oth-ers. There were also cotton markets, like Itapicuru-Mirim, Caxias, Oeiras, Crato, etc.

The extractive economy created ports for the export of rubber from the Amazon region, all with their constellations of auxiliary villages and towns. And finally, a network of cities was established with the development of coffee; most of these would later go into decline, transformed into ghost towns as the frontier moved on, opening up the way to other points of access to the backlands.

These towns and villages, large and small, constituted agencies of an agrarian-mercantile civilization that had the fundamental role of shaping the colonial order of Brazilian society, integrating it into the body of religious and civil traditions of preindustrial Europe and making it turn a profit for the Portuguese Crown. As such, they were centers for the imposition of official ideas and beliefs and the preservation of the old body of western traditions, much more than being creative centers of a tradition of their own.

Therefore, in spite of the immense differences that obtained between European and Brazilian sociocultural formations, both were the fruit of the same civilizing movement. With industrialization, the urban constellation was altered at its base, which was its productive technology, transforming its whole way of being, thinking, and acting. This would also bring about in dependent societies a sequence of mirroring changes of a technical as well as an ideological nature, which here too transformed the character of the civilization itself.

Industrialization and Urbanization

Industrialization and urbanization are complementary processes that usually move along in association, industrialization offering urban employment to the rural population, and these people forming an exodus in search of such opportunities in life. It is not precisely thus, however. External factors generally affect both processes and hinder any linear interpretation that might be given them. In the sixteenth century in England, it was sheepherding that drove the population out of the countryside.

In Brazil several processes already mentioned, especially monoculture and the monopoly of land ownership, brought about the expulsion of the population from the countryside. In our case the dimensions are frightful, given the size of the population and the huge number of people compelled to move. Urban population took a leap from 12.8 million in 1940 to 80.5 million in 1980. Now it is 110.9 million. The rural population has lost substance, having gone from 28.3 million to 38.6 million in the same period and today standing at 35.8 million—reduced in a relative sense from 68.7 percent to 32.4 percent and then 24.4 percent of the total.

As can be seen, we are living through one of the most wrenching periods of rural exodus, all the more serious because no Brazilian city was in any condition to receive that astonishing population contingent. The consequence has been impoverishment of the urban population and enormous pressure in the competition for jobs.

Although there are regional variations and São Paulo represents a large percentage of this transfer, the phenomenon has occurred all across the country. Cities have become swollen and the countryside depopulated, with no harm to agricultural production, which, having been mechanized, has gone on to deliver more and better products. If our program were one of producing only items for export, this would have been admissible. But since the question that history has placed before us is to organize the whole economy so that all can work and eat, this astronomical migration, on the order of 80 percent, has generated huge problems.

In the twentieth century chaotic urbanization has taken place, brought about less by the attraction of the city than by the flight of the rural population. Thus we have reached the point of having some of the largest cities in the world, like São Paulo and Rio de Janeiro, with double the population of Paris or Rome but ten times less endowed with urban services and opportunities for work. It is a mystery, unexplained so far, how the great masses of the poor in Recife, in Bahia with all that brisk merriment, and finally the millions of inhabitants of São Paulo and Rio can survive without work.

Many of these cities were created with a purpose, as happened with old Bahia—Belém do Pará to guard the mouth of the Amazon; Sacramento in the south, across from the nascent Buenos Aires, was kept on a war footing for a century in order to mark the southern boundary of Brazil; and more recently Goiânia, Belo Horizonte, and finally Brasília, created in the center of Brazil in an extraordinary feat of engineering to serve as a central pole to put order into Brazilian life.

This explosive growth entered a crisis in 1982, presaging the impossibility of continued economic growth under the weight of social restrictions that were deforming national development. First was the agrarian structure, dominated by latifundias, which, incapable of raising agricultural production to match population growth and of hiring and paying the rural masses, expelled them in huge numbers from the countryside to the cities, condemning the immense majority of the population to marginality. Second was foreign plundering, which, protected by government policy, strengthened its dominance, making it a partner in industrial expansion, strangling the economy of the country by sucking up all its productive wealth.

In this way Brazil has developed an extraordinary urban existence, bringing forth what could be a new way of life for cities. Tremendous pressures are generated in the abandoned population. Although integrated into urban life and creative about survival, people have maintained their pre-urban culture. True modernization is compromised by the fact that no government has effectively tackled such basic matters as popular education and sanitation.

In our time the main problem for Brazil is to take care of this immense urban mass, which—unable to be exported, as in Europe's solution—must be retrained here. There is finally some awareness that it is no longer possible to leave the population to die of hunger and to slaughter itself in violence, nor for childhood to be given over to vice, delinquency, and prostitution. The general feeling is that we need to make our society responsible for children and the aged. This will only come about through full employment, which presupposes agrarian restructuring, for that is where the opportunities for productive work can be increased the most.

There is no indication, however, that this full employment will happen. The Brazilian social order so fervently defended by politicians and the institutions of government—an order based on latifundia and the implicit right to hold and maintain the land unproductive—has become impracticable. The Rural Democratic Union (UDR), which represents large landowners in Congress, is probably the most powerful organ of government. It is unthinkable to make it admit the principle that no one can keep land unproductive just because of property rights or that land should be turned over to the Union for colonization programs.

Industry, in turn, is oriented more and more toward productive systems that reduce the number of workers and in which every new job entails high investments. This is happening all over the world but is more acutely felt in Brazil because of the mass of unemployed it causes and the disastrous effects unemployment has on society.

Modern industrialization in Brazil had its start in two wartime acts. As a condition for his giving aid with troops and raw materials, Getúlio Vargas demanded of the Allies the building of the steelworks of the Companhia Siderúrgica Nacional in Volta Redonda and the return of iron deposits in Minas Gerais. Out of this, immediately after the war, two dynamic forces for modernization emerged in Brazil. Volta Redonda became the center for naval and automobile production and for all mechanical industry. The Vale do Rio Doce put our mineral reserves at the service of Brazil, opening up world markets to us by exporting these resources. In that way it developed as one of the main enterprises of its type. In addition to these ventures the state created several other less successful ones, like the National Motor Factory and the National Alkali Company.

That policy of state capitalism and basic industrialization has provoked major reaction on the part of privatists and the spokespersons for foreign interests. So it was that when Getúlio Vargas made ready to create Petrobrás and Eletrobrás, a unified campaign in all the media demoralized his government to such a degree that he was himself in imminent danger of being thrown out of Catete Palace. He overcame this with his own suicide, which awoke the nation to the character of the campaign and the interests behind the enemies of his government.

As a consequence, the leaders of the right were unable to attain power and the center-left candidate Juscelino Kubitschek was elected president. With him, substitutive industrialization emerged. In a world in which neither [General Enrico] Dutra [Vargas's successor] nor Vargas had managed to garner any investments, Kubitschek, abandoning the policy of state capitalism, attracted numerous enterprises in the automotive, naval, chemical, mechanical, and other fields to set up subsidiaries in Brazil. To attain this he conceded all kinds of subsidies, such as land, tax relief, loans, and co-signing foreign loans. He did so with such largesse that in many industrial concerns, owners supplied less than 20 percent of the real capital investment (Tavares 1964).

The basis for this policy, formulated by the Center for Latin American Studies (CEPAL), was the erection of customs barriers to preserve the internal market for industries that would be set up here in order to bring about an industrial revolution equivalent to the one that had originally occurred in other countries. On the one hand, the results were highly successful in modernization brought on by these industries as they took the place of imports and moved the whole national economy forward. On the other hand, activity became so concentrated in São Paulo as to make that state a pole of internal colonization as it burgeoned and drew industrial development away from other states. Simultaneously with this process, the metropolitan areas of Brazil absorbed immense quantities of rural people who, having no place in the system of production, became an unemployed mass that gave rise to an unparalleled crisis of urban violence.

The Brazilian state has no program for an economic restructuring that would allow for a guarantee of full employment in the foreseeable future. What is to be done? Continue in the Amazon the genocide of the pioneers? Continue sterilizing the women of Goiás, for example, in order to set aside Brazilian space for someone else? Continue being impregnated with the illusion that the best approach for Brazil is spontaneity, governed by profit-seeking bankers, for the final solution of our problems? How long will this country continue without a project for autonomous and self-sustaining development of its own?

The technocrats of the last few governments have seen a way out only in the sale at any price of the industries created in the past with such great sacrifice, followed by the plunge of Brazilian industry into the world market, confident that it will bring us prosperity, if not for the working people at least for those who are well-integrated into the economic system.

If we were a small nation, our integration into the Colossus would be our destiny. But being what we are, there can be no more postponement of the formulation of a project of our own that will insert us into the global context while preserving our economic autonomy for independent growth. What is lacking in us today is a greater generalized indignation in the face of so much unnecessary unemployment, so much hunger, and so much violence, for they are quite curable with strategic changes in the economic order. Even more lacking is political competence to make use of power in the realization of our potentialities.

Through the efforts of our forebears, history has made us the possessors of a prodigiously rich territory and a human mass stuck in backwardness but thirsting for modernity and progress, and which we cannot hand over to the spontaneity of the world market. The task of new generations of Brazilians is to take this country in their hands and make of it what it should be, one of the most progressive, just, and prosperous nations on earth.

Urban Deterioration

The urban population itself, left to its fate, has found solutions for some major problems. Strange solutions, it is true, but the only ones within people's reach. They have learned to build shantytown favelas on the steepest hillsides, beyond all municipal regulations, but which allow them to live close to work opportunities and to live among others sharing their circumstances, intense social life, and community pride. In São Paulo, where there are no steep hills, the settlements are located on flat land in areas of disputed ownership and have been organized socially as favelas. They resist as best they can any government attempts to dislodge or eradicate them. Whoever can offer a million homes will have the right to speak of the eradication of *favelas*.

Another expression of the creativity of these inhabitants is their taking advantage of drugs as a local source of employment. That "solution," even though so flagrant and illegal, is a reflection of the social crisis in the United States, with its millions of addicts, which produces billions of dollars from drugs and the excess spills over here.

This is the base upon which organized crime operates, offering a mass of jobs in the favela itself as well as a heroic image of its leaders and a highly desirable career model for children. In times gone by it was the illegal lottery called *jogo do bicho* that employed ex-convicts and hoodlums, giving them the conditions of a legal existence. Today it is organized crime as big business that handles the job of addicting and satisfying the addiction of a million users. Anyone who wishes to put an end to organized crime must keep out the subsidy for crime provided by the Americans.

Until then what we have are hollow gestures of short duration, by themselves incapable of solving the problems of the cities. Urban reform is deserving of thought, as urgent today as agrarian reform. Also to be considered is an economy of full employment, but no one has any concrete plans in this respect that could be put into practice.

Another dramatic process experienced by our urban populations is their deculturation. It is almost as serious as the first great deculturation we underwent in our first century of de-Indianizing the Indian, de-Africanizing the black, and de-Europeanizing the European in order to make us what we are. That resulted in a population of pre-urban culture, albeit quite integrated, in which operative knowledge was transmitted from parents to children and in which everyone lived by a civil calendar governed by the Church with well-developed moral models.

The question today is more serious. The struggle within this urban mass is most fierce. They come together eventually in festivals like Carnival and Candomblé ceremonies, releasing their passions by participating in sports and in the cults of the desperate. These marginalized people must not be confused, however, with the long-standing favela populations of the big cities, who are, in fact, their principal victims.

What is normal in hoodlumism is an aggression in which everyone tries to get his due, no matter from whom. There is no family but mere casual living together. Life is based on a matricentric unity of women who bear the children of several men. In spite of all the misery, that heroic mother defends her children and, though hungry, manages to find something to put into their mouths. Having no other recourse, she joins them in rummaging through garbage and begging on the streets of the city. It is incredible that Brazil, which loves to talk so much about its Christian family, has no eyes to see and admire that extraordinary woman on whom the entire life of the poor is based.

A lack of purpose frequently takes over, prostrating multitudes in despair and alcoholism. Often it also deteriorates into anarchy, fleeting gestures of uncontrollable revolt. An elemental set of values shared by all, coming mainly from Afro-Brazilian cults, soccer, and Carnival, rouses their passions. Circumstance periodically brings forth fierce leaders who impose themselves on all in the division of spoils from looting. That situation is aggravated by a lumpen-bourgeoisie of micro-entrepreneurs who live off the exploitation of these impoverished people and control them through professional killers recruited among escaped convicts and cashiered policemen.

The sad part is that these bands set themselves up in the midst of outlaw and favela populations, imposing the harshest oppression to prevent people from escaping their domination. This is what many usually maladjusted poor families want. Paradoxically, what they trust is organized crime, which habitually cleanses the slum of the most irresponsible and violent juvenile delinquents and with the hunting of children by professional killers. Perhaps for this reason, too, they cling to evangelical cults that save men from alcoholism, women from beatings by drunken husbands, and children from all manner of violence and incest. Catholic groups, run by educated priests, rarely appear there. The ones competing most with the evangelicals are the Afro-Brazilian cults, which with their strict hierarchy and elaborate liturgy open the perspectives of a religious career and lives devoted to the cult.

Lately matters have become more complex because traditional institutions have been losing all their power of control and indoctrination. The schools do not teach, the church does not catechize, the parties do not politicize. What is in operation is a monstrous system of mass communication that fills people's heads, imposing upon them unattainable models of consumption, unreachable desires, deepening even more the marginality of these populations and their inclination to violence. The violence unleashed on the streets must have something to do with the abandonment of that population to the bombardment by socially and morally irresponsible radio and television in which the best is what sells the most soft drinks or soap, with no concern for the mental and moral derangement they bring on.

9

Class, Color, and Prejudice

Class and Power

Our typology of social classes finds two conflicting but mutually complementary bodies at the top: business executives, whose power comes from
wealth gained through economic exploitation, and leaders, whose rule
comes from the fulfillment of their duties, people such as generals, deputies, bishops, labor leaders, and many others. Naturally, every wealthy
leader wants to be a business executive and every executive aspires to the
glory of a command that, in addition to his wealth, would give him the
power to determine the destiny of others.

Over the past few decades a new body of strangers has risen up and
spread out in this summit. It is the group of agents for foreign enterprises,
who have come to be the dominant sector of the ruling classes. They employ the most competent technocrats and control the media, shaping public opinion. They elect legislators and governments. They rule, in short,
with an ever-increasing bold impudence.

Below this summit are the intermediate classes made up of minor offi-
cials, professionals, police, teachers, lower clergy, and such. All of them
are prone to paying homage to the ruling classes in an attempt to obtain
some advantage from them. From this class, from the clergy and the few
intellectuals, is where most of those subversive to the established order
emerge. The insurgency itself has been fleshed out by people at its lowest
levels, which is why more priests than any other category of people have
been hanged.

They are followed by subaltern classes made up of a cluster of what
could be called a workers' aristocracy, those who have steady jobs, mostly
specialized workers, and by another cluster of small landowners, agents
for large rural properties, and others.

Below these clusters and forming the widest line on the chart of Brazilian social classes is the great mass of the oppressed classes, the so-called marginals, mainly blacks and mulattos, the inhabitants of favelas and urban peripheries. They are the ditchdiggers, the migrant fieldworkers, the street cleaners, the domestic servants, the petty prostitutes, almost all of them illiterate and incapable of moving up. Their historic aim has been to enter the system, which, this being impracticable, has given them the status of an intrinsically oppressed class whose struggle will have to be one of breaking down the class structure, of dismantling society in order to rebuild it.

This class structure encompasses and organizes all the people, operating as a self-perpetuating system of the social order in force. Naturally, its rule comes from the dominant classes. Its most dynamic sectors are the intermediary classes. Its most combative nucleus can be found in the subaltern classes, and its majority component is made up of the oppressed classes, the only ones capable of cathartic explosions or indirect expression of their revolt. They are most often resigned to their fate in spite of the miserable conditions in which they live and because of their incapacity to organize and confront those in power.

The subaltern classes are formed by those regularly integrated into social life, the productive system, and the body of consumers, and they are generally unionized. Their tendency is more to defend what they have and to get more than to change society. The fourth stratum, formed by the oppressed classes, belongs to those excluded from social life, who struggle for inclusion in the system of production and access to the marketplace. It is really this last body, in spite of its inorganic nature and its antagonisms, upon whom the role of renovator of society falls, that of fighter for the cause of all others exploited and oppressed. That is because it alone has the potential to become part of social life by breaking up the whole class structure. This configuration of antagonistic but interdependent classes effectively means, in fact, organized to stand in opposition to the oppressed classes—slaves yesterday, underpaid today—through the panic-like fright of the threat of a generalized social insurrection that consumes everyone.

Social Distance

In Brazil, in fact, the classes of the rich and the poor are separated from each other by social and cultural differences that are almost as great as those that obtain between different peoples. The physical vigor, longevity, the handsome looks of the few at the top—as an expression of the benefits of social wealth—contrast with weakness, sickliness, premature aging, and ugliness among the great majority, the expression of the penury in which they live. To the refined features, intelligence—a reflection of education—and the aristocratic and cosmopolitan customs of the ruling classes are contrasted the rough appearance, popular knowledge, ignorance, and archaic habits of those over whom they rule.

When an individual succeeds in crossing the class barrier to enter a higher stratum and stay there, it can be noted that in one or two generations his descendants will have grown in stature, become handsome, refined, educated, and they end up blending in with the traditional aristocracy.

Observing the popular mass of Brazilian groupings where one or another stratum predominates, one can see a blatant contrast. The crowd on a beach in Copacabana and the inhabitants of a favela or a suburb of Rio, or even the public at a political rally in Natal or one in Campinas as representative of those opposing classes, would appear to the most untutored observer as distinct forms of humanity.

This social stratification, generated historically, also has as a characteristic the resulting rationale of its structure as a business that gives privileges and nobility to some, making them the masters of life, as it subjugates and degrades the rest as objects for someone else's enrichment. This intentional commercial character makes of Brazil, even today, less a society than a commercial establishment, because it does not structure the population for the fulfillment of their conditions for survival and progress but for the enrichment of a ruling class turned toward the wishes of foreign interests.

These two complementary characteristics—the gulf between the different strata and the international character of the formative process—have conditioned the ruling class to look upon the people as nothing but a workforce destined to use up its strength in productive effort and with no other rights but that of eating, as long as it is working, in order to recharge its productive energies, and that of reproducing in order to replace worn-out workers.

It could not have been different in the case of an authority that was shaped in the struggle with slaves who were considered things and manipulated as purely pecuniary objects in an attempt to derive the greatest possible profit from each "piece." When the slave was succeeded by the sharecropper, then the paid farmworker, the relationship was still impregnated with the same values, which can be seen in the dehumanization of labor relations.

As a consequence, in towns near plantations there is a concentration of a detritus population of old people worn out from work and children given over to the care of their grandparents. The main body of the population of an active age spends its life away on migrant-worker trucks or as housemaids, prostitutes, and so forth. In cities that situation is aggravated but also eased. At the poorest levels one can find families struggling to rise and others getting buried deeper and deeper in poverty, delinquency, and marginality.

Brazilian social classes cannot be represented by a triangle, with a superior level, a nucleus, and a base. They take the shape of a lozenge with a very thin apex of very few people and a neck that grows broader of those who are integrated into the economic system as regular workers and consumers. The whole thing is like an inverted funnel in which the majority of the population is on the fringes of the economy and society, with no regular job and earning no minimum wage.

Given the diversity of regional situations, of prosperity and poverty, the simple movement of a worker from one region to another can represent a substantial rise for him if he manages to come into a more prosperous nucleus.

An investigation I did concerning the living conditions of urban and rural groups in the various regions of Brazil gives us a neat profile of the life of those populations. The criterion used was an index of domestic comfort, measured objectively by household possessions. A tripod for cooking, a pot, a plate, and a few utensils would be worth forty points, while a house full of all items such as television, refrigerator, telephone, and automobile would be worth 2,800 points. Samples from rural homes and urban ones in fourteen cities were used to form the index and show it graphically (Ribeiro 1959; Albersheim 1962).

The ugliest profile is the one from Santarém, in Pará, an extractive region where the mass of the population sinks to the lowest level. The charts show that a move from Catalão, in Goiás—a region of large livestock holdings—to Júlio de Castilhos, in Rio Grande do Sul—an area of farms and plantations—could represent great progress in a person's life. A move to Leopoldina, in Minas Gerais, would worsen the situation.

The best profile is the one from Ibirama, in Santa Catarina, a farming region that has integrated practically its whole population of descendants of German immigrants into the productive system, giving them better living conditions. That was because successive governments, wishing to attract European immigrants to "improve" the race, gave them parcels of land and economic aid, something that had never been done and was even prohibited for Brazilians.

Superimposing the profiles of Ibirama, Mococa, and Santarém shows how spatial variation affects the living conditions of the population and how this is one of the reasons why Brazilians are continuously moving from one place to another.

Those social differences are magnified by the attitude of indifference with which the ruling classes look upon this lode of miserable people from among whom they extract the workforce they need.

One must live on a sugar plantation, a large agricultural spread, or in a rubber extraction center to feel the distance with which an owner or a foreman treats his workers in his disregard for their destiny as people, his unawareness that they might have aspirations, his ignorance of the fact that they, too, possess human dignity.

The susceptibility of the boss to the slightest gesture that might remotely be taken as a sign of disrespect on the part of a worker is in clear contrast to the boorish way in which he treats that worker. This is exemplified by the different criteria in treatment by a policeman or a judge when he has before him a charge of offenses or damages done to a member of the ruling class as opposed to an offense against one of the people.

That and a thousand more syndromes—surviving mainly in rural zones but present in cities also—show how deep has been the process of degradation in character of the Brazilian man of the ruling class. He suffers from the illness of inequality. While the slave or ex-slave is condemned to the dignity of freedom fighter, the masters and their descendants are condemned, on the contrary, to the opprobrium of being fighters for the maintenance of inequality and oppression.

The ruling class divides its conduct into two opposite styles, one governed by the most lively cordiality in relations with their peers, the other marked by indifference in their dealings with those who are their social inferiors. Thus it is that in the same person one can observe two roles being played, depending on whether what is involved is the prescribed etiquette of the hospitable, gracious, and generous host to a visitor or the lordly role in dealing with a subordinate; both are exercised with a spontaneity that can only be explained by the bipartite makeup of his personality.

This corruption of the masters corresponds to a deterioration of the personal dignity of the humbler orders, conditioned to blatant asymmetrical treatment, predisposed to assuming attitudes of subservience and compelled to allow themselves to be exploited to the point of exhaustion. Because of the immutability of their social conditions, they are castes more than classes.

Under these conditions personal dignity can only be preserved through extremely cautious evasive attitudes in order to prevent any misunderstanding. That explains the reserve and mistrust workers have when dealing with the bosses' class. It is the fruit of their awareness that once a shadow is cast over their relationship, all that is left to them is flight, with no possibilities for the demand of any rights. Those who fail to absorb those attitudes are soon let go to wander from plantation to plantation or to head for the cities, if they do not fall into lawlessness or banditry. Most of the time, however, the sociocultural context is sufficiently homogeneous to induce people into accommodation, with escape from it only for the most vigorous of personalities, who because of their very rebelliousness are excluded from plantations.

The most characteristic subproducts of this system were the plantation-owner "colonel" and the plantation-hand *cabra,* produced socially as human types at opposite poles and replaced today by the administrator and the migrant worker. The first markets his production in the large cities, where he lives seasonally and educates his children. He is a man in every meaning of the word, a useful citizen of his nation. The second, born and living within the confines of the plantation in a house made with his own hands, owning only the household articles that he has made himself, devoted from sunup to sundown to the service of his boss, is kept in illiteracy and ignorance. He never attains the minimum conditions for the exercise of citizenship because the plantation itself is his true and only nation. Expelled or running away from it, he becomes a pariah who can only hope to reach the woods in order to escape the boss's punishing arm, to submit, if possible, with even more solicitude to the "protection" of another plantation owner.

Both represent the natural and necessary human products of an order that gives the plantation owner an aura of being its most noble expression and that is demeaned by having the fieldworker as its offal, produced socially to work as a man with a hoe who aspires only to become a foreman in a sugar mill, a rider on a cattle ranch, or a gunman in the backlands.

In this social context democratic institutions with a base in local forms of self-government could never develop. The republican institutions formally adopted in Brazil to justify new ways for the exercise of power by the ruling class have always had the same land-owning group as their agents in dealing with the people. In the rural world the change of regimes never had any effect on the domination of the plantation owners, who, using the function of police repression, the institutions of the Colony, the Empire, and the Republic for their desires, always exercised hegemonic power.

The society that resulted has incurable incompatibilities. Among them are an incapacity to assume a standard of living even modestly satisfactory for the majority of the population of the nation, a lack of aptitude for the creation of a free citizenry, and consequently an inviability for the establishment of a democratic way of life. Under these conditions elections are a great farce in which masses of electors sell their votes to those who should be their natural adversaries. For all these reasons, society is characterized as an oligarchic arrangement that can only maintain itself, artificially or repressively, by squeezing the forces of the majority, condemning that majority to backwardness and poverty.

It was not by chance that Brazil passed from colony to independent nation and from monarchy to republic with no effect on the plantation order and no perception on the part of the people of the changes. All our political institutions are superfetations of an effective power that has maintained itself untouched: the power of the plantation bosses.

The only way out of this self-perpetuating structure of oppression is in the emergence and expansion of the workers' movement. In the cities, unlike the countryside, unionized workers are already acting as free workers as they confront the boss, to the point of being assertive in the presentation of their demands. It is by this route that political institutions can be perfected, giving functional reality to the Republic.

Class and Race

The most frightful distance in Brazil is the one that separates and opposes the poor and the rich. Added to that, however, is the discrimination that weighs on blacks, mulattos, and Indians, especially the first. Nevertheless, black rebellion is much more minimal and less aggressive than it should be. It was not this way in the past. The longest and cruelest struggles that took place in Brazil were the age-old Indian resistance and the struggle of blacks against slavery, which lasted over all the centuries of slavery. Having its start at the beginnings of the slave traffic, the latter struggle ended only with abolition (in 1888). Its main form was flight, for resistance and for rebuilding one's life within the solidarity of the *quilombo* communities, whose numbers grew into the thousands. They were proto-Brazilian formations because the quilombo inhabitant was a black who was already acculturated, knowing how to survive in the Brazilian natural environment, and also because it would have been impossible for him to reconstitute African ways of life. His drama was the paradoxical situation of someone who could win a thousand battles and not win the war—but who could not lose a single battle. That was what happened in all the quilombos, even the most important one, Palmares, which resisted for over a century but fell in the end and was wiped out, its people sold in batches in the south and to the Caribbean.

Still, the most arduous struggle for the African black and his descendants was, and still is, the winning of a place and the role of a legitimate participant in national society. He saw himself incorporated into it by force. He helped build it and that effort broke him, but in the end he learned to live in it only because of his total de-Africanization. The first cultural chore of the Brazilian black was learning to speak Portuguese, which he heard in the shouts of the overseer. He had to do so in order to communicate with his fellow exiles, who came from different nations. By doing so he rehumanized himself, beginning to emerge from his status as a possession that moved, a mere animal or energetic force for work. Miraculously managing to dominate the new language, he not only remade it, lending a singularity to the Portuguese of Brazil, but he also made possible its spread throughout the territory to areas where previously the native language, Tupi-Guaraní, had been mostly heard.

I estimate that Brazil, in its making, used up close to 12 million blacks spent as the main workforce for everything that was produced here and everything that was built here. At the close of the colonial period they constituted one of the largest masses of blacks in the modern world.

Abolition, the most dilatory in history, was the principal cause of the fall of the Empire and the proclamation of the Republic. The ruling classes, however, deftly restructured their system of workforce recruitment by replacing slave labor with immigrants imported from Europe, where the population had become excessive and exportable, at a low price.

The black, culturally conditioned to conserve his working energy in order to avoid being brought to death by the overseer's whip, was in vivid contrast as a working force to the farmhand brought from Europe, already adapted to a system of wages and predisposed to working to the maximum in order to get for himself a plot of land on which he could prosper, free of plantation owners.

The black, feeling himself relieved of the brutality that kept him working in the field under the harshest repression—including preventive punishment, which was not to correct mistakes or laziness but had only the aim of dissuading blacks from running away—wanted nothing but freedom. Consequently, the former slaves abandoned the plantations where they had toiled and took to the road in search of some barren land where they could settle, the same as if they were in a quilombo, planting corn and cassava for food. They subsequently fell into a state of such misery that the black population was substantially reduced, not so much because of the suppression of the annual importation of new masses of slaves to replenish the stock, because this had been slowing over the decades, but much more because of the terrible poverty into which they had been cast. They could not remain in any one place because every time they settled, the neighboring plantation owners got together and called in the police to evict them, since all the land was owned, and thus when they left one plantation they would inevitably land at another one.

The present ruling class in Brazil, made up of the children and grandchildren of the old slave owners, still holds the same attitude of vile contempt where the black is concerned. For their forebears the black slave, the freedman, and the mulatto were nothing but a source of energy, like a sack of charcoal, who when worn out could easily be replaced by the purchase of another. For their descendants, the free black, the mulatto, and the poor white are also held in great contempt because of their innate and inescapable laziness, ignorance, and criminality. All of them are unanimously considered blameworthy for their own misfortunes, explained as a characteristic of their ilk and not as the result of slavery and oppression. That deformed viewpoint has also been assimilated by mulattos and even by blacks who have succeeded in rising socially, who join with the white sector in discriminating against the black masses.

The Brazilian nation, ruled by people with that mentality, has never done anything for the black masses who built it. It has denied them ownership of any piece of land which they could cultivate and live off, schools in which they could educate their children, or any type of assistance. It has given them only a surfeit of discrimination and repression. A large number of blacks went to the cities, where they found a less hostile social environment. They first constituted the so-called African quarters, which were subsequently replaced by the favela shantytowns. Since then, these have been multiplying as the solution in which poor people have found to live and socialize, always under the permanent threat of being dispossessed and driven out.

The rural black, transferred to a favela, must learn the ways of life of the city, where he cannot plant. Fortunately, he finds blacks who have been there for a long time and have already built a culture of their own in which they have expressed themselves with a high degree of creativity. It is a culture made of scraps of what the African had carried in his breast during his long years of slavery, things like musical feelings, rhythms, tastes, religion.

Starting from these precarious bases, the urban black came to be the most vigorous and beautiful force in popular Brazilian culture. This is the base upon which our Carnival is built, the cult of Iemanjá, *capoeira* foot-fighting, and any number of cultural manifestations. The black has taken advantage of every opportunity given him to demonstrate his worth. This occurs in every field that does not require schooling. It is the case with popular music, soccer, and numerous less visible forms of competition and expression. The black has thus, in spite of all the vicissitudes he faces, come to be the most creative component in Brazilian culture and the one who, along with the Indian, most sets our people apart.

The huge sector of blacks and mulattos might well be the most Brazilian component of our people. This is because, de-Africanized in the grinding mill of slavery, being neither a native Indian nor a white from the mother country, he was able to find his identity only as a Brazilian, as a new people made up in the full and happy process of fusion of those who came from different places. Thus blacks do not cling together as a mass fighting for ethnic authenticity but as people intrinsically integrated into the same people, the Brazilian people.

The mulatto, blending biologically and socially with the white world, has been more easily able to approach its erudite culture and has given us some of our worthiest and most cultured figures in letters, art, and politics. Among them are the artist Aleijadinho, the writer Machado de Assis, the jurist Rui Barbosa, the composer Josí Maurício, the poet Cruz e Sousa, the magistrate Luís Gama, politicians like the brothers Mangabeira and Nelson Carneiro, and intellectuals like Abdias do Nascimento and Guerreiro Ramos. Because of his drive and the extraordinary beauty of many—especially mulatto women—the result of hybrid vigor, he had a better chance of rising socially, even though he would progress in proportion to how much he denied his blackness. Placed between two conflicting worlds—that of the black, which he rejects, and that of the white, which rejects him—the mulatto comes to the realization of his drama, where he is two people, which means he is no single one, nobody.

In recent years, as an effect of the success of the American black, which was taken by the Brazilians as a victory of the race but came principally through the rise of a portion of the population of color through education and by an opening up of opportunities for employment, the Brazilian black is gathering the courage to assume his condition as a black with pride.

The same has happened with many mulattos, who have gone over to the black side of their double nature. That step was really quite difficult, given the huge black mass that has been sunk in the most atrocious poverty and with whom they could not blend, a mass representing the popular image of the black whose condition is absolutely undesirable because redounding onto it with all harshness are poverty, illness, criminality, and violence.

This is taking place in a sick society with a deformed conscience, where the black is blamed for his own penury. Under these circumstances his suffering does not awaken any solidarity, much less indignation. As a consequence, the fate of that majority portion of the population is not the object of any specific form of aid to enable it to emerge from poverty and ignorance.

In all Brazil there prevails an assimilationist expectation that leads Brazilians to suppose and desire that blacks will disappear through a progressive whitening. What is happening in fact is a darkening of Brazilians, but it is not coming about so much by the whitening of blacks as by the darkening of whites. In this way we must imagine in the future a dark population in which every family, through genetic imperatives, will occasionally have a coal-black little girl or a pale white little boy.

It is true that with the higher rates of fertility among blacks because of their poverty and the conduct that corresponds to it, blacks would print their mark more strongly on the Brazilian population. It is not impossible that toward the middle of the twenty-first century, in a Brazil of 300 million people, there will be a clear preponderance of blacks and mulattos.

The distinctive characteristic of Brazilian racism is that it is not based on the racial origin of people but on the color of their skin. On that scale black is coal black; the mulatto is already brown and as such half-white, and if his skin is a touch lighter he will then go on to be a part of the white community. It should be added that there is also a purely social or cultural whitening to be noted here. This is the case of blacks who, rising socially with known success, go on to form groups that socialize with whites, marry among them, and in the end are considered white. The Brazilian definition of *black* cannot be applied to an artist or a successful professional. This situation is exemplified by the dialogue of a black artist, the painter Santa Rosa, with a young man, also black, who was struggling to rise in a diplomatic career and complaining about the immense barriers that hindered the rise of people of color. The painter said, very sympathetically, "I understand your case perfectly, my dear boy, I was black once too."

Already in the nineteenth century a foreigner, surprised to see a mulatto in the high position of troop commander, heard the following explanation: "Yes, he used to be a mulatto, but as commander he can't be anything but white" (Koster 1942, 480).

This peculiar form of Brazilian racism is derived from a situation in which miscegenation is not punished but praised. In fact, interracial unions here were never considered a crime or a sin, probably because the populating of Brazil was not done by already formed European families whose white women fought against all intercourse with women of color. We came about in fact from the cross between a few white men and multitudes of Indian and black women.

That situation did not go on to shape a racial democracy, as Gilberto Freyre and many others would like to believe, because of the heavy weight of antiblack oppression, prejudice, and discrimination present. Nor did it happen, of course, because the very expectation that the black would disappear through miscegenation is a form of racism. What is certain, however, is that it stands in great contrast, and a contrast for the better, to purely racial forms of prejudice that lead to *apartheid*.

One must recognize, however, that apartheid has elements of tolerance that are unknown here. If the other party is pushed aside and kept at the greatest possible distance, it leaves room for him to preserve there his identity, continuing to be himself. Consequently, it induces the profound internal solidarity of the group being discriminated against, which enables it to fight clearly for its rights without accepting any paternalism. In assimilationist circumstances blackness is diluted on a broad scale of gradations, which breaks solidarity and reduces combativeness by insinuating the idea that the social order is a natural order, even a sacred one.

The most perverse aspect of assimilationist racism is that it gives itself an image of greater sociability, when in fact it disarms the black in his fight against the poverty that has been imposed on him and conceals the conditions of terrible violence to which he has been submitted. It should be pointed out, however, that the assimilationist ideology of so-called racial democracy mainly affects black intellectuals, leading them into campaigns for the awareness of blacks for social conciliation and for a fight against the hatred and resentments held by blacks. Its illusory objective is to create conditions of life in which the black will be able to take advantage of social capillarity in order to rise through the explicit adoption of the forms of conduct and manners of successful whites.

Every black of extraordinary talent can succeed in his own career, like Pelé, Pixinguinha, or Grande Otelo and countless other athletes and artists, without finding an appropriate expression for the antiracist struggle. Assimilationism, as can be seen, creates an atmosphere of fluidity in interracial relations, but it dissuades the black from his specific struggle, compromising understanding that victory can only be attained through social revolution.

The Cuban Revolution has come to show that blacks are much more prepared to rise socially than is supposed. In fact, a few years of clearly open education and stimulation have rapidly increased the body of blacks who have attained the highest posts in Cuban government, society, and culture. At the same time, the whole black segment of the population, freed from discrimination and racism, has fraternized with the other components of society, markedly deepening the degree of solidarity.

All of this clearly demonstrates that racial democracy is possible but only practicable in conjunction with social democracy. Either there is democracy for everyone or there is democracy for no one, because the oppression of the black condemned to the dignity of the freedom fighter corresponds to the opprobium of the white placed in the role of oppressor within his own society.

10

Assimilation or Segregation

Race and Color

An analysis of the growth of the Brazilian population and its composition according to color is highly expressive of the oppression that the white ruler has imposed on the other components. We estimate at 6 million the number of blacks introduced into Brazil as slaves up to 1850, the year of the abolition of the traffic; at 5 million the minimum number of Indians with whom the edges of Brazilian civilization were coming into contact successively during the same period; and at 5 million the maximum number of Europeans coming to Brazil until 1950. Of these 5 million only half a million entered Brazil before 1850. Let us take a look at their descendants. Looking at the composition of the population in 1950 (the census of 1960 and that of 1970 do not contain any data with reference to race or color), one can verify that Indians living a more or less autonomous tribal life had been reduced to around 100,000 (Ribeiro 1959); blacks would have reached a maximum of 5.6 million, while those defined as brown (mulattos) would be 13.7 million; and "whites" (mainly of mixed blood) would rise to 32 million. Indians unexpectedly tripled from 1950 to 1990, probably because they had adapted to European illnesses and because of the effects of official protection, which has reduced massacres substantially.

In spite of the deformations imposed by the ever so Brazilian confusion of social status and color, such awesome differences in the census could not be for that reason alone or because of differences in the fertility rate but arose because of ecological and social factors. Miscegenation itself must be analyzed with regard to the circumstance that all alien groups were composed principally of men, who had to fight over the women of the land, Indian women. How insignificant was the proportion of white women coming to Brazil is quite well known. Under those conditions the fundamental function as a source of population fell to native women, generally fertilized by white men.

Thus there is a partial explanation for the whitening of Brazilians, since the mixtures of European with Indian make up a lighter yet still dark type, who to the eyes and racial sensibility of any Brazilian are pure white.

The census shows a progressive decrease in the proportion of blacks in the Brazilian population, going from one-fifth to one-twentieth of the population in the last century. This also represented a drop in absolute numbers: after a rise from 2 million to 6.6 million in the fifty years following abolition, the black population fell to 5.6 million in 1950 and still totaled only 7.2 million in 1990. It is to be presumed that many blacks had classified themselves as brown, because every person could choose his color or that of his family group.

Obvious, however, is the contrast in progression between black and white groups. The latter went from 38 percent in 1872 to 62 percent in 1950 and 55 percent in 1990; numerically from 3.8 million to 32 million and to 81.4 million over the same period. The high increment in the white contingent cannot be explained by the growth in European immigration from 1880 onward. The extent of immigration never reached a level that would make it such a decisive influence on the composition of the original population. The demographic explosion of Brazilian "whites" can only be understood, then, in terms of an intense natural growth in absolute numbers. It is prodigiously large in relation to other sectors of the population, and it was favored by better living conditions than those that obtained among blacks and browns; here, too, the tendency to classify all those who had been successful in life as white was at work.

As for the indigenous contingent, we rely on studies of the factors responsible for their extermination, among which the effects of diseases introduced by the Europeans stand out on the biological level, as the conditions of suppression under which they were held have bearing on the social level (Ribeiro 1956a). Little is known regarding the blacks, however, except for an equally deleterious effect from the same factors, with a heavy preponderance of the conditions of oppression over the lethal effects of illnesses. That is because they had already been exposed in Africa to the same circuit of contagious illnesses as had the Europeans. After the abolition of slavery, diseases continued having an effect on the free black as factors in the reduction of his demographic expansion because of the terrible conditions of penury to which he was still subjected. To estimate the weight of this factor, it is enough to consider the misery of the Brazilian population in its poorest groups, difficult to bear for any group of humans and still affecting blacks most harshly.

White versus Black

The census of 1950 allows for some significant comparisons between the living and working conditions of blacks and whites in the active Brazilian population. If we consider, for example, the managerial sector as a whole, it can be seen that the possibilities for a black to attain membership in it are extremely slight, since for every thousand active whites over the age of ten, twenty-three are employers, as against four blacks as owners of a business for every thousand employees.

Comparing the occupational status of the 4 million blacks over the age of ten with the 1 million foreigners registered in the same census, it can be seen that while the first contribute only 20,000 employers, the latter hold 86,000 pieces of property. It can be seen that these foreigners, arriving in Brazil in recent decades as immigrants, found conditions for social advancement more rapidly than did the mass of the existing population and much more rapidly than did the black group.

According to data in the same census, in the grouping of occupations of high esteem, there was one black employer for every twenty-five nonblacks, and one black for every fifty in the liberal professions. Likewise, in lesser professional categories there was one black for every seven factory workers of other colors and, quite expressive, one black for every four other field workers.

Examining the career of the black in Brazil it can be proved that, introduced as a slave, from the very first moment he has been called upon to take on the most difficult tasks, serving as the fundamental base of labor in all productive sectors. Treated as a beast of burden to be worn out with work, with the status of a mere investment meant to produce the greatest profit, he faced precarious conditions for survival. Rising to the status of free worker, before or after abolition, the black saw himself yoked to new forms of exploitation, which although better than slavery allowed him to be integrated into society and the cultural world that had become his only in the status of a subproletarian compelled to fill his former role, which was still mainly that of a work animal.

As for the slave, some far-sighted landowners might have pondered the fact that it would have been more economical to keep their "items" well nourished in order to obtain greater advantage from them over the long run. It even occurred that a black too exhausted for work in the fields was given an opportunity to grow old in a corner of the property, living off the products of his plot, taking care of the lighter tasks required on the plantation. Free, however, no longer belonging to anyone, he found himself alone and persecuted, relying only on his own strength for work in a world where land and everything else had an owner. Thus he had to subject himself to exploitation by masters who did not exploit him more than he had been before, because that would have been impracticable, but who were absolutely unconcerned about the freed black's fate. Under those conditions the free black who had in some way maintained a certain physical vigor could, for that reason alone and being more valued as a worker, settle on some plantation where he could live and breed. The weak ones, the sickly, the prematurely aged from work were simply cast aside like some useless object.

After the first abolition law—the Law of the Free Womb, which freed the children of slave women—the plantation owners in areas with the greatest concentration of slaves ordered that the offspring of their black women be abandoned on roads and in nearby villages, for since these babies were no longer their possessions, the plantation owners felt no further obligation to feed them. In the years following the Law of the Free Womb (1871), dozens of asylums were established in towns and cities in the state of São Paulo to take in those children cast out by plantation owners. After abolition the departure of working blacks who no longer wished to serve their old masters was followed by the expulsion of old and ill blacks from the plantations. Many groups of blacks were concentrated at that time at the entrances to towns and cities, under the most precarious conditions. In order to get away from that famished freedom, they began to let themselves be enticed to work under conditions dictated by the landowners.

With the subsequent development of an agricultural export economy and the consequent abandonment of self-sufficient plantations, which went on to concentrate on commercial crops (especially the cultivation of coffee, cotton, and later artificial fodder), other groups of workers and sharecroppers were expelled, enlarging the mass of residual population in the towns. It was now made up not only of blacks but also of browns and poor whites, all mingled as a mass of "free" farmhands, available for work where labor was needed. This cast-off humanity, predominantly black and mulatto, can be seen even today in urban settings in all latifundist areas, made up of seasonal workers, beggars, biscuit sellers, housemaids, the blind, cripples, sick people, all crowded together in miserable shanties. The oldest, worn out now from farmwork and their uncertain life, take care of the children who are not yet old enough to take part in it.

Under these conditions one must look for the explanation of the blatant discrepancy between the growth of the white contingent and that of the black in the development of the Brazilian population, allowing the first to grow in recent centuries in the proportion of one to nine and the other of only one to two and a half, reducing their presence both in percentage and in absolute numbers; as noted, the number of blacks fell from 6.6 million in 1940 to 5.6 million in 1950, turning to increase to only 7.2 million in 1990.

In cities, too, and even in industrial areas that have absorbed enormous rural masses in the last few decades, incorporating them into the workforce, the integration of the black contingent does not seem to have been proportional to its number in the total population. Research on interracial relations in Brazil reveals that, adding to the case, there are the factors of the lack of preparation on the part of blacks for integration into industrial society and the factors of rejection that render it more difficult for people of color to rise socially (Pierson 1945; Costa Pinto 1953; Nógueira 1955; Ianni 1962; Cardoso 1962; Fernandes 1964).

The situation of the lower status of browns and blacks with respect to whites persists in 1990. The few available data show that 12 percent of whites over the age of seven were illiterate, but for blacks the figure was 30 percent and for browns 29 percent. Furthermore, the annual average income (in cruzeiros) for people over the age of ten was 32,212 for whites, 13,295 for blacks, and 15,308 for browns (*Anuário estatístico do Brasil*, IBGE, 1993). Lamentably, the information regarding color for 1990 is much scantier than for 1950.

Thus the broadening of the bases of society brought on by industrialization does not threaten to break the super-concentration of wealth, power, and prestige as a monopoly of whites because of differentiating conditions that can only be explained historically. These involve the recent emergence of black people from the status of slaves to that of free workers; an effective state of inferiority produced by the oppressive treatment blacks experienced for centuries, with no attempt at compensation; the maintenance of racially discriminatory criteria that have stood in the way of blacks' rising up to the simple condition of ordinary people, equal to the rest, and have made it more difficult for them to obtain an education and to join the workforce of modernized sectors. The rates of illiteracy, criminality, and mortality for blacks are higher, reflecting the failure of Brazilian society to put into practice its professed ideal of a racial democracy that has integrated blacks into the status of citizens undifferentiated from the rest.

Florestan Fernandes points out that "as long as we do not reach that objective we shall not have a racial democracy or even a democracy either. Through a paradox of history the black has become in our time the touchstone for our capacity to forge in the tropics that buttress of modern civilization" (1964, 738).

In spite of the association of poverty with blackness, the profound differences that separate Brazilians and set them in opposition in blatantly contrasting camps are of a social nature. They are what distinguish the privileged circles and well-to-do groups—those who in a general economy of penury manage to reach reasonable levels of consumption—from the enormous mass of those exploited in work or even excluded from it to live on the margins of the productive process and are consequently excluded from the cultural, social, and political life of the nation. The reduction of these differences has constituted the great obstacle facing Brazilian society, the challenge for those aiming for a social reordering that would be an opportunity for the integration of all the people into the system of production and by that route into the diverse spheres of the social and cultural life of the country.

Brazilians of the most obviously black appearance, in spite of being concentrated in the poorest sectors, do not act in a way that is socially and politically motivated by racial differences but by awareness of the historical and social character—even though incidental and surmountable—of the factors standing in the way of their rise. It is not as blacks that they operate in the social picture but rather as members of the poorer sectors, all moved by the same aspirations for economic and social progress. The fact that they are black or mulatto, however, also costs a little extra, because added to the cruelty of the unequal treatment all poor people bear are subtle or open forms of hostility.

It should be pointed out, however, that the very nature of the racial prejudice prevalent in Brazil, as distinct from that encountered in other societies, makes it act more as an integrating force than as a mechanism for segregation. Racial prejudice in the Anglo-Saxon model, falling indiscriminately upon all persons of color no matter what proportion of black blood they might have, leads of necessity to distancing, segregation, and violence through hostility to any kind of community. The color prejudice of Brazilians, falling in a different way, according to the color of the skin, tending to identify a light mulatto as white, leads rather to an expectation of miscegenation—an expectation that is really discriminatory in that it aspires to the lightening of blacks instead of accepting them as they are, even though stimulating integration (Nógueira 1955).

Yet it must be added that as we have repeatedly noted, more than a prejudice of race or color, Brazilians have a deep-seated class prejudice. The enormous social distances that obtain between the poor and those with means is not a result only of their possessions but also of their degree of integration into the lifestyle of the privileged groups—as illiterates or educated people, as possessors of popular wisdom transmitted orally or of modern learning, as the heirs to a folkloric tradition or an erudite cultural inheritance, as descendants of well-placed families or those of humble origin; these dimensions place rich and poor in opposition much more than whites and blacks.

So it is that with marriage and social contact, blacks who rise socially and take on the attitudes, mannerisms, and customs of the ruling class are more easily accepted than a crude and vulgar person would be, whether he be black, white, or mulatto, because of his basic social incongruity and his obvious cultural marginality. Whites and blacks living together under the same circumstances tend to struggle, also together, to overcome poverty, coming together and blending as a uniform social drive, which as they push together for their ascent to better living conditions forces at the same time a social restructuring. Gilberto Freyre (1954) waxes languid as he describes the attraction exercised by dark women over the Portuguese, who were inspired by the legends of the enchanted Moorish maiden, and even in reminiscences of a Lusitanian admiration for the cultural and technical superiority of their ancient Arab masters. Those observations are certainly attractive as extravagances and might even be true. It so happens, however, that they are completely unnecessary as an explanation for the sexual intercourse that has always taken place the world over wherever the European has come across people of color in the absence of white women. This is just how it was in South Africa between English or Dutch men and Hottentot women, whose physical characteristics might have called for a certain reserve. Even so, they mingled for a long time, breeding a large mixed group, which continued until the white population became homogenized through a balanced composition of men and women, creating a cultural and moral environment that was able to work as a barrier against that intercourse.

It should also be pointed out that relations between white men and black slave women have been recorded in all regions and not just those of Portuguese colonization. There to prove it are Americans of mixed blood, for example, more numerous today even than blacks, bred, obviously, through the sexual intercourse of Puritan Protestants and in spite of the absence of any legends of enchanted Moorish maidens.

What the facts seem to indicate is the existence of degrees of permeability of the racial barrier instead of a model of complete abstinence as opposed to another of generalized intercourse. Wherever racially differentiated peoples come into contact a mixed-blood group has been born, in greater or lesser numbers. What makes the conditions of interracial union in Brazil different from those of other areas is the development of reciprocal established expectations, more an incentive than a condemnation. The birth of a mulatto child in Brazilian circumstances is no betrayal either to the black or to the white race and can even become a worthy motive in itself.

This encouraging integrationist ideology of a melting pot is probably the most positive value of Brazilian interracial blending. It will not lead, of course, to a lightening of all Brazilian blacks along the lines popularly hoped for—ultimately racist because it is hoped that blacks will become lighter, that Germans will become darker, that Japanese will normalize their almond eyes—but it does have the value of repressing segregation rather than mixture.

It is to be supposed that along this path the Brazilian population will become more and more homogenized, leading in the future to the participation of all in a multiracial genetic heritage held in common. No one is startled in Brazil by the fact that the color of children of the same parents can go from dark mulatto in one to palest white in another or that they combine the straight black hair of the Indian, the stiff, curly hair of the black, or the silky hair of the white in all ways possible, with different eye openings, shape of nose, form of mouth, or size of hands and feet.

In fact, every Brazilian family of ancient extraction shows in the phenotype of its members isolated characteristics of ancestors, closer or more remote, from the three great formative trunks. Carrying in his genetic heritage all those races, the Brazilian has been able to breed children as varied as all human faces.

What characterizes the Portuguese of yesterday and the Brazilian of the ruling class today is the duplicity of their standards of sexual relations: one for those within their social circle and another completely opposite one for people of the poorer classes. The latter case is distinguished by the casualness in the establishment of sexual relations with a woman of an inferior social status, generally lacking in any romantic tie and moved purely by sexual interest. With no previous courtship, the man of superior social status attempts relations with captivating black, Indian, and mulatto women whenever a propitious moment presents itself. Attachment, love of a lyrical character between people of unequal social levels, is a rare and exceptional occurrence.

Sexual relations under these unequal circumstances can bring forth no intimacy at all, with the woman remaining servile or dependent, just as respectful as before, given her unbalanced social position in relation to the man. When and where she remains in a state of servile dependence, she has to accept the man who imposes on her in order to breed more slaves or the white man who wants to make use of her. Once free, she might hope for more egalitarian relations. Under the existing conditions of poverty, however, she settles for occasional relations or temporary concubinage. With these circumstances the family is structured with the woman at the center as she gives birth to children by different men and undertakes to care for the children, frequently out of touch with the various fathers.

Only when she rises up out of poverty to a certain economic sufficiency does the woman attain the minimal conditions where she can aspire to an independent love life, can give her sexual relations dignity by conducting them in the spirit of a co-participant, and finally has the opportunity to build a stable family life endowed with the religious and legal symbols of social recognition. This new model of relations prevails now for the sector of the black, white, or mixed population that has been integrated into the modern base of national society, but it is still a distant ideal for the large groups of socially marginalized Brazilians.

There is no doubt that over the past few years, thanks to modernization and the spread of new attitudes, inspired especially by the revivalism of American blacks, a vehement affirmation by blacks and mulattos can be observed, finally proud of themselves and sometimes even racist in their blackness as a compensation. The transformation of the patterns of interracial relations seems to be holding out not a simple generalization of all the values that obtain in relations among people of the ruling classes but a softening of the rigidity of the expectations of the latter as to virginity and the limiting of male license for free and irresponsible sexual intercourse with women of an inferior social position.

Under these new conditions the woman of color, who was always a desired and even specially appreciated partner for possible relations, will go on to compete with all other women to set up stable and egalitarian relations. In this way it will be possible one day to overcome the prevalent structure of the Brazilian family, which has always been matricentric. Indispensable for that must first come the elimination of the state of socioeconomic marginality of the population, which is basically the cause of irresponsible paternity. It is probable that there will be a decrease in the ideals of lightening of the black as a form of prejudice but that the tendency will continue as interracial relations continue to play an important role in the integrative process. It might well happen, though, that new and greater tensions will arise, inclined to slow down mingling, with a resistance on all social levels to the massive ascent of the blackest contingent in competition with the less black one, and through the new, more demanding attitude of women of color in the establishment of relations.

The mass of mulatto Brazilians is, however, so large and so broadly distributed across the strata of middle and lower classes that they will now certainly be capable of presiding over the process, working as the generator of new groupings more dark than white, maintaining and stimulating the tendency toward mingling. Their role is all the more important because the privileged groups—predominantly whitish or tending to identify their copper coloration to ancestry that is indigenous rather than black—affected by segregationist ideology, are already showing characteristically racist attitudes of intolerance.

Nevertheless, the vigor of assimilationist ideology, rooted in popular culture and also taught in the schools, and of the attitudes beginning to be generalized among all Brazilians of pride in their multiracial origins and among blacks in their own ancestry will probably permit a successful confrontation with the social tensions deriving from the ascent of the black, which foresees for him an egalitarian participation in national society, because only in that way will it be possible to overcome one of the most dramatic conflicts that tears at Brazilian solidarity.

Immigrants

The contingent of European immigrants integrated into the population of Brazil is estimated at 5 million people, four-fifths of whom entered the country in the last century (on the role of immigration in Brazil see Ávila 1956; Carneiro 1950; Cortes 1954; Diégues Jr. 1964; Ianni 1966; Laytano 1952; Martins 1955; Saito 1961; Waibel 1949; Willems 1946). This sector is mainly composed of 1.7 million Portuguese immigrants who came to join the settlers of the early centuries, who became dominant through the multiplication that came about via their mingling with Indians and blacks. They were followed by the Italians with 1.6 million, the Spaniards with 700,000, the Germans with more than 250,000, the Japanese with around 230,000, and other smaller contingents, mainly Slavs, entering Brazil especially between 1886 and 1930. The various census figures record the current percentages of foreigners and naturalized Brazilians rising from 2.45 percent in 1890 to 6.16 percent in 1900, falling afterward successively from 5.11 percent in 1920 to 3.91 percent in 1940, 2.34 percent in 1950, and 0.8 percent in 1970.

In spite of their being numerically unimpressive, the immigrants' role was quite important, as they formed certain regional groupings in southern areas where they were most heavily concentrated, creating characteristically European environments and populations that were overwhelmingly white. Although important in the racial and cultural makeup of these areas, they did not have any great importance in the formation of any characteristics of the Brazilian population or its culture. When they began to arrive in greater numbers, the national population was already so large numerically and so defined from an ethnic point of view that it was able to begin the cultural and racial absorption of immigrants without any great changes in its makeup.

Consequently, nothing has occurred in Brazil similar to what happened in the River Plate countries, where a numerically small original ethnicity, under the pressure of masses of immigrants making up four-fifths of the total, saw a new physiognomy, characteristically European, imprinted on the national society and culture, transforming them from a new people into a transplanted people. Brazil was born and grew up as a new people, affirming more and more that characteristic in its historical-cultural makeup. What can be noted in the Brazilian case is that on the one hand there is social inequality, expressed racially in the stratification of the inferior position of the black and the mulatto, and on the other hand there is basic cultural homogeneity that transcends regional ecological singularities so much, along with the marks of a variety of racial origins, and also transcends the differences of origin or cultural bases of the various groups.

In spite of the disproportion of the contributions—black in certain areas, Indian, German, or Japanese in others—none of them has been self-defined as a center of extranational ethnic loyalties. This conjunction, built by so many contributions, is essentially one as regards national ethnicity, leaving no place for eventual tensions organized around regional, racial, or cultural unities standing in opposition. One and the same culture takes in all, and a vigorous self-definition that is more and more Brazilian animates everyone.

This Brazilianism is so deep-rooted today that it has resulted in xenophobia on one side and nationalist vainglory on the other. All Brazilians cheer during World Cup matches with feeling as deep as if it were a war between our people and all the other peoples of the world. Victories are celebrated in every family and defeats suffered as personal shame.

In exile I was able to feel how difficult it was for a Brazilian to live outside Brazil. Our country has so much singularity as to make it extremely difficult to accept and enjoy life among other peoples. The mayor of Natal died in Montevideo from pure sadness. I would not learn Spanish, not even enough to buy a box of matches. Some people committed suicide and others went through extreme suffering. One has only to see a gathering of Brazilians among the half million we are exporting as workers to sense the fanaticism with which they cling to their identity as Brazilians and the rejection of any idea of letting themselves stay where they are.

11

Order versus Progress

Original Anarchy

The dialectical counterpart of the aims of the colonial enterprise was the anarchical character, savage and socially irresponsible, of the expansion of the Brazilian nuclei. Acting upon a different reality, which obliged them to seek their own solutions, becoming adjusted to its nature and working at a distant remove from official desires, the colonists almost always acted in an improvised way and in line with circumstances. Being unpredictable, their way developed loosely until through repetition it grew to constitute a norm of action, something to be copied and regulated.

In many fields rules never won out. A good example is that of fornication with Indian women, resulting in a prodigious gestation of people of mixed blood outside any rule that could become canon, allowing and generalizing it. Another example is seen in the bandeira operations, military undertakings the prey of which were Indian slaves to be used or sold. The bandeirante, agent for private violent actions, went on to be an agent of the Crown. It was he who through his actions and with his means made the economic life of poor regions viable and made the physical appropriation of Brazil possible. Even though the official illusion prevailed of giving Indians the noble destiny copiously claimed in official documents, the mother country never placed any serious obstacle in the way of their captivity.

Later on, when the bandeirantes came upon gold, and after that diamonds, in the wastelands where they were roaming, the Crown moved to legalize the possession of mines, imposing forms of payment that grew more and more damaging. In the case of diamonds, the same as had happened previously with tobacco and salt, the Crown decreed a royal monopoly so that no one else should become rich from the new wealth, turning prospectors into smugglers, condemned by the fiscal furor to clandestine exercise of their activities.

We are the result of the collision of that bureaucratic rationalism, which aimed to execute an official program in the new land, with the spontaneity that was shaping it haphazardly under the control and the limitations of tropical ecology and the despotism of the world market.

Who are we Brazilians, made up of so many and such varied human groups? Is the fusion of them all complete in us now? Is it still taking place? Or will it never end? Shall we be condemned forever to be a multicolored people on the racial and cultural level? Will there be some distinctive characteristic of Brazilians as a people, formed as they have been by those coming from everywhere? All these age-old conjectures have no clear answer in concrete action.

In this field of force Brazil has made itself quite the opposite of the Portuguese plan and most surprising for Brazilians themselves. We are here today in spite of the Portuguese and their colonizers—but also thanks to their bringing us together with both the bioracial tiles and the sociocultural mortar with which Brazil is being formed.

So it is that even though we embarked on someone else's plan, we have made ourselves possible as we took a stand against that official project and opposed the designs of the colonizers and their successors. According to their wishes, Indians, blacks, and all of us, their mixed-blood offspring, recruited for the colonial enterprise, would have continued in the role prescribed for us as an overseas proletariat destined to produce exportable merchandise without ever becoming a people with a destiny of its own. Sometimes I think that we are still fulfilling that design, even without the Portuguese, under the gauntlet of the old ruling class of the descendants of slave owners that has succeeded them in the exercise of power and of the new elites, a sector today largely composed of the agents of multinationals. The technocrats themselves, still in their infancy, are already advising governments to plunge even deeper into the spontaneity of the market and the social irresponsibility of neoliberalism.

The greatest fear the Portuguese had in the past was of seeing the slave workforce they had gathered with exclusively mercantile aims, to be used up in production, rising up and attempting to be considered as people with a glimmer of hope for autonomy and self-government. Likewise, the great perplexity of the ruling classes today is that the descendants of those blacks, Indians, and mixed-bloods dare to think that this country is a republic that ought to be ruled by their will since they are its people.

It is no easy task to define the atypical character of our historical process, which does not fit the framework of conceptual schemes put together to explain other contexts and other sequences. In fact, as it rose from the bed of cunhadismo, structured afterward on the basis of African labor, Brazil has been shaped as something quite different from everything else, explicable historically only on its own terms.

Old institutional questions, without having been resolved or passed by, continue as the main factors of backwardness and at the same time are the main driving forces for social revolution. The great historical heritage of Brazil is really the achievement of its very makeup as a people unified ethnically, nationally, and culturally. It is also the failure of our efforts to structure ourselves in solidarity on the socioeconomic level as a people existing for themselves. At the root of this failure of the majorities lies the success of the minorities, who are still in charge. It is their design to shore up old privileges by perpetuating the monopoly of land ownership, by placing profits before needs, and by the imposition of archaic and renovated forms of the population's dependence on its role as an overexploited workforce.

Since there is no sure guarantee that history will spontaneously come to favor the oppressed tomorrow, and there is, on the contrary, a legitimate fear that in the future also, ruling minorities will conform and deform Brazil according to their interests, the task of reaching a maximum of lucidity in order to intervene effectively in history with the aim of making its age-old tendency change course becomes even more imperative. That is our proposal.

The Archaic and the Modern

The passing of the traditional pattern as it became archaic to the modern pattern operates to different rhythms in all regions, but the most progressive people find themselves hamstrung and reduced to a reflex modernization. This cannot be explained, however, by any resistance to change by a cultural order, once a vehement desire for renovating transformation has appeared. This is perhaps the most outstanding characteristic of new peoples, the Brazilians among them. Even rural populations and marginalized urban ones fight resistances to change that are more social than cultural, because both are open to the new. They are, in fact, more backward than conservative. Each path that opens and breaks the isolation of an "archaic island" attracts new contingents into the circuit of internal communication.

Given the cultural homogeneity of Brazilian society, each one of its members is just as capable of communicating with the modernized contingents as he is predisposed to accept innovations. Not tied to any peasant conservatism or to traditional values of tribal or folkloric character, they have nothing that holds them tightly bound to archaic forms of life except the social conditions that bind them to their misfortune. That attitude, receptive to change in comparison to the conservatism observed in other historical-cultural configurations, is not in itself sufficient, however, to promote renovation. The humblest family in the most remote corner of the interior sees an opportunity for freedom in the first truck to arrive. Its youngest members aspire only to become drivers, with all probably wishing to leave rather than stay, ready as they are to be incorporated into the new ways of life.

This is the fundamental result of the process of deculturation of the formative bases of the Brazilian people. Impoverished on the cultural level with regard to his European, African, and Indian ancestors, however, the ordinary Brazilian has been formed as a *homo tabula rasa,* more receptive to the innovations of progress than have been the traditionalist European peasant, the communitarian Indian, or the tribal African.

The future forms that Brazilian culture will have to assume with development will certainly lead to the reinforcement of ethnic-national unity through a greater homogenization of the ways of doing things, interacting, and thinking, but for a long time yet they will carry along local variations, less differentiated than contemporary ones because the specializing factors of the milieu are less powerful than the uniforming ones of productive technology and communication, in spite of the fact that the transforming process is operating on previously differentiated contexts. Thus we will have the possible preservation of something of the mosaic coloring that today enriches Brazil by the addition of differences in landscape and variations in uses and customs from one region to another all across the vastness of our territory.

Resistance to the innovative forces of the Industrial Revolution and the fundamental reason for the tardiness of the latter cannot be found, however, in the people or in the archaic character of their culture but lie rather in the resistance of the ruling classes. This is particularly so as regards their interests and privileges, founded on an archaic structural order, and an unfortunate method of articulation with the world economy, which act as factors for backwardness but are defended wholeheartedly against any change. This is the case of landed property, incompatible with the autonomous participation of the rural masses in modern ways of life and incapable of broadening the opportunities for adequately remunerated work being offered the population. It is also the case of the recolonizing industrialization promoted by international corporations, acting directly or in association with national capital. Even if it modernizes production and allows for the replacement of imports, it only admits the formation of an agency workforce with no other aims than for profits to be transmitted to their bosses. The latter have themselves paid extortionary prices, weighting down the product of national labor with enormous figures of profits and concessions. Its most damaging effect is sending abroad the economic excess it produces rather than applying it here. In fact, if there is any growth in profits, it takes place in foreign countries.

The most serious of these continuities lies in the contrast between the interests of the business management of yesterday and today and the interests of the Brazilian people. It has been maintained for centuries through the control of institutional power and the machinery of the state in the hands of the same ruling class, who ensure the prevalence of a social and legal order resistant to any generalizable progress for the population as a whole. It is what governed the colonial economy, highly profitable for a minority but condemning the people to poverty. It is what today deforms the very process of industrialization, hindering the development here of the transformational role this process has played in other societies. The ruling class are still the ones who, in defense of their anti-national and anti-people interests, allow the implantation of multinational enterprises by means of which post-industrial civilization goes along as nothing but a process bringing peoples who have been historical failures up to date.

Modernized in a reflexive way in spite of its being yoked to this retrograde institutionality, Brazilian society is not configured as an archaic remainder of the western civilization that gave it birth but as one of its external proletariats, conscripted to provide certain raw materials and to produce exportable profits; an atypical external proletariat with respect to historical protagonists as they are designated by A. Toynbee (1959) because it does not possess an original culture and because its own ruling class is the agent of its external domination.

Unlike what occurs in autonomous societies, the people here do not exist for themselves but for others. Formerly they were slave labor for an agro-mercantile export enterprise. Today they are the offering of a labor force seeking work and are a potential market for consumption. Both aspects of the enterprise have always been profitable, even if only for privileged minorities. As such it has maintained the state and enriched the ruling classes over the span of centuries, also benefiting merchants associated with it and the elite of landowners and local bureaucrats. The work force engaged in production as free workers can barely manage to survive and procreate, reproducing only their modest means of existence. The workers conscripted as slaves did not even reach that point because they were nothing but a source of energy that was spent to keep the system whole and to make it produce profits for others.

Nevertheless, that population made up of the descendants of the first groups drawn by the agro-mercantile export enterprise ended up taking on the character of a new national ethnicity, aspiring to autonomy, finally freeing themselves of their colonial bonds. With the first attempts at a break, many native-born masters and all Portuguese reacted with perplexity, pondering how trading establishments could be confused with nations that demanded autonomy and even aspired to becoming authentic citizenries.

When independence was declared, the local ruling class happily nationalized, preparing to profit from the autonomous regime just as they had from the colonial one. Taken over by this class, independence did not represent any decolonization of the system that would permit the transformation of the external proletariat into a people of and for itself, one which would turn to the fulfillment of its own conditions for existence and progress. It represented the transfer of political rule in the person of a Portuguese king with his seat in Lisbon to his son, with the seat now in Rio de Janeiro, from where he would negotiate national independence with the hegemonic power of the time, England. Once the legitimacy of his power was recognized externally and imposed internally, he went on to rule Brazilian society here, a nation now, against the interests of its own people.

Under those circumstances, too, the state presented more continuity than break, structured as political and administrative machinery of repression, destined to maintain the old order, operating along the same lines in the service of the old elite, which was expanded now by the noble families who had come with the monarch and by the nouveaux riches who had arisen with modernization. The people reacted almost all across the country against the narrowness of that independence, demanding the expulsion of the most visible agents of the old order, Portuguese merchants. The cruelest repression made them desist.

The monarchical state became consolidated, renewed itself, and grew over the following decades. Formerly, a few clerics and some colonial administrators, a small number of professional military men and lawyers with university degrees acquired in the mother country had been able to take care of all necessities. Now it became essential to create middle and higher institutions of learning in order to educate new generations of lettered men for the judiciary and parliament, native-born lawyers, military engineers for defense, and physicians to care for the health of the rich. Popular culture and with it most productive techniques would slowly begin to modernize. Since the creation of schools for the elites was not matched by any program for the education of the masses, the Brazilian people remained illiterate.

In spite of all, the new unifying forces did not succeed in annulling the regional differences in national society, which are the forms of adaptation that have become specialized by historical-cultural configurations. Even though they had more things in common than differences, people displayed their own methods of adaptation to nature in the productive process, particular forms of regulation of social and economic relationships, owing to the imperatives of the type of production to which they were dedicated as well as to survival of typical forms of their particular view of the world.

An understanding of each of these variants has bearing on the need to analyze simultaneously both the differentiating role of the adoptive effort and the unifying force of productive technology, two modes of association and ideological creation that conferred a heritage common to all areas (attempts at the classification of the cultural areas of Brazil can be found in Diégues Jr. 1960 and Wagley and Harris 1955). This analysis must be made both synchronically—by means of slices of the historical-cultural continuum so as to bring into focus the relationships that present themselves at a given moment among the modes of adaptation, the forms of sociability, and the world of mental representations—as well as diachronically, with deep historical investigation so as to reach a perspective in time that will permit the verification of how the techniques in use, the working relationships in force, the vision of the world, and other aspects essential to the mode of being of these variants of national society have arisen and become generalized.

Composed like a constellation of cultural areas, the historical-cultural configuration of Brazil fits the pattern of a national culture with a high degree of homogeneity. In each area for generations, millions of Brazilians have been born and have spent their entire lives finding solutions for their vital problems, motivations, and expectations that seem to them to be a natural and necessary way to express their humanity and their Brazilianness. The zones constitute essentially integral parts of a larger society, within which they interact as subcultures, relating among themselves in a different way than they would in relationships with foreigners. Their fundamental unity derives from their all being the product of the same civilizing process, which reached them almost at the same time, from having been formed by the multiplication of one single ethnic proto-cell, and from having always been under the domination of the same controlling center, none of which makes for conflicting ethnic definitions.

In fact, that common governance from the very beginning included all components and, when necessary, made use of a repressive military police force. Even so, because of isolation, specialization, or the action of other forces, some units became sufficiently differentiated to lean toward a breaking away or toward the reordering of the encompassing context, in accord with their immediate interests. As a rule those autonomist tendencies scarcely had a start, returning to unity and uniformity, either because of the pressure of repressive forces or because of the integrative role of the economic system and especially because of the basic cultural homogeneity attained at an early point.

The economic and political system that generated the same kind of stratification and civic arrangement created in each unit the same form of hierarchization, which as seen against society as a whole classified the governing groups for each variant as components of the same power structure, and it has turned them into an essentially solid body facing up to the common threat represented by the enmity of the oppressed classes. Commercial leaders, by virtue of their function as coordinators of productive activities, and the governing class, in the exercise of its role as orderer of social life, could in this way confront all dissociative tendencies and preserve national unity.

It was thus that Brazil established itself as a national society over an immense territory with millions of people: through the growth and adaptive diversification of the original unitary nucleus, along with the simultaneous establishment of local representations of the same governing group in each one of its regional variants. The care of the Portuguese and Brazilian monarchies to reward every locally won eminence with titles of nobility, and the skill of the republican system in making that socioeconomic group its governing elite, preserved at once national unity and maintenance of the system. In that way these forces voided any secessionist impulses, both from regional diversification and from crises of change in the socioeconomic formation, from slaveholding colonial to neocolonial and in the transition from colony to politically independent state.

The counterpart of that unifying task was the ordering of national society in each of its formations with strict obedience to the oligarchic interests, before which the central power itself always limped along, incapable of confronting them in spite of the flagrant discrepancy between their interests and those of the working population. This is what makes the Brazilian ruling classes so like Roman consulates as well as like the local representatives of a foreign power, colonial at first, then imperialist, whom they serve as faithful agents and from whom they derive their authoritative force, and especially like socially irresponsible consulates as regards the fate of the population, who in their eyes did not constitute a people but a workforce or, better yet, a source of usable energy for their commercial activities.

The spheres of state and private power overlap here, occasionally imposing on each other but always looking after the objective stipulations of slavery and land monopoly as the ordering principles of colonial economy. In that interaction there always prevailed the rationale of the Crown's intentional plan, a lame one, it is true, for the anarchic drive of planter, miner, and smuggler; never looking to the simple aspirations of the captive Indian, who wanted his freedom, the black slave, who asked for liberation, the sharecropper, the backlander, the poverty-stricken mixed-blood, who sought to escape oppression and subordination in order to lead a more livable life.

In like manner the conscription of a black workforce came about artificially through the establishment of the broadest and most complex mercantile operation of that era, organized to hunt down millions of blacks in Africa, ship them across the Atlantic, and sell them in Brazilian markets, where they were destined to be wasted coldly and systematically in venal production.

The very independence of Brazil, when it became inevitable, was undertaken by the colonial mother country, which transferred the most active and representative portion of the Portuguese ruling classes and its most competent bureaucrats here. Established here, this class passed for Brazilian and organized independence so well for itself that it continued to rule Brazil for eighty more years. In the course of those decades it confronted and conquered all popular uprisings, killing the leaders or giving them amnesty and incorporating them into the dominating group without resentment.

Ethnic Transfiguration

Ethnic transfiguration is the process through which peoples as cultural entities are born, transformed, and die. We have had an opportunity to study it both through direct observation and through historical reconstruction the different stages of the impact of civilization on Brazilian indigenous populations over the centuries.

An already shaped people will tenaciously resist transfiguration, but it does so precisely by changing as it takes on those alterations that make its existence viable within the context in which it is interacting. There are four basic instances of transfiguration, simultaneous or successive.

First is the biotic, through which human beings, interacting with other living forces, can become radically transfigured. This is the case for the epidemics brought by Europeans, Africans, and Asians to the untainted peoples of the Americas, upon whom an immense depopulation was visited. The germs that the foreigners carried in their bodies did not just victimize but exterminated whoever got close to them.

A second instance is the ecological one, by means of which living beings, through coexistence, affect one another in their physical shape and their vital performance. This case could be exemplified by the introduction of Europeans with their menagerie of cows, sheep, pigs, chickens, etc., in competition for vital resources with the autochthonous population, who on the one hand found their survival facilitated but on the other hand found that the outcome could prove fatal. The introduction of domestic animals in the Aztec and Inca worlds brought about a real replacement of indigenous populations through the breeding of animals.

The third stage of ethnic transfiguration is economic. This stage converts one population into a material necessity for another, resulting in the destruction of both. This is the case for personal slavery, which, tearing people out of their vital context and transforming them into a mere source of labor in the service of others, brings about tremendous human waste. Along with economic interaction we have the web of social relationships, which as they affect the methods of coexistence, community, and broadening or narrowing opportunities for reproduction have also played a deadly role. This interaction is exemplified in the United States, for example, by the agrarian laws of land ownership that produced millions of free farmers. Here, they have produced a proletariat, forcibly urbanizing millions of workers and unleashing violence and unemployment.

A last stage of transfiguration is the psychocultural one, which can decimate populations by removing from them the desire to live, as happened with indigenous peoples who let themselves die because they did not want the life being offered them. Here, too, the ethos or national pride of a population plays a capital role since, once they have been broken, it dissuades them from fighting for survival in any way they could. Social prejudice and discrimination, internalized as basic values, also play an important role in ethnicide.

In any of these instances a people can be transfigured, meaning either dying or being reborn through strategic alterations that render its survival adaptable. In the history of Brazil we have seen the Brazilindians rise up as a group with admirable vigor, both for the destruction of their maternal people as a form of expanding as well as in the appropriation of women in order to reproduce. We have seen something similar occur with blacks, who, taking refuge in the quilombo, reconstituted the life that they had learned to live in the colonial nucleus as a way to regain their dignity and make survival possible.

Foreign immigration, mainly of poor white European workers who had become too numerous for their national economies, also represented a huge threat of transfiguration for the preexisting Brazilian population, as happened in Uruguay and Argentina. In Brazil as these immigrants encountered a population already shaped and ethnically integrated, they barely affected its destiny; almost all that immigrant mass became assimilated, with the newcomers being transformed more than those who were living here. Through all these instances the Brazilian people ended up being shaped as a unique historical-cultural configuration, different from all others.

Such are the Brazilians of today at the stage they are passing through in their struggle for existence. There are practically no more Indians threatening their destiny. De-Africanized blacks have been integrated into society as a differentiated contingent but one not aspiring to any ethnic autonomy. Whites themselves are becoming ever darker and are even proud of it.

All through our five centuries of formative process, the Brazilian people have experienced successive transfigurations, yet always within the configuration of a new people, one already shaped in its larval stage as Luso-Tupi ethnic proto-cells. They have experienced the impact of two technological revolutions, the agricultural and the industrial, which have contributed more than anything else in shaping them. All transformative forces, however, were kept within limits that did not threaten the hegemonies of the ruling classes.

First was the agro-mercantile revolution, which transformed indigenous methods of production, especially through monoculture, and brought on extraordinary prosperity, giving us existence in the world picture and rendering us almost capable of doing without natural reproduction of the population as new members were purchased through slavery.

Second came the Industrial Revolution, which, rendering human muscles obsolete as a source of energy, made slavery impractical, involving society in an extremely serious transformative process in which the black population came to be reduced in absolute numbers and took decades to learn how to live a free and autonomous existence.

The introduction of mechanical devices for steam power, gasoline, and electric engines made us more efficient, not for ourselves but to do the work of providers for the world market. We exported many more goods, minerals, and other merchandise at prices that grew relatively lower, losing value because of the inequality in the economic exchange.

Subsequently, especially in the period after World War II, a huge amount of new merchandise such as medicines, plastics, the means of communication, and forms of recreation tied us even more tightly to the world. We reacted by trying to produce these goods right here in an effort at substitutive industrialization in the place of imports, but we were able to do so only through association with foreign interests, which if they did make us more efficient and modern also made us more profitable and useful for them rather than for us, even implanting an internal colonialism that brought on intense poverty in zones of long-standing occupation.

Over the course of those two steps—one lasting for three centuries, the other for almost two—Brazilian society took on diverse shapes, varying in time and space with the successive modes of adjustment to distinct external imperatives and to different regional economic and ecological conditions. In the first case, it ground up and blended the original indigenous, black, and European bases into a new ethnic entity through the evolutionary routes of modernization or historical incorporation, which was the common path of formation for the new peoples of the Americas.

In the second step, the society that resulted from that long formative process was once more transformed by modernization. Now, in order to incorporate themselves into a neocolonial version of industrial civilization, the contingents that had been homogenized by the deculturation they had earlier passed through under the pressure of slavery had to be readjusted to a new sociopolitical order. It was still ruled by a power structure able to continue the conscription of the population for work through a wage-labor regime, through unproductive enterprises for export articles and in new ones established to take care of the domestic market. That reincorporation of Brazil into the network of the world market, although less traumatic, also called for a certain degree of violence, especially in the repression of popular uprisings that aspired to a profound social reordering and in the preventive control of latent insurgent groups.

The distinctive character of our ethnic transfiguration involves the continuity over the centuries of crucial elements of the archaic social order, the dependence of the economy, and the spurious nature of the old-order culture. That continuity, maintained through both types of modernization and their corresponding socioeconomic formations, caused serious constrictions in development.

Thus the impact of industrialization, operating on archaic structural forms, found itself held back in its capacity for transformation. The system that had prevailed for the conscription of labor—first slavery, then wages—continued to operate under the new conditions as a net that deformed economic growth within industrial capitalism and slowed the integration of the people into the lifestyles of the new civilization. Its most important transformation was moving from a low-energy technological system, one highly demanding of human labor and wasteful of the same, to a system utilizing mechanized technology served by engines and less and less able to absorb the available work force, tending therefore to marginalize it.

Consequently, the Brazilian economy, which has always been famished for labor, today sees its population becoming more than is needed for production. It is the Brazilian worker who is becoming obsolete as an expendable force in the national economy.

We are living today on the eve of even more comprehensive transformations because on the horizon another technological revolution even more radical than the previous ones is rising. If we allow ourselves once again to remain consumers of its fruits instead of masters of its new technology, the threats to our survival and national sovereignty will be even more intense. The ruling classes and their spokespersons have already laid out their plans for continuity through strategic transformations. This is the neoliberal and privatist argument, unanimously defended and propagated by all media and strongly supported by all the forces of the right.

On the cultural level, the two formative periods comprised respectively a colonial culture that flourished and became archaic and a renovated culture that arose through modernization. Traditional Brazilian culture, which gave life to colonial nuclei, was already a culture of a civilization that, corresponding to an urban and stratified social formation, opened up into one sphere that was erudite and one that was popular, with rural and urban variants.

The ruling group, made up of commercial leaders and an elite of clerics, bureaucrats, and military men, all of them urban, was one of the constitutive elements of society, but it operated as a different group on the cultural level, both in the popular culture of the city and in that of the country. As they participated in popular amusements, members of the ruling group did so more as patrons than as part of the functional community following popular beliefs. In truth, that class of the masters was a closed circle of Eurocentric life that followed fashion more than the actual values taken up by metropolitan centers, a circle in which for better or for worse, they became heirs to the literature, music, plastic and graphic arts, and other erudite forms of expression of a culture that, in spite of being someone else's, would come to be their own.

This whole process is worsening, driven in our times by the prodigious power of the culture industry, which through radio, movies, television, and countless other means of cultural communication threatens to make traditional Brazilian culture even more obsolete, imposing on us the mass cultural goods and the accompanying behavior that dominate the whole world. We, who have always been creative in popular arts and everything within reach of the masses, see ourselves more threatened today than ever before by the loss of that creativity and the acquisition of a universalization of dubious quality.

Traditional Brazilian culture being predominant, however, this is what is expressed in our technologically most advanced sectors of production, in the architecture of baronial houses, fortifications, and churches as well as in the art that decorated them. All of them were built in a stylized way as overseas implantations of European civilization, in conformity with the prevailing styles there and only incidentally infused with local elements. There is, to be sure, a Brazilian reaction on the erudite level. It is not any kind of nativism, however. Its creations are human conquests that could have arisen anywhere but fortunately flourished here, in the building of Brasília, the architecture of Oscar Niemeyer, the music of Villa-Lobos, the painting of Portinári, the poetry of Drummond, and the novels of Guimarães Rosa and some others.

Popular culture, based on the folk wisdom of oral transmission, even though divided into rural and urban components, was unified by a common body of understandings, values, and traditions in which everyone shared and which were expressed in folklore, beliefs, crafts, customs, and the institutions that regulated daily contact and work.

Even high culture, influenced as it was by foreign ideas, values, and forms of expression, seemed modern in contrast to old-world cultural forms. That rational modernity marked broad sectors of the urban population, differentiating them from more conservative rural attitudes. But those differentiations along rural and urban lines, archaic and modern, do not negate the spurious character of all erudite and popular culture that corresponds to our being a tropical overseas incarnation of western civilization. Every creative gesture of ours, once sketched out, is condemned to fall into that redoubt, which is the universe to which we belong. It is a matter of a challenge, however, one that involves all creative artists, one that is not a search for the singular or the bizarre but an effort to be the best in the world.

Some of the new transfigurative elements serve as the basis for grand hopes. First of all we have the access of all the people to literate civilization and to the new worldwide systems of cultural intercommunication. This means that from now on, popular creativity will not take place exclusively on the level of soccer, music, and other values and traditions transmitted orally by the population. Second, because of the revolution of "the pill" and orgasmic liberation, the position of women in society has been radically changed; they are still called upon to continue working as they have always done but under better conditions of existence.

The fundamental part, however, is that miraculously, the people, especially the black masses, continue to have eruptions of creativity. This is the case with the worship of Iemanjá, which has been completely transformed over a few years. That black entity, who is worshiped on February 2 in Bahia and March 8 in São Paulo, is carried in procession by the blacks of Rio de Janeiro on December 31. With that happening we have retired ridiculous old Santa Claus, bearded and eating dried European fruits, dragged along in a sleigh pulled by reindeer. In his place arises the first saint since Greece who has sex. One does not go to Iemanjá seeking a cure for cancer or AIDS; one asks for an affectionate lover and for a husband not to beat one so much.

Driven by all those transformative pressures, traditional popular Brazilian culture, having become archaic, is being transfigured into new patterns. These, even though corresponding to the common "western" pattern of post-industrial societies, take on in Brazil peculiar qualities that relate to the specificity of the national historical process. Since these vary by regions, cultural areas operate as structures of resistance to change in an effort to preserve their characteristics, but they can maintain their older traditions only where the predominant cultural profile has become obsolete in the face of the new prevailing economy.

Nevertheless, forced by the new uniformatizing conditions, old cultural areas are becoming more and more homogeneous through the imperative of the general process of industrialization that affects everyone and as a result of the drive toward uniformity by the systems of mass communication, which take the gaúcho of the south and the Amazonian of mixed blood and make them interact reciprocally and be connected to the dynamic centers of the process of industrialization.

This means that despite all, we are a province of western civilization: a new Rome, an active center of neo-Latin civilization, better than the others because bathed in black and Indian blood, a people whose role from here on will be less a matter of absorbing European things than of teaching the world how to live with more joy and more happiness.

IV

Brazilians in History

12

Brazils

After putting together a whole vast theory of history, which I am conclud-
ing with this book, I must confess that the grand historical sequences,
unique and unrepeatable, remain beyond explanation.

What we have arrived at are a few valid generalizations brought out
here and there to shed some light on passages. The search for these generalizations is irresistible as an intellectual adventure, however. It is also
indispensable because no people can live without a theory of themselves.
If they do not have an anthropology to provide it, they improvise it and
disseminate it through folklore.

History, if the truth be told, takes place on the local scene as events that
the people remember and explain in their own way. It is there within the
realm of beliefs held in common and the abrupt rise of collective wills that
things happen. This is why instead of a general picture of Brazilian history
we have put together these regional scenarios.

Copious historical documentation shows that a few decades after the
invasion, a neo-Brazilian ethnic proto-cell that differed as much from the
Portuguese as it did from the indigenous one had taken shape in Brazil.
That embryonic ethnicity, multiplied and spreading as different nuclei—
first along the Atlantic coast and then moving into the interior backlands
or going up tributaries of the great rivers—was what would shape the
social and cultural life of these islands—Brazil. Each one of them was
made singular by its adjustment to local conditions, both ecological and
those governing the type of production, but they always remained genetic
sprouts from the same root.

These islands that make up Brazil worked as agglutinating and acculturating nuclei for the new contingents captured in the new land, those
brought from Africa, or those coming from Portugal and elsewhere, lending uniformity and continuity to the process of ethnic gestation, the fruit
of which has been the basic sociocultural unity of all Brazilians.

I believe that one can distinguish the existence of this neo-Brazilian cultural cell, differentiated and autonomous in its process of development, beginning in the middle of the sixteenth century when the first sugar plantations were established, while commerce was still dominated by dyewood and still a matter of impressing the Indian as a slave for the agro-export sector. It was the destiny and the work of the Brazilindian mamelucos, who—not being Indians or Europeans or anything—were in search of themselves as a new people still in its larval state.

This was a people gestated in the communities made up of Indians torn from their villages to live among the Portuguese and those of mixed blood as settlements began to multiply along the coasts of Pernambuco, Bahia, Rio de Janeiro, and São Paulo, a people with a base in common paternity, even during the time of barter with Indians who remained in their independent villages. The pioneer nuclei quickly evolved to the status of trading-post communities as they began to integrate captured Indians too, structured around a nucleus of mamelucos and functioning as the operational bases of whites who served as ship suppliers, establishing their own relationships of alliance or war with neighboring tribes. Even though imbued with indigenous culture, speaking only the language of the land and structured along semitribal lines, they were still governed by principles of organization that came from Europe. In this way they constituted in fact mutant offshoots of what had come to be an urban and literate civilization.

Out of these communities would come the constitutive groups of all Brazilian sociocultural areas, from the old sugar-producing zones of the coast and the cattle-breeding stations of the interior to the mining nuclei of the center of the country, rubber extractors in the Amazon region, and herders in the extreme south. Covering thousands of miles, that expansion—sometimes slow and scattered, like that of the herders, yet at other times intense and concentrated, as in the mining operations—was multiplying essentially uniform bases across all future Brazilian territory. In spite of seeming so insignificant, that expansion in fact spread like an epidemic, contaminating the surrounding Indians, unmaking them to remake them as islands of civilization. Only much later did they begin to communicate regularly with one another across the immense deserted spaces that separated them.

Across that archipelago, integrating it in a societal way, three connective networks stretched: ethnic identity, which, not being Indian any longer, was becoming proto-Brazilian; the colonial socioeconomic structure, mercantile in character, which linked them to each other by sea and to the Old World as suppliers of dyewood; and a new productive technology that was making them more complex and more dependent on imported articles. Above all that floated an incipient erudite culture, mainly religious, spreading out as a basic model. Just like the Indian Uirá, who went out in search of God and in order to identify himself before the divinity declared: "I am of your people, the ones who eat manioc flour," all we Brazilians could say the same: "We are your people, the ones who eat manioc flour."

Brazilians' ethnic identity can be explained both by the constitutive precociousness of that essential base of our traditional culture and by its vigor and flexibility. This last characteristic will allow it, as heir to the age-old adaptive wisdom of the Indians, to conform still to local adjustments, to all regional ecological variants, and to survive all successive cycles of production, conserving its essential unity. Beginning with those proto-cells and through a process of adaptation and differentiation that has endured over four centuries, the main variants of traditional Brazilian culture have arisen (cf. concepts of rustic culture and backwoods culture in Melo e Souza 1964; rural and folk culture in Redfield 1941 and 1963; caboclo culture in Willems 1947; and creole culture in Gillin 1947).

They are represented by the creole culture, which developed in the communities along the strip of fresh and fertile soil of the Northeast, having the sugar plantation as a fundamental coordinating institution; by the backwoods culture of the areas occupied by the São Paulo mamelucos, first through the activities of hunting down Indians for sale, then by mining for gold and diamonds, and later by large coffee plantations and industrialization; by the backland culture of the sertão, which was based on cattle stations and spread out from the arid Northeast down to the scrublands of the central west; by the caboclo culture of the Amazon populations engaged in the gathering of jungle plants, principally rubber; by the gaúcho culture of livestock herding on the southern plains and its two variants, the Azorean-rural (very similar to the caipira-rustic) and the gringo-rustic-caipira in areas colonized by immigrants, predominantly German and Italian.

In terms of socioeconomic formation, it could be said that these faces of rural Brazil took shape as exogenous products of European expansion. Thus, rural and urban economics, founded on slavery and commerce, respectively, fostered antagonistic, if functionally integrated, social strata. Their driving force was the civilizing process unleashed by the mercantile revolution, which permitted the Iberian peoples to expand overseas and create the first economy of worldwide scope.

Brazil, as a product of that process, developed as the subproduct of an exogenous undertaking of agrarian-mercantile character, which—bringing together and founding the most disparate bases here—gave birth to an ethnic configuration of a new people and structured it as a colonial slaveholding dependency of the mercantile-salvationist formation of the Iberian peoples.

As can be seen, it was not a question of an autonomous unfolding produced at the start of the evolutionary period in which the Indians lived (agricultural revolution) or a question of the type of formation into which it was structured (undifferentiated agricultural villages; this is, not stratified into classes). It was a question of their breakup and transfiguration by way of the historical modernization brought about by a macroethnicity in expansion: the Portuguese mercantile-salvationist one (Ribeiro 1968).

It is simply amazing that those nuclei, so alike and so different, have kept themselves linked in a single nation. During the colonial period each one had direct relations with the mother country and "the natural thing," as occurred in Spanish America, would have been their attaining independence as autonomous communities. But history is capricious and the natural thing did not occur. The extraordinary thing occurred; we made ourselves a nation-people, taking in all those ecological provinces as one single civic and political entity.

Creole Brazil

Being master of a plantation is a title that many aspire to because it carries with it the service, obedience, and respect of many people. And if he is, as he should be, a man of wealth and power, it can well be in Brazil that being master of a plantation is esteemed in the same degree as titles are among the nobility of the Mother Country. (Andreoni 1967)

The sugar plantation, the first form of large agro-industrial export enterprise, was for a time the instrument of viability for the Portuguese colonial undertaking and the basis of the first manner of being Brazilian. Without it, during that period, European occupation of a vast tropical area with no mineral wealth to be found, inhabited by natives who had barely managed to construct agricultural cultures and who did not constitute a workforce that could easily be disciplined and exploited, would have been unimaginable.

Fortunately, sugarcane needed only fertile and fresh tropical soil, and the mill that extracted the mercantile product from the cane juice was a press made of wood and iron, which Portuguese ship's carpenters, the builders of vessels, could easily make. On being transplanted to Brazilian areas, the canefields and mills multiplied in just a few decades, having as their only limits to expansion the availability of a slave labor force in the fields and the breadth of a European consumer market.

The Portuguese, who had already experimented with cane growing on a small scale, using Arab technology on the islands of Madeira and the Azores, were quickly able to expand that production astronomically in the new lands, creating for that purpose a vast system for the recruitment of labor.

No one could have imagined then that an exotic and precious product, destined for consumption by the wealthiest, would increase in production and have its price lowered to the point of becoming accessible to the ordinary consumer as an item of daily use. This was what happened as sugar ceased to be a spice and became an ordinary commercial product. Even so, the figures for its cost and its sale were sufficiently attractive to pay for the expenses of production and the trans-Atlantic transport of the sugar itself and for the overseas transport in the opposite direction of the African slaves who would produce it.

The first sugar plantations appeared in Brazil in 1520 and quickly spread out all along the coast inhabited by the Portuguese. They ended up being concentrated on the fertile black massapé soil of the Northeast and along the shores of the bay in Bahia, laying the bases for a sugar civilization, the urban expression of which flourished in the port cities of Olinda-Recife in Pernambuco and Salvador in Bahia.

A half century later the plantations had multiplied to such a degree that Brazilian sugar production was the principal merchandise of international commerce and its annual harvest was worth more than the exportable product of any European country. In the decades that followed, in spite of war, the resistance of the blacks in Palmares, and the Dutch occupation, the sugar economy and its complements grew even more. The great plantations went from 50 to 100 and to 200. Coming to work them were 10,000, then 20,000, and later 30,000 imported slaves. The volume and value of sugar production grew reciprocally every year until it reached and far outstripped a million pounds sterling.

Around 1650 that increase slowed down and the sugar economy went into crisis with the massive entry into international commerce of production from Dutch plantations in the Antilles. In spite of this, Brazilian production continued to sustain the colonial settlement in the oldest region of occupation. Only much later, after 1700, with the beginning of the gold cycle, did it cease to be the most dynamic sector of revenue for the Crown.

Brazilian society in its creole cultural makeup came into existence around the complex formed by the sugar economy and its commercial and financial ramifications, with all the agricultural and craft complements that made its operation possible. The human mass, organized as a function of the sugar economy, was structured in a socioeconomic formation that was atypical by comparison with American and European ones of the time. It was much simpler, on the one hand, because of its nature as a colonial enterprise destined to fulfill clearly sought economic-mercantile proposals. In it the form of existence, the organization of the family, the power structure were not historical creations with origins in an old tradition but merely the results of options exercised in order to bring efficiency to the undertaking. On the other hand, however, it was much more complex: a population that had arisen out of the racial fusion of whites, Indians, and blacks as a syncretic culture shaped by integration of the most disparate bases and as an agro-industrial economy was being injected into nascent world commerce.

We label as creole cultural areas the historical-cultural configuration that resulted from the implantation of the sugar economy and its complements and satellites on the coastal band of the Brazilian Northeast that extends from Rio Grande do Norte to Bahia. Among its complements are the manufacture of liquor and raw brown sugar blocks, which were the main product of small plantations and destined for the internal market. Among its connections were outstanding commercial tobacco fields and their products, to which small producers without the capital to set up a plantation turned their efforts, but the export value of which came to be onetenth of the value of the sugar harvest. Very much later other agricultural products for export, like cacao, would be added to the first, permitting the spread to other regions of the way of life and work created around the sugar plantation, widening the creole cultural area in that way.

Once formed as a viable form of coexistence, the basic social polarity of the sugar economy—the plantation master and the slave—would constitute a structural base that, adapted to differing productive sectors, would make possible the building of traditional Brazilian society. The plantation owner, in spite of his role as agent for the external exploitation of the population placed under his rule, was still a native entrepreneur. He lived in his great house, built to last and to be passed on to his heirs. In communion with the people of the land he became Brazilian in his habits. He built for himself a domain totally different from any in existence, including those of the few Portuguese who received like incomes.

The slave, Indian or black, who survived the harsh work on the plantation was also being Brazilianized with the same rhythm and just as profoundly. Although poles apart, slave and master had in the end more in common in the language they spoke and their view of the world than slaves shared with their ancestral Brazilian or African tribes. As slaves, however, they constituted the only force in opposition to the system, which, by exercising a constant subversive action, called for permanent reaction by a repressive apparatus. But, incapable of destroying the system — whether to restore archaic forms of existence no longer viable or to implant a precocious socioeconomic formation of greater solidarity — slaves coexisted with it in conflict, reproducing themselves just as they were. Blacks, even when fleeing the plantations to take refuge in the quilombos, continued in a symbiotic relationship with the society with which they were at war, one in which they had been shaped and on which they depended to provide them with the elements that had become indispensable for their existence, such as tools, salt, and gunpowder.

Even though slaves and masters were, in fact, two forms in polar opposition on the social level because of the essential antagonism of their class interests, they were also two mutually complementary alternates within the unequal mutuality of a colonial slaveholding formation. They were still essentially two variant expressions of a culture formed within the canons of European civilization. That unity within diversity compelled the slaveholding culture to generate, through the dynamic of its reciprocal action, new forms of the organization of social life, which simultaneously reaffirmed the all-powerful lordly position of the owner of slaves, who were worth more to him than the whole spread of his property, who exercised many arms and mouths all destined to make that rural factory work, probably the most complex enterprise of the period. The newly arrived black was the brute force for work, brought to the canefield to work from sunup to sundown and oriented by Brazilian blacks specialized in that task.

The patriarchal family of the master, his children, and his closest relatives occupied so exclusively the functions of that Roman-type home that it left no space for any other worthy forms of mating. The master himself and his sons were, in fact, free breeders, there to make pregnant anyone they could. There was no possibility in that environment for blacks and people of mixed blood to have any chance at all of structuring themselves along family lines.

The history of Brazil is, therefore, the history of that original polarity and the ones that succeeded it. It is the one that gave birth to the first civilization of world extension, linking America as a settlement, Africa as the provider of the workforce, and Europe as the privileged consumer and main partner in the business.

Among European peoples the Portuguese were the most competent at implanting an economic system that was not merely extractive or based solely upon pillaging the wealth in American tropical areas. They alone had had any real experience in dealing with slave labor and producing sugar. Only by following in their footsteps and applying Portuguese pioneering experience did other nations also later take up undertakings based on the plantation system (Steward 1960), both in the New World and on other continents.

The Dutch and the French were the most successful in carrying the Portuguese experience forward. Holland was made over, armed, and equipped to defend itself starting out from its tiny territory and using capital acquired in the Antilles. Haiti was the main pearl in the French crown. It was there that the noblemen who built their chateaux along the Loire got their start, forgetting the blacks who had been the fertilizer for all that great aristocracy.

Applied first to sugar and developed there as a structural model, the slave plantation system would subsequently be used for tobacco, indigo, and cacao; for coffee later; and more recently for cultivation of bananas, pineapples, tea, rubber, sisal, jute, and soybeans, these last already under a system of wages.

The Portuguese had become capable at that task thanks to a previous knowledge of the techniques for growing cane, making molasses, and refining sugar, which as noted they had produced on their Atlantic islands before the discovery based on African slave labor and with a new formula for organizing production: the plantation. It was from there that the specialists who built the first Brazilian sugar mills, both technologically and societally speaking, would come, sowing a seed that as it multiplied would give birth to the Brazilian economy as it has taken shape. They had also been prepared for that role by having participated in the European spice trade, sugar being considered a spice, alongside Dutch investors who were mostly Jewish. No less important were their mastery of the techniques of transoceanic navigation and possession of one of the largest commercial fleets of the period. To all this could be added the existence of available financial backing—their own as well as that of Italians, Dutch, Germans, and others, to pay for the new undertaking with an eye on the monetary return it would bring—along with the entrepreneurial spirit that stimulated certain sectors of the Portuguese ruling class.

The Moorish and mixed-blood character of the Iberian peoples also doubtless played an important role. The fact is that as a result of long Arab domination, the Portuguese had made themselves heirs to the Arab technical culture, basically involving navigation, sugar production, and the incorporation of black slaves into the workforce. The Portuguese of the sixteenth century, being in fact Euro-African on the cultural and racial level, were accustomed to living with darker peoples and were more prepared than any others to take in indigenous Americans for sporadic labor as well as to bring in multitudes of black workers who would make the productive plantation system practicable.

From the very start, that system was established by a combination of the monetary interests of the merchants who financed the operation, the entrepreneurs who took direct charge of production, and the Crown, which guaranteed monopoly of the commercial venture as it took for itself along the way the greater share of the profits. Based on all those elements, Brazil took shape as a colonial slaveholding formation, agro-mercantile in character and endowed with enormous potential, which would contribute amply over the ensuing centuries to the building of an economic system extending worldwide and which would go on to organize the lives of millions of people on all continents. In the plantation system there was already a foretaste of the bold capitalist venture that, by breaking up archaic societal units no matter what form they might have had, would engage their members in productive enterprises, either by forced enslavement or "freely" as proletarians.

Sugar production was characterized essentially by the great extension of areas under cane cultivation and by the complexity of the chemical-industrial processing for the making of sugar. It called for the participation of specialized workers and a large concentration of laborers, both groups living on the plantation and completely involved in production and under a rigid work discipline. It was also characterized by the mercantile nature of the undertaking, which attended to the concerns of the external market with the aim of making a profit. All these attributes gave sugar production the character of an agro-industrial undertaking requiring large investments of capital and made it look more like a factory than a traditional agrarian operation, because of the industrial procedures it required and the problems that the management of labor implied.

In the old primitive *banque* mills, one could already find basic struc-

tural elements of the plantation system that would exercise a decisive influence in the deculturation of black slaves and Indians involved in their
work, in the pattern of social relations, in the formation of the family, and
in the whole configuration of Brazilian culture in its local form.

Antonil (João Antônio Andreoni), an Italian Jesuit, left us in 1711 an
excellent picture of the plantations of Bahia that he had visited and judiciously described (Andreoni 1967). Other similar significant testimonials
are those of Gabriel Soares de Sousa for the sixteenth century and of Luís
dos Santos Vilhena for the end of the eighteenth (Sousa 1971; Vilhena
1969). The land, depending on its character, was destined for canefields,
where the greatest number of workers were concentrated, as pasture for
oxen, which in number equaled the slaves, and as plots for the cultivation
of food, mainly cassava and corn. Some land had to be left in virgin timber,
however, in order to provide all the firewood for the mill and, if possible,
also quality wood for buildings. When land came to be in short supply,
neighboring areas would be rented from farmers for the cultivation of
sugarcane, which they would be obliged to turn over to the plantation, or
for the growing of food.

The mill, strictly speaking, comprised various sturdy buildings provided with their respective equipment. The great house, the residence of
the master of the plantation, sometimes attained the grandeur of a baronial mansion, with towers and chapels. The *senzala,* or slave quarters,
where dozens of slaves were housed, was generally in the form of a vast
shed with a thatch roof. The grinding mill, built from large hardwood
timbers and with grinders run by water or animal power, had to be sufficiently large to grind between twenty and thirty cartloads of cane every
day; the cane juice ran out of the grinders into five or six boilers, under
which cord after cord of wood was burned. The weighing table was where
the molasses from the boilers was spread so as to be converted into white
and brown sugar.

The operation of the mill, which produced between 700 and 800 tons
each year on large plantations, called for dozens of field slaves for hoeing
and cutting as well as for carters to carry cane and firewood to the mill and
a large number of black men and women for the work of grinding and the
purifying of the sugar. In addition to this workforce the plantation needed
"a sugar master, a stoker and a substoker, a purger, one bookkeeper on the
plantation and another in town, overseers in the fields and gardens, and a
chief overseer for the whole plantation. And each one of these operators
was paid a salary" (Andreoni 1967, 139). If we add to these specialized
workers the craftsmen indispensable for the functioning of the plantation,

such as brickmakers and carpenters, house slaves and those needed for carts and boats, caulkers, cowhands, and kitchen slaves, one can imagine the breadth and complexity of the workforce that made the sugar agro-industry function.

The plantation system as an organized endeavor is in contrast to both the Spanish American *encomienda* and rural villages with a system of small farms. First in significance in the plantation is the direct and total subordination of the whole population to the single authority of the land-owner, who is also the owner of the houses, installations, animals, people, everything, all under his absolute discretion. That autocratic centraliza-tion along with a strictly mercantile outlook—which led him to treat the people gathered on the plantation, the slaves above all, as simple instru-ments for gain—allowed him to exert pressure for conformity in customs and allowed the imposition of a deculturation greater than in any other system of production. From this the plantation derives its extraordinary acculturative and assimilative efficacy as compared to the encomienda, which always presupposes a certain modus vivendi with the preexisting community, handled by intermediaries, co-participants in two opposite cultural worlds. Enormous, too, is the contrast with herding enterprises, because in these, riders and poor field hands preserved a certain degree of autonomy and spirit, which obliged the landowner to look upon them as people. The contrast reaches extremes when one compares the plantation to rural villages or free farms. These were family groups who existed for themselves, whose activities were mercantile only in a secondary way be-cause their aim was essentially that of fulfilling their own conditions of existence.

The official character of the sugar enterprise—instituted and stimu-lated by the Crown through the concession of land grants and the contri-bution of privileges, honors, and titles—gave the plantation masters a hegemonic power in the established order of colonial life, and it was quite natural that it should be so in view of the economic success of the enter-prise, which made for high profits for the homeland as well as taking excellent care of the occupation of the recently discovered lands, poor in gold, and protecting them against the greed of other nations. Any means put forward in the defense of those interests was weighty and had the greatest possibility of redress.

Thus the power of the plantation owner within his own domains ex-tended over the whole society. Placed in that dominating position, he gained an authority that the nobility itself had never held in the kingdom. Bowing before him submissively were the clergy and the administration from the mother country, all integrated into a single system that governed the economic, political, religious, and moral order. In that sense the system constituted an oligarchy that operated at the governing summit of the power structure of colonial society. Before it only the dependent group of shipowners and merchants who exported sugar and imported slaves—who were also the ones financing the plantation owners—held a certain degree of favor, and there no antagonisms because their disputes were much less relevant than their complementary positions.

The congruity of that all-encompassing structure reinforced the power and the discipline of the plantation, leaving no conditions whatever for revolt or for the expression of demands that might be in opposition to it. On his domains the plantation owner was master and father, upon whose will and benevolence all depended, for there was no authority, political or religious, in existence that was not influenced by him. His family, residing on the plantation, the upholders of Christian virtues, stood as an ideal model of family organization, naturally untouchable by anyone else, even if its stability rested on free access to local women.

Alongside the great house, in contrast to its ostentatious comfort, were the slave quarters or senzala, made up of shacks where the slaves lived a subhuman existence, looked upon only as slaves. The great house, along with the figures of the master, the mistress, the young mistresses, and their personal slave girls or *mucamas,* have received lyrical and nostalgic description in an anthropology always viewing the plantation through the eyes of the owner. We as yet have no trustworthy perspective on the poor whites and free mulattos employed as servants, peddlers, and technicians, nor on the subworld of the field slaves, much less any with adequate interpretation.

The fundamental characteristics of sugar production are extensive land holdings, intensive monoculture, a large local concentration of labor with internal diversification into distinct specializations, a high relative cost of financial investment, and the outside destination of the product; dependence on the importation of slave labor, which cost 70 percent of the profits from export; and the rational and planned character of the operation, which demanded in addition techno-agricultural and industrial conditions of production and an integrated commercial administration with appropriate conditions for commercialization, financial procedures, and fiscal matters.

Some of these characteristics have led many scholars to label it sometimes as slavist and at other times as feudal. If we take into consideration the crucial economic characteristics that make it a commercial undertaking with the aim of producing financial profits, however, it becomes obvious that its nature is that of a mercantile venture. The colonial situation of that venture and the slave makeup of the relationships for production oblige us, however, to characterize it as the slaveholding colonial counterpart of a mercantile-salvationist and socioeconomic formation as shown in the governing metropolitan center (on technological revolutions and respective socioeconomic formations see Ribeiro 1968). In that type of bipartite but operatively integrated formation, one finds the specific form of incorporation for Brazilian society in the nascent economic capitalist system of global extent that was responsible both for the advances the formation presented and for the backwardness and penury it represented. The system as a whole had in its formal contents precisely the most backward and the most modern instruments—slavery and production for the market—of a broadened reimplantation of an economic system of original capitalist accumulation through financial investment and involvement in the international market.

The productive system of the plantation is a characteristic product of the mercantile revolution during the period, which allowed European societies to organize a worldwide economic system. It was not based on the "natural" peasant economy of the European feudal model but on the formation of a new type of agricultural one, concentrated in populous nuclei and run by a centralized system, participating in a more complex mercantile economy and divided into technical and functional specialties.

Compared to the farmer who cultivated his plot with the help of his whole family and carried his harvest to market, the plantation worker was a participant in a productive group, depersonalized, individually linked to the demands of the activities of production, the same as the salaried worker engaged in European manufacturing and, later, the factory worker. The rural worker, integrated into the economic system as a sharecropper on someone else's land—which he brings to life with his work over generations, undertaking complete tasks, from seeding to harvest—aspired basically to the possession of that land, to becoming a farmer and an owner. The plantation worker, on the contrary, employed and under the discipline of a larger, impersonally directed productive unit, of which he is only a tiny part and entrusted with partial and incomplete tasks, aspired to the improvement of his working conditions and a better pattern of life more than to ownership of land. When free, his attitude was closer to the position of a wage earner than that of the sharecropper, more like a factory worker than a peasant.

Because of all that, the plantation productive system cannot be reduced to the nonmercantile system of European feudalism, the shaper of medieval peasant life, or to the modern system of farming. It constituted a new system that must be understood on its own terms. It was an agrarian-mercantile system of slaveholding colonization formed as an integrated combination of centralized relations with an objective of monocultural export production.

In order to attain that objective, the plantation set off a tract of land from nature through the legal institution of land grants, establishing a domain there. Within that possessed space it formed an established system of production through the bringing together of labor, not with an objective of giving life to and procreating a human community in the new settlement but to become organized for the production of export goods. The community thus formed would attend to other tasks, such as biological reproduction, the maintenance of strength for working, and the construction and repair of the instruments of production, but always and implacably keeping in sight its single objective: the production of what was not consumed, so as to take care of external demands. It generated, thus, an authoritarian internal order based on a most rigorous work discipline and at the same time demanding awareness in all those engaged in it. Its methods of action on nature, its forms of organization of interpersonal relations, its vision of the world represented a combination of elements taken from the cultural heritage of each formative group, chosen for their greatest capacity in contributing to the objectives of production or for their capacity to adjust to these.

Under those circumstances it is in the world of the plantation that the fundamental nucleus of the cultural area we have designated as creole took shape. Those who were born in that world or entered it were compelled to become integrated in it as the only way in which they could become members of that society and become human beings in the form prescribed by the needs of production. Creole culture is, therefore, the expression in conduct and customs of the imperatives of the monocultural economy dedicated to the production of sugar.

It had its roots deep in indigenous, African, and European bases from which it chose its circumstantial ingredients, but it placed itself in opposition to them as a new style of life, the constituents of which would look at the world, deal with one another, and act upon their milieu in a completely different way. The plantation owner, his employees, and his slaves, each on his own level, defined by a rigid hierarchy, were transfigurations produced by that new culture, integrated in it with distinct but complementary roles, which together worked to produce and reproduce it, always identical to itself. There emerged in this way a socioeconomic structure completely different from the feudal one, even though archaic and precapitalist. But it took shape not by the plunge of a former imperial area into a feudal nonmercantile regression, as had occurred in Europe, but by an implantation deriving from decisive acts and with a view toward a well-defined project of its own. Once instituted, that project would operate as a new structural model, capable of multiplying the mercantile exploitation of new lands: slaveholding colonialism.

The lordliness of the sugar bosses recalls in many ways that of the feudal aristocracy because of the equivalent powers held over the population who lived on their domains, by the exercise of judicial powers, and by the personal centralization of rule. The two forms become opposite, however, when one remembers that the feudal lord governed a population turned mostly to the fulfillment of its own conditions for survival. The feudal aristocracy fulfilled those conditions essentially by ensuring people's self-sufficiency, because it lived off its broad estates and because its occupation of them is what allowed it to exercise its highest function, which was the military leadership of men recruited on its own fiefs. Its feudal rights, based first on conquest but later consolidated through primogeniture, gave the system stability and assured it a means of life but not of enrichment, because it was important to the aristocracy not to enter into mercantile competition except to avoid conflicts; hence their cultivation of a haughty attitude of a lack of interest in things pecuniary.

Only with the breakup of European feudalism and the restoration of the mercantile network did feudal lords begin to become interested in the economic management of their holdings in terms of capitalist production. But then peasants rebelled against the meddling in their lives and for the right to commercialize themselves and their harvests as owners of their own tracts.

The plantation master, on the contrary, appeared then as the owner of a business that included the land, the installations, and the people of his domain, exercising his command in order to lead them in an exogenous economic activity. He assumed, therefore, a mercantile attitude toward people, especially slaves, less people in his eyes than instruments, efficient or not, profitable or wasteful, for business. In that way he developed a sharp pecuniary sense for change in order to make a profit and get richer; the alternative was to lose it in competition with other autonomous producers in disputes with those involved in the sale of the product and by subjection to complex financial and fiscal systems that exploited it.

The essential difference between the two systems, however, lies in the role and function of the population involved: in the first case, to survive in accordance with one's conception of life; in the second, to produce profits as if in a modern factory and to be integrated into the conditions of life imposed on a subaltern group of a colonial society.

In their later development the feudal system and the plantation system generated entirely different socioeconomic complexes. The first, breaking up as the commercial sector outside it grew, gave way to a free co-participatory peasantry in the nascent capitalist system through ownership of their plots. The second, which evolved along with the slaveholding colonial system that generated it, passed from slavery, which was its most obsolete ingredient, to capitalist forms of workforce effectiveness, with the matter of land distribution never coming to the fore as a crucial point but, on the contrary, always tending toward the concentration of property, the preservation of the entrepreneurial holdings, and a greater strengthening of its character as a commercial and industrial entity.

By the same path the system also preserved its most negative characteristic, that of shaping the economy according to outside demands, which led it not to serve those engaged in it as the workforce but to enrich the owner and to supply the world market. Even after the decline into which sugar production has fallen in the old areas, the plantation continues to represent a good business for those in the position of owner. Its essential failure, as we shall see, lay in its incapacity for opening perspectives for the integration of its working masses into a consumer economy, one capable of giving them a more decent pattern of life.

Playing a relevant role in the formation of this basic nucleus of creole culture was the fact that the plantation master or mill owner resided on the plantation. This would have bearing in lending the world of the sugar plantation another dimension not merely productive and which aimed to provide the proprietary family the comforts and pleasures that their position and wealth allowed them to enjoy. That dimension is what produced the great house on the plantation, with its ample space, its elegant furnishings, its articles for comfort, its "civilization." And it set apart the field slaves—flung into the senzala and worn down like beasts of burden— from the circle of personal maids and household servants chosen from among the black men and women with the most pleasing looks, born on the plantation, to wait on the master's family.

The familial character of the sugar enterprise would lend continuity to that relationship, with generations of masters and slaves succeeding each other under the same governance, more and more attached to one another and more and more specialized with regard to their respective tasks and also more and more imbued with that cultural complex. In that way arose a social heritage of uses, attitudes, and procedures, giving a flavor and consistency to the destinies of those who were born and died in that original world entirely dedicated to producing sugar for export and reproducing ways of life that were so extremely opposite, first between masters and slaves, later between the same masters and a workforce that was no longer slave but held under almost the same conditions of existence.

On the fringes of the plantations the society of the creole cultural area also grew and was differentiated, producing whites and free mulattos devoted to secondary crops and humbler tasks that rarely produced enough to afford slave labor, African slaves at least. That population in the rural zone was made up of families of small farmers and sharecroppers, dedicated to commercial agriculture like tobacco or subsistence crops, the first for export and domestic consumption, the second to be taken to market each week. Some tobacco production increased both in cultivation and in industrialization, calling for the recruitment of workers and a management base. It was no longer the production of tobacco for consumption but for export, which was also used as the main currency of exchange for slaves in Africa. And in towns and cities other groups complementary to this economic system were made up of government functionaries, clerics, merchants, craftsmen, carters, and stevedores.

Specialized and independent communities were formed by fishermen who, by combining native and Portuguese techniques, provided a specific and accessible product for the market. They were scattered in villages along the shore, providing permanent human settlement on the coast. They made up another economy of poverty; fishing made possible a more plentiful diet but did not bring in any wealth.

So oppressive had the rule of the great plantation as a central institution of order become, however, that this whole fringe acted as an auxiliary force for the maintenance of a sugar aristocracy. Every merchant, every priest, and every official of the Crown had as his supreme ideal the day when he, too, would become master of a plantation. And even if they did not get there, they honored those masters with their support, admiration, and respect as the masters of life. That subservience raised the plantation master to the category of the dominant sector of the dominant class, whose hegemony was spread out over the entire society, tying everyone to the hierarchical structure of the plantation and enveloping all in a cohesive and unified system.

Hegemony there was not complete only because plantation owners in turn depended on two other bodies of the ruling class, in the first instance on the parasitic patronage of shipowners and import-export agents who connected the sugar economy to the world market. Also dependent on the prosperity of the sugar economy, which was its source of wealth, this urban patronage imposed itself on the plantation owners, who were tied to it by permanent indebtedness, but all of them acted in defense of common business interests. In the second place the owners were dependent on another body of the ruling class made up of the government aristocracy, who organized, ruled, and defended the colonial undertaking, also doing everything for the sugar economy. Bureaucrats, clergy who wanted charity for the glory of God and the salvation of souls, the military who sought help for defense constructions, the lesser clergy, and even some minor poets, intriguing and speaking ill of others, were in frequent opposition to the immediate interests of the two commercial groups.

As can be seen, from the earliest years we find in Brazil a dominant class divided into two bodies: the commercial and the governmental, the first divided in turn between productive enterprises and dependent businessmen. According to what we have pointed out, these differences, though undoubtedly important, never came to be an insurmountable antagonism, because all the parties concerned essentially formed the homogeneous and cohesive top layer of a single system of external domination and internal exploitation.

Some characteristics of the new society would appear clearly at the threshold of the seventeenth century when the Dutch attacked and seized the principal sugar-producing zone of the Brazilian Northeast. These invaders were the former partners and underwriters of the Portuguese in the establishment of sugar plantations, having practically monopolized distribution. Expelled from the trade by the absorption of Portugal by the Spanish Crown, the Dutch tried to recover through conquest the center of sugar production in their commercial system. After some battles, the new colonial masters peacefully imposed their rule for twenty-five years without any great resistance on the part of the plantation masters.

The fact is, after a century of efforts, the colonists had been formed into a rigidly stratified society that, unlike the original occupiers of the Brazilian coast, relied on subaltern groups who were ready to lend their services to any ruler whatever and had a ruling group ready to negotiate and seek accommodation with any victorious conqueror. In the eyes of many of those owners, it probably seemed better to be subjected commercially to a prosperous Holland than to a bankrupt Portugal in submission to Spain.

The Dutch, with their superior capitalistic development, their position as the real controllers of the European sugar market—sugar only passed through Portuguese ports to have taxes loaded onto it—and the possessors of a financial system that was better endowed with capital seemed to the plantation owners to offer more promising prospects for the betterment of business. And, as a matter of fact, business did quickly improve. The producers, by compromising future harvests, received the necessary financing to reequip their installations, replenish their supply of slaves, and provide their great houses with industrial comforts. The break came only when the Dutch administration, more consistently capitalist, began to demand punctual payment of the credits given, resolving the debts by expropriating the plantations of delinquent debtors. Thereupon some of those most audacious in collaboration during the first phase became ever so patriotic and pious in defense of the Portuguese motherland and the Catholic religion.

The negligent debtors united—leading the population involved as combatants, as had been done before—and expelled the invader. The episode had several consequences, the principal one being the transfer of Dutch capital to the opening of new sugar plantations in the Antilles, which a decade later would contest the world market and which ended up dominating it. During the period of friendly understandings, the Dutch became masters of the techniques of planting and manufacture, acquiring the skills to open this new productive front.

The sugar regime encountered resistance and faced active opposition only on the part of the black slave, who fought for his freedom not only against his master but against all of colonial society united in defense of the system. It was a long and terrible struggle expressed in a thousand different ways—every day by resistance on the plantation, operation of which called for the overseer's fist and lash to impose and maintain the rhythm of work, and periodically by the flight of slaves already familiar with the land to wilderness areas where they took refuge, setting up quilombos.

The most famous of these, Palmares, survived for almost a century, fighting all the way and rebuilding after every raid. In the end it had gathered some 30,000 blacks into different communities and held sway over a vast area located in the richest region of the colony, between Pernambuco and Bahia. Its destruction called for the arming of a force of 7,000 soldiers led by the most experienced fighters in all the colony, mainly from São Paulo.

Palmares, like dozens of other quilombos that rose up in the various regions where slave nuclei were concentrated, was structured within neo-

Brazilian cultural molds and not as the restoration of African cultures. Its houses, crops, language spoken, all of its sociocultural ways of being were essentially the same as those of the entire creole area. In the Northeast, as in the country as a whole, blacks had been deculturated, stripped of their original roots and acculturated into neo-Brazilian ethnicity, which quickly attained a saturation of the African traces it was able to absorb.

Worship based on African religious content, still alive today in the zones that received the largest black contingents, was another strong point of slave resistance. It took shape largely in the big cities, where blacks enjoyed greater independence and where their efforts to rise socially, finding at once resistance and chances of attainment, goaded them all the more. With the deepening of these two opposite yet complementary tendencies and thanks to the freedom that blacks were able to enjoy after abolition, Afro-Brazilian forms of worship took on a growing importance.

The black, who had become integrated into traditional Catholic religious organizations at the end of the colonial period—these being among the few institutions that accepted his participation, although defining his place and his role—went along progressively abandoning them, especially in metropolitan areas, in favor of Afro-Brazilian cults. These are probably more powerful today than at any time in the past. Contributing to this on the religious side was the effort by the Catholic Church to impose a greater orthodoxy on its worship and, on the social side, the conditions of poverty and insecurity that confronted blacks and the humblest groups, who comprise the main body of these cults. In the cities of Bahia, Recife, São Luís, and Rio de Janeiro, *candomblé, xangô,* and *macumba* constitute the most active centers of religious life for poor populations, for blacks and browns and also for whites.

The sugar economy of the colonial Northeast, based on the plantation system, was the most successful form of colonization in the Americas during the first two centuries. In the middle of the seventeenth century, sugar exports were bringing in an annual liquid internal income of over one million gold pounds, a large part of which remained in the hands of the plantation owners. It was applied to the successive expansion of productive capacity, paying the expenses of the factors of production that were imported, especially slaves, and for the maintenance of the external system of financing and commercialization (Furtado 1959, 59–61). In that way an availability for expenses for necessities and luxuries was created, allowing the owners high levels of consumption.

That wealth can be seen mainly in the construction of the cities of Recife, Olinda, and Bahia, which, with the input of wealth coming from mining later on, would emerge as the largest and richest urban centers of the Americas with the exception of Mexico City. The enormous, numerous, and sumptuous churches and convents of those cities, especially those of Bahia, with its brilliant and ostentatious urban life, were the high expression of creole civilization, which was counterbalanced by the grim life and death of the field slave, whose shoulders bore the burden of that opulence.

In the centuries that followed, competition with the new productive zone of the Antilles would displace the Northeast in world markets and bring on a steady deterioration of prices, which would create a chronic crisis in the sugar-growing region. The implanted system would show itself to be perfectly capable of confronting that crisis, however, as well as the exacerbation of its only active contradiction, which was slave revolt, shockingly subversive and offensive to the social order; repression of that was in the hands of the state. Thus the system survived for centuries in spite of a steady decline in profitability. For that reason, however, it was compelled to adopt forms of production that were more and more autarchic, utilizing the available slaves during periods of recession not only to provide the food they ate but also to produce the clothes they wore and to replace worn-out plantation equipment and even household implements. During certain periods when the crisis worsened, the plantation saved itself as a family holding through the sale of a portion of the slaves bred there to agents from the mining region, to which the fulcrum of the colonial economy had been transferred.

The impact of the transforming forces of the Industrial Revolution unleashed an era of social revolutions all over the world before it became crystallized in a stable new social order. Among them can be counted the insurrections, conspiracies, and uprisings that preceded Brazilian independence and those which followed it. They all sought ways to reorder society, ways that by breaking with the constrictive frame of colonial domination and the narrowness of the internal class order would open up for the people better conditions for fulfillment in the emerging civilization. These renovating forces, acting in the context of the creole cultural area, opened up for the first time opportunities for its urban populations to rebel against the old order. As a consequence there was an outbreak of numerous insurrections, of which the leaders, mainly libertarian priests, attracted and activated unredeemed masses from São Luís do Maranhão to Recife and Bahia. In those many outbreaks the underlying tensions never displayed before were noisily expressed. The antipathy of the people was directed at Portuguese merchants, whom they saw as their immediate exploiters; there was the animosity of the poor toward the rich, the antagonism of the native dealer for the foreign one, the resentment of the black toward the mulatto and the hatred of both for the white. The great antagonism that throbbed beneath all these tensions and oppositions, however, was that of slave toward master; but it could scarcely be expressed, because the whites' and mulattos' status of free men united them more than the common denominator of being poor and exploited people, and because the libertarian ideals of the insurgent leaders were limited by the sacrosanct respect for property, slaves included.

In those insurrections a first native leadership arose that was opposed to both colonial domination and the old internal social stratification, which even among free men made for deep differences between rich and poor. Those leaders, however, were terrified of the risks if the social convulsion became generalized and gave the slave masses an opportunity to manifest their age-old rancors, which could drench all society in the blood of a racial war. The image of the revolt in Haiti hung over the Brazilian insurgents, filling almost all of them with terror—with good reason, it is true, given the enormous racial resentment throbbing and held back in the breasts of the majority of the population and which could explode at any moment. José Honório Rodrigues (1954, 38) cites a quatrain sung in 1823 by insurgents in Pernambuco, placing "sailors" (meaning Portuguese in local slang) and the "whitewashed" (whites and their look-alikes) in opposition to blacks and browns:

Marinheiros e caiados
Todos devem-se acabar
Porqus os pardos e pretos
O país hão de habitar.

(Sailors and whitewashed men
will all come to their end
because the browns and blacks
are meant to inhabit the land.)

They already inhabited the land; their aspiration was to rule. It was to remake the social order according to their own plan. It is easy to imagine the well-documented panic and fear brought on by those expressions of the insurgency of blacks and browns if given the opportunity to participate in political struggles. The ruling classes saw here the imminent threat of a "racial war," violent and terrifying because of the age-old contained hatred, which could explode in the form of bloody social convulsions. And in their eyes the threat was all the more terrible because any debate or redefinition of the existing order would inevitably lead to placing in doubt the two basic constrictions: latifundia and slavery.

In those circumstances it is understandable that the whitest and most privileged would end up convinced that their interests coincided with a formal, monarchic, and Portuguese-oriented independence, because only such a regime would be armed with a repressive apparatus and could stand in essential solidarity with latifundia and slavery.

Enclosed within these limits, those helter-skelter revolts of barbers, druggists, bleeders, blacksmiths, tailors, craftsmen, muleteers, and a whole crowd of free poor people armed with blunderbusses, cudgels, and spears could always be overcome and suppressed, sometimes with nothing but the gathering of submissive people from the plantations to reinforce professional troops. At other times, however, it was necessary to wage real war and spill blood.

The main one took place in Pernambuco in 1817, where the insurgents gained power and could only be dislodged after battles where thousands of soldiers fought and which cost hundreds of lives. The victory of the oligarchic order was finally attained over the bodies of nine leaders who were hanged in Pernambuco and four who were shot in Bahia. But not even this calmed the Pernambucans; a few years later new revolts under the command of even more radical leaders were suppressed with the shooting of fifteen patriots. Every crisis that arose in the power structure brought out new popular manifestations, which developed into uprisings. So it was that in 1831 and 1848 the whole creole cultural area went into turmoil several times, bringing on struggles involving thousands of combatants and costing thousands of lives, new imprisonments, executions, and banishments.

Clearly at issue for the urban leaders of the Northeast were the very bases of the social order in force at the time. Among them were the conviction of an imperative need to abolish slavery and a perception of the urgency of land reform that would broaden the economic bases of society. The Pernambucan deputy Antônio Pedro de Figueiredo, in the middle of the nineteenth century, advocated for Brazil the adoption of the North American solution for the land problem:

> Two or three hundred thousand of our fellow citizens, perhaps more, are living on land from which they can be evicted at any moment; the humble vassals of the landowner, whose hatreds, political

party, etc. they are obliged to espouse. With this fact of huge territorial holdings, these new latifundia, we find the basis for the feudalism that holds under its terrible yoke half the population of the
province and at the same time oppresses the other half through the
immense power given it by that mass of obedient vassals. (Quoted in
Rodrigues 1965, 61)

The victory of the old order imposed itself, however, on all rebels, consolidating the Portuguese monarchy and with it slavery and latifundia.
The abolition of slavery would come only decades later. Even though late,
it put the plantation system into a serious structural crisis, but the circumstance of the ex-slave's having no place to go to work for himself in a
world where land was monopolized compelled him to remain in the
canefields. He might change masters, perhaps, so as not to serve as a free
man the one whose slave he had been. Freedom, however, would be reduced to the assumption by that slave of the position of sharecropper; he
would receive a tract of land to work in order to produce the scant food
that no one was giving him now, with the obligation to provide the same
services as before for a payment that would permit him to buy salt, cloth,
and other things indispensable for covering his nudity and satisfying the
elementary needs of his frugal life.

Thus the same structural model developed before abolition to incorporate poor free people into plantation work—the system of sharecropping
or the method of hired hands who worked on other people's land—was
what was presented to the ex-slave as his horizon of social ascension and
national integration.

While slavery was in force, hired hands on plantations played a double
role. They were the lesser partners in the productive process, entrusted
with the less lucrative tasks, such as providing subsistence for the monocultural plantations and the towns. And they were also the landowner's
allies in the repression of the frequent slave revolts. There is documentation indicating that many landowners facilitated the settlement on their
lands of Indians, people of mixed blood, and whites, placing them on the
outskirts of intensive cultivation given over to slave labor, as eventual
auxiliaries of the overseers in the subjugation of the blacks for field work.
With abolition, blacks were added to these poor whites and browns—
who, in order to stress their superiority as men with lighter skin, sometimes became more hateful to blacks than were the wealthy whites. The
integration of both dark- and light-skinned peoples into the marginal mass
of Brazilian society is still taking place in our time, hindered by hostilities

that disguise the fundamental identity of their interests as an exploited class.

This new free man, white or black, formed in the world of the sugar plantation with its distinct hierarchy, remains deep within it and is almost as respectful and servile to the master and to the foreman as was the old slave, simply because he cannot count on any prospects for survival off the plantation. These conditions made the black more resigned to his fate, improved now by his assumption of the dignity of a human being, and made him even more susceptible to a conception of the world that explains the social order as something sacred and that presents the wealth of the rich man and the poverty of the poor as circumstances with no recourse.

The sugar economy experienced a second innovating impact around the middle of the nineteenth century when the Industrial Revolution entered its domain. That came with replacement of mills based on the waterwheel or animal traction by steam-driven installations of enormously greater efficiency and productivity. It began with the establishment of central facilities that received the cane grown in neighboring areas, transforming the old plantation masters into mere suppliers. It was followed by the concentration of land ownership in the hands of these central establishments, which took the form of large modern factories, set up with loans from foreign bankers and organized as stock corporations. The plantation owners who survived in the business as owners or stockholders in the new enterprises moved to the cities, turning over the great house to the administrator and using new means of transportation like the train and, later, the automobile to visit their property periodically.

Another crisis was added to this one, originating in rivalry for the internal market with new sugar-producing zones established in the south in Rio and São Paulo, closer to centers of consumption. In that period a decisive role was taken on by the social position gained and, despite all, maintained by the aristocratic sugar oligarchy, which went on to use its position more and more to demand favors from the government. The sugar industry in the Northeast from then on was maintained thanks to official aid in the form of favorable loans, moratoriums, and market privileges. It ended up, however, being bureaucratized by the ever more imposing interference of official organizations in control of production and marketing. Under these new conditions, as the owner mortgaged lands and machinery— obtaining income guaranteed by the state—what made the survival of the sugar oligarchy possible was mainly its capacity for political action: its control of the local party system and of the votes of its employees. The old plantation owner was replaced by a managerial system of enterprises that fell into the hands of banking firms. The lawyer sons of the old masters, all of them city dwellers now, had as their "plantations" sheaves of shares that were the remains of the family holdings and that now represented the public treasury, of which they had become principal clients.

The area of creole culture, established on the sugar economy, nevertheless took in various ancillary activities that, along with other forms of production, complemented its conditions for existence and produced rural and urban variants of its way of life. Among them can be found various productive specializations that diversified certain portions of the population and certain zones, making up intrusions within the area. Principal ones are the coastal nuclei of fishermen—the Northeastern raftmen with their *jangada* craft—salt workers, the subareas for the cultivation of cacao and tobacco, and oil prospecting around the rim of the bay in Bahia. In spite of their differences in production, these intrusions, by the composition of their groupings of population, by their heritage of lore, norms, and values, represented mere variants of creole culture.

After independence very few changes affected the lives of the wage-earning masses, who remained tied to the plantations under the immediate command of the foremen. Only recently, with events beginning to break up the political hegemony of the sugar barons, have new sources of influential power over the state arisen that threaten to impose a reordering of the system.

In fact, between 1960 and 1964 people began to take a second look at rural working conditions, no longer paying heed exclusively to oligarchical interests. In that way a system of communication was established that defended new values and was represented politically by leaders who spoke a different language. Working side by side in this struggle against the old order were leaders of the left and a new clergy that had reawakened to its social responsibilities. Hundreds of peasants' leagues and rural syndicates were created in this movement, opening the social landscape of the Northeast to political activism as had never occurred before.

In 1963, by those means, a regional minimum wage was attained through a rise in the price of sugar, which was destined to pay that expense, as had been done before for the exclusive benefit of the sugar-factory owners. As might be expected, these subversive measures provoked a most indignant reaction on the part of the bosses, who united in protesting against this "abusive" intervention in their private world, intervention that deprived them of the profits they enjoyed and took away the votes they bought, all of which had permitted them to maintain the privileges they enjoyed as a right of inheritance and on the strength of their political hegemony.

Those transformations seemed to announce the end of the sugar bosses' regime, which had taken place long before on the economic level, but they had managed to maintain its appearance and their prestige through the preservation of their old domination by political processes. It also announced to the sugar-growing Northeast the obsolescence of traditional creole culture as it became archaic and the emergence of a modern culture with an industrial base that seemed destined to reorder the old forms of social life.

Along the way, growing in the illiterate and miserable worker was a new awareness of the world and of himself. Conditions were being created for the replacement of his previous resignation and passivity in the face of the great world of the powerful and the sacred concept of the social order, replacement by an attitude that was more and more out of conformity with the poverty that was now beginning to be explained in secular and dynamic terms. Thus there would soon be fulfillment of the conditions for integration of the rural populations of the Northeast into the ways of life of free workers and for the exercise of their role as citizens of their country.

All these hopes were frustrated, however, with the fall of the reformist government, which had proposed that mobilization, and a return of the power structure by the hand of the military regime to the old oligarchy, defending the perpetuation of its minority interests.

There are those who believe that the suppression of revolt in the Northeast was among of the worst episodes of repression Brazil has experienced and that in it thousands of peasants and their comrades in the struggle were tortured, killed, and dispersed.

Caboclo Brazil

And all those people came to an end or we brought them to an end in little more than thirty years. . . . Of said Indians more than 2 million were dead.

Father Antônio Vieira, 1925–28 (1652)

The area of the tropical forest of the Amazon basin covers almost half the territory of Brazil, but its population barely reaches 10 percent of the nation. Its incorporation into Brazil came about as part of the Portuguese colonial heritage, the unity of a cultural formation founded on the same basic roots, and by the emigration of half a million northeasterners attracted to the Amazon region over the last decades of the nineteenth century and the first of the twentieth for the gathering of rubber from native trees. That territorial, cultural, and human integration has of late come to be seen as organic, thanks to direct communications established along the rivers that run from the central upland plains to the Amazon and the recently opened highways linking Brasília to the great river and about to cut through the Amazon forest from north to south and from east to west.

Today the Amazon region is offering itself to Brazil as its great area for expansion, where inevitably millions of Brazilians are now moving and will continue to move in the future. The forest is being attacked all about its fringes and also within in a powerful demographic movement driven by economic and ecological factors. More than half the caboclo mixed-blood population of the Amazon region has already been dislodged from its dwelling places, tossed into the cities of Belém and Manaus. Because of this all the age-old adaptive wisdom that this population had learned from the Indians in order to live in the forest has been lost.

The new populators are ignorant of all this. They see the forest as an obstacle. Their aim is to cut it down and convert it into grazing land or large commercial plantings. The efficacy of that kind of occupation is doubtful at best, but its capacity for imposing itself is unavoidable precisely because it can rely on government support. The military dictatorship went so far as to subsidize large foreign entrepreneurs attracted by grants of immense parcels of land and with interest-free financing for the projects they were undertaking. It even returned income taxes of large entrepreneurial groups from the south who promised to apply them in the Amazon region. These projects were an abysmal failure. This was not the case with the stealthy invasion of the whole forest by people dislodged from the latifundias and even the minifundias all over Brazil, who are there learning how to live in the jungle and creating a new form of occupation that is yet to be defined.

The Solimões-Amazon river system extends for more than 3,000 miles in Brazilian territory, from the border with Peru to its delta at the island of Marajó. For navigation it represents an inland extension of the Atlantic coast through which large ships can enter. Its principal tributaries increase the navigable extension tenfold, forming a vast river network.

The whole area was originally occupied by indigenous tribes with specialized adaptations to the tropical forest. The majority of them practiced the agricultural techniques of the Tupi groups whom the discoverers first came upon along the Atlantic coast. On some fluvial plains and parcels of land of exceptional fertility and with an easy supply of food obtained through hunting and fishing, there flourished indigenous cultures of the highest technical level, such as those of Marajó and Tapajós, supporting village groupings with a few thousand inhabitants.

They were, however, tribal societies that could be classified as undifferentiated agricultural villages because they had not arrived at the development of urban nuclei, nor were they divided into classes—all inhabitants were equally subject to the tasks of producing food—nor did they have differentiated sectors such as soldiers and merchants. But they enjoyed conditions of broad social intercourse and an extensive domain. Chroniclers who documented those settlements after their first contacts with civilization stressed the size of the populations, which numbered in the thousands for each village, the plentiful food, and the satisfying living conditions they enjoyed. Recent archeological studies are revealing the extraordinary quality of their craftsmanship, especially in molded and colored ceramics.

Such descriptions could be applied only with difficulty today regarding any of the groups populating the Amazon region, engulfed as they are in the vilest penury. In no other region of Brazil does the population confront such harsh conditions of misery as in the caboclo nuclei scattered throughout the forest, devoted to the extraction of plant products and now, in addition, the mineral extraction of gold and tin. Their ways of life constitute a sociocultural variant that is typical of national society, and even though the sector may bear some functional differentiations according to the type of production in which the population is engaged, it displays sufficient uniformity for these to be treated together as a cultural area.

The basic characteristic of this variant is the primitive state of its adaptive technology, essentially indigenous, preserved and transmitted over the centuries without substantial alterations, and the inadequacy of that mode of dealing with nature to develop any satisfactory conditions of life or a minimum integration into modern consumer societies. In fact, civilization has not to date revealed itself capable of developing an adaptive system that can adjust to the conditions of a tropical forest and that could be reproduced as a commercial model assuring economic viability.

In the Amazon region an activity that corresponds to sugar plantations, large commercial agriculture, or cattle ranches is an extractive forest enterprise that is incipiently capitalist: the rubber grove. It can operate economically only as long as it maintains a world monopoly of rubber production and prices ten times higher than the current ones. With the rise of cultivated rubber groves in Asia and the coming of synthetic rubber, the exploitation of native rubber ceased to be economically viable. Since then rubber groves have survived only thanks to state protectionism, which maintains them artificially by subsidizing the rubber bosses but with no concern for the support of the masses of workers involved in the trade. That situation has gone unchanged for half a century, submitting the population of the Amazon region to the greatest misery and without offering them the alternative of becoming involved in other forms of economic production.

An understanding of the way of life of the Amazon populations and the problems that confront them calls for a brief historical examination of how they arrived at their present situation and the principal social forces at work to shape their destiny. That examination will show that the penetration and exploitation of the river valley took place via great accomplishments that were always followed by long periods of lethargy, finally reaching the last one, which has endured now for almost a century. The protagonists of these efforts were a few Portuguese, many neo-Brazilians of mixed blood who came out of those early Brazilian proto-cells, and the Indians engaged as slave labor for all heavy work and demolished by that hard labor.

As a matter of fact, the Portuguese occupation of the Amazon River was initially conducted with the aim of expelling the French, the Dutch, and the English, who had been left out of the Treaty of Tordesillas and who were trying to establish themselves in the area of the river's mouth. For that the Portuguese had to engage in battles and build fortifications. These last began to operate in the region as trading posts, with allied Indians swapping jungle plant products for knicknacks. When the commercial value of the spices obtained in this way—substitutes for the ones Portugal brought from the Indies—was perceived, a deliberate effort to organize and expand the business was undertaken. Since the only workable way of obtaining greater production meant enslaving Indians, compelling them to perform regular work, this was done. The greatest difficulty, however, came with the inevitable contingency of leaving the Indians free to gather the coveted spices, which grew haphazardly in the infinite jungle. The solution consisted in enslaving whole villages, keeping the women and children as practical hostages while the men worked on expeditions that scoured the forest.

The Indians' reaction to this treatment brought on war and the flight of previously allied tribes to refuges where they were safe from slavery. This led to the necessity of hunting for them where they had sought shelter and to the organization of large expeditions that went up rivers in search of the strayed Indians. These were the so-called deliverance troops, an expensive and precarious solution because they always involved more people in war than in work and they killed more Indians than they enslaved, thus reducing the human group they were supposed to bring back.

A better solution appeared to be the installation of missionary nuclei, principally of Jesuits but also of Carmelites and Franciscans, but these had great struggles with the colonizers themselves in the organization of a more rational and profitable solution. An agreement was finally reached: the catechumens of each mission village were divided into three groups. One third were for the services of the priests, these preferably including those recently captured and upon whom it would still be difficult to impose the full weight of slavery. Another third were for the building of public works and the service of authorities of the Crown. And the remaining third were to be distributed among the colonizers in teams for the collection of jungle plants.

For the Indians condemned to even harsher slavery at the hands of the colonizers, the mission regimes, if they did not represent an amenity, were at least more bearable. They allowed people to survive, sometimes to preserve a certain family life when their women were not coveted by some Portuguese or man of mixed blood, and to maintain communal living that made it possible for their traditions to be passed on. But even so, the native population was quickly used up, calling for constant replacements.

Then the period of the transfer of slaves began, initiated by the missionaries to bring down to reduction settlements by persuasion or by force whole Indian villages sheltered along the upper courses of rivers. These formed a mixed group that took in people of different tribes, languages, and customs, all subjected to the civilizing millstone of extractive labor and obligatory service on public works—the construction of fortifications, docks, administrative buildings, mansions—as well as subsistence farming in their own villages and the building of churches and monasteries.

The discipline these jobs imposed and the conditions of community of Indians with different roots led to linguistic homogenization and the compulsory cultural framing of the native into the body of beliefs and way of life of his captors. With these compulsions came the Tupinization of the aboriginal populations of the Amazon region, belonging for the most part to other linguistic trunks but who came to speak the common language, learned not as indigenous tongue but as the speech of civilization, as was happening with almost the whole population of Brazil at the time.

The organization of reduction settlements expanded throughout the river valley, which was becoming Brazilian as masses of native workers were recruited, indispensable for an increase in the production of jungle plant derivatives sold by Portugal all through Europe. These were cacao, still uncultivated, cloves, cinnamon, annatto, and vanilla as well as saffron, sarsaparilla, quinine, *puxuri,* and a great number of seeds, shells, roots, oils, and resins.

The missionary settlements, especially those of the Jesuits, as they concentrated large numbers of Indians, were performing an intensive acculturative action, which permitted the spread of craft techniques such as weaving or building with stone and mortar; use of new types of crops such as rice, sugarcane, and indigo; and the introduction of domestic animals such as hogs, chickens, and in certain areas a start in cattle raising. Yet they had little relevance for the creation of a formula for adaptation to the tropical forest, which still required the original native solutions because of the inadequacy of new techniques in an environment so different from the European. Even the craft techniques played a less than relevant social role because the fine woven goods, the houses of stone and mortar, the European meals were always destined for the tiny ruling group and never reached the workers. The greatest influence of missionary settlements was probably the development of a folkloric and not too orthodox religiosity that resulted in patchwork popular belief based on the syncretism of indigenous shamanism with a vague cult of saints and dates from the Catholic religious calendar.

Living in communities that grew up around centers of royal authority and commerce but relying on their own captive or dependent Indians, the colonizers saw their prospects for wealth limited by the growth of the system of reductions, which gathered together the greatest mass of Indians. Conflicts similar to those in other areas broke out between these two faces of civilization in spite of the modus vivendi they had attained. For a long time the two forces had grown up side by side as different mechanisms for the subjugation of the Indians, both progressively reducing the autonomous tribal population by incorporating them into a system of contagion that decimated them by making them victims of previously unknown illnesses, by war, and by engaging them in work that wore them out.

By this process a new population was arising, heir to tribal culture in what it had of an adaptive formula for the tropical forest. They spoke an indigenous language, even though this had been spread as the language of civilization, learned from whites and from those of mixed blood. They could identify plants and creatures of the jungle, the waters and the forms of aquatic life, sprites and phantoms, according to concepts and terms of the original cultures. They took their subsistence from garden plots of cassava, corn, and a few dozen other tropical plants, also inherited from the Indians. In the same way, like the Indians, they hunted, fished, and brought in small animals, fruits, and roots. They navigated the rivers in canoes and native rafts, built their huts and furnished them with utensils according to old tribal techniques. Also like the Indians, they ate and slept, lived, in short, in the world of forests and waters where they were settling. Like the Indians, finally, they located and collected in the jungle the plants of commercial value that were making neo-Brazilian occupation of the Amazon region viable, and this was their link to the international economy.

More than the transmitters of traditional ways of survival in the damp forest, having developed through millennia of adaptive efforts, the Indians were the wisdom, the nerve, and the muscle of this parasitic society. It was the Indians who knew directions, rowed canoes, opened paths in the jungle, discovered and exploited concentrations of spices, worked the land, and prepared the meals. No colonizer could have survived in the Amazon jungle without those Indians, who were his eyes, his hands, and his feet.

The Portuguese Crown made an effort to stabilize this nascent society by stimulating the cultivation of certain indigenous plants like tobacco, cacao, and cotton. For these productive tasks and also in order to consolidate its rule in the area claimed by the Spanish, it introduced into the Amazon region settlers from the Atlantic islands, mainly from the Azores. That was the only colonizing contingent brought into the Amazon region to transplant a European way of life. They came in organized families, each man bringing his wife, his children, and sometimes a few head of cattle. Initially they formed a few agricultural nuclei, but they were progressively taken over by the ways of life of the region, provoked by the greater value of indigenous formulas of work and food and especially by the economic attraction of the exploitation of jungle plants. So it was that the majority of these nuclei ended up spreading out to engage in the extractive economy. Nevertheless, the existence of local urban markets enabled some of these Azoreans and a few religious missions to establish cattle-raising centers, which enriched the economy with new types of food production and crafts along the strips of native grazing lands of Marajó and Rio Branco. Emerging there were strange herdsmen, a kind of Amazonian "gaúchos," who indiscriminately mounted horses, oxen, or buffaloes to guard their herds, which stood knee-deep in water.

The neo-Brazilian population of the Amazon region was also formed through the crossbreeding of whites and Indian women in the age-old process whereby every man born in the land or brought there bred with Indian or mixed-blood women, bringing forth a racial type that was more indigenous than white. Unable to answer the appeals of the "better people" of the region who asked for Portuguese women, the Crown ended up honoring by law and stimulating through gifts and rewards unions with women of the land. Independent of that official policy, however, crossbreeding had been taking place ever since the earliest times of colonization. For the Portuguese the new aspect consisted in taking a semi-captive Indian as his official wife, setting her children apart as his heirs to the detriment of the group from which she came.

In this way, as tribal life was coming to an end all up and down the river valley, rising up was a new society of mixed-bloods who would constitute a cultural variant differentiated from Brazilian society: that of the Amazon caboclo. His way of life, essentially indigenous as regards ecological-cultural adaptation, was in open contrast on the social level to tribal lifestyles. In their original communities, turned exclusively toward their conditions of existence, the Indians succeeded in obtaining with the same techniques a great abundance of food and in maintaining their cultural autonomy. Transferred to the new nuclei, indigenous adaptation simply permitted one to starve to death, because the new communities were occupied more with the productive tasks of a mercantile nature required by the external market than with those of their own subsistence. Typologically both groups, the subsistence and the mercantile-trading communities, were in opposition to autonomous tribal societies and a communal economy as local nuclei faced a stratified economy turned toward mercantile production and regulated by outside interests.

The full maturing of the new societal structure only came about with a break in the duality that had divided it into missionary reductions and colonizing nuclei. Such came with the expulsion of the Jesuits, which had two crucial effects. First, it knocked down the barriers that prevented the complete subjugation of the heathens and their compulsory integration into the new society as slave laborers. Second, it strengthened the oligarchical class of the nascent caboclo society through the distribution among functionaries and merchants of Jesuit properties along with their houses, crops, and herds of cattle, in addition to their Indians. These successors to the missionaries, those who thus appropriated their holdings—on the island of Marajó alone the priests had more than 400,000 head of cattle—were known from then on as the *contemplados,* those looked kindly upon.

During that period the Portuguese Crown, intent on consolidating its occupation of the Amazon region, made large investments in the area paid for by gold from Minas Gerais, building a network of towns with public services and churches that grew to be quite sumptuous for the region. Some of these, built with stone brought from Portugal, are still standing and are the finest structures in the area and the pride of its urban civilization.

The distributive character of this policy took care first of the aspirations of the colonists, but it created problems later with the withdrawal of interior Indian tribes whom the Jesuits had been attracting to their reductions and integrating into caboclo society by means of compulsory detribalization. Extractive activities declined and an agricultural economy based on tropical species was begun. For a short period of crisis in the world supply of cotton and rice brought on by the North American battles for independence and later by the Napoleonic wars, that economy flourished, creating a few centers of wealth.

The main one was established in Maranhão, outside the Amazon valley but contiguous to it and developed in a parallel way by the same process of integration of Indians into an extractive economy based on jungle plants. The economic success of the undertaking was made possible by the introduction of African slave labor, with which were opened large cultivated areas that came to constitute the principal economic center of the colony at the end of the eighteenth century. Pará also benefited from that boom, receiving a portion of black slaves for its fields of cotton, rice, and cacao. When North American plantings were reestablished, however, both centers fell into decadence, returning to an extractive economy that dominated exports.

Those conditions of exploitation brought on the extermination of the aboriginal populations and created an environment of extreme interethnic tension. But the social order could be maintained thanks to the implantation and implementation over centuries of a vast apparatus of detribalization and forced conscription of Indians for the work. Father Antônio Vieira, of the Society of Jesus, describing in the seventeenth century rivers that he had visited a decade earlier, was horrified at the number of people decimated by the colonists in the name of civilization. He speaks—with exaggeration certainly—of 2 million Indians who were probably lost and would remain lost.

More than repressive action, what explains the maintenance of this hateful system is, on the one hand, the union of active bosses who lived in terror of the possibility of a general revolt by the Indians but were perfectly aware that their only source of wealth was the using up of levy after levy of Indians under conditions of work in which no one could ever survive. And, on the other hand, the servility shown their masters by the caboclos acculturated into the system and its obverse: an attitude of brutal cruelty toward the Indians from whom they had sprung. This posture can only be compared to that of their fellows, the mamelucos of São Paulo, equally fierce subjugators of Indians. Also playing a role of importance was the defenseless situation of "hostile" Indians themselves, torn from their tribes, divided into groups of people of different origins who spoke different languages, had different customs, and were each other's enemies.

For five centuries there was a multiplication of a vast population of detribalized, deculturated, and mixed people who were the principal product and victims of the European invasion. Today there are more than 3 million of those who still hold to their original adaptive culture of forest peoples. They have their origins mainly in the Jesuit missions, which, by confining Indians taken from different tribes, made their original cultures unviable and imposed on them a lingua franca, Tupi, taken from the first native groups the Jesuits had catechized a century earlier in distant regions. In that way the priests had converted an indigenous tongue into the language of civilization as it went on to be the language of the mass of their catechumens. In the course of this process of ethnic transfiguration, people were converted into generic Indians, without a language or a culture of their own and without any specific cultural identity. Joined to them later were great masses of mixed-bloods bred by white men with Indian women; also not being Indians, but speaking Tupi and not getting to be whites, these people fell into the category of caboclos.

The double function of that caboclo mass was to do the work of the extractive exploitation of jungle plants for export to Europe, making the poor economy of the region feasible, and to be used as an instrument for the capture and decimation of autonomous indigenous populations, against whom they developed an aggression equal to or worse than that of the Europeans and the São Paulo mamelucos.

Two waves of violence fell upon the defeated caboclos. The first came with the extraordinary value of rubber on the world market, for which they were recruited as vassals; simultaneously they had thrust upon them people who had come from everywhere for the exploitation of the new wealth. In that instance the caboclos lost their language, taking on Portuguese, but they maintained an awareness of their differentiated identity and their way of life as people of the jungle. The second wave is taking place in our own time with a new invasion of the Amazon region by Brazilian society in its expansion across that forest frontier. The major effect this time has been the expulsion of the caboclos from the land they had occupied, with more than half of them driven off to go hungry in the urban life of Belém and Manaus. The Indians who survived had already learned how to resist vassalage, but the caboclos had not.

The historical process had created three classes of people in the Amazon region, one of which was in the majority and was prepared to assume the whole complex of that society but lacked the sociopolitical capacity to do so. These three categories were formed by tribal Indians, who took refuge in the high headwaters of streams, fighting against all who tried to invade their nuclei of survival in order to steal women and children and condemn them to extractive work. The second was the urbanized population, very heterogeneous but having in common the speaking of Portuguese and the capacity to function as a base of support for the colonial order.

The third contingent was made up of generic Indians, originating mainly in the missions and from the spread of catechumens over the whole area in the gestation of many more generic Indians. It was a question of a new human type, different from the rest, comparable only to the mamelucos of São Paulo. Like the latter, they were extremely combative and were the most competent to run the forest economy.

In fact, they took control several times but were incapable of retaining it and saw themselves defeated and enslaved once again. The São Paulo mamelucos had found a function in a hunt for humans, a hunt that was mercantile in nature, designed for the capture of forest Indians to be sold; and a second function, which was to liquidate the quilombos that were prodigiously multiplying. Such were the tasks of civilization that kept them attached to the colonial enterprise as they transfigured it from then on.

That repressive order was broken in the course of two insurrectionist movements that convulsed the whole Amazon region in the nineteenth century, but since they were challenging national unity itself, they inevitably brought about the cruelest and bloodiest conflagration ever registered in Brazilian history, with a figure of more than 100,000 dead. The first was the so-called Cabanagem in Pará and Amazonas (1834–40), which brought rural and urban populations into revolt, first as an anticolonialist movement and later as a republican, separatist revolution. The Cabanagem made its cause an alternative form of structuring of the Brazilian people and had its origins among the detribalized Indians of the Amazon region. It was the only struggle that, without knowing it, disputed national ethnicity itself, proposing the formation of another nation, that of the *cabanos,* who were no longer Indians, blacks, or Portuguese and who did not identify themselves as Brazilians either.

The Cabanagem managed to take power, dominating the whole province. Coming down the rivers up which the slave hunters had gone before, the rebels destroyed everything they came upon. They seized, occupied, and sacked capitals and principal cities and they interrupted all commerce. The troops who went out in search of the rebels experienced overwhelming defeats. The struggle lasted several years and continued for a few more in isolated centers of resistance where subjection was extremely difficult, but they were defeated in the end.

Two aspects stand out in the struggle of the cabanos. First was its character as a caste war, fought consciously as such by the commander of the forces of repression, who wrote:

All men of color born here are joined in a secret pact to put an end to everything white. . . . It is indispensable, therefore, to place arms in the hands of the others; and it is indispensable to protect the multiplication of whites in all ways. (Quoted in Moreira Neto 1971, 15)

The perception that Indians and caboclos had their ethnic oppressor as an enemy here takes on the cruel aspect of a racist opposition that places all "men of color" in a single category of enemies to be exterminated.

The second aspect to stress is that this evidently victorious insurrection was defeated in the end not only by arms but most of all perhaps by the historical unviability of the struggle of the cabanos. Their revolt against oppression and discrimination built up over the ages was sufficient reason to unleash a war, but even after all their victories it was not sufficient to plan and bring about an alternative program of the social order for the disparate peoples involved in the fight for freedom. Like the blacks in the quilombos, in spite of their primitivism the people led by the cabanos had already been contaminated by civilization. The same civilization that for them meant deadly plagues, slavery, and oppression was also the only practicable way of being articulated commercially with the providers of the goods they could no longer do without, things such as tools, fishhooks, salt, and gunpowder.

Another popular uprising in the settlements of the north was the Balaiada. The *balaios* were essentially rebels from the black masses concentrated in Maranhão for the production of cotton who, equally deculturated and de-Africanized, were fighting like the quilombos for a break in the social order that made them slaves. There were blacks among the cabanos, of course, although these were most often fighting alongside the government troops. It was also evident that among the balaios there were Indians and ex-Indians and many mamelucos from Maranhão.

Too civilized to return to the old tribal forms of autarchic living and too primitive to propose an intentional reordering of society on new bases, the cabanos and the balaios found themselves paralyzed, waiting for the defeat that would destroy them. The privilege of their dominators was that of being able to experience numerous defeats and to survive them and remake the constrictive web. For the cabanos, one single defeat would be their perdition because once brought to submission, they would find their enemy going back to imposing in a reinvigorated and even more hardened way the old oppressive social order. In fact, the greater part of the thousands and thousands of cabano deaths occurred after they had been defeated, with the slaughter of entire Indian villages deemed to be guilty of having fought against the oppressors. That premeditated decimation was paralleled only by those that took place in the sixteenth and seventeenth centuries in the Brazilian Northeast and, like them, could only be classified as a genocidal war for the massive extermination of indigenous populations.

Only during the last quarter of the nineteenth century did the Amazon region experience a period of prosperity motivated once more by the growing value on world markets of one of its traditional extractive products: rubber. The development of the European and American automotive industries turned the rubber from the Amazon groves into an industrial raw material with enormous demand, doubling, tripling in value, and increasing its price more than tenfold. The Amazon region, in its position as the only supplier, transformed its whole economy into an effort to take care of the massive demand. The population concentrated along the banks of the Amazon and Solimões rivers spread out all through the valley, going up streams hitherto untouched, in search of concentrations of native rubber trees and other gummiferous plants of the forest. The cities grew, became opulent, and were transformed. Belém at the delta and Manaus halfway up the Amazon River became great metropolitan centers at the docks of which hundreds of ships tied up, loading rubber and unloading all manner of industrial articles. A railroad was built through the heart of the jungle at an enormous cost in human lives. The Madeira-Mamoré line would link concentrations of rubber trees from Porto Velho up to the River Mamoré on the Bolivian border, a distant region torn away from Bolivia and incorporated into Brazil.

For this productive effort it had been necessary to resolve a preliminary problem: the massive recruitment of labor for the undertaking, which was lacking in the valley—labor capable of enduring the harsh working conditions in the rubber groves. That need was filled by a call on the enormous reserves of labor gathered in the rural Northeast, devastated by a prolonged drought that had caused 100,000 deaths among victims of a primitive and terribly exploitative system of latifundia. Thus began a population transfer that would lead nearly half a million northeasterners to the Amazon region. Disembarking at the two ports of Belém and Manaus, the backlanders were divided among employers already waiting for them. Each allotment, supplied with weapons and munitions for hunting and for protection against Indians and with clothing and the simple instruments for their extractive work, was led upriver and into the jungle to the distant rubber groves. Each rubber tapper entered into service with his purchases and his debts, which would grow greater and greater with the supply of food, medicine, and clothing provided by the company store. It was difficult for a rubber gatherer to manage to pay off that account, which, skillfully manipulated, kept him in a system of virtual servitude for as long as he could endure the terrible conditions of life to which he was subjected.

Rubber, like all products native to the tropical forest, was distributed irregularly and in small concentrations in the midst of an infinity of other species. Even in zones of greater density, the rubber groves were of enormous extent, preventing the population from organizing in sizable nuclei. These conditions determined the dispersal of the Amazon population all along waterways throughout the immense valley, resulting in a demographic density almost like that of a desert and calling for the creation of a system of communication that was based exclusively on river navigation with canoes and rafts.

In that economy the land of itself had no value whatever and the lush jungle that covered it represented only an obstacle to reaching those rare and truly useful species. There was no thought, therefore, of securing legal ownership of the land, as was the case in regions with agricultural or herding economies. What was important in the Amazon region was control of the means of access to the rubber groves and the conscription of the workforce necessary to exploit them. That control did not take on the form of landed property obtained through governmental concessions except accidentally, in the rare cases where it was indispensable and the land was held, in effect, by the one who had the means of transportation. The conscription of labor was managed through the most insidious forms of enticement and maintained by means of the use of force combined with a system of indebtedness from which no conscript could escape.

So it was that rubber gathering was established as an enterprise that had nothing to do with the land. Its element was the river, on which people did not settle as populators but were only present as exploiters until the rubber gave out. Therefore, the endeavor proceeded with its own ways: canoes, the company stores, the ledgers of debts that held the tappers prisoners of the boss. In every rubber grove there would be a group of caboclos exercising the function of foremen who broke in the new arrivals, the "greenhorns." They taught the newcomers how to identify a rubber tree, tap it daily without harming it, collect the latex, and smoke-dry it carefully to form balls of rubber.

Each tapper thus instructed would receive his "road," which was the trail from tree to tree. In the course of five to ten miles, fewer than 200 trees would be found, which when linked by a trail made up the unit of exploitation. The rubber grove is the complex of these roads, usually laid out along a river, hours and even days of travel time from each other, depending on the region. At the mouth of the stream, on guard against any desertion by workers or any loss of merchandise, was the residence of the boss or his agent along with the company store and its dock, its deposit of balls of rubber, its warehouse supplied with liquor, tobacco, foodstuffs, cloth, ammunition, toilet water, and every knicknack that might stimulate a tapper to go into debt.

The tapper had to cover his road twice a day, the first time to tap the trees and fasten bowls to the trunks to receive the latex, the second to pour this into a bucket that he would take back to his hut. With work starting at dawn, by nightfall he was able to give his time to the task of the coagulation of the latex. It should be added that along with being a tapper, he also had to be a hunter and fisherman so as not to be dependent on canned food, which, in addition to poisoning him, put him into debt. And he always had to be on the lookout for Indians lying in wait at some point on the trail, who might bring him down with their arrows. The conflict between Indian and tapper was so intense that the one who saw the other first was the one who killed. To all these afflictions must still be added the incidence of diseases like beriberi, which reached epidemic proportions in the whole Amazon region, and the so-called tropical ailment, principally malaria, which took a high toll in lives and physical disability among the population working in the rubber groves.

Despite all, the misery of the northeastern backlands together with the high price paid for rubber, more than 500 pounds sterling a ton, stimulated that human flow, providing the necessary workforce for the rubber economy. A few arrivals became good hunters and fishermen in the Amazon region and also wily dealers, escaping exploitation and making profits, which on their return to the Northeast let them spread the news of their success, bringing on new migrations. The rest, who were the great majority, were silent about their failure. What made the rubber groves attractive, in fact, were official propaganda and a whole network of recruitment centers maintained in the backlands and the ports, along with the misery of the backlands, which offered no alternative but the Amazon adventure. In that way, after wasting the indigenous population of the river valley, the exploitation of plant life also used up enormous contingents from the Northeast, especially from the backlands.

The prosperity of the extractive economy was abruptly interrupted, however, by World War I. It would never revive because of the entry into world commerce immediately after that conflict of rubber groves planted by the English in Asia. With the price going down to 100 hundred pounds, the exploitation of native groves became unprofitable, wrecking the Amazon rubber economy, which was already 40 percent of the total value of Brazilian exports and employed close to a million people scattered throughout the region. At the peak of extractive expansion (1872), the whole regional urban network had grown to the point of transforming Belém, the second port of the Amazon, into the fourth city of Brazil in population.

The crisis struck like a catastrophe because of inability to place the production stored up during the war and new collections that continued coming down the rivers. Many rubber groves were abandoned by bosses who had fallen into bankruptcy, with all the people employed thrown to their own fate in the jungle wastes. In a short time the population became concentrated once more along the banks of the large navigable rivers, going back to a subsistence economy and conditions of misery more acute than those of the backlands they had fled—and more difficult than those of the Indians because of their needs as "civilized" people to dress themselves, cure their illnesses with purchased remedies, and supply themselves with commercial articles.

Economically marginalized, these "caboclified" backlanders became integrated into the ways of regional life, learning to hunt with bow and arrow in order to save ammunition, to work the land with wooden stakes for lack of hoes, to fish with harpoons, and to eat the food of the land, including turtles and alligators in their diet. In the most backward areas like the Rio Negro region, where the lingua franca was still spoken as the basic language of popular communication, they also came to speak that impoverished and mangled dialect of Tupi. In addition, they became involved in the practices of shamanism and the fears of ghosts in indigenous mythology. They became only imitation Indians, however, because they did not have the latter's motivations or their capacity for adaptation to the tropical forest.

Years later the federal government established certain protective measures for rubber production, principally a monopoly of the supply for the domestic market at subsidized prices. A new extractive economy was then shaped, enticing that miserable population, leading them back into the rubber groves with even more uncertainty than in the past.

With that revival of the rubber groves a new burst of gathering would come during the next world war, giving the Amazon region a brief period of intense activity. This was due to the need for supplying rubber to the Allies, who because of Japanese conquests found themselves deprived of the production from Asian plantations. The federal government then promoted another movement of northeasterners into the Amazon region as the main Brazilian contribution to the war effort. It is estimated that this new migration involved between 30,000 and 50,000 workers. As a matter of fact, Brazilian losses in the so-called Rubber War—both through the misery into which the workers were thrown and the deaths it brought about and through their abandonment in the rubber groves after the conflict—were much greater than the casualties suffered by Brazilian troops in Italy.

The official character of the new waves of extractive activity permitted the rubber dealer to survive by means of favorable banking arrangements, but it attracted rubber workers only because of an absolute lack of any other opportunities for work, and it condemned them to perpetuation of their penury. In those impoverished rubber groves the caboclified backlanders, the same as those newly conscripted, attempted to cultivate a subsistence plot—even though the rubber harvest coincided with the time for preparing the soil for planting—along with hunting and fishing according to traditional Indian techniques in an attempt to improve the conditions of existence. But their economic relations were subject to the bosses, whose own poverty caused them to make the exploitation even more overtaxing. Those conditions of misery and dependency were aggravated by a tacit agreement in effect among the rubber bosses from the beginning never to accept workers with unpaid debts. Anyone who has traveled through the Amazon rubber groves has known those workers who wait for years for the liberating little piece of paper on which the boss has certified that he has been paid for all supplies.

Along with the rubber bosses, the new boom in extractive activity revived another actor in that primitive economy: the river trader. He went where the rubber dealer did not. He was the dealer who carried his merchandise in the boat on which he lived and with which he navigated every river, every channel where there was something to be traded for liquor, salt, matches, cloth, fishhooks, needles, thread, ammunition, and other articles of that nature. The creator of necessities and the instruments for their satisfaction, the river trader was king of the channels. A large part of his business was the embezzlement of the products of the rubber groves, which he spirited away with bold strokes.

Probably no human condition is as miserable as that of those rubber tappers, isolated in their huts, scattered through the jungle, working from morning to evening star, dressed in rags, undernourished, ill, illiterate, and above all disenchanted with their life, which offers them no hope whatever of freedom. Compared to the tribal Indians who preceded them as occupants of the same territory or who still survive in more remote regions, the backward and miserable people are the "civilized" ones, sunk in the worst kind of poverty, brutalized by the very process of civilizing integration to which they have been submitted.

Besides the tappers, the extractive industry of the Amazon region today includes other gatherers specializing in diverse products. These are the balata-gum gatherers, chestnut gatherers, collectors of copaiba balm, rosewood, *passava* palm, *murumu* palm, *timbó* vine, and *tucum* palm, and the hunters of alligators, *priarucu* fish, and turtles, all of them as miserable as the rubber workers.

The great news concerning the peoples who have survived centuries of extermination up till the present is that they are going to survive in the future. Contrary to what we had all feared, their populations have become stabilized and some indigenous peoples are growing in number. They will never reach the tally they had during the first period of European invasion, close to 5 million, half of them in the Amazon region, where colossal rivers sheltered indigenous concentrations that startled the first navigators. Really frightening until today was the swift and steady decline of every indigenous population that came face to face with civilization. But a reversal has taken place. Brazilian Indians already number much more than the 150,000 to which they had fallen in their worst times. Today they go beyond 300,000 and their number is increasing substantially.

As has been seen, the destructive drive of European expansion has moderated, and indigenous populations that were visibly in decline, seemingly heading toward extermination, have now entered a discreet process of demographic growth. In fact, no one had expected this fortunate change. All Brazilian and world anthropology repeated unmistakable data that showed a decline in the numbers of every known tribe every year.

Death seemed to be the fatal destiny of Brazilian Indians and, along with them, all other peoples designated as primitive. Suddenly we began to see a reversal of that picture. The Nambiquara went on to increase, proud and determined to remain on their lands at any price. The Urubu-Kaapor, who reached 400 in 1980, are 700 today. The Mundurucu have now reached a figure of 5,000. The Xavante, who numbered 2,500 in 1946 are 8,000 today.

Some indigenous peoples have reached sufficient numbers to expand and reorganize their cultural institutions. The Tikuna, on the upper Solimões in Brazil and Peru, have already gone beyond 20,000; the Makuxi of the open country of Roraima number 18,000; the Guajajara, who live on the eastern fringes of the Amazon region, are today 9,000; the Kayapó, recently drawn to civilization, are 6,000. The Sateré-Maué, who live on the lakes and islands near the Amazon River, today number close to 15,000.

It is true that some indigenous peoples are diminishing and their chances of survival are minimal. The last thirteen Indians of the Jabuti tribe are seeking brides for their sons among other Indians who speak Tupi-Kawahib. With this they hope that a new indigenous people will arise. The Avá-Canoeiros, who used to number thousands of Indians and dominated the upper Tocantins River, are no more than thirty people. Living in small bands without contact with one another, they were specialists in fleeing the white invasion. Two Indians were recently found speaking an unintelligible dialect of the Tupi language. No one knows who they are, nor will anyone ever know.

The Yanomami, who today constitute the largest untouched people on the face of the earth, have begun to die out, victims of illnesses carried by whites and under the astonished eyes of world public opinion. There are 16,000 of them in Brazil and Venezuela. They speak four variants of a language of their own, with no relationship to other languages, living in hundreds of villages scattered in the jungle, threatened by prospectors who, having discovered gold and other metals on their lands, are demanding that the governments of the two countries give the invaders the right to continue mining operations with primitive processes based on mercury, which pollutes and poisons the waters of the Yanomami.

The survival of indigenous peoples can be explained to a large degree by biological adaptation to the plagues of the whites—smallpox, measles, lung ailments, venereal diseases, and others. Each of these liquidated half the population with the first contact with the frontiers of civilization. Smallpox has disappeared, but several other illnesses continue to do their damage, even though less than in the past simply because medicine itself has made much progress.

Survival can also be explained by changes that have occurred on the frontiers of expansion by national society into the world of indigenous peoples. In spite of being quite aggressive and destructive, people can no longer exterminate entire tribes with impunity, as happened in the past. Only recently the slaughter of a Yanomami village quickly became an international scandal and put an end to the murderous wave.

The forms of content and coexistence have also undergone important changes. Evangelization, cruelly Christianizing and imperially Europeanizing, has lost its ethnocidal fury. There are no longer so many religious missions stealing Indian children from different tribes in order to bring them together in mission schools, which were the most terrible instruments of deculturation and depersonalization. Many of the few survivors of these evangelical schools, having no place in tribal or national society, fell into marginality and prostitution. The paternalism of official protection by the state, brutally assimilationist, either as policy or through ignorance, has been replaced by a more respectful attitude toward the Indians.

The most fearful change occurred with the Indians themselves, whose general attitude of submission and humility following the establishment of peaceful relations has been giving way in many cases to a proud and affirmative posture. Previously, when the newly contacted Indians became aware of the magnitude of national society with its uncountable population dominating immense areas, thus perceiving their own quantitative insignificance, they would fall into a depression that was sometimes fatal. Today they see whites as people who can be challenged.

Under these conditions there has begun to arise a new type of indigenous leadership, without any submission to missionaries, to official protectors, or to any agents of civilization whatever. They know that the immense majority of national society is composed of miserable people who live in conditions worse than their own. They perceive or suspect that their place in national society, if they wished to be incorporated in it, would be even more miserable still. All of that has deepened their natural inclination to remain Indians.

Under certain circumstances the choice between being Indians and engaging with the national context in which they live becomes so fierce that it reaches murderous proportions. This is what leads Indian youths to suicide, as occurred with the Guaraní, who could not bear the hostile treatment shown them by the invaders of their lands. Besides transforming the whole environment, cutting down forests, polluting rivers, ruining hunting and fishing, these civilized neighbors turned upon the Indians all the brutality of a unanimous consensus concerning their incurable inferiority, which ended up being absorbed internally by the Indians, bringing on the waves of suicides. Under such conditions indigenous traditions themselves were sometimes redefined, no longer giving people moral support and confidence in themselves but leading them to disillusionment. This is the case with the heroic myths of the Guaraní addressing the creation of the world, which have been converted into macabre myths where the earth itself appeals to the creator to put an end to life because it has become too weary of eating corpses.

The decline of the rubber economy also killed off the cities that had flourished throughout the Amazon region, bringing on the complete abandonment of some and the deterioration of others. The two regional capitals lost their luxury and show, which had filled them with sumptuous mansions, theaters, and urban works during the prosperous times of high rubber prices. Without any basic production for export, business declined, surviving only as a pivot for speculation and smuggling. The urban population, however, continued to grow, swollen by the influx of groups of rubber workers to the outskirts of towns, where their circumstances were even more miserable than the poorest favelas or rural shacks in the rest of the country. There an underemployed multitude vegetates, displaying conditions of life so extreme that their rates of general and infant mortality have grown worse than the highest ones in the world.

Since the end of World War II a reordering of the economy of the Amazon region has begun, allowing for the participation of a portion of the population in new types of production, such as the cultivation of jute and black pepper introduced by the Japanese and the planting of rice on the flood plains. In the cities a start at industrialization is also providing some opportunities for work, and in some areas mining activities have provided new means for existence. The most important of these have brought thousands of people into the territory of Amapá in search of manganese and smaller groups of tin miners into Rondônia and Amazonas.

The adventure of the prosperous rubber groves at the beginning of the century is being repeated because these immense deposits are being shipped to the United States through a monopolistic enterprise, Bethlehem Steel, for the price of their extraction and transportation. When the exploitation is over, no new source of work capable of occupying the population and no local wealth will remain. The probable consequence will be the onset of a crisis identical to the one in rubber, so that the United States can thereby fulfill its design for power, which is to become the exclusive holder of manganese in the hemisphere. Then Brazil will have to import the mineral that it now gives away for the cost of its extraction and will still be left with a vast worn-out and poverty-stricken population.

The imbalance in the regional economy, the difficulties of integrating the area into the life of the country, and the precarious conditions of existence of its people led the framers of the Constitution of 1946 to earmark a portion of 3 percent of federal income for a program of economic improvement for the Amazon region. In 1950 a commission completed the first five-year plan for development, which since then has been passing through congressional committees without gaining approval. The sums are being applied in the region and represent the principal factor in the balance between the value of its exports and the cost of its imports. The abandonment of planning, however, has transformed those awards into the main source of income used by the ruling classes to enrich themselves through goods and favorable financing controlled by the politicians of the region with the most blatant electoral favoritism. Just as the poverty of the arid Northeast makes a "drought industry" out of federal relief, so the misery of the caboclos of the Amazon region makes "regional development" a lucrative business and a mechanism for the political consolidation of the local oligarchy.

Nevertheless, vitalization of the economy of the Amazon region by promoting revival of the area and its incorporation into national life as a prosperous population is certainly one of the most serious challenges facing Brazil. Once again the existence of that jungle zone—the largest and least populated in the world—has aroused international greed. At one point it was recommended to Hitler as suitable *Lebensraum* for German expansion. Later it was the object of a real project of exploitation camouflaged as an institute for tropical research in which the Americans involved the United Nations. A third attempt at despoilment took the form of a proposal the American government presented to the dictatorship for a ninety-nine-year lease of the area to "study it and text experimentally the techniques suitable for the promotion of its development." The Brazilian government, trapped in this matter of a limitation of its sovereignty in order for Brazil to become a privileged satellite of the American hegemonic system, allowed itself to discuss the issue. Alerted by a reaction of public opinion, however, a group of officers warned the dictatorship that they would not permit the leasing or loaning or any kind of negotiation regarding national territory.

Another attempt was in the language of a hare-brained plan of the futurologists of the Hudson Institute to dam the Amazon River, flooding thousands of square miles of jungle in order to establish hydroelectric facilities that would produce ten times more energy than Brazil consumes. Behind that plan was the more realistic one of creating for the Americans an area suitable for the installation of an industrial civilization in case of a nuclear war.

But the Amazon region is truly the greatest challenge now confronting Brazil. Its occupation has been taking place with a drive of incomparable vigor. States like Rondônia, larger than France, suddenly arise and are populated at an accelerated pace. Ambitious highway projects to cut through the entire forest are carried out in such an inept way that after astronomical investments, they fall into abandonment. Viable dreams of new highways linking the Amazon region to the Pacific, in order to provide China and Japan not only with the native woods that the whole world now receives but with what the great valley will produce in the future, have been sketched out and the prospect of putting them into effect is in sight. A new political class and even a new generation of military men, absorbed with what the economic exploitation of the Amazon can render, are annoyed by the caboclos and the Indians, who occupy only a tiny part of the forest but whom they see as obstacles to progress.

It was possible in the past to liquidate that most poignant Brazilian forest, the one in the Rio Doce valley, converted into scrub pasture under which the soil is an open wound exposed to erosion. It is not impossible that something similar will happen to the Amazon region, even though its gigantic dimensions and its enormous regional variations point to a more dynamic future. Along its rivers, half a million miserable prospectors today searching for gold, tin, or whatever cannot bring in an income equal to a minimum wage. Their only method is based on mercury, which as noted poisons the water, the fish, and the population along the riverbanks. In their footsteps large enterprises are preparing to exploit the mineral deposits of the region, the largest ever known. Will this open up the perspective of creation of a new Minas Gerais, where after ages-long exploitation of mineral wealth, all that remained was a population in poverty and holes in the ground that exposed the inside of the earth to erosion once more?

The plans to revive the old rubber groves and revitalize them in order to provide better opportunities for the forest workers have resulted in conflicts like the scandal that had Chico Mendes as its victim and shook the world. He and his comrades, however, were the only ones pointing out a concrete way to make the Amazon region habitable and profitable, a way that would be quite possible as soon as means were found to sustain human settlements that could be subsidized until plantings of rubber trees matured, along with groves where the fruit trees of the Amazon region could flourish and could offer the world the promise of sweet tastes. This is totally impracticable for the private enterprise system with its inevitable quest for immediacy. It is impracticable also for the caboclos, who would know how to handle it so well, because their misery is such that they must live from hand to mouth.

Backlands Brazil

> Of leather were the doors of the huts, the crude bed made on the hard floor, and later on the couch for childbirth; of leather all cords, the sack for carrying water, the bag or satchel for carrying food, the trunk where clothes were kept, the nose-bag to feed the horse corn, the tether to tie him on a trip, scabbards for knives, saddlebags, and pokes, clothing for going into the forest, the trough for curing hides or refining salt; the material for plugging dams was carried on pieces of leather pulled by teams of oxen, flattening the earth with its weight; tobacco for snuff was also trampled out on leather.
>
> Capistrano de Abreu, 1954

Beyond the northeastern band of fresh and fertile massapé soil with its rich forest covering where plantations were set up, land of a different ecological area opens up. It begins with a still humid broken strip of land and continues into the enormous semiarid extension of the caatingas, or scrublands. Beyond this, penetrating into Central Brazil now, it rises up to form a plateau with open fields that spread out over thousands of square leagues.

This whole area forms a vast midland of sparse vegetation bordered on one side by the forests of the Atlantic coast, on the other by the Amazon forests, and closed in to the south by zones of woods and natural prairies.

Bands of riverine forest cut through the midland, following the courses of the main streams, becoming thick with jungle groves or stands of wax palms, wine palms, and babassu palms where the soil is damper. The usual vegetation, however, is poor, made up of natural grasslands that are sparse and dry with stunted shrubs that reveals in their twisted trunks and branches, their thick, hard foliage the poverty of the soil and the irregularity of the rains. In the open areas and especially in the caatingas, the vegetation reaches complete adaptation to the dryness of the climate, with a predominance of cactus, thorny bushes, and xerophytic plants able to condense the atmospheric moisture of cool dawns and hold in their fibrous leaves and tubers the water of the rainy season.

In the more humid border strips called *agrestes,* then in the caatingas, and finally on the open uplands, a grazing economy developed that was originally associated with sugar production as the supplier of meat, leather, and working oxen. It was always a poor and dependent economy. Relying on the assurance of a growing internal market for its products, however, along with the export of leather, it was able to expand continuously over the centuries. It ended up incorporating an important chunk of the national population into the grazing economy, covering and occupying more extensive territorial areas than any other productive activity.

It also shaped a particular type of population in a subculture of its own, that of the sertão, the backlands, marked by its specialization in grazing, its spatial dispersion, and identifiable characteristics in its way of life, family organization, power structure, typical clothing, seasonal merry-making, diet, cooking, view of the world, and religious leaning toward messianism.

The cattle brought by the Portuguese from the Cape Verde Islands probably arrived already acclimated to extensive breeding without barns or stables, where the animals themselves sought out their own food and water. The first arrivals were installed in the Pernambucan agreste and around the fringes of the bay in Bahia, sufficiently distant from the plantations so as not to harm the canefields. From there they multiplied and spread out in ranches along the rivers, forming riverbank pasturelands. At the end of the sixteenth century Bahian and Pernambucan breeders could already be found in the backlands along the São Francisco River, following it to the south, and north of it into the lands of Piauí and Maranhão. Their herds at that time numbered close to 700,000 head, which would double in the following century.

The expansion of that grazing activity was conducted through the multiplication and dispersal of the ranches, depending on the ownership of the herd and control of the grazing lands. The cattle had to be bought, but the land, belonging nominally to the Crown, was freely given in land grants to those who made themselves worthy of royal favor. In early times the coastal plantation owners received grants on the edge of the sertão, breeding there the cattle they consumed. Later on this became a specialized activity for breeders, who became the owners of the largest latifundias in Brazil. The most famous of these was a Bahian so rich that in his will he left to the Jesuits the resources for masses to be said for his soul until the end of the world.

Through this system, before the cattle could reach any land, it was acquired legally through appropriation by land grants. Since ranches could only be established alongside the rare permanent watering places and not too far from the natural salt marshes where the cattle could satisfy their appetite for salt, and because of the extremely poor quality of the natural pasturage, those land grants came to be immense. Each one of them, with its corrals sometimes separated from one another by days of travel, was in the care of the herders. They kept count of the herd periodically, marking off one head as payment for every three for the owner. In that way the herdsman would proceed to put together the animals for his own herd, which he would take off into more barren lands that were still unexplored and not covered by land grants. The work system of herding, then, was based on slavery but on a peculiar system in which payment was made by supplying the means of maintenance, especially in salt and calves from the herd.

The families of the cowman and his helpers lived at each corral. Helpers were generally apprentices waiting for the day when they, too, would receive a group of cattle to breed and care for. Periodically drovers would pass through, picking up cattle to drive out of the backlands to the coast, where they would be sold. The drovers would bring salt and a few other things needed by the cowmen, accustomed to life in the wastelands, shaped by their herding activities and getting almost everything they needed from the cattle themselves.

The nuclei of people formed by the corrals planted gardens and tamed a few cows for milk, curds, and cheese. Every so often they would butcher a steer, thus guaranteeing for themselves a more bountiful and surer subsistence than that of any other rural Brazilian nucleus. Relationships between the owner of the land and the herders tended to take on a less unequal order than those of the sugar plantation, even though holding to a rigid hierarchy. The master, when present, would serve as best man and godfather, respected by his men but also respectful of their working skills, if not of their personal dignity. At the same time, as happens with pastoral peoples, the specialized activity itself brought out the dash and qualifications of the best cowmen during the daily struggles in the field. Tests of skill and personal valor made herders haughtier than the farmworker or hired hand. The resulting system was closer to the typology of herding relationships the world over than to the working relationships on slaveholding plantations, although similar in the mercantile character of cattle raising and its dependence on the latifundia system.

The breeder and his cowmen had the relationship of a master and his servants. As lord and master, the owner had undisputed authority over their possessions, and sometimes he expected to have it also over their lives and frequently over the women who caught his fancy. Thus the more intense life together and even appreciation for the qualities of workers did not bring the classes closer socially; a hierarchical distance prevailed and arbitrary acts were permitted, even though these were far from anything like the brutality of the relationships that prevailed in areas of creole culture.

The contrast of this attitude with life on the sugar plantations must have made cattle herding more attractive for the poor whites and mixed-bloods of coastal nuclei. In addition, the sugar business, besides calling for enormous capital investments that were beyond the reach of the common people, allowed for only a few specialized workers between the class of the masters and the slave masses. The very rigidity of the working discipline on the plantation must have rendered it unbearable for a free worker and all the more so for people accustomed to the venturesome and vagabond life of coastal villages. For all these reasons, many people of mixed blood must have headed for a herding life as cowmen or helpers in hopes of becoming breeders one day. In this way they provided a constant supply of labor, making the purchase of slaves unnecessary.

Only through this can there be an explanation for the white-looking phenotype of the northeastern, Bahian, and Goiasian cowman on an indigenous base. Such characteristics have sometimes been interpreted as the result of ongoing miscegenation with the indigenous groups of the backlands. This hypothesis seems historically unsustainable given the hostility that has always developed between cowmen and Indians whenever they came face to face.

With cowmen disputing the ownership of tribal hunting territories and turning these into grazing lands, and fighting the Indians to stop them from replacing prey that had grown scarce in populated areas by taking new and larger prey, cattle, conflicts became inevitable. The supposition is also unnecessary because, starting with a few mixed-bloods coming from the villages on the coast—to whom no migratory contingent of blacks or whites was added—we would naturally and necessarily have the genetic imperative of the permanence of racial characteristics and a perpetuation of the original phenotype. All this seems to be true. Anthropology, however, negates history, showing a flat head sunk between the shoulders, which cannot come from nowhere. One must inevitably admit that in stealing women or gathering Indians into the herding lands, the typical phenotype of the original indigenous peoples of those backlands would be imprinted on the cowmen and on northeasterners in general.

In spite of the enormous distances between the human nuclei of these corrals scattered over the deserted sertão, certain forms of sociability did develop among corral dwellers along the same riverbank. The necessity for rounding up and separating cattle running wild in the pastures brought about forms of cooperation like roundups, which turned into contests of skill among cowmen and sometimes ended up becoming regional festivals. Feast days on the religious calendar and worship of patron saints—centered at the chapels and their respective cemeteries scattered throughout the backlands, each with its own circle of communicants, made up of all those living thereabouts—provided regular occasions for a gathering of cowmen's families, which resulted in festivals, dances, and weddings. Beyond this neighborly social contact, which was limited to cowmen from the same area, what prevailed was the isolation of the backlands nuclei, each structured autarchically and turned inward on itself in the immensity of the sertão.

Herding activities under the climatic conditions of backlands covered with poor pasturage and of an extensive area subject to periodic drought shaped not only the life but also the very makeup of people and cattle. Both shrank in stature and became bony and slim. In this association, as they multiplied together, people and cattle were penetrating inland until after three centuries they occupied almost all of the interior sertão. Reduced by slaughter, the cattle took on an aspect of self-regulating merchandise, in spite of getting farther and farther away from the consumer market.

Over the course of this movement of expansion, the whole sertão was being occupied and crossed with roads opened by cattle drives. They would go from one resting place to another, all of which were areas with a permanent water supply and good pasturage to revive the herd. Many of these resting places became villages and towns that grew famous for auctions of cattle coming in from the immense hinterlands. Later the poorer scrublands where cattle could not graze were turned over to the raising of goats, the hides of which found a wide market. These goats multiplied prodigiously throughout the Northeast. Breeding alongside the cattle, they subsequently became the only meat within the reach of cowmen.

Cattle and goat herding grew, with farms multiplying randomly and incapable of absorbing so many people into herding activities, which had no need for many workers. So it was that ranches became breeding grounds for cattle, goats, and people: the cattle to sell, the goats to eat, the people to migrate.

Relying on this excess of labor, the ranchers first stopped paying cowmen in cattle and established a monetary wage system, which with deductions for food and lodging left the worker little pay. Afterward the whole pastoral Northeast began to concern itself with ancillary activities. The most important of these was the cultivation of an arboreal cotton native to the region, *mocó*, the xerophytic character of which allowed it to survive and produce even in the driest areas of the backlands, yielding a boll of long fibers with wide acceptance in the world market. The crop fitted in well with grazing by providing the cattle with seedcake, which was excellent feed, as well as with fodder from the stalks of the workers' subsistence gardens, where the rancher would turn his cattle loose after the harvest.

Every breeder, therefore, tried to be a mocó grower too, putting the families of his cowmen to work at this chore and later relying on people attracted especially by the new crops, bringing even more of them to the semiarid backlands. The cotton growers came onto the grazing lands as sharecroppers; that is, they received a plot of land on which to grow the food they consumed and other plots for harvests of mocó, of which they were to turn in half to the landowner. In that way on every ranch, in addition to the rancher's tile-roofed house with veranda and doors and windows, and the simple houses of his cowmen, there sprouted the miserable thatched huts that housed the cotton workers.

In other areas of the interior Northeast, the surplus population not needed for herding dedicated itself to extractive activities such as the exploitation of carnauba palms for the manufacture of wax and artifacts of straw, always under the same system of sharecropping with the landowner. These activities served to attract hundreds of thousands of workers only because of the misery of the population of the Northeast, for even when combined with subsistence farming, they did provide a minimal income that barely let a person survive.

In some areas of moister soil scattered about in the middle of the sertão—marshes, hills, meadows—some commercial agriculture developed alongside cattle raising. This was the case with the northeastern agreste, cooler and closer to the urban centers of consumption, where grazing was mingled with the growing of food crops without their being completely associated. Where agriculture prevailed, the cattle were fenced in; where grazing predominated, the crops were fenced. That more intensive economy engaged a larger demographic concentration, gathering the population into villages from which they went out to cultivate rented land under a sharecropping agreement and to work on the sugar plantations in cane-cutting teams.

Later on, with the growth in population, the grazing zones became mainly breeding grounds for people, whence came contingents of the labor force needed in other regions of the country. As noted, thus were formed the pioneer groups who penetrated the Amazon jungle to exploit native rubber trees and other gummiferous species. This was likewise what happened with the opening of new agricultural areas in the south, and it also served to enlarge urban populations whenever a burst of civil construction or industrialization demanded masses of unskilled workers.

In that way the backlands became a vast reservoir of cheap labor, living in part from the contributions sent home for the support of their families by backlanders who had left. The bad part, however, is that the people emigrating were precisely those few backlanders who had managed to reach the age of maturity with greater physical vigor and who tended to remain in the more prosperous zones of the south, the ones to whom the poverty-stricken society of their origins had given the wherewithal for education and the capability for work. Thus the most vigorous, most efficient, and most combative human element has been stolen away from the region at the very moment when it should be paying back this social expense.

In spite of these drains on its population, the sertão overflows with the unskilled people needed in latifundia grazing; from a precarious state, its mocó is in full decline, as is the minor extractive activity in which it is engaged; all of this leads to difficult conditions for providing subsistence. It is frightening that this immense offering of labor avid for employment has contributed to the lowering of wages in Brazil, which for unskilled work are the lowest in the world. The presence of these excess human beings is dramatically revealed during the droughts that periodically desolate the region. In those times waves of drought victims emerge from the backlands, parched by the dryness and the scorching sun, filling first the highways and then the towns and cities of the sertão with the somber presence of their misery.

Since the second half of the nineteenth century, the droughts of the Northeast have been considered a national problem that has called for governmental measures for aid and relief. Between federal power and the mass of drought victims, however, stands the powerful and lordly group of the "colonels," the landowners who completely control not only the land and the cattle but the positions of command and the work opportunities available. They are the main electors of deputies, senators, and governors; the manipulators of municipal and state authorities, always solicitous to take care of them and disposed to do everything that lends coherence and breadth to the authority of the landowners, spreading it all over the region. These owners of life, land, and herds are always more disturbed during droughts by the loss of their cattle than by the weight of the catastrophe on their backlands workers and are always predisposed to appropriate the government aid destined for the victims.

In this way the oligarchic order that had monopolized the land through the official award of land grants during the colonial period continues conducting relations with the public powers, according to the ruling groups' interests, managing in the end to put even droughts into their service and make a business out of them. Every drought, and sometimes the simple threat of a dry spell, is transformed into a political operation, which in the name of aid for the victims brings sizable appropriations for the opening of roads and especially the building of dams and cattle-breeding centers. During the last decades enormous federal sums have been set aside to take care of the populations of the Northeast affected by droughts, paying for the construction of thousands of dams, large and small, enriching the large landowners even more by assuring them life-saving water for their cattle during dry periods and plenty of roads to move their herds in search of fresh pasture. These same mechanisms have kept the people of the sertão under the hand of the bosses.

There has even come to be a "drought industry," easily established in an enormous area of low natural rainfall, as the politicians find ways to serve their clientele of businessmen and entrepreneurs, who proceed to live off and enrich themselves from the application of public aid funds, and big cattle breeders, who ask for new dams that increase the value of their lands but that cost them nothing. In spite of the governmental plans to see that the purpose of the dams is always for the irrigation of lands in the form of small family holdings for the growing of subsistence crops, never has a square inch of the lands benefited been set aside with that objective; the irrigated areas are under the control of ranchers for the uses that best suit them. Hence all programs for the relief of drought victims have resulted in initiatives that have consolidated the grazing latifundia, safeguarding the cattle of the ranchers but keeping the inhabitants of the backlands in the same precarious condition, more and more defenseless as they faces economic exploitation more damaging than the droughts.

A first permanent federal organization—the National Department of Works against Drought (DNOCS)—created to attend to the problem of droughts has been transformed into an agency of brazen service for the large breeders and the political bosses of the region; the Superintendency for Development of the Northeast (SUDENE), set up on modern bases and relatively free of favoritism (which would continue to be provided by the first institution), is devoted to the implantation of an infrastructure more capable of activating the regional economy. As was foreseeable, the program encountered the greatest opposition from the ruling groups of the Northeast and could be implemented only after demonstrating that it would not affect the social structure, especially the system of property.

In this way immense resources supplied with a high technical and moral purpose have benefited the Northeast, producing, however, much smaller social effects than even a portion of the same investments might have accomplished had it been possible to reshape the land-ownership structure. All the decisive institutional factors remained in the care of powerful political forces, whose interests are the opposite of those of the backlands population but whose control of the power structure is hegemonic.

Under these conditions of despotic control, the relationship of the man of the sertão with his boss is clothed in the greatest respect and deference, each cowman or farmworker making an effort to demonstrate his serviceability as a servant and his personal and political loyalty. Fearful of any attitude that might make them suspect, they submit to the prohibition of visitors from other ranches and even of any contact with strangers, in addition to a whole series of restrictions on personal and family behavior. Their supreme fear is to see themselves thrown out without a boss and master to protect them from arbitrary acts by the police, judges, the tax collector, and military recruiting agents. Isolated in a sea of ranching latifundia ruled by all-powerful owners, the only agents of public power, they have a real terror of being excluded from the niche in which they live, because that would be the equivalent of falling into a no-man's-land with the status of an outlaw. Paradoxically, that desperate way out is the only one left for the backlander to free himself from the oppression under which he lives; his choice is either to emigrate to other places or to fall into banditry.

In the outworking, an enormous number of people from the sertão have been compelled to increase the number of pioneering groups sent out to open the areas of exploitation beyond the frontiers of territories of long-standing occupation. It has been through their efforts that the barren zones they have penetrated, cultivated, and linked to the market by the most precarious roads have come to be known. But their fate has been that of eternal itinerants, the creators of niches that must inevitably be abandoned when the "legitimate owner" of the lands they have opened up arrives. The bitter experience of successive expulsions has hindered them even in that wilderness from attempting to grow anything with more than an annual cycle, further aggravating their state of poverty. Even though legislation exists for the protection of these pioneers, assuring them ownership of the land after a decade of continuous occupation, its effectiveness depends on access to the services of a registry that is far away and unreachable for the ordinary man of the backlands.

The prevailing system is, therefore, essentially the same as that of the royal land grants during the colonial period, except that now the concession of plots depends on the largesse of state politicians. In all the empty spaces of Mato Grosso and Goiás, Maranhão, Pará, and Amazonas, millions of acres of virgin land have been granted during the past decades to "owners" who have never seen them but who have appeared one day to dislodge as invaders the pioneers from the sertão, who—prodded by an age-old movement of expansion and human occupation of the interior barrens—had reached them, liked them, and settled there permanently.

In the vastness of the midlands, diverse ways of life have been shaped as local and functional adaptations of that expansion in the backlands. Thus along the fringes of the Amazon jungle a human front has come face to face with a virgin forest but lacks the capacity for penetrating it because of a the absence of entrepreneurial and technical means of settlement. Developing there was the harvesting of babassu palm nuts and jungle plants and the cultivation of small subsistence plots. This is still a new pioneering front in its formative phase, beset by new "owners," who, obtaining the newly cleared lands through concessions or squatting, follow in the backlanders' footsteps, always driving them farther along.

Farther to the south in the forests of Minas Gerais, Mato Grosso, and Goiás, the process has already been established. The rancher would make a contract with the pioneers to cut down stretches of forest under the stipulation that after the third food crop, they plant grass. In that way, freely granting the use of the land for a few crops, the rancher obtained for nothing the execution of the most difficult task, that of clearing the forest in order to expand his grazing land. In addition to the brutal exploitation of the peasant masses, this system meant a progressive limitation of the area that could be cultivated, setting apart for the growing of food crops only those areas to be cleared.

Hence instead of there being a growth in the areas of food cultivation, an expansion of fields from the clearing of the forest for that purpose, grazing land was extended. Here one can see another deforming action of those privileged by the system: taking advantage of their ownership of the land in any way they see fit, they even reach the point of denying it the fulfillment of its essential function, which is to feed the population of Brazil.

In the fields of the central west, where there is good pasturage and a regular rainy season, the life of the backlander takes on a different feature. The ranches are fenced in with wire, grazing becomes an orderly business, and the cowman is transformed into a paid worker who must buy his own food, meat included.

Thanks to the quality of the pasturage and crossbreeding with strains from India, the cattle grow more rapidly, take on a broader frame, and provide more meat. In this more advanced grazing system it has become more advantageous for the breeders to exclude beef from the diet of the cowmen. Therefore they do not grow and take on vigor like the cattle but remain skinny and stunted as in the poorer regions. They continue to be disregarded in comparison with the herd as the more expendable and less valuable species. This can be seen in a thousand ways but perhaps most revealingly in the meticulous veterinary measures taken to defend the cattle against epizootics in a world where nothing is done to combat diseases that attack the human population.

Any cowman knows from his own experience the great contrast in facilities available to help an infected bull and the trouble he finds in getting medical treatment for a sick child. Scandalously evident in the milking stalls where the cattle are stabled is the assured plenty of rations for the cows and the niggardliness of the rations on which the peon can depend. Even in the most prosperous grazing areas, the social order thus degrades men, confirming the commercial primacy of cattle-as-merchandise over the human community.

Nevertheless, the situation of the worker paid by a boss looks like a privileged one in contrast to the conditions of the masses of the sertão, concentrated on barren lands or wandering over the countryside in search of eventual work or land to be cultivated, no matter what its condition. The small capacity of the grazing economy for absorption of labor combined with the appropriation of lands by ranchers and with the continuous expansion of grazing activities into forest areas leads the backlands population into a situation of unspeakable poverty.

In vast areas of the interior midlands, large contingents of backlanders dedicate themselves to prospecting for rock crystals, semiprecious stones, gold, and rare minerals. They group together for this in provisional and itinerant campgrounds that spring up and disappear according to the exploitation of each claim, leaving behind only the holes that remain from the digging.

The prospectors display peculiar characteristics, derived both from their backlands origins and from their specialization in mineral extractive activity with its historical vicissitudes of clandestine prospecting for diamonds when these constituted a monopoly of the Portuguese Crown. In response to these conditioning elements, two strange traits developed: an austere manner that admits no break in discipline and that combats theft in a most drastic way; and the adventurous and nomadic spirit of one who works according to the whims of fate. Every man works hard at the job, always driven by the hope of getting rich quickly with the great strike of his life. The real profits, however, are few and are soon gone in profligate spending so as not to spoil his luck, which will look upon him even more generously tomorrow.

For that reason, always present in the prospectors' encampments are the traveling merchants, with their gaudy and superfluous articles for sale, along with the black marketeers, who sometimes underwrite the work but are essentially the local purchasers of the product.

The backlands populations, developing in isolation from the coast, scattered in small nuclei across the human desert that is the midland grazing area, preserve many archaic traits. To these have been added diverse peculiarities from adaptation to the milieu and the productive function they perform or originating in the types of society they have developed. In their bearing and their fatalistic, conservative mentality, these people are in flagrant contrast to the coastal populations, who enjoy an intense social life together and keep in touch with the world. On many occasions that cultural distance is seen to be deeper than the customary difference between country and city dwellers in all societies, making mutual misunderstanding explode into bloody conflicts. In truth, the society of the interior sertão has been at a distance from coastal people, a distance not only spatial but also social and cultural, establishing a difference that sets them apart as though they were distinct peoples.

The traditional man of the sertão is characterized by his simple religiosity, which tends toward fanatical messianism; by his old-fashioned customs, sparse speech, rusticity, and predisposition to sacrifice and violence; and by the moral characteristics of herding groups the world over, like the cult of personal honor, pride, and loyalty to his leaders. These peculiar traits often involve the development of anarchic forms of behavior that encompass vast multitudes, creating social problems of the greatest gravity. Their two principal forms of expression have been the *cangaço,* or banditry, and religious fanaticism, both released by the conditions of penury under which the backlander lives but shaped by the singularities of his cultural world.

Until the middle of the 1930s, with the building of highways through the center of the sertão, the cangaço operated as a kind of revolt typical for the region. It was a form of banditry common to the pastoral backlands made up of bands of *jagunços,* or thugs, wearing the dress of cowmen and well armed, patrolling the highways of the sertão in mounted gangs like waves of severe and violent justice. Everyone making up the band had his own moral justification for being drawn into banditry—one to avenge an affront to his personal or family honor; another to see that justice was done with his own hands because of wrongs endured from a local potentate—all making of banditry an expression of backlands revolt against the injustices of the world. It sometimes resulted in an outburst of a particular kind of savage heroism that led to extremes of ferocity. Such were the famous *cangaceiros* who, on the one hand, made amends to the poor for their poverty with the goods they distributed after each attack, while on the other hand they killed, maimed, and raped in pure exhibitions of fury.

It must be pointed out that the cangaço arose out of the social structure of the sertão, the fruit of the lordly system of the grazing latifundia itself, which incited people to banditry through the attraction of jagunços by the "colonels" to be their *capangas* (bodyguards) and also their avengers. Frequently the ranchers would recruit large bands, concentrating them on the ranches, when two clans of colonels faced each other in the frequent disputes over land. Those capangas, esteemed for the loyalty they developed for their masters, for their personal courage, and even for the ferocity that made them capable of carrying out any order, stood out from the mass of backlanders, receiving privileged treatment from their masters. It must be added that every band of cangaceiros had its protective colonel, who would hide them and protect them on his lands in exchange for security from the band itself and also for its serving him against enemies. These matters were socially conditioned by the system itself, which encouraged and provided incentives for bandit violence.

More relevant still is the fact that the whole population of the sertão, even though disowning the thugs because of the terror they instilled, still saw in them ideal models of honor and valor, sung about in popular verses, models of justice who were elevated and praised. Because of all this the cangaço and its thugs, bloody but pious and in fear of God and the saints of their particular devotion, feared but admired, condemned but also praised, constituted a typical product of backlands society.

Another characteristic expression of the sociocultural world of the backlands is religious fanaticism, which has many roots in common with banditry. Both are expressions coming out of penury and backwardness — forces that, incapable of being manifested in higher forms of awareness and struggle, lead desperate masses astray into unbridled violence and militant mysticism. The fanaticism was based on messianic beliefs held all over the sertão among people waiting to see their savior from poverty rise up one day. He will come with his royal retinue to overthrow the order of the world, restoring to the humble their offended dignity and to the poor their despoiled rights: "The sertão will become sea and the sea sertão." It is a matter of an echo in the Brazilian sertão of the Portuguese messianism regarding King Sebastian.

Periodically there arise announcers of the arrival of the messiah, bringing the people together to fast, pray, and flagellate themselves so that with this purification they will open the path to the reincarnation of old mythical heroes.

One of those thaumaturges in Pedra Bonita, Pernambuco, called for the blood of innocent children to be poured onto a rock and thus to awaken King Sebastian and his knights, who would materialize there with the armies that had fallen in the crusades against the Moor. Another, José Lourenço do Caldeirão, led in Ceará the cult of a miraculous ox, the urine of which was gathered with veneration as a most efficient medicine against all illnesses. Others led endless marches out of the sertão of starving multitudes of pilgrims, who exorcized and flagellated themselves in hope of miracles. Yet others attracted huge pilgrimages to their seats, where they prayed, confessed, counseled, and especially cured the incurably ill and gave hope to the hopeless.

Sometimes the results of these focal crescendos—as occurred in the Juazeiro of Father Cícero—were the enticement of backlanders to work for years and for nothing on the land of relatives of the miracle worker. Frequently they took on more tragic aspects, as in the events provoked by Antônio Conselheiro toward the end of the last century. Gathered around that thaumaturge, who combined the passion of a prophet with the talents of a social reformer in Canudos in the sertão of the upper São Francisco River, was a vast backlands population fired up by his mysticism. The neighboring landowners immediately saw the intrinsically subversive character of those worshipers. What would follow that surge of biblical religious fervor was the abandonment of farms by workers who served there, and the result would inevitably be the division of landholdings if the evil was not eradicated.

They failed to contain matters, however, because of the leadership powers of Antônio Conselheiro, founded on his capacity to instill in the backlands masses the hope of salvation and of a better life on earth itself. Once activated, people were transformed and leaped out of their traditional resignation and humility into extreme combativeness. Every backlander who approached the thaumaturge was transformed into a gleaming seeker of divine justice, ready to devote himself solely to prayers and to reconstruction of the social order on new bases.

Canudos, the center of the sacred gathering, attracted men from neighboring areas and already had more than a thousand houses when the landowners demanded intervention by state troops. These were defeated. The authorities of the state of Bahia then called upon the army, which sent two large contingents. These were also defeated by the fanatics, who thus gained weapons and ammunition for even stronger resistance. The idea then arose in urban centers, aroused by the problem and scandal of the military victories of those backlands thugs, that it was a matter of a gang of monarchists in rebellion against the republican regime and under the direction, perhaps, of Portuguese agents.

In 1897 a whole army was assembled to fight the hamlet of Canudos. It was supplied with all the instruments of war, including heavy artillery. That modern professional army was able to defeat the obstinate resistance of the fanatics only after heavy fighting, and it was able to do so only at the price of wiping out the whole population. The episode was famous for its sinister image and also for the white-hot picture of that dispute between the two faces of Brazilian society left us in Os Sertões (published in English as Rebellion in the Backlands), by Euclides da Cunha, written as a grim indictment of the government involved in it.

It was a repugnant victory. Shameful. It was, in reality, counterproductive compensation for the munificent costs of combat, defeats, and thousands of lives, the capture of that human trash, at the same time pitiful and sinister, somewhere between tragic and obscene, as they passed before one's eyes in a long stream of carcasses and rags. (Cunha 1945, 606)

The memory of Canudos has also been perpetuated in the oral tradition of the sertão populations, who took in the few survivors of the massacre and heard from them and retained the heroic episodes of resistance and struggle—and, above all, the lesson of hope in the teachings of the Conselheiro, the Counselor, for the possibility of creating a new social order without large landholders or authorities.

In recent years the isolation of the backlands has been broken as the all-powerful landowners have been disarmed by the federal government, and their ranches have been cut through by roads with thousands of trucks bringing in people, merchandise, and new ideas at the same time as the people of the sertão are being reached by radio and village movie theaters that are familiarizing them with the great world outside.

In those penetrated backlands where a central political authority has now been able to enforce law and justice, even though it can still be done only with the connivance of the local colonels, there is no longer any place for thugs and fanatics. The social tensions tend to be structured along new lines. Political disputes themselves are no longer exclusively the result of family quarrels or contests for prestige among colonels who call on the loyalty of their men; they take place rather between opposing camps of national leaders that recruit the landowners and their dependents into political parties, opposing each other in everything except the maintenance of the landowning system from which all of them, in the end, draw their votes and the majority of their leadership cadres.

More recently a new polarization of forces has been shaping up, putting into opposition on one side the traditional parties, supporters of the old oligarchic order, and on the other side reform movements based on the independent vote of the urban masses. While this polarization prevailed, the people of the backlands were summoned to an alternative by new political voices, which, leaping over the fences of ranches and coming to them over the radio, encouraged them to fight for their own cause.

Called upon to take a position in this new polarization, the man of the backlands is gradually acquiring greater social awareness. Contributing to this, too, are migrant backlanders who return to their lands, bringing from the south the image of progressive regions where more humane and just treatment, freer and more open customs, and especially a higher standard of living prevail. All these ingredients are actively at work to broaden the mental horizons of the people of the backlands and to call on and reorient the energies that had previously been turned toward banditry and mysticism.

It must be pointed out, however, that the awakening of the backlanders' awareness of their own cause has not yet taken on the aspect of a generalized rebellion. But it has already reached a posture of nonconformity that stands in contrast to traditional resignation. It has not reached the point of explaining social life in realistic terms of interest, opposing and, rarely, placing in doubt the sacred picture of the world that explains, through fate and divine help, the wealth of the wealthy and the poverty of the poor. Their nonconformity is shown mainly in attitudes of withdrawal: the idealization of the past as a wonderful age in which the cowman was paid in cattle and in which the land was free for the one who wished to live on it and work it; the idealization of life in other regions of the country where the living is easy and where with little effort a man can eat well and live with dignity. And there is the hope of seeing emergence of a new governmental paternalism more sensitive to their cause than to the interests of the landowners. But these attitudes have led to the abandonment of the backlands for other rural areas and the cities and to redemptivist politics rather than active pressure for a reordering of backlands society.

For the masses of the grazing backlands, that basic and passive nonconformity still prevails, which can be explained by the age-old monopoly of the land and by excessive population growth in a socioeconomic framework that renders impossible technological innovation capable of bringing about progress and plenty. These conditioning elements bring forth a narrow dependence of the backlander on the rancher, which operates as a mechanism of consolidation for the system.

In spite of the penury in which they live, both the backlanders employed as cowmen and the hired hands or tenant farmers who till someone else's land in a system of sharecropping feel permanently threatened with being thrown off the land along with their families and hence falling into the even more miserable status of rural displaced persons. Below every person who succeeds in getting a job in the productive system, there exists a marginalized mass that is even more miserable and into which anyone could fall.

These conditions render extremely difficult any political organization of backlands populations lost in the desert of vacant lands or swallowed up in the latifundia system. These people are born, live, and die confined to other people's land, taking care of cattle, houses, fences, and fields that have jealous owners. Even the miserable shack in which they live, built by their own hands out of mud and straw from the fields, does not belong to them. Nothing stimulates them to improve it, nor will the landowner allow them to make it better by planting fruit trees or breeding farm animals, because he does not want to have to indemnify them when they are to be turned out.

This situation of the farmworker or cowman of the backlands contrasts with the circumstances of the village peasant of feudal Europe, who lived in a community where his parents and grandparents had been born and died, always working the same land, all involved in a continuous effort to provide their own subsistence, paying the rents owed their lord but always improving their conditions of life and work in the niche where they were located in order to make it steadily more habitable. No matter how many years or generations he has remained on a piece of land, the backlander is always a temporary worker subject to being displaced at any moment without any explanation or rights. Therefore, his home is a hut in which he is only a tenant; his plot is a marginal garden capable only of assuring him the vital minimum to avoid dying of hunger; and his attitude is one of reserve and mistrust, which is fitting for a person living on someone else's land, begging pardon for existing. When, in spite of all his care to live unnoticed, he becomes the object of attention, it is to have new iniquities thrust upon him, which he must bear, aggravating his misfortunes even more.

Thus, only the free farmer who works as a tenant on someone else's land or settles on unoccupied land or in hamlets reaches the minimum conditions of social interaction that permit him to develop politically and to assume the behavior of a citizen. Only these show their rebellion against the landowning system by openly suing for ownership of land.

That movement underwent rapid expansion by means of leagues and rural syndicates—the latter mainly on sugar-factory plantations, where great masses of wage-earning farm workers are concentrated—organized by urban leaders of diverse political orientation, ranging from Catholic priests to Communist militants. They were founded, however, on the precarious base of transitory political circumstances. When these were overturned by the military coup, the sertão sank once more into the despotism of the large landowners.

In the last thirty years a technological discovery has opened up new perspectives of economic life for the broad open areas. It has been shown that these immense plains could offer perfect conditions for the growing of soybeans or wheat if the acidity could be corrected. Therefore the *cerrados* are being invaded by groups of large planters from the south along with a huge amount of machinery for the cultivation of cereal crops for export. A few backlanders are learning to be tractor drivers or specialized workers at these large agricultural centers. For the human mass of the backlands, this new wealth has offered no hope whatever.

I can picture a string of northeasterners, adults and children, ragged, heads covered with their hats of straw or leather, squatting and looking in awe at the huge machines turning over the old earth of the plains.

Rural, *Caipira* Brazil

> Penetrating the forest hunting for Indians, men and women, the latter for the exercise of his lusts, the former for the profit of his interests . . . he does not even know how to speak [Portuguese] . . . nor is he any different from the most barbarous wild Indian except in saying that he is a Christian and in spite of having been married for a short time he is accompanied by seven Indian concubines.
>
> **Bishop of Olinda on Domingos Jorge Velho, the bandeirante captain who wiped out the quilombo of Palmares, 1694**

While the sugar nuclei of the Northeast were growing and becoming wealthy, the population of São Paulo was bogged down in an economy of poverty. Not having any large sugar plantations, which were the wealth of the period, the area had no black slaves either, and rarely did any ship go as far south as the anchorage of São Vicente. At the end of a century and a half the most important nuclei of São Paulo were hamlets of mud or adobe huts with straw roofs.

The leaders who were the local authorities and in charge of the bandeiras, the expeditions that devastated the inner backlands, lived with their families at locations in the interior under equally poor conditions. Each one was served by captive Indians, who cultivated cassava, beans, corn, squash, and tubers to eat along with meat from the hunt or fish that were caught, and who grew tobacco for their pipes, annatto, pepper for condiment, and some other native plants.

With their families and in dealings with the bandeirantes too, they spoke only the lingua franca, which was a variant of the language of the coastal Tupi Indians. Indigenous also were the techniques for gathering firewood and for hunting, fishing, and picking of wild fruit on which they lived. Household articles such as hammocks for sleeping, kneading troughs, gourds, strainers, etc. differed little from those in use in Indian villages.

Although their luxuries, as compared to tribal life, consisted of simple clothing, salt, pork rind, a few metal tools, firearms, tallow candles for illumination, an occasional tidbit like a block of brown sugar, and the cane liquor they distilled, they nevertheless retained a haughty bearing. Each family spun and wove crude cotton for their sleeping hammocks and clothing for everyday wear—baggy pants topped by a loose jacket for the men, blouses tucked into full, long skirts for the women. They all went barefoot or wore simple slippers or sandals. The garments served to cover their bodies in contrast to those of the Indians, who were wont to leave theirs in full view without modesty, ornamented with annatto and genipap.

That poverty, which formed the base of both their motivations and their customs and shaped the character of the old bandeirantes, was what made them a band of adventurers always ready for any bold task, always more predisposed to pillage than to production. Every bandeirante leader worth his salt could raise hundreds or even thousands of men under arms, and the truth is that the immense majority of them consisted of Indian bowmen.

Nothing else was needed, however, since the enemy to be faced consisted of hostile tribal Indians, tame missionary Indians, or quilombo blacks who were practically unarmed. Their subsistence economy with a Tupi tribal base served admirably to support those hundreds of fighting Indians, who needed only huts they made themselves, garden plots they cleared themselves, and hunting and fishing, which they also took care of. The fundamental contributions of the bandeirantes to these nuclei were a military discipline superior to a tribal one and the mercantile motivations, also more fitting for the circumstances.

It is probable that the Indian drawn to these bands, after being removed far enough from his tribe so as to dissuade him from returning, would have been integrated into these groups without any difficulty because of their almost tribal simplicity. He would not have been placed under rigid working discipline as on a plantation but had the alternation between effort and leisure to which he was accustomed. His status was probably quite close to what he would have encountered, for example, as a captive Indian of warlike tribes like the Guaikuru, serving a chieftain as a slave. In both cases he would find a well-defined social role and a possibility of integration into a new cultural world, which would be tolerable even though less desirable than the tribal one. The greatest inconvenience was the impossibility of having a woman (because these would always be fought over) or a family life.

That rudimentary, poor way of life was the result of the social retrogressions of the deculturative process. The bandeirante had lost the communitarian village life of his Portuguese side, along with the patriarchal discipline of traditional agrarian societies, the plow, and a diet based on wheat, olive oil, and wine. On the indigenous side he had lost the autonomy of the egalitarian village, with everything focused on its own subsistence, the equality in social relationships of a society not stratified into classes, the solidarity of the extended family, and the skills of artisans whose intent was to live by the rhythm with which their ancestors had always lived.

The bandeirante nuclei, attached to an external mercantile economy and motivated by ambitions for enrichment, did not wish merely to exist like the Indians with whom they were almost mingled. Integrated into the divisional structure of the colony, they aspired to be part of the ruling group, to give themselves consumer luxuries and the power to influence and command. Armed with a rudimentary technology, but one far superior to the tribal one and assembled from European and indigenous elements, the bandeirantes exercised their destiny: to pounce upon the people and things of the land, capturing and pillaging whatever was within reach, in order to prove themselves socially.

For all these reasons the São Paulo mamelucos—as men of the jungle and sertão superior even to the Indians themselves—became the terror of free tribal groups and Indians catechized by the Jesuits and later of runaway blacks and those gathered in quilombos. For a century and a half the bandeirantes became hunters of Indians, first to be the workforce in their settlements and villages and later as merchandise to be sold to sugar plantations. In that way they depopulated the villages of agricultural indigenous groups over immense areas, in the end going to hunt them down thousands of miles inland, wherever they might have taken refuge.

Having become skilled at these practices, the bandeirantes at the beginning of the seventeenth century attacked the prosperous Jesuit missions in Paraguay, where tens of thousands of Indians, settled and disciplined for farming, herding, and artisanry, offered themselves as most tempting booty. The catechumens were especially valuable at that time because of the lack of black slaves on whom the plantations of Bahia depended; the Dutch had control of the sources of supply in Africa. But in addition to Indians to enslave, the bandeirantes found church decorations, tools, and other items of value in the Jesuit missions, along with a great many head of cattle.

Entire missions, among the richest and most populous, like Guaíra (western Paraná), Batim (southern Mato Grosso), and Tapes (Rio Grande do Sul), were thus destroyed by the São Paulo bandeirantes, who pillaged their possessions and enslaved their Indians. It is thought that the bandeirantes sold more than 300,000 Indians, mainly from the missions, to plantation owners in the Northeast.

These undertakings to raid the Jesuit missions of Paraguay sometimes called for the mobilization of all the bandeirantes available along with their trustworthy Indians. The largest of these groups would be made up of 2,000 to 3,000 people, a third of them "whites," who were doubtless almost all mamelucos. Going along were men, women, old men who could still walk and fight, and children, all divided into families, like a vast mobile city, settling down along the way, making gardens and hunting and fishing in order to eat but always pushing on to attack the missionary Indians in their redoubts, defeat them, and take them captive. In addition to the nucleus of combatants with its military hierarchy and incipient legal and religious establishment, the bandeira proceeded through the backlands with a whole retinue of auxiliaries who carried the burdens of supplies and tools, Indians who hunted and fished and gathered food, and sertão scouts who blazed trails and showed the way.

Thus, at a time when the nations disinherited in the division of the world were resorting to the maritime piracy of corsairs, the bandeirantes, who were the disinherited of Brazil, were also plunging into pillage with equal violence and greed. Left out of the economic process of the colony where almost everyone was involved in the lucrative and peaceful chores of sugar plantations and cattle ranches, the São Paulo bandeirantes ended up with a specialty as men of war. Every time the Indians put up major resistance to the opening up of a new area, the suppressing hand of the bandeirantes was called upon. Likewise, when there was a slave revolt or when a group of blacks rose up and established in a quilombo a solid resistance to local forces, the bandeirantes were called in.

In that way fighting units of bandeirante leaders and their fighting Indian warriors went beyond the impenetrable backlands that were their usual field of action to all the prosperous regions of the country, contracted to dislodge Indians or to destroy quilombos. Some of these sinister bandeirantes ended up remaining in different regions as cattle breeders or farmworkers. The majority, however, returned to their refuge, rejoining the difficult and primitive life of their people. They formed a society that, because it was poorer, was also more egalitarian, where masters and captive Indians got along as leaders and soldiers rather than as masters and slaves.

Miscegenation was widespread because there was almost no one among men of rank who was not of mixed blood. Under those circumstances the son of an Indian woman slave and her master grew up free among his equals, who were not people with a tribal identity like his mother, much less *mazombos*, as Portuguese were called, but so-called mamelucos, the product of previous mixtures of Portuguese with Indian women, proud of their autonomy and their valor as warriors.

The family structure was patricentric and polygynic, dominated by the chief, a domestic group with people of different generations—basically the father, his women and their respective offspring, and their relatives. The Indian women brought into the group as captives were concubines of the father and his sons. Only little by little was religious marriage undertaken for the establishment of the mother of the legitimate children among the women of each man. In their wills, many old bandeirantes would consign the quota of their sparse possessions that was to fall to their legitimate children, and what was left to be distributed among the others, with the boastful explanation that they considered as their children all those whose mothers said they were.

The work program, aimed at sustenance and not commerce, was almost the same as that of a tribal village. Falling to the women were the tasks of housekeeping, planting, gathering, gardening, preparing meals, caring for children, washing clothes, and carrying loads; to the men fell the sporadic tasks that called for great expenditure of energy, such as clearing, hunting, and war, but which permitted long periods of rest and leisure after each activity. During the long inactive periods of waiting for expeditions into the sertão, the men remained at home, restless, like warriors on alert. In that atmosphere there were frequent outbreaks of bloody conflicts. Those habits gave the early inhabitants of São Paulo the reputation of headstrong and lazy people.

In spite of that primitivism, sixteenth-century São Paulo was also an implant of western European civilization, a world mercantile emporium, a slaveholding colonial enclave of the Iberian mercantile-salvationist formation. Because of all these qualities it was in flagrant contrast to the tribal organization of undifferentiated agricultural villages with which it interacted without joining them. On the contrary, it imposed its domination on them and led them to physical extermination, causing the advent there of a different people in the territory they had previously occupied.

As a civilization, it was a late transplant of a Romanness reshaped by successive transfigurations on the Iberian peninsula, which at a certain moment took on form and vigor to expand as a conquering macroethnicity. In that sense, repeated in São Vicente—as in all of Brazil as well—were the situations where Carthaginian and Roman conquerors imposed their language, religion, and culture on the Celtic-Iberian peoples, transforming them ethnically into Portuguese. In both cases we have the same modality of movement from one evolutionary stage to another, the step that takes place through the historical incorporation of a people into a conquering macroethnicity with the loss of their own cultural autonomy.

This means that in São Paulo a rise from tribalism to civilization did not take place but rather a formation, with people torn away from tribes, of an emerging ethnicity that was born umbilically tied to an exogenous society and culture and was shaped by and dependent on them. São Paulo arose, therefore, as a historical-cultural configuration shaped by the crossing of people of differing racial bases and by the integration of their cultural heritages under the governance of the dominating one, which in the long run would impose the preponderance of its genetic characteristics and its culture.

As a mercantile outpost, São Paulo was a module in the transatlantic network of production and commerce connected by oceangoing ships. Its principal merchandise consisted of captured Indians to be sold as slaves to sugar-growing centers in the Northeast and other parts as well. Capistrano de Abreu, referring to São Paulo, said that Brazil, before it was an importer, was an exporter of slaves. But even though this was for the internal market, it was in interaction with a mercantile circuit that allowed for the provision of imported products, principally weapons and tools. The very business of selling Indians as slaves was part of the world traffic in slaves and had its rhythm and success determined by the hazards of the capture and export of Africans.

As a formation, São Paulo was not a reincarnation of progressive stages of human evolution. It was a colonial slaveholding formation structured as a contemporary and coeval counterpart of the Iberian mercantile-salvationist formation. That historical-evolutionary position is what imposed, on the one hand, its basic characteristic of a society stratified into antagonistic classes in rural and urban components, the latter freed of the tasks of pure subsistence in order to occupy themselves in other functions, and on the other hand, its role as an agent for the spread of Iberian civilization and the imposition of its domination over all Brazilian territory.

The great hope of the Paulistas in their forays into the sertão was always that of coming upon deposits of gold, silver, or precious stones. This also goaded the Portuguese Crown as it strove to see that its chunk of the Americas produced the same wealth that the Spaniards were taking out of Mexico and Peru. So it was that the bandeiras could obtain official support and even some help for the expeditions looking to discover precious metals.

Gold finally appeared in the backlands of Taubaté, first in poor veins, which only stimulated the search, and later on in prodigiously rich deposits in the hills of Minas Gerais, the exploitation of which would transform all of Brazilian colonial society and, carried to Europe, would alter the monetary pattern. Pandiá Calógeras estimated the wealth taken out of Brazil during the colonial period at 1,400 tons of gold and 3 million carats of diamonds (Calógeras 1938, 60–61).

Such were the mining areas discovered by the São Paulo bandeirantes in the mountains of the interior of the country at the dawn of the eighteenth century in Minas Gerais (1698), then in Mato Grosso (1719), and later in Goiás (1725). With the very first news of the discovery of gold, multitudes poured into the mining areas from all over Brazil and later from Portugal as well. In only a few years those deserted regions were transformed into the most densely populated area in the Americas, with a concentration of close to 300,000 inhabitants by around 1750. The rich came with all their slaves, claiming large mines; the middle class came with what they had and the poor with just a few blacks, with only one, or with none but also in search of their fortunes. The human migration reached such numbers that the Crown faced the contingency of having to restrain it by passing successive decrees in order to avoid an exodus from plantations and towns of old settlement.

The exploitation began with alluvial gold, which was mixed in with the sand and gravel of streambeds ("profit" gold) and in the banks ("shallow" gold). There it was simply a matter of washing and pounding the sand in order to find the nuggets and turn them into gold dust. Later on it was the turn of "gravel" gold, which was found in the mountains. With that it became necessary to use a more complicated process, which involved channeling water for washing and separating the pebbles and, frequently, the crushing of stones in which the gold was embedded. Finally, there was also the exploitation of mined gold, where veins had to be followed into the earth, calling for more work and more sophisticated techniques.

Initially, however, the amount of gold that was found on the surface of the ground, which could be had just by panning, was enormous. That ease of exploitation led to the rapid petering out of alluvial beds, obliging prospectors to move their camps to new locations. Some of the first centers of exploitation were so rich that huts were built right over the gold-bearing ground and had to be torn down later to continue with the washing of gravel. In that way camps were formed that became villages and later towns, literally founded on gold, like Vila Rica, Cuiabá, and Goiás, among many others. Built from that rich mud, even today these cities show people pounding the earth of an old ruined adobe wall in search of nuggets.

The influx of people into the mining areas and the greed with which they set about searching for gold brought on grave social problems, hunger, and conflicts. Copious historical documentation shows how one could die of hunger or barely survive by eating wild roots and the foulest of animals with his hands full of gold. They also report conflicts among miners, arising mainly between bandeirantes and newcomers. The former, considering themselves to have greater rights as the discoverers of all that new wealth, fought against the invasion of Bahians, Pernambucans, and other Brazilians as well as against the Portuguese attracted by the mines. The so-called War of the Emboabas, or outsiders (1710), was the most serious confrontation of this type.

Only one decade after the discovery, the colonial authorities established themselves in the new regions with effective power, becoming capable of compelling crop cultivation in order to provide subsistence, of squelching conflicts, and of settling disputes over control of waters for sluicing and over the ownership of the richest areas.

Thereupon a fierce struggle began between the native-born entrepreneurs and the Portuguese ruling class, with the first making an effort to retain and increase their holdings against the assessing extremes of the Crown. The inclination to spirit the gold and diamonds and the withholding of taxes prevailed from then on as the deepest feeling in the hearts of the miners and as their particular form of rebellion. The Crown reacted with extra taxes, punitive demands, confiscation, and repression, but it was never able to deal with illegal possession or smuggling, which were the Brazilians' defense against the plundering. The population responded with conspiracies, sometimes quickly crushed but at other times calling for the mobilization of thousands of soldiers to put them down. The main such uprising, which broke out in 1720, ended with the drawing and quartering of Felipe dos Santos and the burning of rebels' houses.

Also during the first half of the eighteenth century, discovery of a rich diamond region brought on new human movement. In the eyes of the Crown, however, the wealth was too great to remain in the hands of Brazilians. A royal monopoly was decreed. Accordingly, diamonds would be exploited first by those under contract to the Crown and later directly by agents of the mother country. The royal monopoly, in spite of being decreed and imposed by means of the largest repressive apparatus of the colonial period, did not prevent clandestine prospecting for diamonds. This continued, ending up with the formation of a characteristic social type, the prospector, who still today maintains traits of independence, reserve, and rebellion that can be explained by those clandestine origins.

The first populators built and abandoned settlements continuously as the veins were discovered and petered out. But they soon formed centers, at first in the nearest resting places, where stands were set up that later became inns and warehouses. There everyone bought tools and utensils, salt, gunpowder, cloth, provisions, and cane liquor, paying for it all in ounces of gold dust, which was the currency of the region. That wealth attracted importers, escorts bringing from the coast columns of slaves tied to one another, drovers who carried all manner of merchandise on donkeys. Some of those rest areas became settled, developing into towns and villages capable of furnishing the population with the necessities of religion and justice along with merchandise. In that way the basis of what would become a broad and prosperous urban network was built up with extraordinary speed.

The slaves in the mine works lived all gathered together in huts set up in the area, working under the strict vigilance of inspectors and overseers, who were on guard against the purloining and even swallowing of the larger nuggets and especially of diamonds. The slaves enjoyed certain prerogatives as compared to those in the canefields, however, with an opportunity to cultivate their own plots and sometimes to buy their freedom, if they reached an unusual level of production. In that world requiring a great variety of technical aptitudes, many skilled blacks became craftsmen. To them are owed the first iron forges, indispensable in mines for the manufacture of working tools, for shoeing the drovers' mules, and for cart wheels.

In the mining zones Brazilian society took on particular characteristics as a branch of the São Paulo trunk through the influence of Brazilians coming from other areas, through new European contingents incorporated into it, and also through the presence of a large mass of slaves, both African and native, brought from the old sugar-producing areas. The main conforming element of that cultural variant was the initial economic activity of mining and the local wealth that it generated, creating the conditions for an urban life more complex and splendid than in any other region of the country.

The opening up of the mining regions had some external consequences of importance in addition to the movement of populations. It brought about the transfer of the colonial capital from Bahia to the port of Rio de Janeiro—which had been a poverty-stricken settlement like old São Vicente—laying the groundwork for a great administrative and commercial center on the southern coast, in the immediate area of which a new nucleus of agrarian economy was developed. It stimulated the expansion of northeastern grazing into the areas along the São Francisco River and the west-central region, assuring a new consumer market at a time when the Northeast was in decline. Finally, in the southern region conquered by the bandeirantes with the destruction of the Jesuit missions, it made possible occupation for cattle grazing, which endeavor spread out over the plains, and especially for the breeding of mules, which supplied almost all land transport in colonial Brazil.

Thus, in addition to representing a new economic activity of greater profit than previous ones, mining brought about the integration of colonial society, assuring thereby the basic requirement of national Brazilian unity over a vast territory that had now been penetrated.

A half century after the mineral discoveries, the region of Minas was already the most populous and richest of the colony, with a broad urban network. Over the following decades it would vibrate with a brilliant social life, served by majestic public buildings, spacious churches of exquisite baroque architecture, two-story mansions, and cobblestone streets embellished with bridges and fountains of carved stone.

Simultaneously there developed a lordly class of royal and ecclesiastical authorities, wealthy merchants, and mine owners, both Brazilian and Portuguese, served by a wide circle of professional military men, bureaucrats, magistrates, auditors, tax collectors, and clerks. Within this circle everyone had a cordial manner of "urbanity without affectation," according to a European observer. The men wore jackets and black flannel trousers from Manchester; the women allowed themselves the luxury of following

French fashions. They produced architecture and painting of the highest quality, creating a Brazilian variant of the baroque, lyrical literature, and even libertarian politics. They read revolutionary thinkers and composed erudite music, magnificently orchestrated.

The mining activities that maintained this urban luxury also favored the creation of a broad intermediate group between the wealthy citizens and the poor workers in the diggings. They were artisans and musicians, many of them mulattos and even blacks, who now managed to attain a decent pattern of life and to disassociate themselves from subsistence chores in order to be completely involved in their specialties. To attend to this group, trade organizations modeled on the Portuguese ones were founded, which became powerful centers in the defense of professional interests, bringing separately into association goldsmiths, stonemasons, carpenters, wood-carvers, blacksmiths, actors, sculptors, painters, and other artisans.

Religious activities governed the calendar of social life, ruling all inter-actions among the diverse social strata. This was done through various brotherhoods organized by caste, which brought together free blacks, mulattos, and whites, separating them into different groups but also bringing all of them together in the social life of the colony. Each had its own church, which was its pride, a private cemetery, and the right to funerals with the participation of its own clergy and its professional mu-sicians. Blacks, too, even slaves, created their own organizations, devoted like the others to some saint. This was the case of the sumptuous Sanctu-ary of the Rosary of the Blacks in Ouro Preto.

The sustenance of that urban population called for the creation of di-versified agricultural enterprise, supplying provisions of meat, brown sugar, cheeses, smoked pork, and many other products. A small portion of the slaves was destined for these tasks, given their massive engagement in mining operations. The agricultural tasks were mainly undertaken by free blacks and mulattos and the poorest whites, unable to get into mining since it was now no longer a simple matter of panning but involved dig-ging mines and leveling gravel mounds, which called for large capital in-vestments.

Working principally on other people's land because of a monopoly en-joyed by the upper class, these truck farmers must have worked under some system of sharecropping, like the farmers in the sugar regions, who were dedicated to providing food for the towns and villages of the North-east. Beneath those intermediate strata was the humblest group, free blacks and mulattos, represented in the poorest brotherhoods but integrated into them at least. They were domestic workers or manual laborers upon whose shoulders fell the heavy work. At the bottom of the stratification, as the most exploited group without any representation or rights, came the large slave mass of workers in the mines, on the farms, and in carting. A conspicuous apparatus of repression kept watch in every town over those miserable people in order to prevent the flight of slaves, the vagrancy of freedmen, which could lead to assaults and above all rebellion.

Sedition arose, however, in the upper class itself, from which emerged an educated elite who proposed formulating and establishing an alternative system to that of the colony and a reordering of its society. It was a question of the most daring libertarian attempt in colonial Brazilian history, as it foresaw the building of a republic on the model of the United States, one that would abolish slavery, decree freedom of trade, and promote industrialization. The insurrection would break out in 1789, piggybacked onto the revolt of the miners against colonial exploitation, a revolt that intensified with newly announced taxation on diminishing wealth. It was the misnamed Inconfidência Mineira (mines conspiracy), which in spite of its failure through betrayal reveals to us the strength of a nascent nativist sentiment and also the maturing of a republican ideology capable of reordering society on new bases.

Tiradentes (Tooth-puller), the principal figure of the movement, a professional military man, always carried a copy of the United States Constitution in order to show how social and economic life should and could be reorganized after freedom from the Portuguese yoke. Arrested because of a betrayal, all the conspirators except Tiradentes himself were exiled to Africa, where they died; he was hanged after three years in jail and then quartered and displayed in the places where he had previously conspired, as an example and warning to the population.

After a few decades of intensive and disorderly exploitation, the deposits in Minas Gerais and later those in Goiás and Mato Grosso began to peter out. The miners returned to their old haunts, washing once more the gravel that had already been worked or examining abandoned sites for what they could pilfer. All in vain: the gold was waning and with it the society founded on the dissipation of easy wealth. The miners persisted, however, struggling with aging slaves they could not replace, and going into debt, but always continuing because of their incapacity for going into any other kind of activity. The problem lay in determining what could be produced in those mountainous wastelands, how to transport it to the distant coast, and to whom it could be sold, since the only wealthy market had been that of the mines, impoverished now.

At the end of the eighteenth century urban life still seemed to have vitality that came from the artistic brilliance it had attained, from the polish it had acquired, from the worldly customs it cultivated. But these were now expressions of decadence that would soon disappear as everyone sank into the shameful poverty in which inhabitants of the former gold and diamond cities in Minas still vegetate.

Nor had Portugal succeeded in creating new sources of production to hold onto the prodigious wealth it had garnered. An economically complementary pact with England, the Treaty of Methuen, which guaranteed minimal duties on port wine and Portuguese olive oil in exchange for free trade in English manufactured goods, saw almost all the gold transferred to London bankers. The breadth of the transfer can be estimated through documentation of the period, which indicates weekly Portuguese payments of up to 50,000 pounds in gold for the imports received by the mother country and Brazil from English industries. That gold would go to help pay for the wars against Napoleon and especially to finance the expansion of England's industrial infrastructure.

With the decline in mining, the whole region sank into an economy of poverty, with the resultant cultural regression. Miners became small farmers, hiding their poverty on their farms. Local artisans who made rustic clothing and utensils went back to obtaining a plot of land and with it an autarchic subsistence economy. The presence of European and African groups in Minas society, however, allowed for the development of certain techniques, like the smelting of iron, construction, fine carpentry, and a fabric industry, as well as for a certain level of bookish erudition that prevented Minas society in decline from regressing into the rusticity of its São Paulo trunk.

Its historic calling would be industrialization, for which it was perhaps as qualified as were the colonies in North America. In fact, only industrialization would be able to open new horizons of productive use for the accumulated capital and especially for the masses previously engaged in mining, who were now languishing in the decaying towns and poverty-stricken countryside. The truth is that the industrialization taking place at the time in the governing centers of world economy involved technical knowledge that not even Portugal possessed, as well as requiring international contacts and financial resources that were probably beyond the possibilities of a colonial province stuck in the heart of the continent. The fundamental obstacle to realization of that plan, however, resided in an express prohibition. As it turned out, attempts in Minas to set up crude factories appeared in the eyes of the Crown to be so against its interests that it had all of them destroyed by colonial troops, and it was decreed in 1785 that they were never to be rebuilt.

Thus a progressive disintegration took hold of the economy and the society that had built its towns and villages in the mining region, forming the largest demographic grouping and the largest urban network in the colony. Former mine owners and merchants became large-scale farmers; artisans and employees became owners of unoccupied lands. Ruralized town dwellers spread out into the countryside, choosing land no longer for its wealth in gold but for its qualities for farming and living. They became small subsistence farmers, breeders of cattle, horses, donkeys, and pigs, scattered across the vastness of the valleys that wove their way through the hills whence gold had previously been taken.

Seeking to maintain their social standing, many family groups who had been rich before but whose wealth had diminished emigrated with their slaves to land grants they attained in barren territories. There they reconstituted nuclei of autarchic life, proud once more of relying on commerce only for providing them with salt, hiding their poverty behind that vanity. That noble group of clans continued making a cult of a certain erudition. Fathers taught their male children to read and write, sometimes initiating them in the rudiments of Latin and classical literature. Even the popular classes maintained for some decades certain cultural traces of European urban origin, like erudite music, in the centers of ruralized town dwellers. Into the nineteenth century, musicians skilled in string quartets startled the German scholar Karl von Martius, who crisscrossed the region with invitations to gatherings of pure genteel taste in the middle of the backlands of Minas Gerais.

Urban life deteriorated, leaving dead towns where houses were sold at prices much lower than the cost of building them, where businesses established in large stores had empty shelves, where people lived on credit and in debt, more and more miserly, showing their old glitter only during religious processions organized according to the old ways, in which they all wore their only threadbare set of Sunday clothes. This was the Minas Gerais of decadence: conservative, reserved, mistrustful, taciturn, and bitter. The most profitable activity, since it was the only one paid in money, would come to be the surviving bureaucracy of a few public positions, fought over by the best people.

With the creative impulse of the bandeirantes having led them to become miners exhausted, the whole economy of the vast south-central region went into stagnation. It had sunk into a culture of poverty, bringing back to life forms of archaic living of the old São Paulo pioneers, forms that had remained latent, ready to reemerge with a crisis in the productive system. The population scattered and settled down, struggling to attain a minimum level of satisfaction of necessities.

The balance was reached in a variant of rural Brazilian culture that became crystallized as a *caipira,* or rustic, cultural area. It was a new way of life that was gradually spreading out from the old mining areas and the ancillary centers of craft production and maintenance, substituting for manufactured goods, draft animals, and other items. It ended up expanding, speaking the Portuguese language finally, over the whole forest area of the south-central region of the country, from São Paulo, Espírito Santo, and the state of Rio de Janeiro along the coast to Minas Gerais and Mato Grosso, extending farther still to neighboring areas of Paraná. In that way the former area of activity of the old bandeirantes in their hunt for Indians and in search of gold was transformed into a vast region of caipira culture, occupied by an extremely dispersed and disconnected population. In essence, drained of its mineral wealth and with the commercial system that had energized it in shambles, the bandeirante spirit became "feudalized," abandoned in the neglect of a rustic caipira culture.

The only reliable resources for that declining economy were the huge availability of unemployed labor and unpopulated land devoid of any value—land that the better-off could obtain through the concession of large land grants and that poorer and improvident people could occupy only as squatters. On that base a natural subsistence economy was established, since its production could not be commercialized except within minimal limits. In this way an itinerant agriculture spread, with people cutting and burning new groves in the forest for each annual planting, along with a complementary exploitation of the land, waters, and forests through hunting, fishing, and the gathering of fruits and roots. With nothing to sell, there was nothing people could buy, which meant reverting to the autarchic life of an economy based on domestic crafts that satisfied necessities, which were compressed to extreme limits on every possible level.

Those new ways of life were important for the dispersal of population over large areas, with family groups living at greater distances from one another. It did not lead to segregation, however, because new forms of intermittent sociability were shaping units of solidarity. In that way the rural "neighborhoods" were formed, defined by an informant of Melo e Souza (1964) as "little nations," or groups with a unifying sociability deriving from the territorial base where they were settled, from the feeling of locality that identified them and set them apart from other neighborhoods, and from the participation in a collective way in forms of work and leisure.

For these rarefied populations, which as a general rule needed only family members for their daily living, certain solidifying institutions took on importance as they permitted exchange and collaboration with other nuclei in undertakings that called for greater concentration of efforts. The principal one of these was *muxirão,* which institutionalized mutual help and joint action through the gathering of the inhabitants of a whole neighborhood to undertake the heavier tasks that were beyond the capability of family groups. Thus the inhabitants of a neighborhood would come together successively to help each other in clearing the forest for gardens, for planting, and for weeding as well as for winnowing crops of rice and beans and eventually for the construction or repair of a house, the rebuilding of a bridge, or the maintenance of a road. Whenever the task was of immediate interest to one of the inhabitants, he would take on the duty of providing food and at the end of the work would arrange festivities with music and drink. In that way the muxirão became not only an association for work but also an opportunity for festive leisure, a pleasant gathering.

The neighborhoods with the greatest solidarity would organize themselves further in higher forms of sociability around the cult of a powerful saint, whose chapel would be the local pride for the frequency with which it was the focus for masses, festivals, auctions, always followed by a dance. Each nucleus, in addition to its subsistence production, which absorbed almost all of its labor, produced a few articles for the incipient market, such as cheese, dairy products, brown sugar loaves, manioc flour, bacon, sausages, grains, chickens, and pigs. To this could be added crude cotton cloth made at home, which came to serve as the unit of exchange in that nonmonetary economy.

The caipira population, gathered into neighborhoods, fulfilled its minimal requirements for survival in this way. Those who broke away from that social system to penetrate the more deserted backlands were always threatened with descent into lawlessness and were suspected of incest and all manner of cultural alienation.

Caipira rural life, organized in that fashion, made for a satisfactory balance between periods of continuous labor and leisure, which allowed people to attend to their frugal wants and even to take care of the sick, the weak, the insane, and unproductive dependents. It also conditioned the caipiras to a culturally limited horizon of aspirations, which made them seem to be unambitious and improvident, lazy and vagrant. In fact, it demonstrated their integration into an economy that was more autarchical than mercantile and that, besides guaranteeing their independence, followed their mental pattern of placing greater value on the alternation of hard work and leisure in the traditional way than on a pattern of a higher way of life through involvement in rigidly disciplined systems of work.

Only by means of these conditions of economic recession did the poor white and mixed-blood population and free mulattos have access to land—not through any institutional reforms that guaranteed ownership to the possessors but simply because, with mercantile links broken by the nonexistence of a purchasing market, the monopoly of land ownership would temporarily cease to have meaning as an additional mechanism for conscription of a work force for commercial agriculture.

The freedom that was incidental to this autarchical existence would last only a short time, because a viable export economy would raise its head in another form: through large agricultural enterprises. With these came the legal denial (1850) of access to ownership of land by simple occupation and cultivation; the new law involved obligatory forms of purchase or documentation showing ownership, which were out of the reach of the caipira.

Indeed, after the decades of greatest recession (1790 to 1840), there arose and spread new forms of agro-export production, initiating a slow process for the regrouping of caipira populations into mercantile economic bases. This happened with the emergence of new commercial crops for export, like cotton and tobacco and later coffee, which revived the caipira regions. Roads were improved and systems of transport by mule train were reestablished. Simultaneously, an institutional reordering was being implanted on the civil and ecclesiastical levels: neighborhoods were transformed into districts, settlements into towns, provided now with a certain administrative apparatus that began to examine the legality of land occupation. Spontaneous religiosity was institutionalized with the erection of chapels and later of parish churches with permanent vicars. Finally, state power was installed with police services that were able to put an end to both spontaneous and paid banditry, which had become widespread, attracting adventurers and wastrels.

That penetration of public power did not come, however, as an extension of justice or as a guarantee of the common good. The state penetrated the caipira world as the agent of the landowning class and essentially represented a new subjection. From then on it became imperative that every person place himself under the protection of a landowner with a voice before the new power, so as to avoid arbitrary acts by which he would be threatened in the future. For that reason he became a *compadre* or tenant or follower or elector—generally all of them—of someone who could assure him the necessary protection.

In that way the oligarchical rule that remonopolized the land and brought about the uprooting of the caipira possessor with the help of the administrative and political legal apparatus of the government gained strength and coherence, going on to demand the loyalties of the caipira as well. Just as had happened to the man of the sertão, the caipira's greatest fear from then on was to see himself torn away, with no powerful master who could intervene, if necessary, between him and that impersonal, anti-popular, all-powerful order that was advancing over his world.

The basic factor of that social and economic reordering was the reestablishment of the mercantile system and with it a rise in the value of property. This unleashed disputes over lands of the best quality, near transportation networks, useful for the more and more widespread commercial crops of cotton and tobacco and for the new plantings of coffee that were beginning to take hold. Notaries became active in that process, authenticating titles of old land grants, genuine or false, and bringing about the dispossession of former occupants.

A whole urban juridical apparatus was placed at the service of that concentration of property. Holdings broken up by the successive inheritances of extensive families were reconstituted through the purchase of unusable parcels. Land surveyors became active and forced those who could not pay in money to pay in land. Squatters multiplied, bribing judges and recruiting police forces from the towns to dislodge caipira families, declaring them invaders of the lands where they had always lived. Placed outside the law and suffering police persecution, in the end they were driven off the land as its commercial exploitation became viable.

With the prodigious increase in coffee planting, this process of social reordering accelerated. The caipira was compelled to become a tenant as a paid farmworker or to seek refuge as a sharecropper, moving to more remote areas or to lands where owners did not have the resources to grow the new crops. The caipira clung to this way out with all his might, trying to become a sharecropper, going halves with the owner who financed him, or thirds, working on his own account but paying a third of his crop to the landowner for the use of the land. That status allowed him to preserve an autonomy in the rhythm of his work and afforded him conditions under which he could maintain his forms of adaptation and life. It assured him, furthermore, the status of a quasi-landowner, treated as such by salesmen, with a guarantee of credit from harvest to harvest, which was not given to one who worked for wages.

The implantation of the new productive system was gradual, allowing for some time the coexistence of commercial crops and traditional farming. That was because in the beginning, the production that was mercantile in character affected only the central activity of the landowner, not taking up all the land and even allowing for a reserve labor force on the plantation itself, one which could be called upon for tasks demanding a larger number of workers.

Soon, however, the new system took on strength and coherence, going on to seek out and dislodge caipira from any wasteland where he was hiding and, through a continuous expansion of areas occupied by the plantation economy, obliging him to face once more the choice of employment as a paid farmhand or new dislocations in search of still more backward areas appropriate for sharecropping. Sharecropping itself was becoming less satisfactory, limited to the poorest lands and those farthest from the market and burdened with new exigencies. Among these was the so-called *cambão*, or yoke, a form of unpaid work that obliged the caipira and his family to give the landowner days of work free and additional days for every mount animal he possessed.

In spite of all these obstacles, the caipira, despoiled of his possessions and successively expelled from his land, continued to resist submission to the plantation regime. His whole experience made him identify working with a directed rhythm as a denial of his personal freedom, which would make him the same as a slave. Even after the abolition of slavery (1888), that criterion of value remained, considering work with an established timetable and the ringing of a bell under the direction of an authoritarian foreman as humiliating.

The caipira was becoming marginalized, clinging to a status and independence that was not viable without ownership of land. Thus, in spite of the existence of millions of underemployed caipiras, the plantation system first had to promote intensification of the traffic in black slaves and later had to call for massive European immigration, which placed thousands of workers at the disposition of large-scale commercial agriculture.

Confined to the most sterile lands, sunk in poverty, the caipira impassively watched the arrival and settling as tenants on the plantations of swarms of Italians, Spaniards, Germans, and Poles, who took the place of blacks in the fields, accepting a status that he had rejected. The new masses, however, came from old, rigidly stratified societies that had disciplined them for paid work, and they saw in their status as tenants a path upward that would one day perhaps find them as small landowners. The caipira, unprepared for directed work, culturally predisposed against it, long disillusioned about ever becoming a landowner, resisted in his sharecropper's redoubt, which for him was the status closest to the unattainable ideal of a farmer on his own land.

Monteiro Lobato's pages revealing to cultured groups in the country the figure of Jeca Tatu passed on a true image of the caipiras but with a false interpretation, in spite of the richness of his observations. In his early portraits, Lobato sees them as vermin on the land, a kind of incendiary plague that sets fire to the woods, destroying enormous forest wealth in order to plant their measly gardens. That caricature served only to stress the laziness, the slovenliness, the despondency that made Jeca Tatu answer any proposal of work as "not worth the effort." He is described in his characteristic pose, squatting on his heels in an ungainly way, puffing smoke from his pipe, spitting to the side. The one thus describing the caipira was a landowner-intellectual of Buquira, who was bitter over his own failed attempts to include the caipiras in his grandiose plans.

What Lobato did not see at the time was the cultural trauma in which the caipira was living, marginalized by the theft of his lands, resisting involvement in tenant farming and the compulsory abandonment of his traditional way of life. It is true that later on Lobato came to understand that the caipira was a natural and necessary residual product of the agro-exporting latifundia. He, too, then proposed agrarian reform.

The plantation system that was being implanted and was inexorably expanding for the production of export items created a new world where there was no longer any room for the nonmercantile ways of life of the caipira or for the preservation of his traditional beliefs, his archaic customs, and his family-based economy. With the spread of that new system, the caipira saw his forms of neighborly solidarity and comradeship disappear as not viable, to be replaced by commercial relationships. He watched the atrophy of homely crafts along with the replacement of homemade fabric by factory-woven products, and with these came soap, gunpowder, and metal tools, which no one made at home any more and which they now had to buy.

The agricultural occupation of the land, the fencing of the large estates with barbed wire, the expansion of pastures, and the presence of cattle, all changing the ecological conditions, made hunting and fishing impossible. Thus the caipira lost the complementary nourishment that permitted him to better his frugal and wanting diet. By the end of the process installing the plantation system, penetrating even into the barren lands where he had taken refuge in flight from compulsory involvement, the caipira was attempting to preserve a condition that had become obsolete and impractical.

The final blow to the life of the traditional caipira, who in the end was becoming completely marginalized, came with the growth of an urban market in meat, which made the exploitation of the most remote areas practical. Lands both rich and poor were turned over to cattle raising. From then on every caipira garden, permitted because it meant clearing the forest or underbrush, was followed by the planting of grass and the automatic removal of the area from the system that had previously prevailed, in order to turn it over to grazing. The old latifundia properties that had become autarchic with the help of groups of caipira families gathered into neighborhoods were depopulated and turned over to cattle. On these breeding ranches a tiny group of cowmen replaced the former resident population, which thus found itself expelled. The new procedure, within reach of the large landowners provided with the least resources because it made use of the caipira himself and even of sharecropping as a means of eliminating him, had the important effect of a progressive limitation of land for agriculture.

As a result, masses of caipiras were obliged to face new options. Now they were not even offered an opportunity to be taken on as tenants. They faced a choice among remaining on their own sharecropping plot, which was becoming quite precarious but on which they could still eke out a subsistence; joining the groups of invading occupiers of others' land; gathering in barren lands as reserve workers to serve the depopulated ranches as teams for intensive work; or joining the urban marginalized masses, aspiring to become proletarians.

The basic institution of caipira culture crumbled with the impact of the renovating wave represented by the new forms of agricultural and herding activity that were mercantile in character. The living of the caipiras was destroyed, however, without any compensatory forms of accommodation for rural groups that might afford them a place and a role in the new structure. That role could have been their integration in the category of small landowners, which might have permitted them to take on technological innovations, enhancing their aspirations as they became integrated into the national economy. Monopoly of the land based on the domination of the center of power by the agricultural oligarchy did away with that outlet.

A caipira who has preserved his traditional culture is a rare survival today, limited to the most remote areas, those least integrated into the productive system. Nevertheless, the number of autonomous rural workers, sharecroppers or small tenant farmers in the great majority, is over 5 million. They are no longer those caipiras whose ways of life are archaic and poor but satisfactory in their eyes. They make up a vast group that is marginal to the structure of society and they experience the most difficult conditions of life, inferior even to the near minimums of the caipira economy. And they are yet worse off because they subsist within sight of superior conditions of life, which they know about or which they can appreciate and which act to shape the ideals of their aspirations. It is impossible for them to become integrated into those new forms of consumption, however, because of the narrowness of their own social structure, based on the latifundia system of property, incapable of improving the conditions of life for the mass of sharecroppers and also unable to incorporate them as wage earners. In that way they fall into the status of contingent workers, the so-called *bóias-frias* (cold leftovers).

The rapidity with which sharecroppers in different regions have become interested in the rural syndicate movement over the past few years, anticipating the organization of paid farmworkers, indicates on the one hand their greater independence and capacity for autonomous conduct and, on the other, the degree of awareness of their own misery and of their revolt against the social order that maintains it. That mass of millions of caipiras, who are the true peasants of Brazil because they are age-old claimants to ownership of the land they work, seem to be waiting for the appearance of ways of struggle that will give their nonconformity expression and will unleash rural rebellion.

With the establishment of the large coffee plantings, the plantation system attained new heights, comparable only to the heyday of the sugar plantations. Its most important effect was to make Brazil viable once more as an agricultural exporting unit of the world market and as a prosperous import market for industrial goods. Another effect of the coffee culture was the shaping of a new form of productive specialization and the configuration of a different way of existence for Brazilian society. Culturally, the new form was basically caipira, but other dimensions were added to that trunk through the incorporation of a large slave mass during the first phase and later through the contribution of European immigrants, integrated en masse into the group of tenant farmers. Those bases would also receive elements taken from other Brazilian cultural variants through the convergence on plantations of people from the diverse regions of the country.

Coffee growing, which had been conducted on a small scale all over Brazil as a limited operation for local consumption, took on economic meaning with the first large groves planted in the mountainous area near the port of Rio de Janeiro. The success of exports—which grew from 3,178 sacks in the decade following 1820 to 5,163 in the one after 1880— quickly boosted the new crop into the leadership it would maintain from then onward as the mainstay of economic activity in Brazil, going from 18.4 percent of the value of exports during the first of the decades mentioned to 61.5 percent in the second. For establishment, the coffee enterprises relied on an abundant availability of proper soil and of slave labor, underexploited ever since the decline of mining, and also on an adequate system of transport and commercialization.

The entrepreneurial model that was first established was the slaveholding plantation, which as in the sugar plantation system had a great expanse of land, a high degree of specialization and rationalization in its productive activities, a mercantile character in the product for export, and a need to concentrate major contingents of rigidly disciplined slave labor on large plantations. It also called for enormous financial investments, especially for the acquisition of lands, which were rapidly increasing in value, and for the purchase of slaves and their replacements once the simple installations for improvement were in place on the plantations themselves. A coffee grove, as a permanent planting, demands a great concentration of labor in the preparatory phase of clearing the forest and calls for special care during its first four years. From then on it needs a large number of workers only on the occasion of the harvest.

Under those circumstances the slaveholding plantation could always count on an oversupply of workers utilized in chores of subsistence and craftsmanship. It was thus structured as a large autarchic unit in which agro-mercantile work was surrounded by a series of ancillary activities, the personnel of which could all be mobilized for the harvest.

The slaveholding coffee plantations of the mountainous areas near Rio de Janeiro soon extended into the valley of the Paraíba and from there spread out progressively into the forests of Minas Gerais, Espírito Santo, and especially São Paulo. The largest of these were communities of 500 to 2,000 people, mostly slaves, producing almost everything they consumed, from slaves' clothing, houses, and provisions to the installations and furnishings of the plantation itself. But they also acquired many industrial goods for the consumption of the owners' families as well as for the work.

The recruitment of slave labor for coffee growing was first undertaken regionally with the acquisition of surplus blacks from the mining areas. The success of this enterprise brought on the promotion of a veritable drainage of slaves from other areas in decline, such as the cotton fields of Maranhão and the sugar plantations. Added to all this later was the direct importation of close to a half million Africans. In spite of these sources, coffee plantations experienced a permanent shortage of labor by virtue of their intense rhythm of expansion and the wearing out of slaves in the field, evidence of the miserable conditions of life and work to which they were subjected. During the five years immediately preceding the prohibition of slave traffic (1850), close to 250,000 African slaves officially entered Brazilian ports, costing approximately 15 million pounds sterling, the equivalent of more than 36 percent of the value of exports.

During that phase the owner lived on the plantation, presenting the same picture of contrast as in the Northeast between baronial mansion and slave quarters. He was also attended by a large number of household servants, to which were sometimes added European tutors for the education of his children on the plantation and resident priests for religious services.

Beginning in the second half of the nineteenth century, when coffee was already dominating the Brazilian economy, coffee growers came to constitute a more and more powerful national oligarchy. It became more authentic and stronger than the sugar oligarchy because it dominated the whole economic complex of coffee, from planting to export—whereas sugar growers had always been under the control of the parasitic patronage of exporters—and above all because the coffee growers quickly learned how to use their political power in defense of their economic interests.

The proximity of the imperial court facilitated the exercise of that influence, which ended up becoming hegemonic. It was in that hegemonic, lordly group that the Brazilian empire based the nobility that sustained it, distributing titles and recruiting cabinets heads and ministers of state from it. Thus the coffee growers became the barons, viscounts, counts, and marquises of the empire, the noble counterweight of the slaveholding system, aware that they would not survive abolition, which indeed proved to be the case when abolition became inevitable because of the pressure of urban public opinion.

Abolition, however, representing the simple return to the slave of own-ership of himself, was important for two crucial economic effects and for the deepest social consequences. On the economic plane it expropriated the major portion of capital of the principal landowning class, ruining it, and leading to a broader redistribution of income through the remunera-tion of work by wages. The financial ruin of the coffee barons brought about an abrupt substitution in owners of the coffee groves with positive consequences for the whole economic system, given the modern character-istics of the new entrepreneurs and the advantages they had in not having to invest resources in the purchase of slaves.

The second effect had even deeper social consequences through the elevation that it permitted in people's standard of living, principally in sectors where there was competition for workers, as was the case with coffee. For slaves, abolition represented an opportunity to exercise a choice regarding their future and for recognition of the human dignity and self-respect they had been denied. That freedom, however, would be lim-ited by the monopoly of land ownership, which would oblige slaves to hire out in the service of some landowner and to cling to the low level of consumption to which they had always been subjected.

The fact was, the black slave had been conditioned by all his previous experience to resist being wasted in work, which he tried to avoid by any means possible as an elementary way of self-preservation. He had also become habituated to a most frugal diet and minimal possessions, which were reduced to the clothes on his back. He had been further reduced in his own being by the impossibility of maintaining any family ties, since his women also belonged to someone else and his children, too, were the property of the master.

With his basic motivations deriving from that conditioning, the free black began his integration into the role of free worker. His inevitable reaction was to reduce the obligations of disciplined work to the minimum indispensable for providing his most elementary needs. Under those con-ditions, no stimulus represented by a rise in income would move him. The basic value he cultivated was that of ease and recreation. His level of aspirations had been dulled by the inculcation of values that limited in the extreme the number of things he considered desirable and fitting for the human condition. The construction of a new self-image would be reached only by following generations, who, growing up free, would become pro-gressively more energetic and ambitious. In that way the black took up work in the field once more as a free wage earner and performed with even less efficiency than he had as a slave, and when he found himself near areas of unoccupied land he preferred becoming a caipira, joining a subsistence-economy nucleus, rather than taking on the status of a paid permanent farmworker.

Through this process, with abolition there was an increase in the marginal absentee group that fled work on the plantations. To the original caipiras—whites and mulattos, sometimes former owners or occupiers, perennial litigants for the lands on which they worked—was added this new group of marginalized people. The latter were in an even more precarious state, because instead of demanding ownership of the land and a level of dignity higher than that of tenant, all they wanted was to survive, to take care of their very limited horizon of aspirations. Under these circumstances, as they enlarged the marginal mass, these contingents of freed blacks made up a subproletariat that, besides being more miserable, found itself segregated from the first group, predominantly white and of mixed blood, because of racial prejudice, which would make it difficult for all of them to reach an awareness of the exploitation of which they were both objects.

Abolition and the republican regime, doing away with slavery and then with the nobility, did not weaken the reign of coffee, which grew more and more powerful. It was ruled now by coffee growers who made themselves the great founding fathers of the republic and had a new labor system—work was gradually becoming the preserve of paid workers. It was coffee growing under the tenant system that led toward monoculture, based on a division of labor whereby the agricultural concerns of the plantation were turned over mainly to European immigrants and the other chores to occasional workers from outside the plantation. Clearing of forests for the planting of new coffee groves was in the care of mobile groups whose specialty it was and who generally worked as contract laborers, often freed slaves or former sharecroppers. The harvest, calling for a greater concentration of workers, was also done with the help of outsiders recruited from the same sources, who ended up settling in the neighborhood of plantations as a reserve labor force.

New plantations were already opening in the forest areas of the interior of São Paulo, sometimes anticipated by rail lines that opened a path to the west. The introduction of European labor on coffee plantations was a slow process, attained through the pertinacity of coffee growers intent on a solution for their greatest problem, a shortage of workers, aggravated first by the prohibition of the slave trade and then by abolition. The first attempts to subject the immigrant to a revived system of the old sharecropping brought on consular complaints and scandals in the European press, to which Brazilians are especially sensitive. The attempts had been too hasty; in spite of the conditions of poverty prevalent in Europe, the immigrants would not accept coexistence with slaves. Only after abolition was a regular and sizable supply of European workers established, which at the end of the nineteenth century reached 803,000 workers, 577,000 of them from Italy.

That availability of European labor matched the advance of industrial capitalism, which was uprooting from the countryside and drawing to the cities more people than the factories could use. Every country touched by the process was exporting millions of people. First they emigrated from the British Isles, then from France, later from Germany and Italy, and finally from Poland, Russia, and the Balkan countries. Presenting itself there was an offering of European workers cheaper than African slaves and also more efficient because of their adaptation to the new productive systems.

Their entry into the labor market of Brazil, besides representing the solution for the problems of coffee growing, had several other effects. Among them was that it proved a dissuasive factor in the silent and bloodless battle that caipiras and freed slaves were fighting for the status of farmers. There was a devaluation of the native worker; in the face of availability of this more qualified workforce, he was losing out in the competition and finding himself prevented from attaining the few better-paying positions that the system would create. Finally, there was the effect of channeling the migration of northeastern backlanders to the rubber groves of the Amazon region because their natural route, which would have been movement to the south, was blocked by the saturation of European immigrants responding to the call for labor on the large plantings. Another result of the massive incorporation of foreign workers was that of holding up the proletarianization and consequently the politicization as factory workers of the old caipiras and ex-slaves, who would have the opportunity to rise up to the more dynamic sectors of the modernized economy only after the supply of European labor was exhausted.

The tenants were contracted in Europe with passage for their families furnished, a guarantee of help in maintenance for the first year, and the receipt of a plot of land for their subsistence gardens. To those conditions it was later necessary to add an annual fixed wage and variable extra earnings, depending on production. Since the expense of their passage was paid for by the government, only the other conditions weighed directly on the plantation owner. Those privileges, significantly superior to those offered the caipira, were explained by the capacity of the tenants—assisted by the consular corps and backed by the press of their countries—to demand better working conditions. In fact, it was the immigrant tenant who, through that setup, introduced a system of wages in Brazilian rural life, accepting a rigorous working discipline but, as compensation, making owners pay them in cash and pay them more. Motivated by a broader horizon of aspirations and relying on a better adjustment to work for wages, immigrants produced more and worked harder. Some managed, after a few years and thanks to their capacity for saving, to free themselves from the status of tenant and to become small tradesmen. Their sons, Brazilians already, would become factory workers in the nascent industrial centers.

The new plantations, structured in accord with the tenant system, progressively became monocultural, and they simultaneously they added to the crop another element: the company store. There the plantation owner became a merchant in order to provide the tenants with everything they needed—but also to recoup most of the wages he paid. In that way the most advantageous money contracts were undone for the rural worker as he was subjected to two reductions: first, inflation, which substantially diminished the value of the coffee-planting contracts, which were generally for four years; and second, exploitation in the supplies furnished by the company store. Under these circumstances the tenant could manage to save only at the price of a great reduction in expenses, with the majority of tenants yoked to the system through unpayable debts and watching the yearned-for opportunity of becoming farmers vanish forever.

Under the tenant system, the plantation owner is now an absentee. He lives in the city and runs his property through administrators. He still maintains in the republican regime, however, the hegemonic position won in the empire, with an oligarchic patrician class that places the whole of governmental machinery at the disposal of the coffee growers, perpetuating itself in power. The very autonomy of the states, about which the first republic was so zealous, can be explained by that continuing effort of the coffee grower to subject everything to his interests. Among these matters was transfer to the states of control and facilities for the disposition of unoccupied lands, which was of such great importance in areas of coffee growing.

In addition to the control and political rule whereby almost all civilian presidents and the majority of ministers have come from their ranks, the coffee planters not only maintained but improved their old mechanisms for defense of their class. Principal among these was probably control of the exchange rate—which changed every time the international price of coffee fell—in order that they be paid the same amount in local currency. Following on this devaluation of the currency were foreign loans destined to defend it, which meant a continuous increase in the nation's foreign debt but which permitted the transfer of export sector damage to the broad group of importers, made up of the entire population in a country without industry and which depended on international commerce for almost everything.

Later on those procedures would be carried to extremes with the policy of "valorization," which consisted of the purchase through foreign loans of harvests for storage as resources by state governments. With the crash of 1929, new methods were imposed in the face of the impossibility of obtaining international loans.

The federal government was then induced to assume the role of purchaser. When the stocks reached fabulous amounts, widely known to be impossible to sell, the government was brought to the position of having to buy coffee to be burned in order to maintain international prices. The principal effects of that policy—besides socialization of the damage done by transfer to the masses of losses resulting from subsidizing of coffee growers—were the constant expansion of plantings and with this increases in the sale of coffee, aggravating the problem all the more. Another consequence was the policy's effect as an indirect subsidy of the establishment of coffee growing in other countries through its maintenance of attractive prices, whereby Brazil ended up losing its almost monopolistic position.

Those mechanisms—leading to reduction of public income but also to spending to pay for the purchase of harvests and to cover resulting budget deficits—brought on enormous inflationary pressure, from which only the exporters managed to escape. No force could oppose those hegemonic interests, however, and their lack of regard would lead to even more serious crises through the recession that would result from abandonment of plantings, the main source of remunerated work and almost the only sector for the investment of capital.

The coffee oligarchy, as holder of major political power during both the imperial and the republican periods, was responsible for some of the most deeply entrenched deformations of Brazilian society. The main one derives from the oligarchy's ongoing dispute with the state over the appropriation of national income; from its deep-seated discrimination against blacks, slave or free, against the caipira nuclei that resisted it, and also against the poor masses in the cities, who were growing more numerous. In that dispute and in that lordly discrimination, one should look for the reasons why Brazil was so visibly behind other Latin American countries, and all other peoples with the same level of development, in both the abolition of slavery and the imposition on the state of an obligation to assure a primary education for the people and to extend to rural workers the right to unionize and strike.

Independence and republican status, which in almost all of America provided a deep national effort for elevation of the cultural level of the population, preparing it for the exercise of citizenship, did not assume an equivalent effort in Brazil. That disregard for popular education and slight interest in the problems of well-being and health of the population can only be explained by the baronial attitude of the plantation owners and by the peaceful transition, presided over by that same ruling class, from colony to independence and from empire to republic. Without any change in leadership, simply an alteration within the same patrician oligarchic group, that attitude also perpetuated the old social order.

Under these conditions all democratic participation in political life was reduced to oligarchical pressure groups fighting for control of what affected their interests. In that republic of landowners, the problems of the public good, of justice, of access to land, of education, of the rights of workers were debated along with democracy, freedom, and equality; that is, as mere themes for parliamentary rhetoric. The machine functioned substantially only for the greater consolidation of power and greater enrichment for the rich. Since the social result of this policy was a vexing backwardness, as compared to the United States for example, an attitude developed among the ruling classes that involved open discontent with their own people, whose black or mixed-blood status was invoked to explain the backwardness of the nation.

As a consequence, added to the economic motives were ideological incentives for the realization of enormous public investments with the aim of attracting white tenant farmers to the country as reproducers destined to "improve the race." And they did not want any Portuguese, because the oligarchs' alienation had also turned against their Portuguese ancestors; convinced of their own racial inferiority, members of the oligarchy explained their individual successes as exceptions.

By examining the expansion of the coffee economy, one can see that it was a particularly mobile frontier, involving millions of people and progressing from the Rio de Janeiro coastal areas to the west. That movement at first reached the forests of the state of Rio de Janeiro, then those of Espírito Santo, later the forest area of southern Minas Gerais, and finally that of São Paulo. The march continued to northwestern Paraná, penetrat-

ing Paraguayan territory, and later into Mato Grosso do Sul and Rondônia.

That moving wave spread out, enveloping pockets occupied by hostile
Indians until then untouched by civilization in the forests of Minas Gerais
and Espírito Santo (1910) and São Paulo (1911), as well as old forms of
economic occupation like caipira nuclei, quickly sweeping away everything before it. It advanced with the help of railroads and highways that
linked it to ports, bringing into the forest an internationally articulated
commercial system, establishing towns and villages where it was set up. In
that way it played a modernizing and integrating role that ended up creating the broadest economic area in the country and the one with the greatest density of population.

Coffee did not spread out into new forest areas while also maintaining
those already occupied, however. Its rearguard has always been the desert,
and that fact reveals the real moving force behind its drive. With land as
the most abundant and relatively the least onerous factor for coffee production, it is there that, whenever possible, entrepreneurial savings are
made. The virgin forest is cut down and new coffee groves are planted
with no cultural cares weighing on the entrepreneur, using and wasting the
land in a technologically primitive way that has almost transformed agriculture into extractive activity. Thus only in areas of exceptional fertility
do coffee groves remain as a truly permanent crop. The common procedure has always been to open up areas for planting in hopes of obtaining
harvests for a decade or less, until a freeze destroys the plants or the coffee
grove gives out because of wasting of the soil.

Operating through that extractive process, coffee growing was structured like a living frontier that kept moving ahead, taking with it capital,
labor, and wealth and leaving behind enormous devastated and eroded
areas. There grazing would be organized, generally in the hands of a different owner, who would try to make grass grow where coffee had been
before. The new economy could not maintain the same level of employment of labor, however, nor could it utilize the railroad that had crossed
the forest at great expense and very high social costs or the urban network
that had been set up. In that way the whole region went into decay, shaping a typical landscape of decline, with dead towns and forming a different
society and culture of poverty. New agricultural production was eventually brought into force in some areas, as happened in places that became
important producers of sugar and alcohol. In Paraná the option of wheat
and soybeans was the solution because the best lands were subject to
frosts. The price of that reversion was the decline of a rural zone of gener-

alized prosperity into a different monocultural panorama that sent more than a million farmworkers off in search of new areas as far away as Rondônia.

In order to estimate the social cost of that waste of land, we only have to compare the number of workers who would be employed in cutting down the forest and planting coffee with the reduced number later, when they had only to care for the plants and make the annual harvest, and later yet, when the worn-out land is turned over to cattle grazing. The population of a hundred workers needed in the first stage goes to thirty in the second and to only one in the last—explaining how and why the moving frontier of coffee, made up of millions of workers, always keeps going forward, leaving behind a kind of human desert and consequently the death of towns, railroads in deficit, failed businesses.

In certain areas with the poorest soil, like northeastern São Paulo and some zones in Paraná, the towns born of the clearing and planting scarcely had time to mature because of the speed with which the boom passed through. They died before they could grow, with their unfinished churches, housing never completed, declining commerce, and all who were attached to those things thrown into poverty.

In Paraná coffee found a promised land in the Londrina region because of the quality of the soil and especially because the occupation of the land was not done through latifundia. The zone was colonized by an English company in a system of smallholdings that involved thousands of families as owners, intent on defending land that was theirs. The resultant society stands in vivid contrast to coffee lands under the latifundia system and reveals its unique qualities in the people's standard of living, the growing prosperity of the towns and their commerce, and in independent political behavior, in contrast to the that in old oligarchies in Paraná and São Paulo. Outside the zone of Londrina, however, the moving frontier of coffee has continued advancing through lands already impracticable and generally with an expansion of latifundia holdings. In the past few years, that wave, which has only the River Paraná before it, has begun to penetrate Paraguay.

Something that did not happen to Brazil as a whole happened to São Paulo, which saw itself subjected to a disproportionate number of foreigners, who overwhelmed the inhabitants. In 1950 foreigners, mainly Italians and their descendants, were more numerous than the original inhabitants of São Paulo. That demographic burying has been matched by a Europeanization of mentalities and customs.

Modern Art Week, which was a reaction to that overwhelming presence, was also, through its style, the most expressive form of that Euro-centrism. Yet it was all to the good because almost all of those people ended up being nicely Brazilianized. Here and there remain a few loony leftovers who still have not left the holds of the ships on which their grand-fathers arrived. They have lost their original homeland and they are wan-dering in search of a roost. Their only compromise is with themselves and for the advantages they can obtain. They have no notion of, much less any pride of accomplishment in, the building and independence of this big country, which they found already made. As a consequence, just as the Argentines do now with their *cabecitas negras,* they have come to look down on workers from the Northeast and even caipiras from São Paulo, whom they contemptuously call Bahians.

I once heard a São Paulo politician say that the illiteracy and backward-ness in São Paulo is the fault of that Bahian presence, and he proposed paying those people's passage back to their points of origin. Fortunately, he represents a minority.

13

Southern Brazils

Gaúchos, Rustics, and Foreigners

Those Indians are nothing but gaúchos.

Gaúcho saying

The expansion of the old bandeirantes also reached and occupied the southern region previously under Spanish domination and incorporated it into Brazil. In interaction with other influences, however, it brought about such a complex and unique cultural area that it cannot be considered a component of Sao Paulo culture. Different from other areas shaped by the bandeirantes—such as the mining region with its natural caipira economy and the areas involved in the expansion of coffee growing, which in spite of their socioeconomic differentiation present a common cultural base— ways of life arose in the southern region so differentiated and so divergent that they cannot be included in that configuration or even treated as a homogeneous cultural area.

Southern Brazil's basic characteristic as compared to other Brazilian cultural areas is its cultural heterogeneity. The modes of existence and participation in national life of its three principal components not only diverge broadly from one another but also differ from those of other areas of the country. These are the *matutos* or rustic farmworkers, of mainly Azorean origin, who occupy the coastal strip from Paraná southward; the present-day representatives of the ancient gaúchos of the plains areas along the River Plate frontier and herding pockets in Santa Catarina and Paraná; and finally the Gringo-Brazilian formation of descendants of European immigrants, who constitute an island in the central zone and are advancing into the two other areas.

The coexistence and interaction of these complexes works actively in the sense of homogenizing them, mingling characteristics and customs from one to another. The distance that obtains between their respective cultural heritages, and especially between their systems of agricultural production—the archaic farming pattern of the matutos, the cattle herding of the gaúchos, and the gringo settlers' intensive farming practices on smallholdings—works, however, as an element that establishes their differences. Even in the face of the homogenizing effects of the modernization deriving from industrialization and urbanization, each of these complexes tends to react in its own way, integrating into the new forms of production and life with different rhythms and ways, making for distinct modes of participation in the national community.

Southern Brazil came into civilization through the hand of the Spanish Jesuits, who made their Christian-Guaraní republic flourish in today's southern mission lands. It is true that they envisioned objectives of their own, clear alternatives to Portuguese and Spanish civilization, which acted to their own detriment as agents of civilization as through their successes and their failures they worked for the consolidation of those alternatives.

The Jesuits created one of those rare utopian models of social life that effectively made possible new forms of human existence. In spite of their antipagan inspiration, the model of social structure that they created was characterized by a high feeling of social responsibility for the native population they attracted. Unlike the colonial slaveholding formation, which treated the Indian as an energy factor to be used up in mercantile production, the Jesuit model sought to assure him of an existence of his own within a community that existed for itself—that is, one basically concerned with its own subsistence and development.

It would have two other distinctive characteristics, however, that had unexpected effects. On the one hand, there was the detribalizing efficiency of the Jesuit model, which allowed it quickly to attract to its missionary nuclei thousands of Indians; on the other hand, there was its economic efficiency in the production of articles for regional and external markets, which allowed the missions to maintain an active commercial interchange whereby they provided themselves with everything they could not produce.

The concentration of great masses of deculturated and culturally uniform Indians motivated for disciplined work had the effect of unleashing upon the missions all the fury of the São Paulo mamelucos, who looked upon these communities as an enormous supply of Indians to be easily hunted down. The first missions were thus wiped out by the enslavement of their catechumens for sale to the sugar plantations of the Northeast. Then later, the mercantile success of the new missions, their character as an alternative to the colonization under way, brought on envy and greed locally and in the mother country itself, which impulses ended up provoking the expulsion of the Society of Jesus. The consequence was for the ex-catechumens to be brought into vassalage by the large landowners who had appropriated the missions. Hence the missions contributed to the formation of southern Brazil in two ways. In the first instance, they offered a supply of slaves who could be exported or subjugated and from whom a local subaltern population was created—the first gaúchos—serving as a workforce in the mercantile exploitation of cattle herding. The second mission contribution came with appropriation by Brazilians of the land and cattle of the missions' territory and through the compulsory assimilation of a large portion of the people living there.

The fundamental driving force in the formation of southern Brazil was, however, the Portuguese colonial enterprise that had been set up at an early date with the explicit aim of extending its hegemony to the River Plate. That aim, initially reached through the bandeirante operation of turning Indians into slave merchandise, establishing the first trans-Brazilian mercantile circuit, was followed soon after by the establishment of the Colony of Sacramento on the River Plate.

In the next century the Portuguese project was seriously threatened with failure by a lack of economic viability, since the exploitation of wild cattle for the export of leather and tallow was mainly under the control of colonists from areas of Spanish domination, who attracted southern nuclei into their orbit of influence. The threat was overcome, however, by a new economic viability that arose with the emergence of the new, rich market of the mining region for live cattle as oxen, for riding horses, and for pack and harness mules.

The fact that Indian slaves in the seventeenth century and livestock in the eighteenth were both merchandise that could transport themselves to market, no matter how distant and over any roads or trails at all, would give the far south economic conditions that would link it to the north and center of Brazil.

The petering out of the mines represented a new challenge for southern Brazil, which saw itself condemned to a premercantile regression or a search for extra-Brazilian forms of economic viability if new means of linkage to other regions of Brazil did not appear. These arose with the introduction by people from Ceará of the technique for making jerked beef, which not only gave new value to southern herds but also linked them to northeastern and Amazonian markets and, later on, to those in the Antilles.

The economic integration of southern Brazil was reached, as can be seen, through the creation of successive mercantile links that tied it more to the rest of the country than to the neighboring Spanish American provinces. All those links, however, would not have been sufficient to guarantee a real incorporation if, in addition to them, there had not been other forces for unification at work. Outstanding among them, as we have seen, was the power politics of Portugal in the drive to carry its hegemony to the River Plate, conducted both through maintenance of the Colony of Sacramento and enormous effort in colonization of the area with Azorean immigrants and through decades of diplomatic negotiations for the establishment of borders.

Contributing to this as well was the "Portuguese" posture of the Luso-Brazilians in the extreme south as they faced the "Castilian" stance of the Spanish Americans opposite them, establishing ethnic identities that were all the deeper because they were continually put to the test. That self-identification was further reinforced by association with the hegemonic disputes of the mother countries, which compelled every rancher not only to define himself clearly as being of one side or the other but also, once his identity had been established, to defend his flag, making a military redoubt of his ranch.

In spite of these integrative forces, more than once it was necessary to appeal to force of arms in order to keep southern Brazil tied to Brazil. As the only effective nuclei of population on this immense uninhabited frontier, Portuguese and Castilians faced each other over long centuries, under deep tensions, with conflict periodically breaking out into skirmishes. As part of those tensions and the disputes they generated, Brazil saw itself at various times involved in wars along the Plate, moved on some occasions by its own expansionist ambitions and on others as part of a grouping of nationalities confronting each other in a process of self-differentiation, unification, and the establishment of borders.

The central power also had to combat and suppress by force of arms movements that aspired to autonomy for the region, much more vigorous and better orchestrated than those in other areas. Diverse factors came together to activate these separatist tendencies. Among them was the fact of being a vast and distant region with its own undeniable interests; government's failure to attended to these adequately brought on disruptive tensions that led to breaks with the central power. Added to this was the circumstance of being far removed from the rest of Brazil and under the intellectual and political influences of culturally advanced centers like Montevideo and Buenos Aires. Under these conditions it was inevitable that aspirations for independence should arise, inspired sometimes by the concept that the south could realize its potentialities better as an autonomous nation than as a federal state and motivated at other times by daring political ideologies, like the antislavery struggle and the republican campaign of the so-called *farrapos* or ragamuffins.

The condition of being the southern Brazilian frontier, bringing about concentration there of the major portion of national troops, on the one hand gave continuity and function to the old combative urge of the gaúcho of the skirmishes. On the other hand, it conferred on Rio Grande do Sul greater power in the makeup of the nation than its economic importance warranted, making inevitable the imposition of southern candidates for central power when the choice went beyond institutional means and had to be decided by military considerations.

Paradoxically, a role would also be played in the Brazilianization of the extreme south by the massive influx of immigrants from central Europe, promoted after independence. Placed in the uninhabited zones between the southern borders and the main nuclei of the country, they activated those areas economically, contributing to the viability and modernization of the southern economy and giving it the capacity for better forms of interchange with the rest of the nation. Without that presence, foreign but compelled to identify itself as Brazilian, without their posture of people more peaceful and hardworking than disorderly and given to gaúcho antics, it would have been more difficult to incorporate those southern Brazils into the whole; and especially to incorporate them as a component equal to others and prepared, like the rest, to live a common destiny within the same national framework—as was indeed accomplished.

Brazilian gaúchos have a historical background in common with other River Plate gaúchos. They came out of the ethnic creation of mixed-blood populations by Spanish and Portuguese males with Guaraní women. They were specialized in the exploitation of cattle, domestic and wild, which were multiplying prodigiously on the natural prairies on both sides of the River Plate. The main group took shape in the Tapes region through missionary Indians who were Guaraní or had been made Guaraní by the Jesuits and who later mixed with Spaniards and Portuguese. Another source was the neo-Guaraní nucleus of Paraguayans from Asunción, who expanded over the Argentine plains along with the cattle that would occupy the pampa. A third source was the offspring of the Portuguese settled in the Colony of Sacramento (1680) on the River Plate.

The first group, after the devastating attacks by the São Paulo bandeirantes in the seventeenth century, and especially after the expulsion of the Society of Jesus (1759), became a diaspora, trying to escape the Spanish and Portuguese who wanted to bring them into vassalage, but they ended up being incorporated into the proto-cells of the nascent national societies through compulsory involvement in the labor force. The last were agents in the regathering of the remnants of former catechumens and their later integration into the four ethnic-national blocs of the Plate basin.

The cattle that had multiplied on the eastern shore had been brought there mainly by the Jesuits. They were bred with the greatest care, being one of the main ingredients for the settlement of the natives, who if they had a regular supply of meat could dedicate themselves to agriculture and crafts, freeing them from hunting and fishing. Along with cattle of other regions, that Jesuit herd, expanding enormously, would come to be the apparently inexhaustible source of the "maritime cattle" from which both missionary Indians and people from the other bank of the Plate, and later bandeirantes and Portuguese, would come to gather stock.

The prodigious herds became the hunted prey of a population that lived off them, just as the Indians of the North American prairies lived off their buffalo. Initially people all treated the cattle as prey, but some soon became specialized in pastoral life. Thus, the Indians of the region ended up as horsemen and beef eaters, but they remained hostile to one another and also attacked the Guaraní mission Indians, the whites, and the population of mixed blood. The latter made up the first gaúcho nucleus as they switched from being hunters of cattle for food to being dealers in leather, working from then on to exploit the herds for hides.

Three factors in the formation of the gaúcho base can be listed: first, the existence of a herd that belonged to no one on land that belonged to no one; second, mercantile specialization in its exploitation; and third, the degree of Europeanization of a mixed-blood portion of the population, which meant they needed imported articles and were capable of establishing a system of exchange in order to swap hides for merchandise (Ribeiro 1970).

Both the Guaraní toponymy of the entire territory of the maritime cattle (present-day Uruguay) and the historical documentation—superficially examined—indicate that those gaúchos spoke Guaraní better than Spanish, being in that respect culturally closer to the bandeirantes of the sixteenth and seventeenth centuries (Holanda 1956, 108–18) and to today's Paraguayans in their language, their means of adaptation to nature for providing their subsistence, their forms of association, and their view of the world.

That Guaraní base is what probably forged the gaúcho proto-ethnicity, which populated the land through natural reproduction, turned other contingents Guaraní, and later came to be the main ethnic base of southern populations. Afterward, under the influence of exogenous shaping forces, that base was divided, merging with the emergent national entities as Argentines, Uruguayans, Paraguayans, and Brazilians.

Originally those gaúchos did not identify themselves as either Spanish or Portuguese, just as they did not consider themselves Indians, making for a nascent ethnicity that was open to being joined by contingents of Indians who had been detribalized by the action of missionaries or slavery, of new people of mixed white and Indian blood thrown into marginality, and of poor whites distanced from their roots.

These were the original gaúchos, made culturally uniform by herding activities as well as through the unity of language, customs, and common usage. Items they used in common were unsweetened maté, tobacco, hammocks for sleeping, and their own peculiar garb characterized by the *xiripá* and the *poncho; bolas* and lasso for hunting and roundup; tallow candles for light; and the metal artifacts, principally knives for cutting meat, the tips of lances, spurs, bits, and a few utensils for boiling water and cooking.

The incorporation of a portion of these gaúchos into Brazilian ethnicity was a later process, deriving from the struggle of the bandeirantes to take part in the exploitation of southern cattle, from the competition between Spanish and Portuguese for domination of the region now on the Brazilian side of the River Plate, and especially the integration of the south into the market providing beasts of burden for the gold mines.

The first Brazilian penetrations into the area occurred in the first half of the seventeenth century with the bandeirantes' predatory action against Tape and other Jesuit nuclei in search of Indians. This did not lead, however, to any occupation, only allowing the intruders to learn about the region, to herd Indians for the slave trade, and to cause those who escaped them to scatter. The Portuguese came afterward—in an official effort at colonization—founding first São Francisco (1660) and Laguna (1676) to dominate the plains of Curitiba, where cattle left by the Jesuits bred, and later the Colony of Sacramento (1680) on the bank of the River Plate. That distant military establishment, aiming to extend Portuguese colonial rule, maintained itself in enemy territory mainly through the economic viability conferred upon it by its participation in the leather trade using wild herds of maritime cattle.

At the beginning of the eighteenth century, the Paulistas returned along with the Curitibans to settle in the region as breeders. They intended then to herd and own cattle and later to breed horses and mules to sell in the new market that had arisen in the gold-mining zones. Breeding of mules is so specialized and so much the opposite of extractive exploitation of wild cattle that one cannot imagine it having arisen spontaneously in the region. The gaúcho providers for the mines were probably only intermediaries for the real breeders. The latter were most likely ranchers in Corrientes and Santa Fe in Argentina who had become specialized in the production of pack animals for the silver mines of Potosí. The decline in Spanish mining operations, preceding the rise of Brazilian operations, probably creating an oversupply of mules for export, which found a new market in Minas Gerais. Only much later could the breeding of work mules in Rio Grande do Sul have begun.

Throughout the area, breeders recruited people accustomed to working with the wild or gaúcho cattle, people who spoke Guaraní, which the bandeirantes from São Paulo could understand, and who cultivated plots of cassava, corn, and squash and made manioc flour like all peoples of the Tupi trunk. These gaúchos, incorporated into the neo-Brazilian nuclei that were beginning to be founded in the countryside, served as cowhands and wranglers, ox trainers, and breeders of horses and mules.

The new type of exploitation—which did not look to leather alone but to the whole animal and to more complicated production, such as of dray oxen and riding and pack mules to be taken along with the cattle drive to the mines—was what settled the neo-Brazilian populations in the southern countryside, progressively incorporating a gaúcho contingent into Brazilian society.

I am quite aware of the scant documentation for the hypotheses set forth here. Nevertheless, they seem valid as the first steps in an investigation and necessary for the explanation of the formation of the Brazilian gaúcho. This cannot be attributed simply to the fact of a southward movement of bandeirantes and their Indians along with the addition of a few Spaniards, much less to a progressive maturation of the civilization of the Charrua and Minuano tribes, the former having been occupants of the plains. These Indians, of a preagricultural culture, were on the wane, victims of diseases and hunted in great raids by the whites who occupied their territory, until they disappeared. Some of their women eventually bore children of mixed blood, who no doubt became integrated into the gaúcho culture. A few men, enslaved, may have had the same fate. They were too different culturally from the Guaraní-shaped nuclei of mission Indians, Paraguayans, River Plateans, and proto-Brazilians to blend and coexist with them.

The integration went on through a clear and persistent effort by the Portuguese Crown—applied in this case by the bandeirantes—for the occupation and appropriation of the area. This was carried out through two procedures: the installation on the coastal strip of families brought from the Portuguese islands, mainly the Azores, to constitute a permanent nucleus of Portuguese presence, and the concession of land grants in the plains region where grazing areas were established, which progressed with unusual profusion. The Azoreans were joined by Portuguese soldiers—recruited mainly in Rio de Janeiro, São Paulo, and Minas Gerais—sent to the Colony of Sacramento and to the former territory of the Seven Villages of the Missions.

The legal appropriation of the land would begin to turn grazing grounds into ranches, establishing on them an owner and his gaúchos. The distribution of land grants, which began in the regions of Viamão and the Rio Grande, extended later to the plains along the River Pelotas, reaching afterward to the Laguna zone on one side and on the other to the area of the old Jesuit missions. Continuing its march of appropriation, the operation later integrated into the landowning system the fields of Ibicuí in the south and Coxilha Grande in the west.

For a long time the activity of these ranchers involved rounding up the wild cattle on their land into herds or bringing them from old cattle areas and, later, the breeding of horses and mules. They always worked with an eye on the horizon, alert for Castilian attacks. The broad band of undetermined frontier, moving according to pressure from one side or the other, was more of a threat to the ranch and its cattle than to the nation itself. In that way every rancher, on either side of the border, became a military chieftain, dug in on his ranch with his gaúchos, always ready to take part in raids that would allow him to protect his herd and sometimes increase it with what he could snatch from the other side.

Subjected to predatory exploitation for leather for export and to hunting by wild dogs, which were also multiplying on the plains, feeding on calves and newborns, the source of cattle that had seemed inexhaustible was continuously being reduced. The ranchers then began to struggle on both sides of the undefined border to keep cattle in their own pastures. The first to do this were the Paulistas, who found a market for live cattle at the mines hundreds of leagues inland. Then all of them began to do so at the end of the eighteenth century when production of jerked beef began. On the Spanish side the new product became the main article for export as food for the slaves in the Antilles. On the Brazilian side it became more and more valuable as meat for the mining populations and later for the commercial agriculture that succeeded them and for plantations in the Northeast.

The gathering of cattle onto ranches also gathered the gaúchos as cow-hands and as fighters for their bosses, who were their leaders. Over the following decades, with diplomatic agreements for the establishment of a border, progressive pacification took place in the areas closest to the line, giving birth to Uruguay as a vast territory placed between the contenders, Brazil and Argentina. After the convulsive period of external wars and the struggles for national unification that roused the countryside all along the River Plate, Brazilian ranches entered a phase of relative tranquility.

At that time the increase in jerked beef production enhanced the value of cattle and created an industry out of their exploitation, increasingly turning grazing into less of an adventure and more of a rational business. Jerked beef brought to the herding environment, however, a new look characterized by work with a regular and intensive rhythm, regulated by a timetable and rigid obligations, to which the free-roaming gaúcho could not adjust. Therefore, black slaves were introduced, the labor force of the time in all work that used people up.

These communities of salters, with their workers and their slaves, in flagrant contrast to the social structure of the plains, constituted a pre-industrial enclave that in the future would spread, with abattoirs and meat-packing plants as the new governing centers of herding activity. From then on it was no longer the rancher-chieftain who ruled regional life but a more complex mercantile-industrial complex, susceptible to official regulation, defended against smuggling, and prepared to introduce tech-nological innovations such as barbed-wire fences on the plains.

With that process, the rancher was ceasing to be the political leader, going back to being the boss of his gaúchos. The benefits for the latter lessened along with his ration of meat for barbecues and maté for his gourd. The gap between the social roles of the old gaúcho—the wrangler of cattle belonging to no one on land belonging to no one—and that of the new gaúcho—a cowhand hired on the ranch to attend to the boss's cattle—was becoming progressively wider. The gap was lessened, how-ever, through a continuation over decades of the pattern of leader-gaúcho relations caused by the convulsive effects of battles for national unification.

The southern political leaders—Brazilians because by location they were not Castilian and were opposed to the latter in long-standing disputes but also opposed to the distant empire, which had no vision of or sensitivity to their problems—made up an ethnicity that was not entirely identified with a remote Brazilianness that was still only beginning to spread out. Their border battles and their independent stance toward the empire kept all of the plains area on a war footing for decades. It caught fire in fights among leaders in the famous raids called *califórnias,* in which parties fought over land and cattle, and in disputes with farmworkers and merchants of Azorean origin who had settled along the coast and were tied to the central authority in an attempt to impose order on the plains. And there were groups of one kind and another who were against imperial rule, favoring a republic or any sort of government that would attend to their aspirations better.

While that environment of war prevailed, with the plains divided into commands and militias under the leadership of rancher-chieftains always ready to fight, the gaúcho—less a ranch worker than a soldier—held certain privileges in food and treatment. When the ownership of land and herds was consolidated, the plains pacified, and the ranches later fenced in with barbed wire, the new sedentary gaúcho was compelled to take on his new role as a simple ranch hand. A horseman still, he proudly herded the boss's cattle, skilled in his task and in his coordination of mount and herd. Progressively less well paid, however, he ate less and lived more miserably. The immense free range of former times was now divided rectangularly into ranches and subdivided into corrals. Between the ranches, stretching out as a no-man's-land, was the corridor between divisional fences, rising and falling over the sloping pasturelands as a means of communication and of separation between the private worlds of the ranches.

The gaúcho riding a fiery steed, wearing *bombachas* and boots and a hat with chinstrap and silver-ornamented hatband, carrying a revolver, dagger, and leather money pouch, with bolas wrapped around his belt, bandana around his neck, a sash around his body at midriff, and Chilean spurs at his heels, is today either the boss dressed up like an old rider or a member of some city folklore club. The rancher's home has become a comfortable house; even the barn, as the pride of the ranch, has a tile roof and is filled with hooks where harnesses are hung. Only the gaúcho's shack is just the way it used to be, and inside it life is more miserable.

Introduction of thoroughbred breeding bulls, of animal husbandry technology, and of improved pasturage has brought on a change in the cattle, which have put on weight, become more docile, and begun to give milk. The herds have grown; cattle have been joined by sheep. New areas have been taken over to expand intensive herding, with the cattle half-stabled, their growth controlled by diets focused on genetic excellence. The difference between cows and cowmen has come to be like the difference between the owner's cattle—their eugenics, health, and feed the object of all kinds of worries—and stray cattle; there is greater care for the herd and the greatest indifference with respect to the human contingent.

There remain, however, as cultural survivals, certain forms of personal dealings between rancher and gaúcho that recall the relationship between the leader and his fighter. Together occasionally to display horsemanship during the roundup, joining in contests of mastery of the bolas or lasso, wrangling wild cattle, betting on races—as happens in other herding areas as well—they maintain a relationship that is cordial, if markedly respectful and unequal, as is proper in the relationship between boss and worker. The maté-drinking circle is always a part of it and is the circle of the gaúcho's social companionship, sometimes joined by the boss to see that his orders are carried out and to assign new duties. Some habits remain, like the pleasure of the gaúchos' boss in male company, which brings every rancher to live surrounded by worker hangers-on. They are the ones who mix the maté, heat the water, and test the brew for him; the ones who roast, cut, and serve his steaks for him; the ones who set his rendezvous with the prostitutes of the area. The working gaúcho looks askance at and does not look kindly upon that one real intimacy, with its intrigues and fawning.

Yet, the ranch hand, even so, is a privileged person in the human landscape of the plains. With the increase of cattle there came an increase in the human population, some of whom were dislodged from ranches as too numerous for the simple worker requirements of herding chores. Gathering in barren lands or where the corridors stretch out into living quarters that constitute rural slums, they have thus become gaúchos in reserve, workers available when the rancher needs to recruit men at roundup time, to run a fence, or at shearing time. They work for a handout, underemployed but prolific odd-job workers, whose families grow up in poverty, the victims of undernourishment and infections—in short, all the ailments of poverty—as one more by-product of the latifundia herding system.

The major part of that population of dismounted gaúchos has switched to being workers on other people's land, land not taken up with herding, through a system of sharecropping. They are the autonomous rural workers of the south as opposed to ranch workers, just as the caipira of the central region is in opposition to the paid workers on large agricultural enterprises. Equally dependent on the landowner, who lets them have land to cultivate, collecting a half or third of their harvest as well as their personal and political loyalty, these neo-gaúchos, too, see the state and the government as an all-powerful and arbitrary entity with which the bosses have an understanding, which places the authorities effectively in the owners' service as a system of militias, police forces, and inspectors, destined to maintain the order of things just as it is.

When the network of appropriation of lands unravels with the occasional abandonment of a ranch, that loose population ventures an invasion of the unoccupied land, counting on remaining on the occupied plot until the police and lawyers come to stitch up that tear in the seamless weave. Under those circumstances, neither the ranch hand gaúcho nor the sharecropping gaúcho, both immersed in the latifundia herding system, attains the minimal conditions for the autonomous conduct of a citizen. They are men who belong to their bosses, fearful of losing a link that to them seems to be a haven in face of the threat of seeing themselves thrown into even more difficult conditions. In the crude taverns scattered along the corridors, listening to the radios that are always turned on and commenting on the news between rounds of maté and cheap liquor, that marginal subhumanity of shack dwellers lives its civic life. They argue about politics and politicians. They talk about agrarian reform. They are always serious and severe. One does not see there the relaxed cheerfulness of festivals on the ranch, where ranchers and their guests do more dancing, laughing, and celebrating than do the gaúchos assigned to serve the barbecue, all to the old tunes and the sound of the harmonica, the concertina, and the guitar. It is in those highway redoubts that a new awareness of his destiny is being forged in the gaúcho and that a spirit of rebellion, still diffuse and inconsistent, is taking shape.

Just as has been happening in the herding backlands of the Northeast, the ranch of the south is a breeding ground for cattle and its encampments are breeding grounds for people. The population of those shantytowns is made up mainly of old men who have been worn out in the struggles or herding or sharecropping and of children who are starting out in the same drudgery, all undernourished, ragged, and barefoot. Most of the young and healthy people emigrate to other rural areas or to the cities in search of a better future. In that way, with industrialization Rio Grande do Sul has experienced a profound process of urbanization, watching a huge mass of the underemployed, beggars, and prostitutes multiply in cities and towns. For that reason it has also become the populator of the rural zones of neighboring states and the southern plains of Mato Grosso. The gaúcho influence is visible in the whole area with the use of maté, the taste for barbecued ribs, and the particular regional accent of the border country with its overlay of Guaraní words.

Over the past few years, with the rise of a broad national market, the southern region has been specializing in temperate agricultural production, facilitated by its ecological and climatic conditions. There has thus arisen the growing of wheat as a substitute for imports, of rice, and of soybeans for export, all cultivated on a large scale with modern techniques and a certain degree of mechanization on the slopes previously given over to herding. In some rare cases, this development of activities takes place within the herding latifundia system itself. As a general rule it takes up only part of the workable land, the rest being reserved for traditional herding, which continues to be the main line of production.

For the new crops, instead of the traditional forms of sharecropping (halves and thirds), a system of rentals paid by the tenant in money has been introduced. The tenant is frequently a city man with greater business experience, who works with a base of official and private bank financing. The pioneering character of this activity and the urban background of the tenants involves a certain adventurism responsible for serious deformations—above all through the incapacity of this group to contribute to any revision of the landowning system, or at least to a modernization of the working relationship in a way that would organically integrate the rural population in a more prosperous economy. Utilizing machinery and more modern agricultural techniques, they have contributed more to the marginalization of the gaúcho than to his better integration into the most productive sector of the agrarian economy.

The high price of rentals—which seems to constitute one of the principal factors limiting production—is caused by the monopoly of land in the hands of the old latifundia class. Collecting heavy rents, these landowners take advantage of the modernization of the countryside by building comfortable houses and making improvements on their ranches, not as active entrepreneurs but as a drain on modernization. Meanwhile, one of the main obstacles to orderly expansion of southern wheat and rice crops is that the huge expenses of planting new crops, machinery, help, irrigation, and fertilizers is undertaken by simple entrepreneurs who work on other people's land. Other obstacles with heavy production costs and resulting in sacrifice of the land are the recommended association of these crops with others, or crop rotation according to modern techniques.

It must be pointed out that even under such conditions, these activities involve new working opportunities and better pay conditions for a portion of the rural masses, mainly at harvest time, for which there is generally less mechanization. Its most important social effect is perhaps a diversification of southern agricultural society with the broadening of an intermediate sector between landowners and their gaúchos that has been extremely narrow until now. Such are the semiskilled workers recruited for the tasks of agricultural mechanization, improvement of harvests, and marketing. The very degree of mechanization of these crops, however, works toward reduction in the possibilities for employment, which, in association with the monopoly of land ownership, has contributed to keeping the greater part of the rural population in a state of marginality; they continue to be left out of herding activities and are also too numerous for the labor needs of the new agricultural economy.

Another historical-cultural configuration has been created in southern Brazil by the populations brought over from the Azores by the Portuguese government in the eighteenth century. The objective of that colonization was to implant a permanent Portuguese occupying nucleus, in order to justify the appropriation of the area under the nose of the Spanish government and also for the colonists to serve as a faithful rearguard in the fighting taking place along the border. These Azoreans came with their families to reconstitute their island way of life in the south of Brazil, attracted by rewards that were quite special for the period. They were promised grants of plots of land marked out as the property of each married couple. On settling, they were to receive supplies, a rifle and ammunition, working tools, seeds for planting, two cows, and a mare as well as food for the first year. For the impoverished people of the islands, that generosity looked like an assurance of wealth. Groups settled on the coastal strip, on land along the banks of the River Guaiba, and on the coast of Santa Catarina.

This Azorean colonization was a failure on the economic level, as would be inevitable. Isolated in small niches along the deserted coast, unprepared for agricultural work on unknown lands, they were condemned to subsistence farming because they had no consumer market for their crops. After using up their maintenance supplies, they must have looked at one another and wondered what they should do. They had been called there to be farmers in a land where the white man only accepted the status of a master directing slaves. Giving in to their fate, however, they ended up learning the uses of the land at their disposal through communion with groups already shaped by the proto-Brazilian cells that were expanding along the Santa Catarina coast.

They became rustic matutos, adjusting to a way of life that was more Indian than Azorean, working the land through a slash-and-burn system, planting and eating cassava, corn, beans, and squash. Even in the crafts practiced today in the nuclei of their descendants, one cannot perceive any Azorean peculiarities. It is essentially the same as with caipira populations; people did what they had to do to supply their needs in cloth of domestic weave, pottery, and tools.

Some enterprising Azoreans, however, escaped "caipirization," either moving ahead with their own cultivation of grains, mainly wheat, or becoming merchants dedicated to dealing in provisions for people in the herding areas. In that way a mercantile movement was born that made viable the hamlets that were arising and began to integrate them into the incipient economic system of the region.

Their contribution to neo-Brazilian culture was negligible because the culture had been saturated with all the characteristics of Portuguese heritage that it could absorb. Their influence in regional culture and their social role, however, was decisive for the linguistic "Portugalization" and the cultural Brazilianization of the area and, most especially, in their status as a nucleus loyal to Portuguese and later on imperial power, which was needed along frontiers that were so markedly Castilian on one side and so independent, with loyalty to autonomous leaders, on the other.

When the region became embroiled in the melees of local leaders fighting over land and cattle in frontier battles, and especially in the autonomist struggles, republican in inspiration, against imperial centralism, the matuto population played a capital role. Being the natural opposite of the fiery gaúchos of the herding countryside because of their agricultural, sedentary, and peaceful way of life, their aim was to impose order along the frontier. They functioned thus as a base from which imperial forces could leave to subdue local leaders, to which they could retire when attacked in order to resupply, and whence they could recruit a portion of their troops.

The lands granted the Azoreans—reaching greatest value in the areas of rising of regional markets but fractionalized by a succession of inheritances in other areas—are seen today as zones of latifundia and minifundia, the first structured as a plantation economy and the second as a subsistence one. With that development, the matutos on plantations became mainly rural sharecroppers, with characteristics quite similar to those of the caipiras, going on to form a national labor reserve, disdained in the region because of their rude customs and their clinging to non-salaried forms of work. Those not involved in the plantation system or holding onto small parcels were obliged to move out to the settlements along the corridors or to the cities, increasing the mass of marginalized southerners.

Some groups of these matutos became specialized in new productive activities that arose with the broadening of the national market. These were the nuclei of fishermen along the coast and coal miners in the interior. Both lived under the most precarious of conditions, without a doubt making up one of the Brazilian groups most victimized by tuberculosis and infant mortality.

The marginalized matutos and the gaúcho masses all fell into a culture of poverty that led them to uniformity because of the simplicity of their equipment for life and work. They lived in shacks built by their own hands with the humblest of materials, which might be mud, palm leaves, or thatch in the rural areas and packing cases, cardboard, and discarded metal sheeting in suburban zones. In place of the ceramic, wicker, fiber, and leather artifacts they formerly made, they now use tin cans from dumps for storage and eating and drinking.

Illiterate in a society that is now half-integrated into literate systems of communication, these marginalized populations are even losing their age-old folkloric traditions, forgotten and replaced by new elemental forms of understanding and values that are heard through the radio and oral transmission. Under these conditions, a cultural homogenization processed by poverty—just as a uniform deculturation was processed through slavery in the past—is unifying the most diverse Brazilians by means of the common denominator of poverty, with a community of habits and customs reduced to their simplest expression and with a spreading out by modern means of communication that reaches them with accessible music and with appeals to an inaccessible consumerism.

That homogenization is drawing them together, too, as they face the future with their common destiny, confronting the social order responsible for their being left out of the occupational system and the pattern of life of the groups integrated into modernized sectors of national society. Their forms of expression, tending toward insurrection, are still elemental but have a tendency to become exaggerated. As among European peasants during the first phases of their marginalization by the mercantile-capitalist reordering, the rebellion of these Brazilian marginal masses, in the south as well as elsewhere, finds only anachronistic cultural forms of expression, almost always cloaked in a messianic guise.

The main one broke out between 1910 and 1914 in the border region between the states of Paraná and Santa Catarina because of suspension by the respective regulatory authorities of the legitimacy of appropriation of vacant lands. When the dispute arose between the two states over rule of the contested area, matters remained juridically in suspense, bringing on popular movements of occupation by the matuto population and an enlargement of holdings by plantation owners.

Given the hunger for land on the part of the rural masses thereabouts, the area was quickly populated, with the opening of any number of clearings in the forests, where families of claimants tried to conquer a niche and organize an economy of independent farmers. The violent reaction by the two contending states to that invasion, and later the armed intervention of the federal government, placed those populations in an illegal position, creating the conditions for the outbreak of a subversive uprising of the kind similar to those that took place in other parts of the country. Studies of this emergence of messianism can be found in Maria Isaura Pereira de Queiroz (1957, 1965) and Maurício Vinhas de Queiroz (1966).

Like those other movements, this one was defined as monarchist because the latifundia order that it wanted to bring down with fire and steel was called republican. Like the others, it was also messianic because on its cultural horizon, reform of the society founded on latifundia property was viewed as a reordering of the world that was legitimate in sacred terms. Messianism arose here as the cultural expression of a social reordering taking place through the invasion of the land. That concrete action brought back significance and meaning to old popular religious beliefs that had always been held in the region but that were now called upon to inspire new leadership for a holy war destined to bring about a restructuring of society.

The subversive character of the movement was immediately identified by local plantation owners and was defined as such by the two systems of regional authority. Although impeded from exercising their function as legitimizers of the appropriation of the unoccupied land, the state authorities considered the occupation of forest land an inadmissible abuse as the occupiers opened plots there and organized their ways of communal life. Finally, the invasion of the lands was interpreted by the federal authorities as revolutionary because it was throwing a huge area into convulsions, because it had brought occupiers and state troops face to face in conflicts where the latter were being defeated, because it was defined as a movement for the restoration of the monarchy, and most especially because it questioned the legitimacy of the constitutional form of land appropriation.

It was under these conditions that the age-old worship officiated over by itinerant "monks" was transformed and took revolutionary shape. These professional preachers did not belong to any religious congregation but gathered together wherever simple people were passing, to pray with rosaries and novenas and to spread popular versions of the most dramatic Catholic beliefs and biblical traditions, especially those referring to the threat of punishment and cataclysm or the hopes of collective salvation and restoration of the golden age.

Once the forests were peopled by matuto possessors and by caboclified foreigners, an environment arose that was more propitious for the wanderings of the so-called monks. They were received and heard everywhere with devotion by a population whose beliefs became heated and who saw them as miracle workers able to heal incurable illnesses; as priests qualified to perform marriages and last rites, to forgive sins, and to point the way to the path of salvation; and as seers capable of foretelling the future.

Having become counselors and guides — both in religious beliefs and in other matters — for those holding the lands, these monks were their leaders when conflicts began to break out. Under this leadership the fight to maintain possession against a legal order that was trying to expropriate their land was transformed into a holy war that developed simultaneously in two spheres. The first involved battles against state troops and later against the national army. The second was the effort at reordering society according to values embedded in deep layers of popular tradition, respectful of the property of the faithful who were in first possession and affirming the right of each to the fruits of his labor, leading to a communitarian economy regulated by an organization of labor that prescribed the duties of each person and by redistributive system that assured everyone of his essential needs.

Under the tension of the struggle, the matutos led by the monks organized their whole social life along those lines, from war to work and religion, self-disciplined under a strict warrior-priestly hierarchy, impregnating all activities with a redemptionism that subjected everything to the judgment of the monk, the only authority capable of establishing the way to collective salvation.

Various people were able to fill the role of "monk" before and after the messianic revolt of the Contestado, or Witness, because they were really in the old popular tradition of the "Awaited One," who would come to reorder the world and put an end to injustice, poverty, illness, and sadness. During the course of the struggle the nuclei in revolt were organized in "holy quarters," which attempted to reproduce the paradise lost and to anticipate the paradise awaited. In those nuclei, which brought together a population previously dispersed among plantations or gathered in miserable shacks, an intense community spirit developed, markedly egalitarian, and a natural economy was established in which commerce was proscribed except for the acquisition of goods from outside the nuclei in revolt. Within them, thousands of combatants came together (between 5,000 and 12,000), armed with long knives, shotguns, and later rifles they managed to capture in battle. They fought and worked with the drive of people who were trying at once to defend a life on earth that looked like the earthly paradise and to seek eternal salvation.

In fact, matutos did have something to defend: no longer just the land they now occupied but the way of life they had created—in spite of the war and because of it—which assured them opportunities for leisure, for worship governed by calls to prayer, and for religious festivals of a popular nature, such as processions, weddings, and baptisms, which took place almost daily. In spite of the prohibitions on dancing and consumption of alcohol, and the punishment of adultery and prostitution, life in those "sacred quarters" was merry and festive as it had never been for that population emerging from the latifundia system, where they had lived in isolation or in miserable shantytowns dependent on surrounding latifundia holdings. The allure was even greater, perhaps, in the opportunities for an intense communal social life, presided over by egalitarian ideas, and in its nonmercantile structure, which permitted members of each nucleus to devote themselves collectively to the fulfillment of their conditions for existence.

In contrast to their previous situation of being a subaltern group subjected to the work regime of the plantations and ranches, which had allowed only perpetuation of their miserable living conditions, the new structure—assuring access to land for all, providing incentives for collective organization of work, and regulated by egalitarian criteria of distribution—guaranteed them a healthy diet and a joie de vivre they had not known until then.

Because of all this, the eradication of the "sacred quarters," made up mainly of matutos and a few German, Polish, and Italian immigrants and their most impoverished descendants, was one of the most difficult campaigns for the Brazilian army, which had to mobilize thousands of men and arm them with heavy artillery in order to stand up against the guerrilla warfare of the "fanatics." The latter were defeated only after three years of combat in which close to 3,500 people were killed. The plantation order was restored at that price, compelling the matutos to accept the place and role prescribed for them in it.

Even today, among the humble groups of the matuto areas, a belief in the return of the monk survives. He will reestablish plenty and happiness, make the old young, the ugly beautiful, and will render God visible to all. In 1954 a messianic germ grew active in the region, bringing together several matuto families in worship for the return of the monk and obliging the authorities to intervene once more in order to make them accept their fate.

Similar uprisings have taken place in other places where latifundia land has been broken up, creating a disputed area between Minas Gerais and Espírito Santo. The landless flocked there, too, demanding their bit of land, but they were dispersed before someone like a new Contestado could arise. A similar episode took place with the Muckers of Rio Grande do Sul.

The struggles of these matutos, those of Canudos, the Cabanagem, those of the Muckers, and hundreds of others have in common a trait that must be emphasized. They have all demanded land to occupy and on which to eke out a living, and by the same token they all show that they are perfectly capable of creating sufficiency, if not prosperity, and a happy and satisfactory social life. The other trait that should be stressed is the capacity of the ruling order, backed by police and army, to stifle these demands in order to reimplant the sad world of the latifundia order that starves and degrades.

The third historical-cultural configuration of the southern region is made up of Brazilians of Germanic, Italian, Polish, Japanese, Lebanese, and various other origins, brought in as immigrants in the nineteenth century, mainly during its final decades. Although Brazilians like all the rest because they would not know how to live in the homelands of their parents and grandparents and because they are Brazilian in their fundamental loyalties, they make up a differentiated sector of the population by their form of participation in national society. They are distinguished by bilingualism, with the use of a foreign tongue as the language of the home, with habits that still link them to their European roots, and most of all in a rural way of life founded on polycultural small properties, intensively cultivated, and a higher educational level than the general population.

European settlement, initiated during the imperial period, was in answer to an attitude common to the Latin American oligarchies that came to power after independence: a cultural alienation that made them look upon their own people with European eyes. Like Europeans, they viewed the blacks and mixed-bloods who made up the greater part of the population with suspicion, and they blamed the prevalent backwardness of their countries on the racial inferiority of people of color. Under the pressure of that complex and its heavily demeaning identifications, they inaugurated a campaign for radical replacement of their own people, where practicable, by eugenically better ones. And these would be the light-skinned populations from central Europe, who at that time were moving in large contingents to North America, assuring its progress. The colonization enterprise was one of the objectives most persistently pursued by the imperial government, which spent enormous resources on it, assuring the settlers passage, facilities for establishing themselves and for their maintenance, and grants of land. Similar conditions had never been offered to Brazil's own caipira population, who at the time formed large masses marginalized by the latifundia system.

The gringo population resulting from that movement for whitening by colonization today occupies a vast island in the center of the states of Paraná, Santa Catarina, and Rio Grande do Sul and spreading out into neighboring territories, with small enclaves enclosed in other regions, like the nuclei in Espírito Santo and São Paulo. To the east they come face to face with the old Azorean settlements in the coastal areas; to the west and south with gaúcho herding activities. They influence and are influenced by both these contiguous areas, giving and receiving adaptable cultural contributions, but rarely do their descendants become matutos or gaúchos except for those who, finding themselves marginalized, become a part of a culture of poverty common to the whole region—and to almost all of Brazil—through the same uniformity in their regression to the simplest and most primitive forms of subsistence and life.

The gringo cultural pocket formed by immigrants coming from different European and Asian ethnicities shows great social uniformity in its way of life and in the human landscape it has created—colored, however, by differentiations that allow for distinctions between German subareas and Italian ones, between Polish and Russian ones, and between all of them and the Japanese. The social uniformities come essentially from the way in which the colonies have been formed through land grants of smallholdings for family exploitation and from the professional skills the immigrants brought for the practice of small-scale agriculture. The cultural uniformities come from the segregation in which they lived during the early decades as implants in a profoundly different society with which they did not intermingle. Also playing a salient role in the formation of the gringo island was the circumstance that the southern settlements were not limited to grazing or latifundia agricultural areas, thus avoiding the power and arbitrariness of the great landowners.

Each group could therefore organize its own life autonomously, establish its schools and churches, and constitute its authorities, shaping the early generations still in the spirit and according to the traditions of their immigrant parents and grandparents. Living in isolation, they would gain mastery of the Portuguese language only much later, as a means of communication with Brazilians and among colonists of different linguistic backgrounds. Tensions inherited from the European world also placed these ethnicities in opposition to one another through discrimination that made for even greater segregation. The Japanese nuclei of colonists, installed outside the southern area and often concentrated in proximity to large urban centers as suppliers of vegetables, had a parallel development, marked by even greater self-segregation.

The first generation of immigrants faced the hard task of subsistence as they cleared the virgin forest, sometimes confronting hostile Indians, building their homes and roads, and experiencing a stern and arduous life. Their struggle was made even more difficult by the lack of a regular market for their produce. The great initial task they fulfilled was defining the productive activities with which they could best become integrated into the national economy. Only the penury that the peasantry of their countries of origin faced—uprooted from the countryside by the reflexive effects of the Industrial Revolution or caught up in the crises of the consolidation of European nationalities—could explain the tenacity with which they faced up to such difficult conditions. Here, however, they were landowners; of virgin lands that had almost no value, true, but fertile land that they were confident would become valuable through their own efforts.

The succeeding generations, beneficiaries of the results of these pioneering sacrifices, found much more propitious conditions. They were already children of the land, accustomed to the jobs they had to do. Their problem began to be one of the availability of land where they could open new clearings for the families that were multiplying. In principle, however, all the territory around the settlements, made up of land that was vacant or available at a low price, acted as a frontier open to their expansion.

During the period of transition between the pioneering phase and the stage of prosperity, some of the more isolated gringo populations also had a bout of lawlessness that was messianic in character, although different from such movements elsewhere in the country because of the biblical-

Protestant orientation in this case and the cultural content coming from German folk traditions. Such were the events that took place in 1872 with the messianic eruptions of the Muckers (Puritans) along the Rio dos Sinos, twenty-five miles from the provincial capital of Porto Alegre in Rio Grande do Sul, led in the main by a prophetess who also established an egalitarian and fanatic community. During its critical period, this revivalist movement brought on a succession of crimes and assassinations, and it was only eradicated with the slaughter of its believers.

In spite of their isolation, they knew quite well that if they lived here, they would have to change their country of affiliation as well as change themselves, giving up European patterns in customs, language, and aspirations. The successive groups of newcomers served as a contrast with the earlier immigrants' accents and their ignorance of the distant cultural world from which their families had broken away. But at the same time, living among Indians, matutos, and gaúchos reminded them how different they were from the early occupants of the land, for whose miserable way of life they could feel no attraction whatever. These other groups of people were, on the one hand, their forebears and, on the other, the Brazilians they knew. They felt themselves to have formed a third entity, incapable of being reduced to either of the others.

That situation of the ethnic marginality of the colonization nuclei, principally those of the Germans, Japanese, and Italians, was exploited before and during the Second World War by the governments of their countries of origin, creating serious conflicts of ethnosocial loyalty. With that objective, the Nazi and Fascist movements as well as the Japanese government set up strong propaganda services and fostered the rise of terrorist organizations dedicated to intense ideological, nationalist, and racist indoctrination.

Thus was created a traumatic situation that gave rise to serious differences between Luso-Brazilians on one side and Gringo-Brazilians and Nippo-Brazilians on the other. The conditions of relative segregation in which these nuclei developed and their cultural and linguistic conservatism facilitated that dissociative action. To confront the problem it was necessary to mount a massive official nationalizing action, which—as always happens in cases like these—had disastrous results, aggravating the conflict of loyalties all the more. It did fulfill a decisive assimilating function, however, compelling the teaching of the vernacular language in schools, breaking the isolation of communities, and recruiting Gringo- and Nippo-Brazilian youths for service in the armed forces. Taken to the large urban centers, these youths broadened their cultural horizons and their view of Brazil itself, contributing upon their return home to the facilitation of a national identification that was now becoming imperative.

The diverse areas of European settlement today form a region with its own physiognomy, with people gathered into villages for the concentration of inhabitants in commerce, church, and school. Entirely new roads lead out across the Brazilian countryside, passing between densely populated and carefully maintained plots on both sides. These rural towns form networks that are centered on cities, their production diversified and adjusted to the conditions of the market, adding industrial activities to craft-based agricultural ones. In that way a prosperous regional economy was implanted on a Europeanized cultural landscape within the relative Luso-Brazilian uniformity of the country.

The Gringo-Brazilian nuclei became important centers for the production of wine, honey, wheat, potatoes, rye, hops, and European fruits and vegetables along with corn for fattening hogs and manioc for the production of starch. The crops of the temperate zones were added to the national economy in this way; old farm plots flourished; and most of all, these people demonstrated the high pattern of life that could be established by nuclei of small property owners when they were able to cultivate the land intensively and benefit from its produce rather than commercializing it. Looking at the areas in question, it is clear that this small-farm economy allows for the maintenance of a much larger population than the herding zones and even the agricultural areas based on latifundia, and it assures a high standard of living as well.

In their expansion, however, the settlements ran up against the world of latifundia, seeing their movable frontier thus come to a halt. With no means to intensify their production, they entered an uneconomic subdivision of lots, with two and afterward four families on areas originally meant for one. It is minifundia that today harasses the Gringo-Brazilian population just as much as the latifundia that hems in its expansion.

Because of that obstacle of latifundia, a marginal population has also arisen in the very heart of settlements in the most prosperous agro-economic region of the country. They are the so-called caboclos of the southern settlement area. Caboclified gringos, not owning any land, they have regressed to a culture of poverty, blending in with the matutos of Azorean origin and with the gaúchos of the shantytowns in the struggle for land on which to sharecrop. Their habits of work and leisure, their diet, the shacks that serve them as dwellings, the penury in which they live, all commingled, reduce them all to one single group: the marginal people of the southern region.

This distinction has become so obvious today that the colonist in the gringo region is a small landowner and the caboclo is someone without land. Mingled in each category are Brazilians of gaúcho, Azorean, or foreign extraction, distinguished basically by their position with regard to ownership of the land they cultivate.

That group of caboclified gringos, like other marginalized groups in the country, constitutes a labor reserve operating as a subclass below paid farmworkers in rural areas and below those integrated into the workforce with regular jobs in the cities. The existence of that social stratum, into which all are threatened with falling if they lose their jobs, has two quite serious social effects. It works to reduce the combativeness of peasants and factory workers for the betterment of their living conditions and to induce conformity through underscoring that even the humblest worker still has something to lose; he can fall into an even more degrading situation. On the other hand, for those marginalized at the lowest level of misery, already as low as they can get, it constitutes an incitement to revolutionary rebellion, for only a profound social reordering can open up better prospects of life.

In the last few years intensive industrial development with origins in family craftsmanship has arisen in the zone of settlement, which has already attained the status of a network of middle-level industry dedicated to metallurgy, weaving, chemicals, leather, ceramics, and glassware. Some of the old gringo colonial villages have been transformed in this process into important regional industrial centers, places like Caxias, São Leopoldo, Novo Hamburgo, Blumenau, Joinville, and Itajaí. The old colonists, transformed into entrepreneurs, have not limited themselves, however, to their original areas. They have established their industries in regional capitals too, becoming the main modern entrepreneurs in the south of the country. That industrial development has brought about the integration into the labor force as factory workers of sizable contingents of marginalized populations, gringos as well as gaúchos and matutos.

The leap from small farming to crafts and later to factory industry was made possible by the colonists' knowledge of simple European productive techniques—more complex, however, than those used by other Brazilian nuclei. But it can be explained mainly by bilingualism, which gave them access to better sources of technical information and made possible European contacts that permitted importation of equipment and qualified personnel when necessary and obtaining assistance in the implantation and expansion of their industries. It should be pointed out that this industrial boom took place during the same period when a large textile plant was brought into one of the most backward regions of the country (Minas Gerais) but fell into disuse for lack of capacity for technical maintenance and lack of modern entrepreneurial spirit.

The social and economic progress of Gringo- and Nippo-Brazilian settlement, as well as their simultaneous integration into national markets as producers and consumers, gave rise to new horizons of human relations and better conditions for cultural integration. Today the image conjured up by gringo or Japanese Brazilians is not confused with the marginalized population or with the latifundia oligarchy; it is associated with the urban populations of modern and progressive life in which they are involved as workers. At the same time, they are persuaded that they no longer belong to the cultural world of their ancestors in view of the fact that this, too, has changed, making unreal for them any ethnic identification not Brazilian.

In these new situations of contact and in light of this new understanding, the self-identification of the descendants of colonists as Brazilians has progressed, differentiated in their way of participation in national life by their origins and their experience, but Brazilians and nothing else. Only the Japanese, marked by differentiating racial characteristics, have tended not to find their assimilation recognized, even when complete, as has happened with those who have been urbanized. This characteristic, which was painful while Brazilians identified the Japanese as a backward people, has been losing that content in view of the growing prestige of Japan and the cultural and economic success of the Japanese Brazilians. In fact, they probably make up the immigrant group that has risen and modernized the most rapidly. It is not rare for the grandson of a Japanese peasant to be an engineer, industrialist, or executive in one of the large Japanese firms established in the country recently or that his granddaughter is a teacher or a doctor.

14

The National Destiny

Birth Pangs

Brazil was ruled first as a slaveholding establishment, exotically tropical, inhabited by native Indians and imported blacks, and then as a consulate in which a subcategory of Portuguese people including African and Indian blood was living the destiny of an external proletariat within a foreign possession. The interests and aspirations of its people were never taken into account because attention and care was paid only to looking after the requisites for the prosperity of the exporting establishment. What was stimulated was the drawing out of Indians from the forests or the importation of more blacks brought from Africa to enlarge the workforce, which was the source of profits for the mother country. There was never a concept of a people here that took in all workers and attributed to them any rights, not even the basic right of working to feed oneself, clothe oneself, and have a home of one's own.

That primacy of profit over necessity engendered an economic system moved by an accelerated rhythm of production of what the external market demanded, based on a workforce sunk in backwardness, and moved by greed, because no attention was paid to the production and reproduction of the conditions for existence.

As a consequence there always existed side by side commercial prosperity, which at times was the greatest in the world, and a generalized poverty of the local population. The society was, in fact, nothing but a conglomeration of multiethnic peoples coming from Europe, Africa, and right here, activated by the most intense miscegenation, by the most brutal genocide of tribal peoples, and by radical ethnicide in the deculturation of the indigenous and African contingents.

In that way, paradoxically, the ideal conditions for ethnic transfiguration were attained through the forced de-Indianization of the Indians and de-Africanization of the blacks, who, despoiled of an identity, would see themselves forced to invent a new ethnicity that took in all of them. So it was that a growing human mass was being blended, one that had lost its face: they were de-Indianized ex-Indians, and especially mixed-blood, black, and Indian women, ever so many of them with ever so few white Europeans using them to multiply prodigiously.

The Portuguese nucleus—formed by the few Lusitanians who arrived during the first century and by the even rarer women who came here, looking down on all the others from the height of their prejudice as people from the kingdom and because of the power of their weapons—operated for the economic despoilment of all others and tried to impose on all their ethnic form and their civilizing face. Surprisingly enough this nascent entity, despite being an overseas Portugal, shaped within itself a people who have been fighting ever since for self-awareness and to realize their potential.

That mass of mulattos and caboclos, Lusitanized by the Portuguese language they spoke, by that view of the world, were giving shape to Brazilian ethnicity and simultaneously promoting their own integration into the form of a nation-state. It was already mature when it received large contingents of European and Japanese immigrants, which made it possible for them to proceed to be assimilated, all of them, into the status of generic Brazilians.

Some, especially the Japanese, by maintaining unmistakable physical marks of their origins, have as a consequence a certain resistance to full assimilation or to recognizing it, even when it has taken place completely. They never cease to be Japanese Brazilians because they carry it on their faces. Other immigrants—Italians, Germans, Spaniards—in spite of being light-skinned and bearing intricate surnames, have been easily assimilated and their status as Brazilians has been fully accepted. Some, like the first-generation Brazilian General Geisel, have even been exasperated and mystified as to why the Indians, here for so many centuries, insist that they themselves are not Brazilians.

The Arabs have been the most successful immigrants, quickly becoming integrated into Brazilian life and attaining positions in the government. They have even forgotten where they came from and their miserable life in the countries of their origin. They are blind to the fact that their success can be explained to a large degree by the casual attitude they have in addressing and working with the local society: armed with prejudices and incapable of any solidarity, detached from any loyalty and family or social obligations. All of this allows them to concentrate their entire effort on getting rich.

The attitude of these immigrants is frequently one of disdain and incomprehension. Their tendency is to consider poor Brazilians responsible for their own poverty and to view the racial factor as what sinks the descendants of Indians and blacks into misery. They even state that the Catholic religion and the Portuguese language have contributed to Brazil's underdevelopment. They ignore the fact that they arrived here as a result of crises that rendered them superfluous, discarded from the workforce in their homelands, and that here they found a huge country already opened, with fixed frontiers, autonomously governing its destiny.

Fortunately, none of these contingents has sufficient coherence to present itself as an ethnicity fighting for domination of the total society or seeking an autonomous destiny. Contrary to what happens in other countries that hold within their population groups that are clearly opposed to identification with the national macroethnicity, in Brazil, in spite of the multiplicity of racial and ethnic origins of the population, such intractable and separatist contingents disposed to organize themselves in isolation are not to be found.

What tears apart and separates Brazilian components is the stratification of classes. But that is what at a deeper level unifies and articulates as Brazilians the immense and predominantly darker masses, much more solidly joined together as such than as carbon-dark blacks or plaster-light whites, because neither of these defects is curable. The most brilliant spokesman for that deformed view held by certain descendants of immigrants was the scholar Hermann von Ihering. In his passion to defend his German countrymen, who were at war with the Indians who had always lived on the territories granted for settlement, he lent his scientific prestige to two campaigns: that of asking the government to exterminate the Indians as a requisite for progress and civilization, and that of accusing the Brazilian people, who had built this country that gave him shelter, of being incapable of any enterprise.

The present Indians in the State of São Paulo do not represent an element for work and progress. As in other states of Brazil, too, one cannot expect serious and continuous work from civilized Indians and since the savage Caingangs are an impediment to the colonization of the backland regions which they inhabit, there would seem to be no other means with which to have recourse but their extermination.

The conversion of Indians has not given any satisfactory result; those Indians who joined with Portuguese immigrants have only left a bad influence on the habits of the rural population. It is my conviction that it is essentially due to these circumstances that the State of São Paulo has been obliged to bring in thousands of immigrants since it cannot count in any efficient and sure way on the services of that indigenous population for the tasks that its agriculture requires. (Ihering 1907, 215)

Other interpreters of our national characteristics see the most varied defects and qualities, to which they attribute causal values. One example is sufficient. For Sérgio Buarque de Holanda they would be our characteristics inherited from the Iberians—Hispanic arrogance and Portuguese laxness and plasticity as well as an adventurous spirit and appreciation of loyalty in both, and in addition a greater pleasure in leisure than in commerce. From the mixture of all these ingredients has probably resulted a certain slackness and anarchy, lack of cohesion, disorder, indiscipline, and indolence. But probably deriving from them also is the tendency toward despotism, authoritarianism, and tyranny.

Since all of these are defects, we ought to agree that we are a sorry case. Can that be true? I very much fear that it is not. Much worse for us, perhaps, and Sérgio recognizes it, would have been the opposite of those defects—servility, humility, rigidity, a spirit of order, a sense of duty, a liking for routine, gravity, circumspection. These might well have made us even worse because they would have taken away the creativity of the adventurer, the adaptability of someone who is not rigid but flexible, the vitality of someone who faces fate and fortune with daring, the originality of an undisciplined people.

There is also a lot of talk about Brazilian laziness, attributed both to indolent Indians and runaway blacks and to the corrupt ruling classes. This is all exceedingly dubious in view of the fact of what has been done here. And much has been done, like the building of a whole urban civilization during the centuries of colonial life, incomparably more vigorous than the one seen in North America, for example. The question arising is how to understand why the North Americans, so poor and backward, praying in their wooden churches without any prominence in any area of cultural creativity, rose fully into industrial civilization while we sank into backwardness.

The cause of that discrepancy must be sought in other areas. The bad thing here, the effective cause of backwardness, is the way in which society is structured, organized against the interests of the population, who are always bled in order to serve designs that are alien and even opposed to their own. There is not and never has been a free people here, one that ruled its own destiny in search of its own prosperity. What there has been and what there still is is a mass of workers exploited, humiliated, and offended by a dominant minority that is frighteningly efficient in the formation and maintenance of its own plan for prosperity, always ready to squelch any threat of reform of the effective social order.

Comparisons

What is Brazil among other contemporary peoples? What are Brazilians? As a people of the Americas they stand in contrast to those peoples who have watched the intrusions without losing their former cultural integrity altogether, like Mexicans and those of the Andean highlands, whose peoples came from high civilizations and have lived the drama of cultural duality and the challenge of fusion into a new civilization.

Another contrasting bloc is that of transplanted peoples, who represent in the Americas nothing more than the reproduction of European peoples and landscapes. The United States and Canada are, in fact, more like and more related to white South Africa and Australia than to us. Argentina and Uruguay are other transplants, invaded by a European wave that sent 4 million on top of the mere 1 million who had devastated the country and gained independence, burying the old Hispano-Indian formation. The question remains why, with the same economy and with even richer production of grain, meat, and wool, did they not attain the prosperity of Australia and Canada, which grew rich with much less? Could it be that old Cromwell and the institutional forms he created, still obtaining in the north, are what make the difference?

The other Latin Americans are, like us, new peoples in the making—an infinitely more complex task, because it is one thing to reproduce a spiritless European world overseas and distinctly another to embark upon the drama of reshaping high civilization. A third challenge, quite different, of ours is reinventing the human being, creating a new breed of people different from all that exist.

If we look outside, Africa stands in contrast to us because it is still living the drama of its Europeanization, following its own leadership for freedom, and evincing more horror at the tribalism that survives and threatens to explode than at recolonialization. These are illusions! If the surviving Indians in Brazil have resisted all the brutality for 500 years and continue to be themselves, their equivalents in Africa will resist too, to laugh in the face of their neo-Europeanizing leaders. More distant worlds, like those of Asia, more mature than Europe itself, are being structured in a new civilization, retaining their being and their face.

We Brazilians in this picture are a people in the making but impeded from doing so. We are a mixed-blood people in flesh and spirit, for miscegenation here was never a crime or a sin. We were made through it and we are still being made that way. The mass of natives originating in miscegenation lived for centuries with no awareness of themselves, sunk in nobodyness. That was how it was until they were defined as a new ethnonational identity, that of Brazilians, a people in the making, in search of its destiny even today. Looking at them, hearing them, it is easy to perceive that they are, in fact, a new Romanness, a late but better Romanness, because it has been washed in Indian and black blood.

Indeed, a few Roman soldiers who were encamped on the Iberian Peninsula Latinized the pre-Portuguese there. They did it so firmly that their sons maintained their Latinness, their face, resisting centuries of oppression by Nordic and Saracen invaders. After 2,000 years that effort has leaped across the Ocean Sea and come to Brazil to shape the neo-Romanness that we are.

It should be pointed out that in spite of the fact that they were made through a fusion of such different roots, Brazilians are today one of the most linguistically and culturally homogeneous and also one of the most socially integrated peoples on earth. They speak the same language without dialects. They do not contain any groups demanding autonomy or clinging to a past. We are open to the future.

There are nations in the New World—the United States, Canada, Australia—that are mere transplants of Europe onto broad spaces overseas. They offer no novelty in this world. They are the excess populations who no longer found any room in the Old World and came here to repeat Europe, reconstituting their native landscapes in order to live with more repose and freedom, to feel at home. It is true that they sometimes become creative, reinventing the republic and Greek elections. But rarely. They are, strictly speaking, our opposite.

Our destiny is to join with all Latin Americans in our common opposition to the same antagonist, which is Anglo-Saxon America, in order to bring together, as is happening in the European Community, the Latin American Nation dreamed of by Bolívar. Today we are 500 million; tomorrow we will be a billion. This is a human contingent obviously sufficient in size to incarnate Latinness in future humanity in the face of Chinese, Slavic, Arab, and neo-Britannic blocs.

We are new peoples still engaged in the struggle to make ourselves as a new human breed that never existed before. It is an exceedingly difficult and arduous task but also one that is beautiful and challenging.

If the truth be told, we are the new Rome—a tardy, tropical Rome. Brazil is already the largest of neo-Latin nations in population size and it is beginning to be so in artistic and cultural creativity also. It must become so now in the domination of the technology of future civilization in order to become an economic power with self-sustaining progress. We are building ourselves in the struggle to flourish tomorrow as a new civilization, of mixed blood and tropical, proud of itself—happier because it is more enduring; better for incorporating within itself more humanities; and more generous for being open to all races and all cultures and because it is located in the most beautiful and luminous province of the earth.

Bibliography

Albersheim, Ursula. 1962. *Uma comunidade teuto-brasileira—Ibirama, Santa Catarina*. Rio de Janeiro: CBPE/Ministério da Educação.

Anchieta, José de. 1933. *Cartas, informações, fragmentos históricos e sermões do padre Joseph de Anchieta (1554–1594)*. Rio de Janeiro: ABL/Civilição Brasileira (Cartas Jesuíticas III).

———. 1958. *De gestis mendi de saa*. Edição bilingüe, tradução do pe. Armando Cardoso. Rio de Janeiro: Arquivo Nacional.

Andreoni, João Antônio (André João Antonil). 1711. *Cultura e opulência do Brasil por suas drogas e minas*. 1ª ed. Lisboa: Officina Real Deslandesiarta.

———. 1967. *Cultura e opulência do Brasil por suas drogas e minas*. Vol. 2. São Paulo: Companhia Editora Nacional (Roteiro do Brasil).

Araújo, José de Souza Azevedo Pizarro e. 1945–51. *Memórias historicas do Rio de Janeiro*. 10 vols. Rio de Janeiro: INL/Imprensa Nacional.

Ávila, pe. Fernando Bastos de. 1956. *L'immigration au Brésil*. Rio de Janeiro: Agir.

Azevedo, João Lúcio d'. 1930. *Os jesuítas no Grão-Pará, suas missões e a colonização*. Coimbra: Imprensa da Universidade.

———. 1931. *História de Antônio Vieira*. 2 vols. Lisboa: Liv. Clássica Ed.

———. 1947. *Épocas de Portugal econômico: Esboços de história*. Lisboa: Liv. Clássica Editora.

Baião, Antonio. 1939. *História da expansão portuguesa no mundo*. Vol. 2. Lisboa: Ática.

Blásquez, Antônio. 1931. *Cartas avulsas (1550–1568)*. Rio de Janeiro: Academia Brasileira de Letras (Cartes Jesuíticas II).

Boiteaux, Lucas Alexandre. 1912. *Notas para a história catharinense*. Florianópolis: Typ. da Liv. Moderna.

Bonfim, Manuel. 1929. *O Brasil na América*. Rio de Janeiro: Francisco Alves.

———. 1930. *O Brasil nação*. 2 vols. Rio de Janeiro: Francisco Alves.

———. 1931. *O Brasil na História*. Rio de Janeiro: Francisco Alves.

———. 1935. *O Brasil*. São Paulo: Companhia Editora Nacional (Brasiliana, vol. 47).

Borah, Woodrow. 1962. "Population decline and the social and institutional changes of New Spain in the middle decades of the sixteenth century." In *Akten des 34. Internationalem Amerikanisten-Kongresses*. Copenhague.

————. 1964. "America as model: The demographic impact of European expansion upon the non-European world." In *Actas XXXV Congreso Internacional de Amencanistas*. México.

Boxer, Charles R. 1963. *A idade de ouro do Brasil.* São Paulo: Companhia Editora Nacional.

Brandão, Ambrósio Fernandes. 1968. *Diálogos das grandezas do Brasil.* Rio de Janeiro: Edições de Ouro.

Buescu, Mircea. 1968. *Exercícios de história econômica do Brasil.* Rio de Janeiro: APEC Editora.

Caldas, João Pereira. 1900. "Roteiro do Maranhão a Goyaz pela capitania do Piauhy." *Revista do Instituto Histórico e Geográfico Brasileiro* (Rio de Janeiro), 62, parte 1ª: 60–161.

Caldeira, Clovis. 1960. *Menores no meio rural (trabalho e escolarização).* Rio de Janeiro: CBPE.

Calógeras, J. Pandiá. 1927. *A política exterior do Império.* 2 vols. São Paulo.

————. 1938. *Formação histórica do Brasil.* 3ª ed. São Paulo.

Camargo, José Ferreira de. 1957. *Êxodo rural da Brasil.* São Paulo.

————. 1968. *A cidade e o campo.* São Paulo.

Canstatt, Oscar. 1954. *O Brasil, a terra e a gente.* Rio de Janeiro: Irmãos Pongetti.

Capistrano de Abreu, João. 1929. *O descobrimento do Brasil.* Rio de Janeiro: Ed. da Soc. Capistrano de Abreu.

————. 1954. *Capítulos de história colonial (1500–1800).* Rio de Janeiro: Ed. da Soc. Capistrano de Abreu.

————. 1975. *Caminhos amigos e povoamento do Brasil.* Rio de Janeiro: Ed. Civilização Brasileira.

Cardim, Fernão. [1584] 1980. *Tratados da terra e gente do Brasil.* Belo Horizonte/ São Paulo: Itatiaia/EDUSP.

Cardoso, Efraim. 1959. *El Paraguay colonial: Las raíces de la nacionalidad.* Buenos Aires/Assunção.

Cardoso, Fernando Henrique. 1962. *Capitalismo e escravidão no Brasil meridional—O negro na sociedade escravocrata do Rio Grande do Sul.* São Paulo: Difel.

Carneiro, Édison. s.d. *Candomblés da Bahia.* Rio de Janeiro.

Carneiro, J. Fernando. 1950. *Imigração e colonização no Brasil.* Rio de Janeiro: Faculdade Nacional de Filosofia, cadeira de geografia do Brasil (Publicações Avulsas n° 2).

Cascudo, Luís da Câmara. 1954. *Dicionario folclore brasileiro.* Rio de Janeiro: INL.

Castro, Josué de. 1946. *Geografia da fome.* Rio de Janeiro.

Cava, Ralph dela. 1970. *Miracle at Joaseiro.* New York/London: Columbia University Press.

Cook, Sherburne, and Woodrow Borah. 1957. "The rate of population change in Central Mexico, 1550–1570." *Hispanic American Historical Review* 37, no. 4: 463–70.

Correa Filho, Virgílio. 1969. *História de Mato Grosso.* Rio de Janeiro: INL.

Cortes, Geraldo de Menezes. 1954. *Migração e colonização no Brasil.* In separate da *Revista de Serviço Público.* Rio de Janeiro: Depto. de Imprensa Nacional.

Cortesão, Jaime. 1943. *A carta de Pero Vaz de Caminha.* Rio de Janeiro: Ed. Livros de Portugal.

————— (org.). 1956. *Pauliceae lusitana monumenta histórica.* Lisboa: ed. comemorativa do 4º Centenário da Cidade de São Paulo, Real Gabinete de Leitura do Rio de Janeiro, vol. 1 (1494–1600), partes 5–8.

—————. 1958. *Raposo Tavares e a formação territorial do Brasil.* Rio de Janeiro: Serviço de Documentação/Ministério da Educação e Cultura.

—————. 1964. *Introdução a história das bandeiras.* 2 vols. Lisboa: Portugália.

Costa Pinto, L. A. 1948. "A estrutura da sociedade rural brasileira." In *Sociologia* (10, 2/3). São Paulo.

—————. 1953. *O negro no Rio de Janeiro.* Rio de Janeiro.

Cruls, Gastão. 1938. *A Amazônia que eu vi. Obidos—Tumucumaque.* São Paulo.

Cruz, Ernesto. 1963. *História do Pará.* 2 vols. Belém: Universidade Federal do Pará (Coleção Amazônica).

Cunha, Euclides da. 1945. *Os sertões (Campanha de Canudos).* Rio de Janeiro: Francisco Alves.

Curtin, Philip D. 1969. *The Atlantic slave trade: A census.* Madison/London: University of Wisconsin Press.

Daniel, pe. João. 1976. *Tesouro descoberto no rio Amazonas.* Separata dos *Anais da Biblioteca Nacional,* vol. 95. Rio de Janeiro.

Davatz, Thomas.1941. *Memórias de um colono no Brasil (1850).* São Paulo: Martins (Biblioteca Histórica Brasileira).

Dias, Carlos A. 1981. "O indígena e o invasor: A confrontação dos povos indígenas do Brasil com o invasor europeu, nos séculos XVI e XVII." *Encontros com a Civilização Brasileira* 28: 201–25. Rio de Janeiro.

Diégues, Manuel, Jr. 1960. *Regiões culturais do Brasil.* Rio de Janeiro: CBPE.

—————. 1964. *Imigração, urbanização e industrializaçã.* Rio de Janeiro: CBPE.

Dobyns, Henry F., and Paul Thompson. 1966. "Estimating aboriginal American population." *Current Anthropology* (7, 4). Utrecht, Holland.

Dourado, Mecenas. 1958. *A conversão do gentio.* Rio de Janeiro: Liv. São José.

Dreys, Nicolao. 1839. *Notícia descriptiva da província do Rio Grande de São Pedro do Sul.* Rio de Janeiro: Typ. Imp. e Const. de J. Villeneuve e Cia.

Ennes, Ernesto. 1938. *As guerras nos Palmares.* São Paulo: Companhia Editora Nacional (Brasiliana, vol. 127).

Faoro, Raymundo. 1958. *Os donos do poder. Formação do patronato político brasileiro.* 2 vols. Porto Alegre: Globo.

Fernandes, Florestan. 1949. *A organização social dos tupinambás.* São Paulo: Progresso Editorial.

—————. 1952. *A função social da guerra na sociedade Tupinambá. Revista do Museu Paulista,* n.s., vol. 6. São Paulo.

—————. 1964. *A integração do negro à sociedade de massas.* São Paulo.

Franco, Francisco de Assis Carvalho. 1953. *Dicionário de bandeirantes e sertanistas do Brasil (séculos XVI, XVII e XVIII)*. São Paulo: comissão do IV centenario da cidade de São Paulo.

Frank, Andrew Gunder. 1964. "A agricultura brasileira: Capitalismo e o mito do feudalismo." In *Revista Brasiliense* 51. São Paulo.

Freyre, Gilberto. 1935. *Sobrados e mucambos*. Rio de Janeiro: José Olympio.

———. 1954. *Casa-grande e senzala*. 2 vols. Rio de Janeiro: José Olympio.

Friederici, Georg. 1967. *Caráter da descoberta e conquista da América pelos europeus*. Rio de Janeiro: INL.

Furtado, Celso. 1959. *Formação econômica do Brasil*. Rio de Janeiro.

Gandia, Enrique de. 1929. *História crítica de los mitos de la conquista americana*. Buenos Aires: Ed. Juan Roldan y Compañia.

Geiger, Pedro Pinchas. 1963. *Evolução da rede urbana brasileira*. Rio de Janeiro: CBPE.

Gillin, John. 1947. "Modern Latin American culture." *Social Forces* 25.

Gorender, Jacob. 1978. *O escravismo colonial*. São Paulo: Ática.

Guerreiro Ramos, Alberto. 1957. *Condições sociais do poder nacional*. Rio de Janeiro.

Guimarões, Alberto Passos. 1963. *Quatro séculos de latifúndio*. São Paulo: Fulgor.

Harris, Marvin. 1964. *Patterns of race in the Americas*. New York: Walker and Company.

Hemming, John. 1978. *Red gold: The conquest of the Brazilian Indians*. London: Macmillan London Ltd.

Holanda, Sérgio Buarque de. 1945. *Monções*. Rio de Janeiro: Ed. Jornal do Comércio.

———. 1956. *Raízes do Brasil*. Rio de Janeiro: José Olympio (Documentos Brasileiros 1).

———. 1977. *Visão do paraíso*. São Paulo: Companhia Editora Nacional (Brasiliana, vol. 333).

———. 1986. *O extremo oeste*. São Paulo: Brasiliense.

Ianni, Octavio. 1962. *As metamorfoses do escravo. Apogeu e crise da escravatura no Brasil meridional*. São Paulo: Difel.

———. 1966. *Raças e classes sociais no Brasil*. Rio de Janeiro: Civilização Brasileira.

Ihering, Hermann von. 1907. "A anthropologia do estado de São Paulo." *Revista do Museu Paulista* 7: 202–57. São Paulo.

Kloster, W., e F. Sommer. 1942. *Ulrico Schmidl no Brasil quinhentista*. São Paulo: Pub. da Soc. Hans Staden.

Koster, Henry. 1942. *Viagens ao Nordeste do Brasil—Travels in Brazil*. São Paulo: Companhia Editora Nacional (Brasiliana, vol. 221).

Labrador, José Sánchez. 1910–17. *El Paraguay católico*. 3 vols. Buenos Aires: Imprenta de Coni Hermano/Comp. Sud-Americana de Billetes de Banco.

Laytano, Dante de. 1952. *A estância gaúcha*. Rio de Janeiro: Serviço de Informação Agricola n° 4, Ministério da Agricultura.

Leal, Victor Nunes. 1948. *Coronelismo, enxada e voto*. Rio de Janeiro.

Leite, pe. Serafim. 1938–50. *História da Companhia de Jesus no Brasil*. 10 vols. Lisboa/Rio de Janeiro: Liv. Portugália/Civilização Brasileira.

———. 1940. *Novas cartas jesuíticas*. São Paulo: Companhia Editora Nacional (Brasiliana, vol. 194).

———. 1956–58. *Cartas dos primeiros jesuítas no Brasil (Monumenta brasiliae, 1538–1563)*. 3 vols. Coimbra: Comissão do IV Centenário da Cidade de São Paulo, Tip. da Atlântida.

———. 1960. *Monumenta brasiliae IV 1563–1568*. Coimbra: Tip. da Atlântida.

———. 1965. *Novas páginas de história do Brasil*. São Paulo: Companhia Editora Nacional.

Léry, Jean de. 1960. *Viagem à terra do Brasil*. São Paulo: Martins (Biblioteca Histórica Brasileira, vol. 7).

Lima, Ruy Cirne de. 1935. *Terras devolutas. História, doutrina e legislação*. Porto Alegre.

Lisboa, João Francisco. 1901. *Obras*. 2 vols. Lisboa: Typ de Mattos Moreira & Pinheiro.

Lugon, Clovis. 1968. *A república comunista cristã dos guaranis*. Rio de Janeiro: Paz e Terra.

Macedo Soares, José Carlos. 1939. *Fronteiras do Brasil no regime colonial*. Rio de Janeiro: José Olympio.

Machado, José de Alcântara. 1943. *Vida e morte do bandeirante*. São Paulo: Martins.

Magalhães, Couto de. 1935. *O selvagem*. 3ª ed. Rio de Janeiro.

Malheiro Dias, Carlos (org.). 1921–24. *História da colonização portuguesa do Brasil*. 3 vols. Porto: Lit. Nacional.

Mancilla, Justo, e Simón Masseta. 1951. "Relación de los agravios que hicieron algunos vecinos y moradores de la villa de S. Pablo . . . ." In Jaime Cortesão (org.), *Manuscritos da Coleção de Angelis*, 1: 310–39. Rio de Janeiro: Biblioteca Nacional.

Marchant, Alexander. 1943. *Do escambo a escravidão*. Rio de Janeiro: Companhia Editora Nacional (Brasiliana, vol. 225).

Martins, Romário. 1899. *História do Paraná (1555–1853)*. Corytiba: Typ. da Liv. Econômica.

Martins, Wilson. 1955. *Um Brasil diferente. Ensaio sobre fenômenos de aculturação no Paraná*. São Paulo: Anhembi.

Matos, Raimundo José da Cunha. 1979–81. *Corografia histórica da província de Minas Gerais (1837)*. 2 vols. Belo Horizonte: Arquivo Público Mineiro.

Matos Guerra, Gregório de. 1946. *Florilégio da poesia brasileira*. Org. F. A. Varnhagen. Rio de Janeiro: Pub. da ABL (Coleção Afrânio Peixoto).

———. 1990. *Gregório de Matos*. Ed. James Amado. 2 vols. Rio de Janeiro: Record.

Meggers, Betty. 1971. *Amazonia: Man and culture in a counterfeit paradise*. Chicago: Aldine.

Mello Franco, Afonso Arinos de. 1936. *Conceito de civilização brasileira*. Rio de Janeiro: Companhia Editora Nacional (Brasiliana).

Mello Moraes, A. J. de. 1858–60. *Corographia histórica ... do Império do Brasil*. 5 vols. Rio de Janeiro: Typ. Brasileira.

Melo Neto, José Antonio Gonsalves de. 1947. *Tempo dos flamengos, documentos brasileiros*. Rio de Janeiro: José Olympio.

Melo e Souza, Antonio Candido de. 1964. *Os parceiros do Rio Bonito. Estudo sobre o caipira paulista e a transformação dos seus meios de vida*. Rio de Janeiro: José Olympio.

Mendonça, Marcos Carneiro de. 1963. *A Amazônia na era pombalina*. 3 vols. Rio de Janeiro: IHGB.

Milliet, Sérgio. 1939. *Roteiro do café*. São Paulo.

Montenegro, Abelardo F. 1959. *História do fanatismo religioso no Ceará*. Fortaleza: Ed. A. Batista Fontenele.

Montoya, pe. Antonio Ruiz de. 1892. *Conquista espiritual*. Bilbao: Imprenta de Corazon de Jesus.

Moreira Neto, Carlos de Araújo. 1960. "A cultura pastoril do Pau D'Arco." In *Boletim do Museu Paraense Emilio Goeldi*. Belém (Nova Série, Antropologia nº 10).

———. 1971. "A política indigenista brasileira durante o século XIX." Tese de doutorado, Faculdade de Filosofia de Rio Claro. 2 vols.

Morus, Thomas. 1941. "Utopia." In *Utopias de Renascimiento*. México: Fondo de Cultura.

Newen Zeytung auss Presillg Landt (1515). 1914. "A nova gazeta da terra do Brasil." *Anais da Biblioteca Nacional* 33: 1–27. Rio de Janeiro.

Nimuendaju, Curt. 1939. *The Apinayé*. Washington: Catholic University of America.

———. 1946. *The Eastern Timbira*. Berkeley/Los Angeles: University of California Press.

———. 1950. "Reconhecimento dos rios Içana, Ayarí e Uaupés—Relatório apresentado ao Serviço de Proteção aos Índios do Amazonas e Acre de 1927." *Journal de la Société des Américanistes* 39: 125–82.

———. 1952. *The Tukúna*. Berkeley/Los Angeles.

———. 1987. *As lendas da criação do mundo como fundamentos da religião dos Apapocuva-Guarani*. São Paulo: Hucitec/Edusp.

Nina Rodrigues, Raimundo. 1939. *As colectividades anormais*. São Paulo.

———. 1939a. *O alienado no direito civil brasileiro*. São Paulo: Companhia Editora Nacional.

———. 1945. *Os africanos no Brasil*. São Paulo: Companhia Editora Nacional.

Nóbrega, Manuel da. 1931. *Cartas do Brasil (1549–1560)*. Rio de Janeiro: ABL/ Officina Industrial Graphica (Cartes Jesuíticas 1).

————.1954. *Diálogo sobre a conversão do gentio.* IV Centenario da Fundação de São Paulo, Lisboa.

————. 1955. *Cartas do Brasil e mais esontos do pe. Manuel da Nóbrega (Opera omnia).* Coimbra: Acta Universitatis Conimbrigensis.

Nógueira, Oracy. 1955. "Preconceito racial de marca e preconceito racial de origem." In *Anais XXXI Congresso Internacional de Americanistas.* Vol. 1. São Paulo.

————. 1960. "Cor de pele e classe social" in vários autores. *Sistemas de plantaciones en el Nuevo Mundo.* Washington.

Paes Leme, Pedro Taques de Almeida. 1954. *Nobiliarchia paulistana histórica e genealogica.* 3 vols. São Paulo: Martins.

Paula, José Maria de. 1944. *Terra dos índios.* Rio de Janeiro: Imp. Nacional.

Perdigão Malheiros, Agostinho M. 1976. *A escravidão no Brasil.* 2 vols. Petrópolis, Vozes.

Pierson, Donald. 1945. *Brancos e pretos na Bahia.* São Paulo.

Pinheiro, José Feliciano Fernandes (visconde de São Leopoldo). 1946. *Anais da Província de São Pedro.* Rio de Janeiro: INL/Imprensa Nacional.

Pinto, Álvaro Vieira. 1956. *Ideologia e desenvolvimento nacional.* Rio de Janeiro: ISEB.

Prado, Eduardo da Silva. 1917. *A ilusão americana.* São Paulo.

Prado Júnior, Caio. 1942. *Formação do Brasil contemporâneo.* São Paulo: Brasiliense.

————. 1966. *A revolução brasileira.* Rio de Janeiro: Brasiliense.

Queiroz, Maria Isaura Pereira de. 1957. "O movimento messiânico do Contestado e o folclore." In *Anais da II Reunião Brasileira de Antropologia.* Bahia.

————. 1965. *O messianismo no Brasil e no mundo.* São Paulo: Ed. Dominus.

Queiroz, Maurício Vinhas de. 1966. *Messianismo e conflito social.* Rio de Janeiro: Civilização Brasileira.

Raiol, Domingos Antonio. 1970. *Motins políticos.* 3 vols. Belém: Universidade Federal do Pará.

Ramos, Arthur. 1940. *O negra brasileiro.* São Paulo: Companhia Editora Nacional (Brasiliana, vol. 188).

————. 1942. *A aculturação negra no Brasil.* São Paulo: Companhia Editora Nacional (Brasiliana, vol. 224).

————. 1943–47. *Introdução a antropologia brasileira.* 2 vols. Rio de Janeiro.

————.1946. *As culturas negras no Novo Mundo.* São Paulo: Companhia Editora Nacional (Brasiliana, vol. 249).

Rangel, Inácio. 1957. *Dualidade básica da economia brasileira.* Rio de Janeiro.

Redfield, Robert. 1941. *The folk culture of Yucatan.* Chicago.

————. 1963. *El mundo primitivo y sus transformaciones.* México.

Reis, Arthur Cezar Ferreira. 1931. *História do Amazonas.* Manaus.

————. 1954. *O seringal e o seringueiro na Amazônia.* Rio de Janeiro.

Ribeiro, Darcy. 1956a. "Convívio e contaminação. Efeitos dissociativos da de-população provocada por epidemias em grupos indígenas." In *Sociologia* (18-1). São Paulo.

———. 1956b. "Culturas e línguas indígenas do Brasil." In *Educação e Ciências Sociais* (2-6). Rio de Janeiro.

———. 1959. "Projeto de pesquisa sobre os processos de industrialização e urbanização." *Educação e Ciências Sociais* (4-5): 113–18. Rio de Janeiro.

———. 1968. *O processo civilizatório—Etapas da evolução socio-cultural.* Rio Janeiro: Civilização Brasileira.

———. 1970. *As Américas e a civilização—Processo de formação e causas do desenvolvimento desigual dos povos americanos.* Rio de Janeiro: Civilização Brasileira.

———. 1970a. *Os índios e a civilização—A integração das populações indígenas no Brasil moderno.* Rio de Janeiro: Civilização Brasileira.

———. 1971. *El dilema de América Latina—Estructuras de poder y fuerzas insurgentes.* México. Siglo XXI.

———. 1988. *The Americas and Civilization.* Petropolis, Brazil: Editora Vozes.

Ribeiro Pires, Simeão. 1979. *Raízes de Minas.* Montes Claros: Minas Gráfica Ed.

Rocha Pombo, José F. da. 1905. *História do Brazil llustrada.* 10 vols. J. Fonseca Saraiva/Benjamim de Aguila.

Roche, Jean. 1969. *A colonização alemã no Rio Grande do Sul.* 2 vols. Porto Alegre: Globo.

Rodrigues, João Barbosa. 1890. "Paranduba amazonense." In *Anais da Biblioteca Nacional,* vol. 14. Rio de Janeiro.

Rodrigues, José Honório. 1954. *O continente do Rio Grande.* Rio de Janeiro: Ed. São José.

———. 1965. *Conciliação e reforma no Brasil.* Rio de Janeiro: Civilização Brasileira.

———. 1979. *História da história do Brasil.* São Paulo: Companhia Editora Nacional (Brasiliana, vol. 1).

Rodrigues do Prado, Francisco. 1839. "História dos índios Cavalleiros ou da nação Guaykurú." *Revista do Instituto Histórico e Geográfico Brasileiro* 1: 25–57. Rio de Janeiro.

Romero, Sílvio. 1943. *História da literatura brasileira.* 5 vols. Rio de Janeiro: José Olympio.

———. 1954. *Folclore brasileiro.* 3 vols. Rio de Janeiro.

Rosenblat, Angel. 1954. *La población indígena y el mestizage en América.* 2 vols. Buenos Aires: Ed. Nova.

Saint-Hilaire, Auguste de. 1939. *Viagem ao Rio Grande do Sul (1820–1821).* São Paulo: Companhia Editora Nacional (Brasiliana, vol. 167).

Saito, Hiroshi. 1961. *O japonês no Brasil.* São Paulo: Ed. Sociologia e Política.

Salvador, Frei Vicente do. 1888. *História do Brasil (1550–1627). Annaes da Biblioteca Nacional* 13: 1–261. Rio de Janeiro.

———. 1982. *História do Brasil (1500–1627)*. São Paulo: Itatiaia (Reconquista do Brasil, vol. 49).

Santiago Dantas, bel. F.C.D. 1877. *Ligeira notícia sobre as operações militares contra os Muckers na província do Rio Grande do Sul*. Rio de Janeiro: Typ. da Gazeta de Notícias.

Santos, Milton. 1955. *Zona de cacau*. Salvador.

Schmidel, Ulrich. 1947. *Derrotero y viaje a España y las Indias*. Buenos Aires/México: Calpe Argentina SA.

Schupp, pe. Ambrósio. s/d (1957). *Os Muckers*. Porto Alegre: Ed. Liv. Selbach.

Sepp, pe. Antonio. 1951. *Viagem às missões jesuíticas e trabalhos apostólicos*. São Paulo: Martins (Biblioteca Histórica Brasileira).

Serra, Ricardo Franco de Almeida. 1844. "Extracto da descripção geographica da província de Mato Grosso feita em 1797 por . . . ." In *Revista do Instituto Histórico e Geográfico Brasileiro*, vol. 6. Rio de Janeiro.

Silva, cel. Ignacio Accioli de Serqueira. 1919–40. *Memórias históricas e políticas da província da Bahia*. 6 vols. Bahia: Imp. Oficial do Estado.

Simonsen, Roberto. 1937. *História econômica do Brasil (1500–1820)*. 2 vols. São Paulo: Companhia Editora Nacional (Brasiliana, vols. 100 e 100a).

Sodré, Nelson Werneck. 1963. *Introdução à revolução brasileira*. Rio de Janeiro.

Sousa, Gabriel Soares de. 1971. *Tratado descritivo do Brasil em 1587*. São Paulo: Companhia Editora Nacional (Brasiliana, vol. 117).

Southey, Robert. 1862. *História do Brasil*. 6 vols. Rio de Janeiro: B. L. Garnier.

Souza Leite, Antonio Attico de. 1898. *Fanatismo religioso, memória sobre o reino encantado na comarca de Villa Bella*. Juiz de Fora: Typ. Mattoso.

Spix, J. B. von, e C. F. P. von Martius. 1938. *Viagem pelo Brasil*. 3 vols. Rio de Janeiro: IHGB/Imp. Nacional.

———. 1938a. *Atlas*. Rio de Janeiro: IHGB/Imp. Nacional.

Staden, Hans. 1942. *Duas viagens ao Brasil*. São Paulo: Pub. da Soc. Hans Staden.

Steward, Julian H. 1949. "The native population of South America." In *Handbook of South American Indians*, vol. 5. Washington: Smithsonian Institution.

———. 1960. "Perspectivas de las plantaciones" in vários autores. *Sistemas de plantaciones en el Nuevo Mundo*. Washington.

Studart, barão de. 1910–23. "Documentos pare a história do Brasil e especialmente a do Ceará." In *Revista do Instituto do Ceará*, vols. 24 (1910), 34 (1920), 35 (1921), 36 (1922), 37 (1923). Fortaleza.

Taunay, Affonso de E. 1922. *Na era das bandeiras*. São Paulo: Melhoramentos.

———. 1924–50. *História geral das bandeiras paulistas*. 11 vols. São Paulo: Typ. Ideal H. L. Canton–Imp. Oficial do Estado.

———. 1936. *A guerra dos bárbaros*. Separata do n° XXII da *Revista do Arquivo*.

———. 1941. *Subsídios para a história do tráfico africano no Brasil colonial*. Rio de Janeiro: Imp. Nacional.

———. 1952. *Ensaio de carta geral das bandeiras paulistas*. São Paulo: Melhoramentos.

Tavares, Maria da Conceição e outros. 1964. "Auge y declinación del proceso de sustitución de importaciones en el Brasil." In *Boletin Económico de América Latina* (9-1). Santiago de Chile.

Torres, João Camilo de Oliveira. 1962. *História de Minas Gerais.* 5 vols. Belo Horizonte: Difusão Pan-Americana do Livro.

Toynbee, Arnold J. 1959. *Estudio de la historia (Compendio).* 2 vols. Buenos Aires.

Valente, Waldemar. 1963. *Misticismo e religião. Aspectos do sebastianismo nordestino.* Recife: Instituto Joaquim Nabuco de Pesquisas Sociais.

Valverde, Orlando. 1964. *Geografia agrária do Brasil.* Vol. 1. Rio de Janeiro.

Varnhagen, Francisco A. de. 1854–57. *História geral do Brazil.* 1ª ed. 2 vols. Madri: Imprensa de V. de Dominguez/Imprenta de J. del Rio.

——. 1962. *História geral do Brasil.* 5 vols. São Paulo: Melhoramentos.

Vasconcelos, Diogo de. 1948. *História antiga de Minas Gerais.* 2 vols. Rio de Janeiro: INL.

——. 1948a. *História média de Minas Gerais.* Rio de Janeiro: INL.

Vianna, F. J. Oliveira. 1956. *Evolução do povo brasileiro.* Rio de Janeiro.

Vieira, pe. Antônio. 1925–28. *Cartas do padre Antônio Vieira, coordenadas e anotadas por J. Lúcio de Azevedo.* 3 vols. Coimbra: Imprensa da Universidade.

——. 1951. *Sermões.* 15 vols. Porto: Lello e Irmãos Editores.

——. 1951a. *Em defesa dos índios — Obras escolhidas.* 5 vols. Lisboa: Liv. Sá da Costa.

Vieira da Cunha, Mário Wagner. 1963. *O sistema administrativo brasileiro, 1930–1950.* Rio de Janeiro.

Vilhena, Luís dos Santos. 1969. *A Bahia no século XVIII (Recopilação das notícias soteropolitanas e brasílicas).* 3 vols. Salvador: Ed. Itapuã.

Vitória, Francisco de. 1696. *De indis y De iure belli* em *Relectiones morales.* 1ª ed. Colonia: ed. Augusti Boetii.

——. 1943. *Las relecciones de indis y de iure bell.* Washington: Imprenta de la Union Panamericana.

Wagley, Charles, and Marvin Harris. 1955. "A typology of Latin American subcultures." *Amencan Anthropologist* 57, nº 3: 428–51.

Waibel, Leo. 1947. "O sistema de plantações tropicais." In *Boletim Geográfico* (5-56). Rio de Janeiro.

——. 1949. "Princípios de colonização européia no Sul do Brasil." In *Revista Brasileira de Geografia* (11-2). Rio de Janeiro.

——. 1958. *Capítulos de geografia tropical e do Brasil.* Rio de Janeiro.

Willems, Emílio. 1946. *A aculturação dos alemães no Brasil. Estudo antropológico dos imigrantes alemães e seus descendentes no Brasil.* São Paulo: Companhia Editora Nacional.

——. 1947. *Cunha — Tradição e transição em uma cultura rural no Brasil.* São Paulo.

About the Translator

Gregory Rabassa is internationally acclaimed as the translator of the Latin American writers referred to as the "Boom" generation. He won the National Book Award for his translation of *Hopscotch*, by Julio Cortazar and has been awarded numerous distinctions and honors, including the Alexander Gode Medal of the American Translator Association, the Governor of Arts Award from New York, the Wheatland Prize for Translation, and Literary Lion of the New York Public Library.

Professor emeritus at Queens College of the City University of New York, he continues to teach courses in Latin American literature and translation. He holds an honorary doctorate from Dartmouth College and received the Order of San Carlos from Colombia for his translations of the works of Gabriel García Marquez.

Gregory Rabassa has specialized in the study of the black character in Brazilian fiction and was the recipient of a Fulbright-Hays dissertation scholarship that allowed him to complete dissertation research in Rio de Janeiro. He has translated numerous Brazilian writers, including Clarice Lispector and Nélida Piñon. He has had a lifelong interest in the works and life of Padre Antonio Vieira, the Luso-Brazilian preacher, missionary, and statesman, and he received a Guggenheim fellowship in 1988 to continue his study of Vieira's works.

Rabassa's believes that "translation is natural writing and not an analysis, and that too much thought about technique might dull and stultify the results." This translation of *The Brazilian People* does justice to Darcy Ribeiro's original Portuguese text, with all its expressive idiosyncrasies, its departures from contemporary U.S. norms of political correctness, and its intrinsic poetry and epic hyperbole. Darcy Ribeiro could have wished for no better translator than Gregory Rabassa, who has the gift of translating not just the words but the pulse of a text. For an author writing more a philosophy or aesthetic of the Brazilian people than a scientific text, the match with this translator was appropriate. Rabassa has stated that "the translator must become the author's other. The writer stays himself but is now writing in another language and therefore at least partially in another culture." Although the book was translated after Ribeiro's death, without the benefit of consultation with the author, the translator of *O Povo Brasileiro* has again stretched the possibilities of language, allowing readers of the target text to "hear" the voice of the "other" in the way that the author's own Portuguese language readers would have heard him.

Elizabeth Lowe is associate director of the Center for Latin American Studies at the University of Florida. A former student of Gregory Rabassa's at The City University of New York, she translates Brazilian and Spanish American fiction into English. She translated Darcy Ribeiro's novel *The Mule* and worked closely with Ribeiro in the last two years of his life on plans for the translation of his collected works into English.